Consumer Theory

Consumer Theory

H. A. John Green

ACADEMIC PRESS New York San Francisco
A Subsidiary of Harcourt Brace Jovanovich, Publishers 1978

First published 1971 by Penguin Books
Revised edition first published in the United Kingdom 1976 by
The Macmillan Press Ltd

ACADEMIC PRESS, INC.
111 Fifth Avenue, New York, New York 10003

ISBN 0-12-298150-2

LIBRARY OF CONGRESS CATALOG CARD NUMBER: 77-838900

PRINTED IN HONG KONG

To Barbara

Contents

Preface to Revised Edition

This book is a revised version of the one originally published by Penguin Books in 1971, of which stocks were exhausted in 1974. Since a number of colleagues have been kind enough to say that they require the book urgently in their teaching, I thought it best, when the Macmillan Press undertook to re-publish it, to confine the revision to the correction of errors of which I was aware. The most substantial change is the rewriting of Section **T.4** on the composite commodity theorem in the Technical Appendix: the proof in the original version of the book is wrong.

Readers of this revised edition may be interested in two works which were not available when I wrote the original version. The coverage of *Static Demand Theory* by Donald W. Katzner (New York: Macmillan, 1970) is similar to that of my book, but it is very definitely for the 'specialist', as defined on page 16 below. The survey article on 'Models of Consumer Behaviour' by Alan Brown and Angus Deaton (*Economic Journal*, December 1972) is accessible to any reader of this book who spends a few minutes learning vector notation, as explained in pages 58–72 of Chiang (see the bibliography on page 17 below). The first of these works attaches considerable importance to indirect utility functions (cf. pages 138–9 below) and expenditure functions, and in the second there is a long section on the demand for durable goods (cf. pages 175–80 below).

Though this book is designed for a fairly wide class of readers (see page 16 below), it had its origin in a course in microeconomic theory given for many years to first-year graduate students at the University of Toronto. I hope that this revised edition will prove useful to students and teachers in similar courses in other universities in North America.

Canterbury, Kent
November 1975

H. A. J. G.

Preface to Revised Edition

Chapter 1
Introduction

It is obvious that the individual family or household is of crucial importance in the economic system. Consider the effects of: (i) its decisions to buy or not to buy specific consumption goods; (ii) the timing of its purchases of durable consumption goods, and the amount it decides to save; (iii) its decisions to hold wealth in one form rather than another. And ultimately: (iv) the efficiency of an economic system must be judged by its responsiveness to the preferences of individuals.

In this volume we offer an account of the ways in which economists have sought to explain the three types of decision mentioned above. We discover at an early stage that what in most textbooks of price theory is called the 'theory of consumer behaviour' or the 'theory of demand' extends no further than (i) above; it is relevant, strictly speaking, only to such problems as that faced by the housewife doing her weekly grocery shopping. But the analysis of this type of problem is fundamental, and occupies Parts One and Two of the book.

We are unwilling, however, to leave it at that. The methods of analysis developed in Parts One and Two are also applicable to the way in which the consumer plans his consumption over time ((ii) above and Part Four), to the forms in which he holds his wealth when faced by uncertainty ((iii) above and Part Five), and to the evaluation of the price mechanism as it affects consumers ((iv) above and Part Six).

Part Three is a connecting link between Parts One and Two and Parts Four to Six. It shows how the theory of consumer behaviour assists those who seek to *forecast* demand, and develops further techniques useful in the later parts.

A brief word on methodology is in order. Economics is not a subject in which one can, as in the physical sciences, decisively reject a theory by means of a crucial experiment. The theories developed in Parts Two to Five of this volume, which form a reasonably cohesive whole, have performed fairly well when confronted with data. If the basic assumptions about individuals on which they rest appear implausible, this is no reason for either alarm or complacency. In many instances we are obliged to say that this is the best (meaning the only) theory of individual behaviour we have; one does not reject it unless one has something better to put in its place. But there are several areas in which the theory of individual behaviour is clearly in need of development, as we shall indicate.

It is hoped that this book will be of interest to two classes of readers: (i) the undergraduate, who has taken at most a course in the principles of economics, and whose mathematical preparation does not extend beyond O-level; (ii) the graduate student, or the undergraduate with a special interest in èconomics, who has mastered the techniques expounded in the books recommended in the Notes on the literature at the end of this chapter, or who has taken a year of calculus.

The mathematical level of the text is designed for class (i) (henceforth called the 'general reader'). But the *notation* (no more) of derivatives and partial derivatives is introduced, explained and used; it is so useful a device that it would be absurd not to do so.

Passages which, whether or not they require no more mathematical knowledge than that of the general reader, are of interest primarily to class (ii) (henceforth called the 'specialist'), have been dealt with in three ways. Some have been included in the text, but set in small type, some have been placed in footnotes, and the long mathematical arguments are to be found in the Technical Appendix.

At the end of Chapters 1–16 and the Technical Appendix is a section entitled Notes on the literature. At the beginning of most of these is a paragraph containing the titles of books or articles which the general reader is either urged to read because they are basic and readily comprehensible sources or advised to consult if he has difficulty with technical material in the chapter. There are also bibliographical notes for the specialist related to the individual sections of the chapter. The Notes on the literature also contain bibliographical details of works referred to, and of passages quoted with or without attribution, in the text.

All readers are urged to attempt **all** the exercises.

To summarize, the general reader should (i) read the text, except for those sections which are in small type, (ii) read those items which appear in the general parts of Notes on the literature and (iii) do the exercises. He may omit (unless curiosity overcomes him) the footnotes, the specialized parts of the bibliographies and the Technical Appendix, which are designed for the specialist.

Notes on the literature

If the reader would care at this stage to sample the flavour of the subject, good brief surveys are to be found, for the general reader in W. J. Baumol, *Economic Theory and Operations Analysis* (3rd edn, Prentice-Hall, 1972, ch. 9), and for the specialist in J. M. Henderson and R. E. Quandt, *Microeconomic Theory* (2nd edn, McGraw-Hill, 1971, ch. 2) or H. S. Houthakker, 'The present state of consumption theory' (*Econometrica*, vol. 29, no. 4, pp. 704–40, 1961).

Two textbooks, which introduce the reader to most of the mathematical techniques used in this book, are highly recommended: R. G. D. Allen, *Mathematical Analysis for Economists* (Macmillan, 1938), and A. C. Chiang, *Fundamental Methods of Mathematical Economics* (McGraw-Hill, 1967, chs 1–13).

The device of appending Notes on the literature to each chapter is borrowed from Peter Newman, *The Theory of Exchange* (Prentice-Hall, 1965).

The specialist will find valuable additional exercises in Samuel Bowles and David Kendrick, *Notes and Problems in Microeconomic Theory* (Markham, 1970, Units 1 and 2).

Part One
Fundamentals

Chapter 2
The Rational Consumer

2.1 The consumer and his decisions

When we speak in this volume of a 'consumer' we shall not always mean a single individual. Typically we shall mean a household or family unit, which makes decisions, either collectively or by an agreed delegation of responsibility (e.g. Father buys the car, Mother buys the groceries, the children buy their records and comics) on a variety of matters affecting the well-being of the household and its members. Examples of such decisions are: how much to spend on groceries each week and how to spend the grocery budget in detail, how much work to do and of what kinds, how much insurance to carry, what durable goods to buy and when to buy them, how much to save and in what forms to hold one's savings.

All these types of decision, and more, will be discussed in later chapters. But we must learn to walk before we can run, and initially we confine our attention to a limited type of decision. We assume that the household has decided to set aside a sum of money to be spent on a particular date on commodities to be used up during a particular period (say a week or a month); at the beginning of the next period, a new set of purchases must be made. We abstract from the numerous difficulties involving *time* (which will concern us in Part Four) by assuming that the household possesses no stocks of these commodities and (as already indicated) carries no stocks over to the next period. For practical purposes, therefore, there is no distinction between *purchase* and *consumption*. And we abstract from *uncertainty* (the subject of Part Five) by assuming that the consumer knows exactly what he will get if he makes a certain set of purchases, and that he knows the prices of all commodities and all other circumstances relevant to his decision.

2.2 Rationality

An assumption which pervades the theories of consumer behaviour to be discussed is that consumers behave *rationally*. Since the economist's use of the term 'rational' is a special one, let us first see what is meant by the term and then ask ourselves what we think of the assumption.

To the economist, rational behaviour is behaviour in accordance with a systematic set of preferences. We shall try to make this idea precise by developing it formally. Consider first the *set* or collection S of alternatives from which a choice is to be made. The *elements* or *members* of the set are the different *bundles* or market baskets of commodities (x, x', x'', . . .) which the consumer can afford, given the prices of the commodities and the size of his budget.

Now we define a *binary relation* on the set S. This means that we recognize the possibility of finding a *pair* of elements (hence the term 'binary') in the set of which we can say that one member of the pair is related in a certain way to the other. For example, if we take S to be the set of all human beings, living or dead, instead of a set of bundles of goods, we may be able to find a pair of elements of S (e.g. James Mill and John Stuart Mill) and say 'James Mill was the father of John Stuart Mill'. Then 'fatherhood' – or more exactly 'is or was the father of' – is a binary relation defined on the set of human beings.

In the consumer's case the binary relation which permits us most easily to develop a preference ordering is illustrated by the statement *Bundle x is regarded by the consumer as at least as good as bundle x'.* The binary relation is 'is regarded by the consumer as at least as good as', a mouthful which will be abbreviated to the symbol R. Thus xRx' means exactly the same thing as the italicized statement above.

We require three axioms concerning the relation R in order to state our definition of rational behaviour. The first is, in words, that if, from any set of alternatives S, we select *any* pair of elements, the consumer either prefers one member of the pair to the other or is indifferent between them. Formally we state this assumption as:

Axiom **1** (Completeness): *For all* x, x' *in* S, either xRx' *or* $x'Rx$ *or both.*

The implications of this axiom can be appreciated if we reflect that each of the statements xRx' and $x'Rx$ must be either true or false. Thus quite independently of Axiom **1** there are four *logical* possibilities, shown in the table below.

xRx'	$x'Rx$	
True	True	Written as xIx'
True	False	Written as xPx'
False	True	Written as $x'Px$
False	False	Excluded by Axiom **1**

The last of the four possibilities, in which xRx' and $x'Rx$ are both false, so that x and x' are not comparable in the consumer's preference ordering, is ruled out by Axiom **1**. One, and only one, of the remaining three possibilities must hold, and it seems natural to give each a name. If each of the alternatives x and x' is (regarded by the consumer as) at least as good as the other, this can only mean that he is *indifferent* between them. This can be abbreviated to xIx'. Thus xIx' is defined as xRx' and $x'Rx$. Similarly if x is at least as good as x' but x' is *not* at least as good as x, then the consumer must *prefer* x to x'. This can be abbreviated to xPx'.

Using the definitions of R, P, I and Axiom **1**, it is easy to prove the following immediate (and common-sense) consequences or:

Corollaries: *For all* x, x' in S:

(a) *one and only one of* xPx', $x'Px$, xIx' *holds*;
(b) xIx;
(c) *if* xIx', *then* $x'Ix$.

The next axiom expresses an intuitively reasonable property of the preference ordering with regard to groups of *three* alternatives in S: if x is (regarded by the consumer as) at least as good as x', and x' is at least as good as x'', then x must be at least as good as x''. The relation R is then said to be *transitive*:

Axiom **2** (Transitivity): *For all* x, x', x'' *in* S: *if* xRx' *and* $x'Rx''$, (written as $xRx'Rx''$), *then* xRx''.

One would expect the foregoing definitions and axioms to have certain common-sense consequences or *corollaries* (e.g. that if x is preferred to x' and x' is indifferent to x'', then x is preferred to x''). This is indeed the case; there are eight such corollaries, of which the example just given in parentheses appears as (j):[1]

Corollaries: *For all x, x', x'' in S*:

(d) if $xPx'Px''$, then xPx'';
(e) if $xIx'Ix''$, then xIx'';
(f) if $xRx'Px''$, then xPx'';
(g) if $xPx'Rx''$, then xPx'';
(h) if $xRx'Ix''$, then xRx'';
(i) if $xIx'Rx''$, then xRx'';
(j) if $xPx'Ix''$, then xPx'';
(k) if $xIx'Px''$, then xPx''.

We have now defined a *weak preference ordering* of the elements of the set S, which permits us to *partition* the set. To 'partition' a set is to divide it up exhaustively into *disjoint subsets.* A 'subset' of S is a set, all of whose elements are members of S; two sets are 'disjoint' if they have no elements in common. The subsets into which S is partitioned are termed *indifference classes*: the consumer is indifferent between any two elements in any one 'indifference class'. The indifference classes can be ranked in order of the consumer's preference. The ordering is 'weak' because we permit indifference between any two distinct alternatives in S. (A *strong* preference ordering is one in which, of any distinct alternatives x and x', either x is preferred to x' or x' is preferred to x).

We are now in a position to define rational behaviour, and it is easiest to think of it negatively. It would not be rational to choose x from a set of alternatives if there were another alternative x' in the set which was preferred to x. This is ruled out by Axiom 3.

Axiom 3 (Rational Choice): *If x is chosen from a set of alternatives* S, *then for all x' in* S, xRx'.

Note that this axiom is in a sense incomplete. If there are alternatives

1. The method of proof is similar for all these corollaries, and may be illustrated by proving (d). We are to prove that xPx''. Suppose xPx'' is false: then $x''Rx$. But $x'Px''$, so that $x'Rx''$, and by Axiom 2 $x'Rx''$ and $x''Rx$ imply $x'Rx$. But this contradicts xPx'. The supposition that xPx'' is false has led to a contradiction. Therefore xPx'' is true.

in S which are indifferent to x it does not tell us how x is selected from the indifference class to which it belongs.

2.3 Are consumers rational?

We shall not take the view than an examination of such fundamental assumptions as rationality is unnecessary because, whatever irrationality individuals may display, the behaviour of large numbers of individuals in a market closely approximates what it would be if each of them were rational. Empirical studies of market behaviour are surely not so good as to justify complacency. And we believe that a theory which works well at the level of the individual is a better theory in itself, and also likely to work better at the market level, than one which does not. Moreover, the assumption of individual rationality is the basis not only of *positive economics*, concerned with explanation and prediction, but also of *normative* or *welfare economics*, concerned with evaluation and recommendation. In welfare economics, the individual occupies the centre of the stage, and there is no question of individual irrationalities 'cancelling out'.

How then shall we proceed to judge the assumption of individual rationality? The definition of rationality given in the last section is so general that it is not possible for a consumer's observed choices to be inconsistent with it. Even though on a succession of dates the consumer's budget, the commodities available and their prices were all unchanged, yet he chose a different bundle each time, it could be argued that all the bundles chosen belonged to the same indifference class. Only a larger set of axioms, including those to be introduced in the next chapter, can be contradicted by actual choices.

Let us then take the direct approach of asking the consumer about his preferences. On our present assumption that he knows exactly what he is getting when he makes a purchase, unfamiliarity and complexity should not prevent him from being able to compare any two bundles. But suppose that on two different occasions he says first that xPx' and then that $x'Px$. We may say either that he has no preference ordering on which to base a rational choice or that his preference ordering has changed between the first occasion and the second. Without wishing to discourage the search for a theory of individual behaviour which takes account of irrationality, we note with Hicks that 'no simple alternative of equal fertility ... (to the assumption of rational behaviour) . . . is available, none that is so rich in consequences that can be empirically applied'. Moreover, empirical hypotheses about market behaviour based on individual rationality are quite successful even when preference orderings are assumed to remain unchanged. A theory based on rationality which takes account of changes in preferences should work even better.

But before we turn to possible reasons for changes in preferences, an interesting argument against the assumption of transitivity should be considered. Suppose that a consumer 'really' prefers x' to x, but the difference is so slight as to be below his threshold of perception, and he tells us that xIx'; similarly he 'really' prefers x'' to x', but shrugs and tells us that $x'Ix''$. Now when he is asked to compare x and x'', his cumulated preference for x'' over x is perceived, and he says that $x''Px$. We have xRx' and $x'Rx''$, but xRx'' is false, so that Axiom **2** is contradicted. We must admit that the theory could be improved, though at the cost of considerable complexity, if the consumer's imperfect powers of discrimination were taken into account.

2.4 Changes in preference orderings

Since man is a developing animal, a learning animal and a social animal it would be absurd to assume that the preferences of any members of any household remain unchanged over time and unaffected by their environment. Such considerations are peripheral to standard textbook discussions of consumer behaviour and will for the most part remain so in this one. But we cannot in all conscience proceed without some discussion of three outstanding possible reasons for changes in preferences.

(*a*) *Advertising*

Galbraith has recently argued that promotional advertising has a dominant influence on consumers' choices. Most economists would claim that a consumer's choices are determined by his preferences and the information available to him. We have assumed provisionally in section **2.1** that information about the nature of goods and the terms on which they are available is complete. As to preferences, the issue is the extent to which the consumer can be said to have a mind of his (or her) own. We would point out only that the more highly a product is favoured in *existing* preference orderings, the less will be the cost of promoting it, and the greater will be the chance of success. The Ford

Motor Company's Edsel is a frequently quoted example of the failure of promotional advertising. The fate of the mini-skirt, still in the balance at the time of writing, will provide a further indication of the degree of autonomy of consumers' preferences.

The question may be clarified if we consider a recent theoretical development on which we shall lay great stress in later chapters. This is that preferences among bundles of *goods* are not a fundamental determinant of choice, but are derived from preferences among the bundles of *characteristics* supplied by these goods. Ford could not persuade people to buy the bundle of characteristics embodied in the Edsel, and one hopes that the characteristics of the midi-skirt will prove equally unacceptable.

It has often been observed, however, that advertising is more concerned with persuading people to switch from one 'brand' of a 'commodity' to another than from one commodity to another. (One wonders by how much the proportions in which brands are sold would in fact change if brand advertising were drastically reduced, but that is another matter.) If one interprets the different brands of a commodity (e.g. toothpaste) as goods which supply the same characteristics in different proportions, a good part of brand advertising may be interpreted as an attempt to *inform* people of the characteristics of a given brand. To the extent that this is so, a switch of brands is quite consistent with unchanged preferences with regard to characteristics. What happens is that the *information* available to the consumer changes.

The reader must judge whether the foregoing constitutes an adequate defence of the neglect of advertising in the standard theory of consumer behaviour. (We should point out, however, that Baumol takes advertising outlay as one of the determinants of sales, and that this is frequently done in empirical studies.) If a theory which took account of the information available to the consumer were developed (and such a theory would depart from the simple assumptions of section **2.1** because it would naturally recognize the existence of uncertainty), advertising would of course be incorporated as a source of information.

(*b*) *Choices of other consumers*

It is obvious that the preferences of one consumer are affected by what others consume. At one level 'it is enough . . . to imagine what would happen to any one man's desire for a telephone if those of all his friends were permanently disconnected' (Graaff). At another 'we know that he often buys things he does not particularly enjoy consuming in order to produce an impression on the Joneses, or avoids things that he would enjoy for fear of being thought common' (Joan Robinson). These last two phenomena have been termed the 'bandwagon effect' and the 'snob effect' respectively.

At the level of the individual consumer these interactions have been disregarded in most theoretical writings. They have, however, been recognized as vitally important in welfare economics, and it has not escaped notice that they must be taken into account when the theory of individual behaviour is applied to the behaviour of many individuals in the market.

(*c*) *Prices and preferences*

Of course changes in prices affect *choices*, by altering the set of alternative bundles of goods that the consumer can afford with a given budget. But does a change in the price of a commodity affect a consumer's preferences among alternative bundles?

It is arguable that economists are justified in neglecting prices as a significant *independent* determinant of preferences. To the extent that a high price leads a consumer to believe that few others will buy a product, his reaction may be accounted for by the 'snob effect' in (*b*) above.

To those who follow the slogan 'you get what you pay for', the price of a product may be regarded as a source of information. Satisfied with the reputation of the manufacturer or dealer and fortified by a certain faith in the competitive system, they argue that a product could not cost more if it were not 'better' in some respects relevant to most people's preferences.

There are also sceptics who consult *Consumer Reports* in North America or *Which?* in the United Kingdom to make sure that rankings of brands by price and by quality are not widely disparate. A list of dramatic discrepancies between the two rankings is a major feature of *Consumer Reports*' own advertising.

In the next chapter we resume the exposition of the usual theory of the behaviour of the individual consumer, from which the matters discussed in this section are absent. We suggest, without having anything original to offer, that the theory could be improved if the information available to consumers and their interactions were taken into account.

Exercises

1. Which of the following binary relations are transitive?
On the set of all human beings, living or dead:
(a) 'is (or was) the father of';
(b) 'is (or was) a lineal descendant of';
(c) 'is (or was) the brother of'.
On the set of all places on the earth's equator:
(d) 'lies to the east of'.

Notes on the literature

The reader will find Chapter 2 of Peter Newman's *The Theory of Exchange* a very useful companion to our Chapters 2 and 3, which owe a great deal to Newman's careful exposition.

2.2 Chapter 2 of K. J. Arrow, *Social Choice and Individual Values* (2nd edn, Wiley, 1963), in which the logic of relations was first applied to economics, may also be consulted by the reader who has trouble with this section.

2.3 Of the two methodological positions contrasted at the beginning of this section, one is to be found in M. Friedman's *Essays in Positive Economics* (University of Chicago Press, 1953), reprinted in part in W. Breit and H. M. Hochman (eds.), *Readings in Microeconomics* (Holt, Rinehart & Winston, 1968, pp. 23–47), and the other, which corresponds more closely to our own, in P. A. Samuelson's contribution to the discussion on 'Problems of methodology' (*Amer. econ. Rev.*, vol. 53, no. 2, pp. 231–7, 1967), and in T. C. Koopmans, *Three Essays on the State of Economic Science* (McGraw-Hill, 1957, pp. 135–42). The quotation from J. R. Hicks is to be found in his *Revision of Demand Theory* (Oxford University Press, 1956, p. 18). An off-beat theory of market behaviour based explicitly on individual irrationality is to be found in Gary S. Becker, 'Irrational behaviour and economic theory' (*J. polit. Econ.*, vol. 70, no. 1, pp. 1–13, 1962). The imperfect powers of discrimination of the consumer were stressed by W. E. Armstrong:

see, e.g., 'The determinateness of the utility function' (*Econ. J.*, vol. 49, no. 195, pp. 453–67, 1939).

2.4 (a) J. K. Galbraith's views are expressed in *The New Industrial State* (Hamish Hamilton, 1967). The reader may care to look at J. E. Meade's review of this book (*Econ. J.*, vol. 78, no. 310, pp. 372–92, 1968). The 'goods-characteristics' analysis is the work of K. J. Lancaster, and will be discussed at length in Chapter 10 below. On advertising as a determinant of sales, see Baumol, *Economic Theory and Operations Analysis*, ch. 10. A paper which takes account of the information available to the economic agent, but which will mean little to the reader at this stage, is Roy Radner's 'Competitive equilibrium under uncertainty' (*Econometrica*, vol. 36, no. 1, pp. 31–58, 1968).
(b) The terms 'bandwagon effect' and 'snob effect' are Leibenstein's, and their implications for market behaviour are discussed in Section 9.5 below.

2.5 The quotations in the text are from J. de V. Graaff, *Theoretical Welfare Economics* (Cambridge University Press, 1957, p. 43), and from Joan Robinson, *The Accumulation of Capital*, (Macmillan, 1956, p. 389). An interesting attempt to introduce interactions among consumers into the analysis of individual saving behaviour was made by J. S. Duesenberry, *Income, Saving and the Theory of Consumer Behaviour* (Harvard University Press, 1949).

Chapter 3
The Consumer's Preferences

3.1 The consumption set

The alternatives from which the consumer chooses consist, according to the assumptions of sections **2.1** and **2.2**, of a set of bundles of goods to be bought on a particular day and used up during a particular period. If there are n distinct goods, and we decide which good is to be regarded as the first, second, and so on, a bundle can be identified as consisting of, say, 3 units of the first good (3 loaves of white bread), 2 units of the second good (2 loaves of brown bread),... and 2 units of the nth good (2 pairs of black shoelaces), or simply as (3, 2,..., 2). In referring to bundles in general terms we identify x, x', x'',... respectively as $(x_1, x_2,..., x_n)$, $(x'_1, x'_2,..., x'_n)$, $(x''_1, x''_2,..., x''_n)$, where for example x''_2 is the number of units of the second good in the bundle x''.

It is often useful to assume for expository purposes that there are only two goods, and to employ geometry in the analysis. Thus if $x = (x_1, x_2) = (3, 2)$ we can represent it in Figure 1 by the *point* x reached by travelling 3 units in a positive direction (i.e. to the right) from the origin O (representing the bundle (0, 0)) along the x_1–axis, and then 2 units in a positive direction (i.e. upwards) parallel to the x_2–axis. It is sometimes convenient to think of a bundle as a *vector*, that is a straight line possessing length and direction. In Figure 1 the vector corresponding to the bundle x is the straight line from (0, 0) to (3, 2); the arrowhead indicates the direction.

Let us now turn our attention from the set of alternatives from which the consumer chooses on a particular occasion to the wider set of all alternatives that must be contemplated if we consider all possible budgets and sets of prices. What is the nature of the set of all bundles on which his preference ordering is defined?

This set must of course include bundles large enough for very large

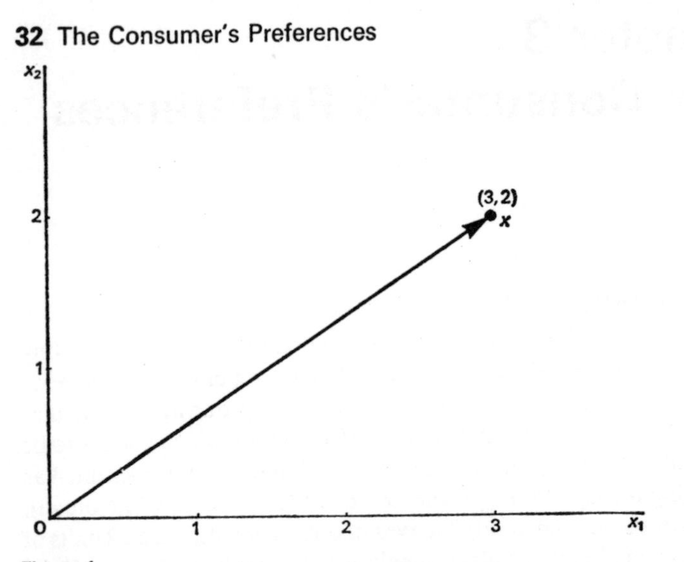

Figure 1

budgets and low prices. But very *small* quantities of all goods may be inadequate to permit the consumer (or all members of the household) to survive. It makes no sense to speak of preferences among bundles below the survival level, since if only such bundles can be afforded the consumer will cease to exist. Thus there will be bundles close to the point $(0, 0, \ldots, 0)$ to which the preference ordering does not apply. (The precise *shape* of this set of bundles will be discussed later in this chapter.)

Are we to allow bundles which are very close together? Some goods (like butter) are perfectly divisible; others (like eggs) are not. But a household that buys 5 eggs, 6 eggs and 5 eggs in successive weeks has purchased on the average $5\frac{1}{3}$ eggs per week, so that there is some justification for permitting $x_1, x_2, \ldots, x_n$ to be any (non-negative) *rational* numbers (i.e. numbers which can be expressed as the ratio of two whole numbers). There is no similar justification for admitting *irrational* quantities (like π or $\sqrt{2}$) of indivisible commodities, but it is very convenient to take the further step nonetheless and let $x_1, x_2, \ldots, x_n$ be any non-negative *real* numbers (i.e. any numbers, rational or irrational,[2] that can be measured as a distance along a straight line).

2. The notions of rational and irrational *number* and rational and irrational *behaviour* are of course quite unrelated, though they do have a common ety-

Powerful analytical methods can then be used, and adjustments can be made later.

We are now in a position to define the consumption set C, from a subset S of which, determined by his budget and the prices of goods, the consumer will on each occasion make a choice. The consumption set consists of all bundles $(x_1, x_2, \ldots, x_n)$, in which $x_1, x_2, \ldots, x_n$ are non-negative real numbers, which permit the consumer to survive. He has a weak preference ordering (defined in Section **2.2**) on the elements of the consumption set.

3.2 Non-saturation

As we saw on page 25 above, the assumption of a weak preference ordering alone is not sufficient to permit us to derive any testable hypotheses about a consumer's actual choices. In the remainder of this chapter we make further assumptions which lead to such hypotheses.

The first assumption is that the consumer prefers more of each commodity to less. More precisely, if bundle x contains at least as much of every commodity as bundle x' and more of at least one commodity, then x is preferred to x'. This is a plausible enough assumption in most cases – the commodities consumed are 'goods' rather than 'bads' – but there are ways of dealing with cases in which it does not hold (see sections **7.2** and **8.3**).

It will be useful to have a shorthand way of comparing the quantities in pairs of bundles

$$x = (x_1, x_2, \ldots, x_n) \quad \text{and} \quad x' = (x'_1, x'_2, \ldots, x'_n).$$

Two obvious symbols are:

$$x = x' \quad \text{if } x_1 = x'_1, x_2 = x'_2, \ldots, x_n = x'_n;$$

the two bundles are then identical, containing equal quantities of each commodity (we write simply $x \neq x'$ if they are not identical); and

$$x > x' \quad \text{if } x_1 > x'_1, x_2 > x'_2, \ldots, x_n > x'_n,$$

so that x contains more of every commodity than x'.

There are two important intermediate cases. If x contains at least

mological origin. The basic meaning of the Latin word *ratio* is 'a calculation'. It was also used to mean the faculty which calculates (i.e. the reason) and the relationship (or ratio) between two numbers.

as much of every commodity as x', and we do *not* wish to exclude the possibility that the two bundles are identical, we write:

$$x \geqq x' \text{ if } x_1 \geqq x'_1, x_2 \geqq x'_2, \ldots, x_n \geqq x'_n,$$

but if x contains at least as much of every commodity and *more of at least one commodity*, so that the two bundles are *not* identical, we write:

$$x \geqslant x' \text{ if } x_1 \geqq x'_1, x_2 \geqq x'_2, \ldots, x_n \geqq x'_n \text{ and } x \neq x'.$$

The assumption of non-saturation may now be written formally as the following axiom.

Axiom **4** (Non-saturation): *For all x, x' in the consumption set* C, *if $x \geqslant x'$, then xPx'.*

In what follows, the indifference classes defined in section **2.2** will be of great importance. Though our assumptions do not yet guarantee that any two distinct bundles will be indifferent, we shall now state, prove and then interpret a result about indifference classes.

Proposition **1** ('downward-sloping indifference curves'): *For all x, x' in* C, *if xIx', then neither $x \geqslant x'$ nor $x' \geqslant x$.* (The formal proof is very easy, and is left to the reader as an exercise.)

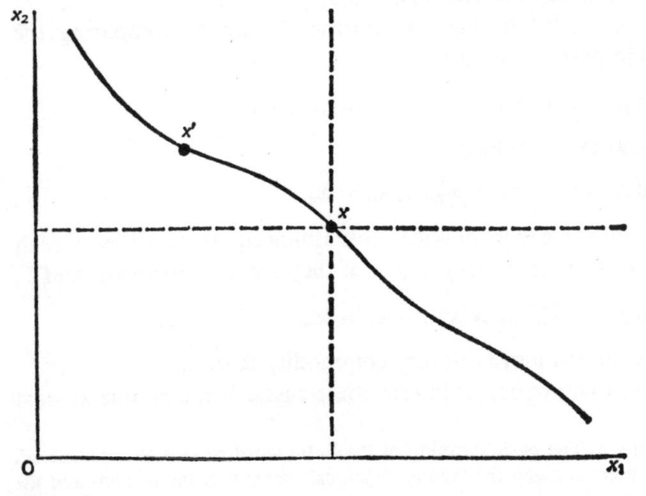

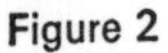
Figure 2

To see what Proposition **1** means, consider Figure 2. Let us suppose either that there are only two commodities x_1 and x_2, or that we are considering a set of bundles containing equal quantities of all commodities other than x_1 and x_2. Given the point representing bundle x, where must we place the point corresponding to a bundle x' which is indifferent to x (but not identical with x)? By Axiom **4** it cannot contain at least as much of each commodity and more of at least one commodity, or it would be preferred to x. That is, x' cannot lie in, or on either boundary of, the quadrant (bounded by dotted lines) 'north-east' of x. Similarly, x' cannot lie in, or on either boundary of, the quadrant 'south-west' of x. Thus it must lie within (not on the boundary of) either the 'north-west' or the 'south-east' quadrant with reference to x.

If there is a continuous line or curve consisting of points all indifferent to x, application of Proposition **1** at each point implies that it must everywhere slope downward to the right, as shown (hence the name given to Proposition **1**).

3.3 Continuity of preferences

It is a nuisance to have to be concerned with matters of continuity, but a great convenience to be able to use the methods which the assumption of continuity permits. But since continuity is of technical rather than of economic interest, general readers may prefer to skip to the paragraph following Axiom **5** on p. 38.

In Figure 3, draw the straight line or ray from the origin to the point x in the consumption set C. By Axiom **4**, every point above x on this ray is preferred to x, and x is preferred to every point below it on the ray. Now consider any other ray from the origin which enters the consumption set C. Start on this ray at a point to which x is preferred[3], and move outwards until a point is reached at which you can move no further without reaching a point which is preferred to x. Call this point x'. All points above x' on this ray are preferred to x; x is preferred to all points below x'.

Consider the set of all points like x' on all rays from the origin which enter the consumption set C. We call this set the *boundary set* of x, B(x). It is the set of all points x' on rays from the origin with the property that for any other point x'' on the ray Ox', if $x'' \geqslant x'$, then $x''Px$, while if $x'' \leqslant x'$, then xPx''.

3. There will always be such a point, since x cannot be the origin by virtue of our exclusion from C of all bundles that do not permit the consumer to survive.

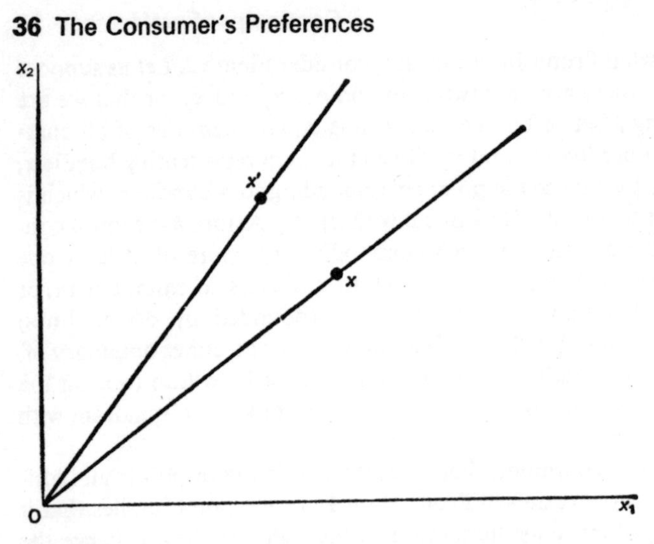

Figure 3

What is the set $B(x)$ like? Firstly, if x' and x'' are both in $B(x)$, it is not possible for one to contain more of *all* commodities than the other.

For suppose that in Figure 4 $x'' > x'$. Then one could find a point x''' on Ox' above x' and a point x'''' below x'' on Ox'' such that $x'' \geqslant x'''' \geqslant x''' \geqslant x'$.

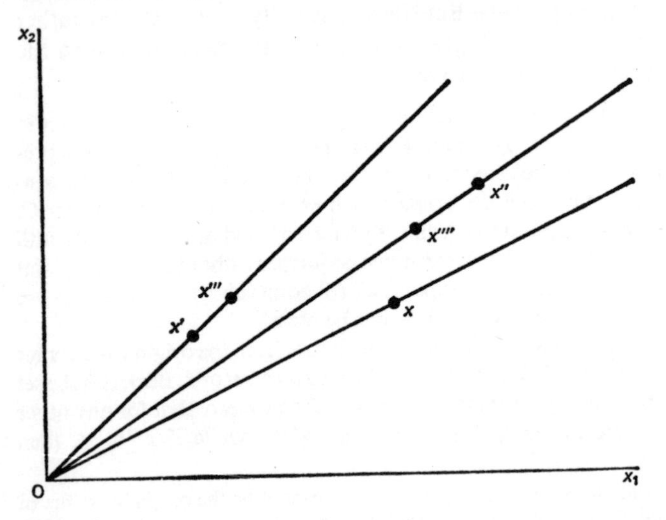

Figure 4

By construction $x''Px$ and xPx''', so that $x''Px'''$ by Corollary (d), Section 2.2. But since $x''' \geqslant x''$, by Axiom 4 $x'''Px''$ – a contradiction. We cannot, however, prove that x'' cannot lie *due east* of x'. Thus while $x'' > x'$ is ruled out, $x'' \geqslant x'$ is not.

Secondly, the set B(x) forms a continuous set of points. This means that if x' and x'' are two points in B(x), then no matter how close together they are there must be a point *between* them.

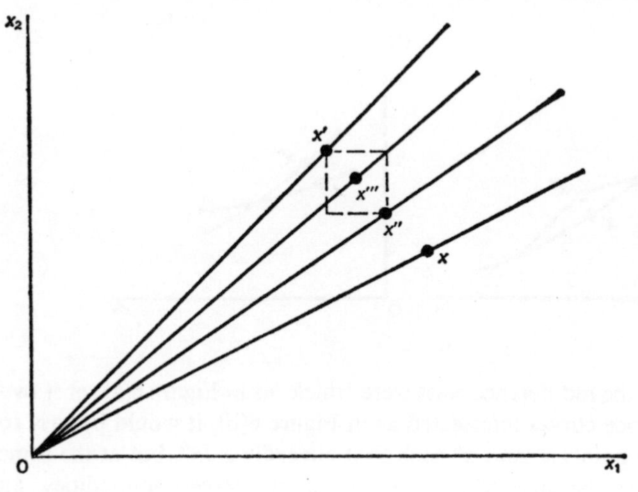

Figure 5

Let x' and x'' in Figure 5 be in B(x). No matter how close together x' and x'' are, there is a ray between Ox' and Ox'', and on that ray is a point x''' in B(x). We have just shown that neither $x' > x'''$, $x''' > x'$, $x'' > x'''$ nor $x''' > x''$ is possible. It follows that x''' must lie in or on the boundary of the rectangle (or its n-dimensional equivalent) of which x' and x'' are the corners. If x'' lies due east or due south of x', x''' must lie on the straight line joining them. This is what we mean by saying that there must be a point 'between' x' and x''.

Now although the assumption of perfect divisibility of commodities, together with Axiom 4, ensures that the set B(x) has no 'holes' in it, this is *not* what we mean by continuity of the preference ordering. On our present assumptions the consumer may regard any member of B(x) as better than, worse than or indifferent to x. As we move along a ray we may go abruptly from points worse than x to points better than x, without passing through a point indifferent to x. The assumption of continuity is simply that this does not happen, since all bundles in $B(x)$ are indifferent to x.

Axiom 5 (Continuity of preferences): *For all x' in the boundary set* $B(x)$ *associated with x, $x'Ix$.*

We have now assumed the existence of continuous indifference curves like that shown in Figure 2 above. In two dimensions an indifference class must indeed be a line or curve.

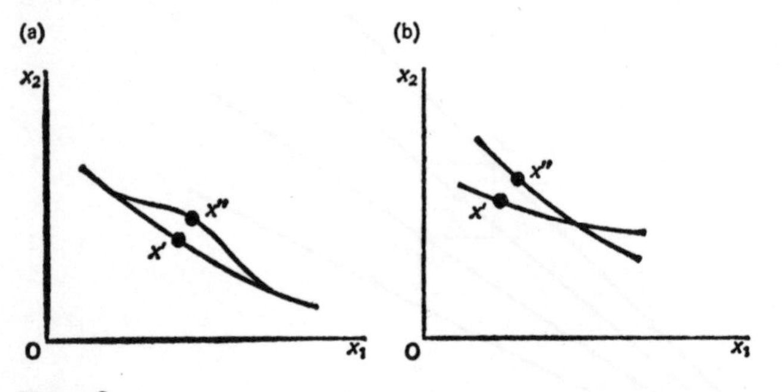

Figure 6

For if the indifference class were 'thick' as in Figure 6(a), or if two indifference curves intersected as in Figure 6(b), it would be easy to find two points x' and x'' such that allegedly $x'Ix''$, but at the same time $x''Px'$ because $x'' > x'$. (If there are *three* commodities, an indifference class is a two-dimensional surface, and in general it is an $(n-1)$-dimensional surface if the number of commodities is n.)

We are now in a position to be a little more specific about the lower boundary of the consumption set C. We assume the existence of an indifference class, the *bare survival set*, any bundle in which barely permits the consumer to survive. With less than the quantities contained in a given bundle in the set, he would starve or die of exposure. He prefers any given bundle in the bare survival set to any smaller bundle, but no preference ordering exists on the bundles which do not permit survival.

3.4 Convexity

All we have so far assumed about indifference curves is that they exist and slope downward to the right. The assumption of convexity relates to their curvature.

The usual assumption that indifference curves are (smoothly) 'convex to the origin' has a visual interpretation. In Figure 7, one imagines an eye at the origin looking up at the curve and seeing it as convex.

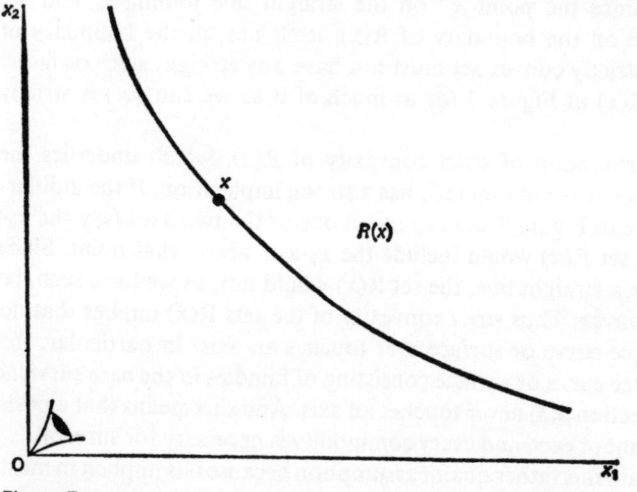

Figure 7

A more rigorous way of defining convexity is to focus on the *set* of points regarded by the consumer as at least as good as x. This set, R(x), consists of all points x' in C such that $x'Rx$.

A set is said to be *convex* if, for all x', x'' in the set, every point between x' and x'' on the straight line joining x' and x'' is also in the set. It is *strictly convex* if every such point is in the interior (i.e. not on the boundary) of the set. Compare Figure 7 with Figures 8(a) and 8(b).

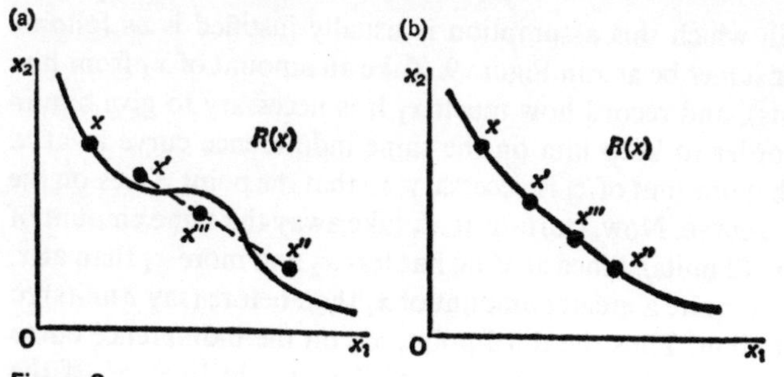

Figure 8

In Figure 8(a) R(x) is not convex, since there are points like x''', on the straight line joining x' and x'', which lie outside R(x). In Figure 8(b), that part of R(x) which is shown is convex but not strictly convex, since the point x''' on the straight line joining x' and x'', which are on the boundary of R(x), itself lies on the boundary of R(x). A strictly convex set must not have any straight sides or faces. The set R(x) in Figure 7 (or as much of it as we can see) is strictly convex.

The assumption of strict convexity of R(x), which underlies the indifference curve in Figure 7, has a strong implication. If the indifference curve in Figure 7 were to touch one of the two axes (say the x_2-axis), the set R(x) would include the x_2-axis above that point. Since the axis is a straight line, the set R(x) would not, as we have seen, be strictly convex. Thus strict convexity of the sets R(x) implies that no indifference curve or surface ever touches an axis. In particular, the indifference curve or surface consisting of bundles in the bare survival set (see Section **3.3**) never touches an axis. And this means that a positive amount of each and every commodity is necessary for survival.

We retain this rather quaint assumption because it is implicit in most of the literature. Surprisingly, the techniques for dealing with cases in which the sets R(x) do touch the axes (and the consumer does *not* buy a positive quantity of every commodity in the shop!) have been developed only fairly recently, and are neglected in most textbooks. We shall introduce these techniques in section **7.2**, but for the time being we state the following Axiom.

Axiom **6** (Strict convexity): *For all x in* C, *the set* R(x), *consisting of all x' in* C *such that $x'Rx$, is strictly convex.*

The way in which this assumption is usually justified is as follows. Let the consumer be at x in Figure 9. Take an amount of x_2 from him (e.g. 2 units), and record how much x_1 it is necessary to give him in return in order to keep him on the same indifference curve as at x. Suppose that one unit of x_1 is necessary, so that the point x' lies on the indifference curve. Now, starting at x', take away the same amount of x_2 as before (2 units). Since at x' he has less x_2 and more x_1 than at x, he will now require a greater amount of x_1 than before (say 2 units) to compensate him. Thus the third point, x'', on the indifference curve will lie to the right of the extension of the straight line xx'. If the amounts of x_2 taken away were made smaller and smaller, and the foregoing argument held everywhere, the indifference curve (the lower boundary of the set R(x)) would approach the convex-to-the-origin indifference curve of Figure 7. But we have not yet ensured that indifference curves will be *smoothly* convex to the origin as in Figure 7.

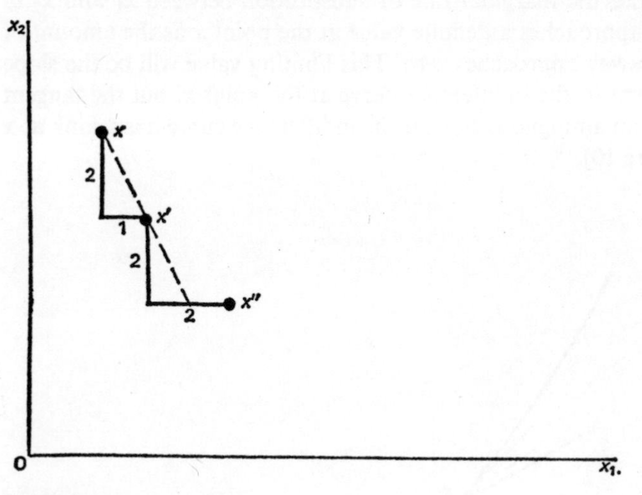

Figure 9

Before we discuss smoothness, it will be useful to introduce the concept of the marginal rate of substitution.[4] As we move from x to x' in Figure 9, one unit of x_1 is substituted for 2 units of x_2 at the margin, and we say that the marginal rate of substitution of x_1 for x_2 is 1 : 2, or $\frac{1}{2}$; alternatively (if we move *back* from x' to x), the marginal rate of substitution of x_2 for x_1 is 2.[5] As we move from x' to x'', the marginal rate of substitution of x_1 for x_2 is 1, and the marginal rate of substitution of x_2 for x_1 is also 1. Thus as we increase x_1, keeping the individual on the same indifference curve, the marginal rate of substitution of x_2 for x_1 falls (from 2 to 1 in the example just given).

4. I believe that Newman is fighting a losing battle in trying to change this term, which has been in universal use since Hicks introduced it over thirty years ago.

5. I cannot bring myself to say, as Hicks would, that the marginal rate of substitution of x_1 for x_2 is 2.

This is how we must express the familiar 'diminishing marginal rate of substitution'.

Now we shall discover in later chapters that it is often necessary to consider what happens if we make infinitesimally small movements along an indifference curve. It is convenient to assume, in this connexion, that the marginal rate of substitution between x_1 and x_2 in Figure 9 approaches a definite value at the point x as the amount of x_2 taken away approaches zero. This limiting value will be the slope of a tangent to the indifference curve at the point x, but the tangent will have an ambiguous slope if the indifference curve has a kink at x (see Figure 10).

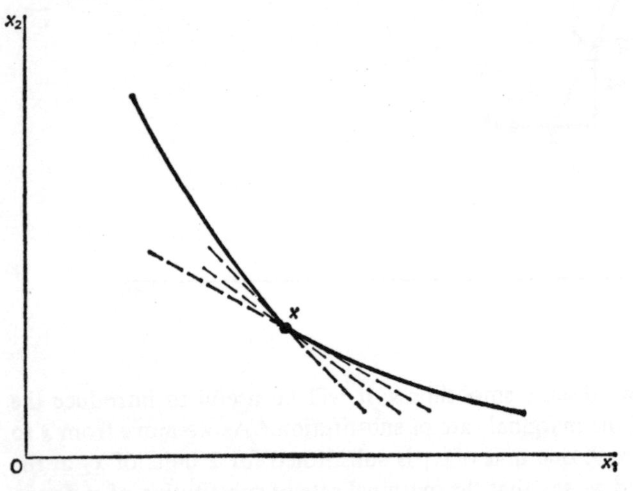

Figure 10

The existence of a unique marginal rate of substitution between all pairs of commodities at every point x, together with Axiom **6**, thus implies that indifference curves are everywhere *smoothly* convex to the origin.

Axiom **7** (Smooth indifference curves): *At all points x in* C, *the marginal rate of substitution between any pair of commodities is uniquely determined.*

The implications of Axioms **5**, **6** and **7** taken together can be summarized, in part, as the following proposition.

Proposition 2: *For any pair of commodities x_i and x_j, given the quantities of all other commodities, the marginal rate of substitution of x_j for x_i is a continuous and strictly decreasing function of x_i.*

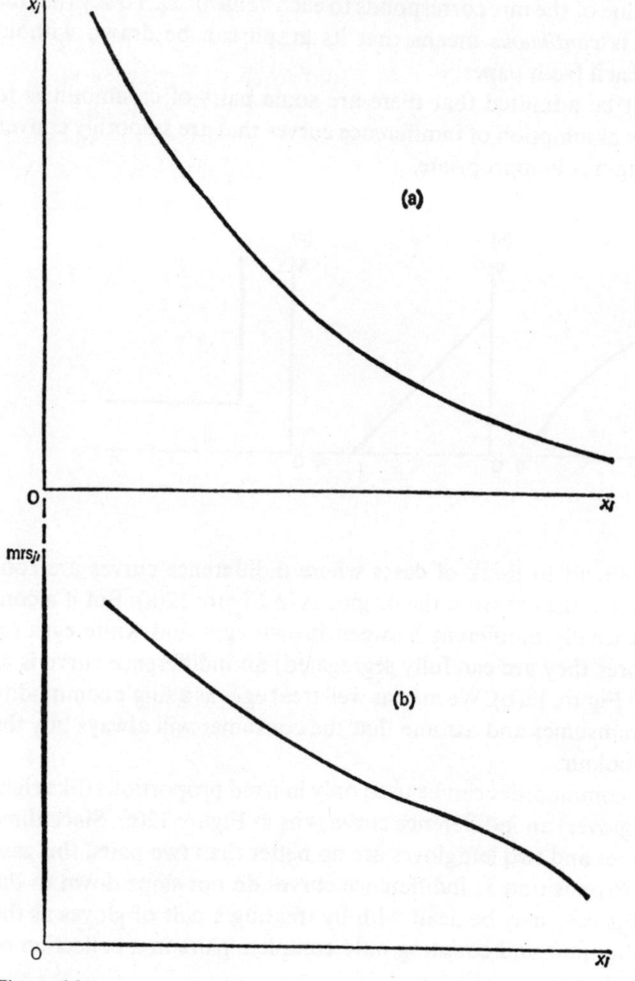

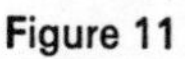
Figure 11

This proposition is illustrated in Figures 11(a) and 11(b). As we increase x_i and decrease x_j (holding the quantities of all other commodities constant) in such a way as to keep the consumer on the same indifference curve, the marginal rate of substitution (mrs) of x_j for x_i always decreases. To say that the mrs is a *function* of x_i means that a *unique* value of the mrs corresponds to each value of x_i. To say that the function is *continuous* means that its graph can be drawn without taking pencil from paper.

It must be admitted that there are some pairs of commodities to which the assumption of indifference curves that are smoothly convex to the origin is inappropriate.

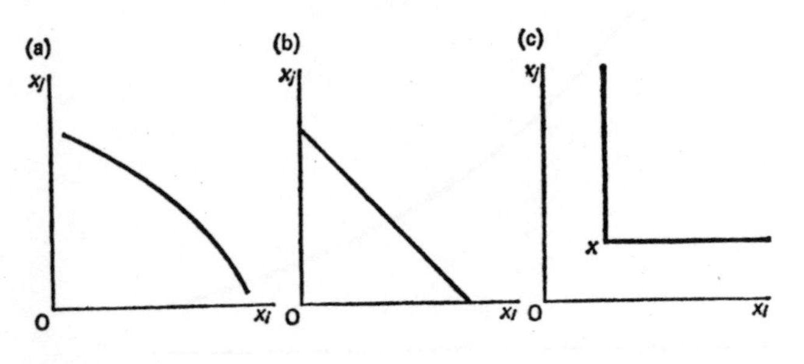

Figure 12

It is difficult to think of cases where indifference curves are concave when looked at from the origin, as in Figure 12(a). But if a consumer is totally indifferent between brown eggs and white eggs (in some stores they are carefully segregated) an indifference curve is as shown in Figure 12(b). We may as well treat eggs as a single commodity for this consumer and assume that the consumer will always buy the cheaper colour.

If two commodities can be used only in fixed proportions (like right and left gloves) an indifference curve is as in Figure 12(c). Since three right gloves and two left gloves are no better than two pairs, this case violates Proposition **1**; indifference curves do not slope down to the right. This case may be dealt with by treating a pair of gloves as the commodity unit and counting only complete pairs in a collection of assorted gloves.

Our description of the structure of the consumer's preferences is now complete. In the next two chapters we show how testable hypotheses about behaviour can be derived.

Exercises

1. Prove Proposition **1.**

2. What is implied about a consumer's preferences if $x \geqq x'$?

3. Which of the following is convex or strictly convex?

   (a) a solid sphere;

   (b) a solid cube;

   (c) a doughnut (with a hole).

4. If $y = \sqrt{x}$, where x can be any positive real number, is y a *function* of x?

Notes on the literature

As with Chapter 2, the most useful single companion to this chapter is Newman, *The Theory of Exchange*, ch. 2. Some of the technical matters are beautifully expounded by T. C. Koopmans, *Three Essays on the State of Economic Science* (McGraw-Hill, 1957), in the first essay of his book.

3.2 The notation used here for comparing quantities in different bundles is common but not universal. Sometimes '$\geqslant$', '$>$' and '$\gtrsim$' are used for our '$>$', '$\geqslant$' and '$\geqq$'.

We have used the term 'non-saturation' to mean two things that are sometimes distinguished:

(a) that it is not possible for the consumer to have so much of everything that he is completely saturated and

(b) that he is also not 'locally' saturated at any point, as he would be, for example, if he were indifferent between two units and three units of a commodity, but preferred four units to either two or three (see Koopmans, *op. cit.*, pp. 30, 47).

3.3 It is not always assumed that the consumer is indifferent among alternative ways of barely surviving (see Koopmans, *op. cit.*, p. 34).

3.4 The 'marginal rate of substitution' was introduced by J. R. (now Sir John) Hicks in the first chapter of *Value and Capital* (Oxford University Press, 1939 and 1946). The first three chapters of this work are compulsory reading, but the references to utility (which we do not take up until Part Two) may bother the reader at this stage.

Chapter 4
Demand Functions

4.1 The budget constraint

We have assumed that the consumer sets aside a certain sum of money or 'budget', M, for his purchases on a particular date. Goods are available to him at positive prices which he cannot alter no matter how much or how little he buys. Since the essence of a budget is that it must not be exceeded, he is subject to the limitation that the total money value of his purchases must not exceed M. If we call p_i the price of the ith commodity (i runs from 1 to n), $p_i x_i$ is his expenditure on the ith commodity. Thus the budget constraint is

$$p_1 x_1 + p_2 x_2 + \ldots + p_n x_n = \sum_{i=1}^{n} p_i x_i \leqq M.$$

It is again useful to have a short-hand notation. The term *vector* is used not only geometrically to mean the directed line corresponding to a list of numbers as in Figure 1, but also to mean the list of numbers themselves. Thus $p = (p_1, p_2, \ldots, p_n)$ is a vector of prices and $x = (x_1, x_2, \ldots, x_n)$ is a vector of quantities. Two vectors of equal dimensions (i.e. consisting of lists of numbers of equal lengths) like p and x have an *inner product*, defined as $p_1 x_1 + p_2 x_2 + \ldots + p_n x_n$ and written as $p.x$. This inner product is nothing but total expenditure, so that the budget constraint can be written alternatively as

$$p.x \leqq M.$$

If there are only two commodities, the budget constraint can be shown geometrically as limiting the consumer to a triangle, as in Figure 13.

Let $M = £100$, $p_1 = £2$ and $p_2 = £5$. If the whole of M is spent, the consumer may buy $50x_1$ and no x_2, or $20x_2$ and no x_1, or any combination of x_1 and x_2 on the straight line joining (50, 0) and

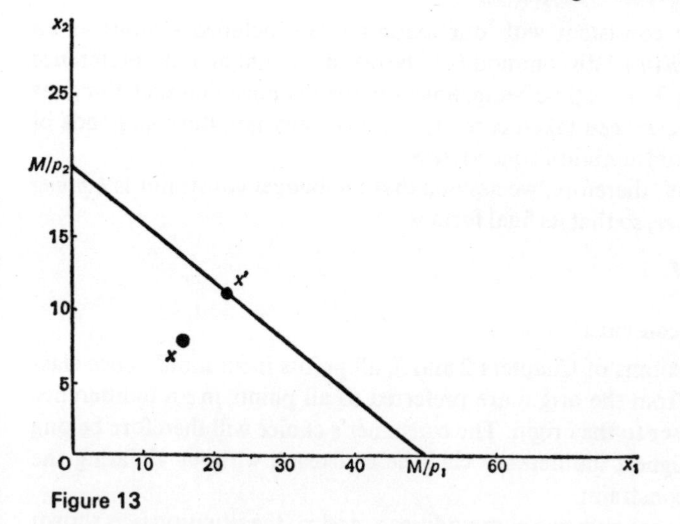

Figure 13

(0, 20). The equation of this 'budget line' is obtained by solving $p_1 x_1 + p_2 x_2 = M$ for x_2,

$$x_2 = \frac{M}{p_2} - \frac{p_1}{p_2} x_1 = 20 - \tfrac{2}{5} x_1.$$

Will the consumer spend his whole budget? He is not compelled to do so and if he does not he may presumably carry the unspent balance over to the next period or use it for another purpose. It will be recalled, however, that the selection of this particular budget was assumed to be part of a wider decision process (see section **2.1**) in which provision for other dates and requirements was made. If this process is efficient, there will be no slack in the household budget we are now considering.

In fact, our Axioms **3** and **4** compel us to conclude that the consumer *will* spend his whole budget. For if a point like x below the budget line in Figure 13 were chosen, there would be points like x' in the budget triangle containing more of both goods than x, so that $x'Px$ by Axiom **4**. To choose x would then be inconsistent with Axiom **3**.

If this very strong result makes the reader suspicious, let us point out that diversion of part of the budget to, for example, savings *could* be made consistent with our axioms if we included savings as an *additional* $(n+1)$th commodity to be taken account of in the preference ordering. For the time being, however, it is assumed that such things as saving have been taken care of, and that only non-durable goods of current consumption concern us.[6]

In brief, therefore, we assume that the budget constraint is *binding* or *effective*, so that its final form is

$$p.x = M.$$

4.2 The consumer's choice

By the axioms of Chapters 2 and 3, all points in an indifference class further from the origin are preferred to all points in an indifference class closer to the origin. The consumer's choice will therefore belong to the highest indifference class he can reach without violating the budget constraint.

If there are only two commodities x_i and x_j, the situation is as shown in Figure 14. The highest indifference curve attainable is the one that touches the budget line at x in Figure 14.

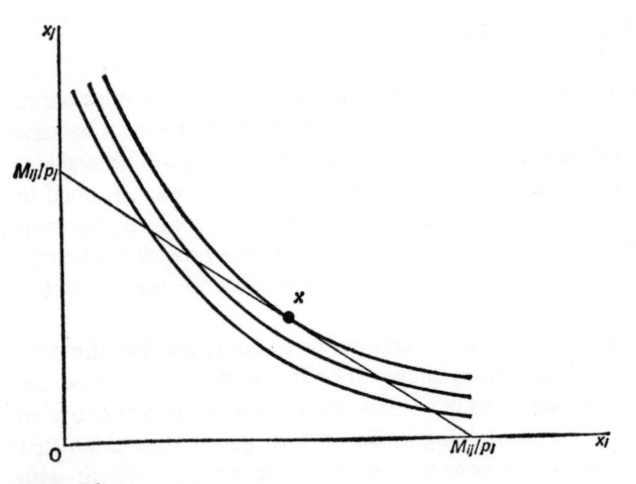

Figure 14

6. The implications of this assumption are considered further in section 11.2 below.

If there are more than two commodities, let x_i and x_j be any two of them. When the consumer has made his choice of all n quantities, subtract from M his expenditure on all commodities other than x_i and x_j, and let M_{ij} be the amount that is left. If we now draw indifference curves relating to x_i and x_j alone (holding the quantities of all other commodities constant at their chosen levels), a budget line is obtained as for Figure 13 above (p. 47),

$$x_j = \frac{M_{ij}}{p_j} - \frac{p_i}{p_j} x_i.$$

The situation for x_i and x_j will be exactly as in Figure 14.

At the point x the budget line is tangent to the indifference curve, so that their slopes are equal. Along the *budget line*, the change in x_j per unit change in x_i is equal to p_i divided by p_j. For if, by moving along the budget line one can buy two more units of x_j by buying five units less of x_i, the price per unit of x_i must be two-fifths of the price per unit of x_j. At the point x on the *indifference curve*, the rate of change of x_j per unit change of x_i is the marginal rate of substitution of x_j for x_i, which we write as mrs_{ji}.[7] Therefore at x, $\text{mrs}_{ji} = p_i/p_j$.

It will be recalled that Axiom **6** implies that no indifference class in the consumption set ever touches an axis. It follows that no point of tangency of a budget line and an indifference curve can ever be on an axis, so the consumer will always choose a positive amount of every commodity. (This odd assumption will be relaxed later: see sections **7.2** and **8.3**.)

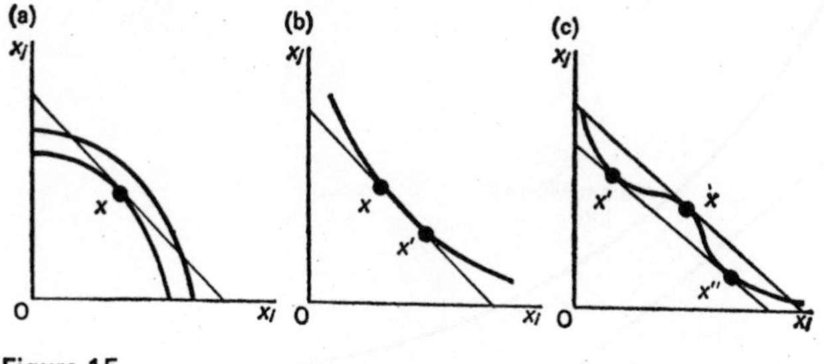

Figure 15

7. Since both the budget line and the indifference curve slope downward to the right, the *slopes* are negative, and equal to $-p_i/p_j$ and $-\text{mrs}_{ji}$ respectively.

What is the significance of the assumptions that the indifference curves are everywhere strictly and smoothly convex to the origin (Axioms **6** and **7**)? In Figure 15(a), x is a point of tangency of an indifference curve with the budget line, but since indifference curves are concave to the origin, x is the *worst* point on the budget line, not the best. In Figure 15(b), the indifference curve has a straight segment ($R(x)$ is convex, but not strictly convex), and the rational consumer may choose any point on the line xx'. In Figure 15(c), the indifference curve has both concave and convex stretches. The point of tangency at x is not the best point on the upper budget line, and there is nothing to choose between the points of tangency x' and x'' on the lower budget line.

Thus it is only when indifference curves are strictly convex to the origin that there is a unique point of tangency, between an indifference curve and a budget line, corresponding to the bundle of goods that stands highest in the consumer's preference ordering. (The assumption that indifference curves are smoothly convex to the origin, rather than kinked as in Figure 10 on p. 42 above, is a convenience in that, as is there pointed out, the marginal rate of substitution is then uniquely determined at each point.)

Our theory has nothing to say about what the consumer will do if his budget and the prices of goods do not permit him to survive, as in

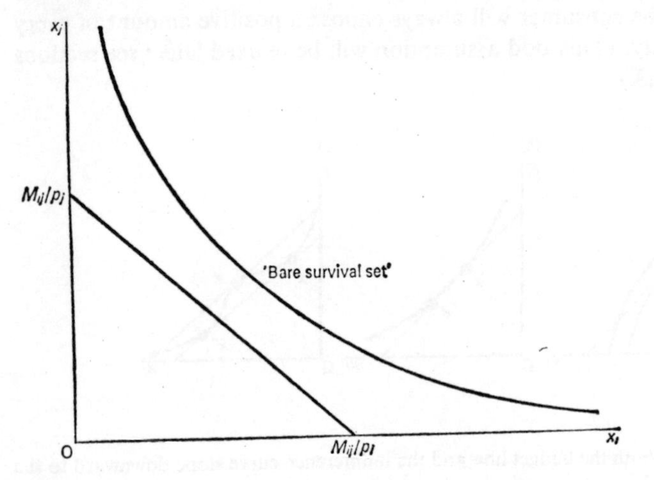

Figure 16

Figure 16. It is to be hoped that such cases do not often arise, though we shall have occasion to consider the possibility later in our discussion of welfare economics. For the time being we assume that the consumer can always afford bundles in his consumption set.[8]

Let us summarize the results of sections **4.1** and **4.2**. If a consumer satisfies Axioms **1** to **7**, and is faced with a budget constraint $p.x \leqq M$ in which all prices are given and positive, then:

1. he will spend his whole budget M;
2. he will buy a positive amount of each commodity;
3. at the chosen point, for each pair of commodities x_i and x_j, $\text{mrs}_{ji} = p_i/p_j$.

4.3 Fundamental properties of demand functions

A *demand function* of a single consumer is a relationship between, on the one hand, the amount of a commodity he is able and willing to buy, and on the other hand his budget and the prices of all commodities. To say that x_i is a *function* of $M, p_1,\ldots, p_n$ means (see p. 44 above) that to each set of values of M and $p_1, p_2,\ldots, p_n$ there corresponds a *unique* value of x_i. This is clearly the case for all commodities on our assumptions. The values of M and p define a budget area in which a single point is preferred to all others, and is chosen. This point represents a unique quantity of each commodity. Thus demand functions *exist*, and we write

$$x_i = f_i(p_1, p_2,\ldots, p_n, M) \quad (i = 1, 2,\ldots, n).$$

This expression says that the *dependent variable* x_i is a function of all the *independent variables* $p_1, p_2,\ldots p_n, M$ that appear in parentheses after the functional symbol f_i.

The reader will find that in the literature '*income*' (written as Y, I or sometimes M) usually appears as an independent variable instead of the budget. We do not wish at this stage to worry about definitions of 'income', and we certainly do not wish to identify the consumer's budget with his 'income'. We shall, however, find that if we assume, purely for convenience, that *the consumer's budget M is always the*

8. Technically, we assume that the *intersection* of (i.e. the set of points common to) the consumption set and the budget area is not empty (as it is in Figure 16).

same proportion of his 'income' Y, many of the results we shall state continue to hold if 'budget' is replaced by 'income', and we shall so indicate when appropriate. For example, if $M = cY$, M is uniquely determined by Y, so that if x_i is a function of p and M it is also a function of p and Y, and we can write

$$x_i = g_i(p_1, p_2, \ldots, p_n, Y) \quad (i = 1, 2, \ldots, n).$$

Note that we use a different functional symbol (g_i instead of f_i) since the list of independent variables has changed.

The first property of demand functions (apart from their existence) that follows from our axioms is that they are free from *money illusion.* A consumer is said to suffer from money illusion if an increase in his monetary means causes him to feel better off and buy more regardless of what has happened to money prices.

Our axioms rule out this phenomenon. For if, for example, the budget doubles *and* the prices of all commodities double, the budget area is unaffected, and so therefore is the chosen bundle of goods. This point may be illustrated by the numerical example on page 46 above. If M, p_1 and p_2 are all doubled, becoming £200, £4 and £10 respectively, the equation of the budget line is still $x_2 = 20 - \frac{2}{5}x_1$, exactly as before. On the assumption, discussed at length in Chapter 2, that the consumer's preference ordering has not changed, the chosen point x does not change, nor does the chosen quantity of any commodity.

Thus if M and all prices are changed in the same proportion, the quantity of each commodity demanded is unchanged. This means that for any (positive) value of k

$$x_i = f_i(p_1, p_2, \ldots, p_n, M) = f_i(kp_1, kp_2, \ldots, kp_n, kM).$$

Such a function is said to be *homogeneous of degree zero*. A function is homogeneous of degree r if, when all the independent variables are multiplied by k, the result is to multiply the dependent variable by k^r (k to the rth power). In the case of our demand functions, x_i remains unchanged: it is multiplied by 1. Since for all values of k (except $k = 0$), $1 = k^0$, the demand functions $f_i(p_1, p_2, \ldots, p_n, M)$ are homogeneous of degree zero. If M is always the same proportion of Y, to multiply M by k is also to multiply Y by k, so that the demand functions $g_i(p_1, p_2, \ldots, p_n, Y)$ are also homogeneous of degree zero.

Without using symbols, we can say that demand for any commodity is homogeneous of degree zero 'in' the budget and all prices, and also (if $M = cY$) in 'income' and all prices.

Note that since k can be *any* positive number, we can set it equal to, $1/p_1$ or $1/M$, for example, so that

$$x_i = f_i\left[1, \frac{p_2}{p_1}, \ldots, \frac{p_n}{p_1}, \frac{M}{p_1}\right] = f_i\left[\frac{p_1}{M}, \frac{p_2}{M}, \ldots, \frac{p_n}{M}, 1\right].$$

The quantity of any commodity demanded is uniquely determined by the n *ratios* formed by dividing each of the $n+1$ independent variables by any one of them: one quotient is always unity. But if we wish to write x_i as a function of n such ratios *only*, f_i can no longer be used, and a different functional symbol must be defined for each set of ratios selected. Thus:

$$x_i = h_i\left[\frac{p_2}{p_1}, \ldots, \frac{p_n}{p_1}, \frac{M}{p_1}\right] = k_i\left[\frac{p_1}{M}, \frac{p_2}{M}, \ldots, \frac{p_n}{M}\right].$$

4.4 Demand curves and own-price elasticity

A useful way of describing a demand function is to give the values of its *elasticities*. 'Elasticity' is a measure of the responsiveness of a dependent variable to changes in an independent variable.

In demand theory, the most familiar elasticity (often referred to as *the* elasticity of demand) relates the quantity of a commodity demanded to changes in its own price. To distinguish this concept from other elasticities to be defined in the next section, we call it the *own-price elasticity of demand.*

It is best explained by means of a *demand curve* (Figure 17), which represents x_i as a function of p_i. As we have seen, x_i is a function of the budget and prices of all goods, not only of p_i, so that if the demand curve is to be a legitimate construction we must assume that the independent variables other than p_i (as well as the consumer's preferences) remain unchanged during the analysis. Then we can write $x_i = d_i(p_i)$. (For some purposes it is convenient to treat price as the dependent variable and quantity as the independent variable; see sections **8.1** and **9.5**.)

It saves confusion if we refer to a movement along a demand curve in response to a change in price (e.g. a movement from A to B in

Figure 17) as a *change in the quantity demanded.* The term *change in demand* is best reserved for cases in which the demand curve shifts, as when a change in the budget or in some price other than p_i causes more or less to be bought at a given price. A movement of the whole demand curve in the direction of the arrows would be an increase in demand, altering the functional relationship $x_i = d_i(p_i)$.

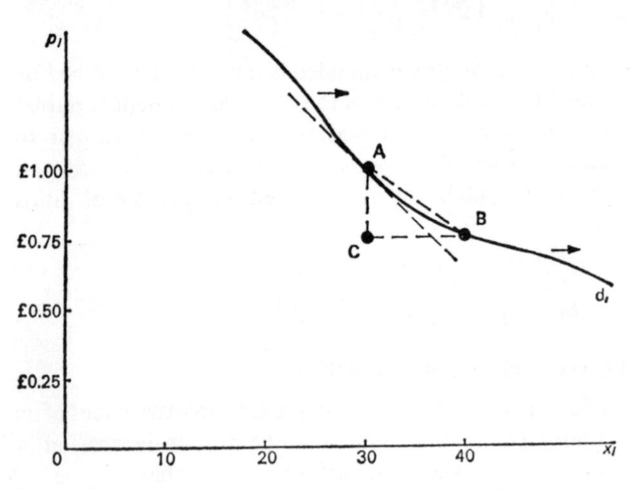

Figure 17

One way of measuring the own-price elasticity of demand is as the percentage change in x_i divided by the percentage change in p_i, or (writing Δ for 'the change in') as

$$\frac{\Delta x_i}{x_i} \div \frac{\Delta p_i}{p_i}, \quad \text{which obviously equals } \frac{p_i}{x_i}\frac{\Delta x_i}{\Delta p_i}.$$

But there are serious objections to this formula. In the first place, using the illustrative numbers in Figure 17, the value of the elasticity as we go from A to B is

$$\frac{40-30}{30} \div \frac{£0{\cdot}75-£1{\cdot}00}{£1{\cdot}00} = 33\tfrac{1}{3}\% \div -25\% = -1{\cdot}33,$$

whereas if we go from B to A, we get

$$\frac{30-40}{40} \div \frac{£1{\cdot}00-£0{\cdot}75}{£0{\cdot}75} = -25\% \div 33\tfrac{1}{3}\% = -0{\cdot}75.$$

More important is that it is very convenient for a measure of this elasticity to have the properties (which this measure lacks) that:

(a) if a change in price leads to a change in quantity that leaves expenditure ($p_i x_i$) unchanged (unit-elastic demand), elasticity equals minus one;

(b) if a fall in price increases quantity but reduces expenditure and a rise in price reduces quantity but increases expenditure (inelastic demand), elasticity is between zero and minus one;

(c) if a fall in price increases expenditure and a rise in price decreases it (elastic demand), elasticity is between minus one and minus infinity.

Our numerical example illustrates this deficiency in the formula. Between A and B demand is unit-elastic as defined in terms of expenditure, since $30 \times £1{\cdot}00 = 40 \times £0{\cdot}75 = £30{\cdot}00$. But as measured, demand is elastic ($-1{\cdot}33$) as we go from A to B and inelastic ($-0{\cdot}75$) as we go from B to A.

Two words of warning before we try to clear up this difficulty. Firstly, because price and quantity normally change in opposite directions as we move along a demand curve, Δx_i and Δp_i have opposite signs, so that by the formula elasticity is negative. We shall retain the minus sign; but it is conventional in describing the own-price elasticity of demand to ignore it and say, for example, that an elastic demand curve has an elasticity greater than one (rather than 'less than minus one'). Secondly, for the case of vertical (completely inelastic) and horizontal (perfectly elastic) demand curves, the formula is quite satisfactory. Elasticity is zero in the former case, and approaches (minus) infinity as the demand curve approaches the horizontal in the latter case.

We shall not review the alternative measures of 'arc elasticity' (the elasticity over a stretch of the demand curve) that have been devised to overcome the difficulties we have described. Instead we shall use the same formula but confine ourselves to the elasticity at a *point* on the demand curve. We therefore seek the value of $(p_i/x_i)(\Delta x_i/\Delta p_i)$ as Δp_i approaches zero. A standard notation is available. When x_i is a function of p_i alone, the *derivative* of x_i with respect to p_i, written as dx_i/dp_i, is defined as the limit approached by the ratio $\Delta x_i/\Delta p_i$ as Δp_i approaches zero. In Figure 17, dx_i/dp_i at the point A is the value approached by ratios like $\text{CB}/-\text{AC}$ as AC gets shorter and shorter;

its value is given by the slope of the tangent to the demand curve at A.

Thus we can define the own-price elasticity at a point on the demand curve as $(p_i/x_i)(dx_i/dp_i)$. It can be verified (see Technical Appendix, section **T.1**) that on a stretch of a demand curve where $(p_i/x_i)(dx_i/dp_i)$ is everywhere between zero and minus one, demand is inelastic, as defined above in terms of the behaviour of expenditure when price changes. If $(p_i/x_i)(dx_i/dp_i)$ everywhere equals minus one, or is everywhere between minus one and infinity, the behaviour of expenditure is appropriate to unit-elastic or elastic demand respectively.

But our formulation of own-price elasticity needs to be sharpened slightly. It must be emphasized that dx_i/dp_i is the symbol for a derivative only when x_i is a function of the *single* independent variable p_i. If x_i is a function of severable variables, the limit of the ratio $\Delta x_i/\Delta p_i$ as Δp_i approaches zero, *and* the values of all independent variables other than p_i are held constant, is called the *partial derivative* of x_i with respect to p_i, and written as $\partial x_i/\partial p_i$. Since we wish to emphasize that x_i is a function of the $n+1$ variables $p_1,\ldots,p_n$, M, it is better to define the own-price elasticity of demand as

$$\eta_{i,p_i} = \frac{p_i}{x_i}\frac{\partial x_i}{\partial p_i}.$$

4.5 Cross-elasticities and budget-elasticity

Elasticities of demand must now be defined for the other independent variables. The *cross-elasticities of demand* measure the responsiveness of the demand for x_i to changes in the prices of other goods:

$$\eta_{i,p_j} = \frac{p_j}{x_i}\frac{\partial x_i}{\partial p_j}$$

is the limit, as Δp_j approaches zero, of $(\Delta x_i/x_i) \div (\Delta p_j/p_j)$, i.e. of $(p_j/x_i)(\Delta x_i/\Delta p_j)$, with M and all other prices held constant.

x_i is said to be a (gross[9]) *substitute* for x_j if $\eta_{i,p_j} > 0$, which implies that $\partial x_i/\partial p_j$ is positive, so that x_i and p_j move in the same direction. An increase in p_j would normally reduce x_j, so that if x_i increases it is being *substituted* for the more expensive x_j. x_i is said to be a (gross)

9. This is to distinguish them from the *net* or *Hicksian* substitutes and complements to be introduced in the next chapter.

complement for x_j if $\eta_{i,p_j} < 0$; in this case the demand for x_i falls along with x_j as x_j becomes more expensive.

Finally, the *budget elasticity of demand* and the *income elasticity of demand* are defined as

$$\eta_{i,M} = \frac{M}{x_i}\frac{\partial x_i}{\partial M} = p_i\frac{\partial x_i}{\partial M} \div \frac{p_i x_i}{M}; \qquad \eta_{i,Y} = \frac{Y}{x_i}\frac{\partial x_i}{\partial Y} = p_i\frac{\partial x_i}{\partial Y} \div \frac{p_i x_i}{Y}$$

($\eta_{i,M}$ is the limit, as ΔM approaches zero, of $(\Delta x_i/x_i) \div (\Delta M/M)$, i.e. of $(M/x_i)(\Delta x_i/\Delta M)$; similarly for $\eta_{i,Y}$.) The assumption that $M = cY$ implies that if Y rises by 10 per cent M rises by 10 per cent, so that $\Delta M/M = \Delta Y/Y$. From the definitions of the two elasticities they must then always be equal:

If $M = cY, \quad \eta_{i,M} = \eta_{i,Y}$.

If $\eta_{i,M} < 0$, which implies that $\partial x_i/\partial M < 0$, so that an increase in the budget reduces the demand for x_i, x_i is said to be an *inferior good.*

With all prices given, the value of $\eta_{i,M}$ indicates whether the proportion of the budget spent on x_i will rise or fall as the budget increases. This will first be proved, and then illustrated by a numerical example.

With p_i given, $p_i\ \partial x_i/\partial M$ is the rate at which expenditure on x_i will increase for each extra pound in the budget; it may be called the *marginal propensity to spend* on x_i. The quantity $p_i\ x_i/M$ is simply the proportion of the budget spent on x_i, or the *average propensity to spend* on x_i. Thus the budget-elasticity of demand is defined as the marginal propensity to spend on x_i divided by the average propensity to spend on x_i.

Now it is well known (see Technical Appendix, section **T.2**) that for any pair of average and marginal quantities (cost, revenue, productivity, propensity to spend ...), as the independent variable (output, sales, input, budget, ...) increases

$$\text{average} \begin{Bmatrix} \text{rises} \\ \text{stays the same} \\ \text{falls} \end{Bmatrix} \text{when marginal} \begin{Bmatrix} > \\ = \\ < \end{Bmatrix} \text{average.}$$

Now if $\eta_{i,M} < 1$, $p_i\ \partial x_i/\partial M < p_i\ x_i/M$, so that the marginal propensity to spend (mps) is less than the average propensity to spend (aps). Thus aps, the proportion of the budget (M) spent on x_i, falls as M rises and rises as M falls. Such goods are often called *necessities*.

If $\eta_{i,M} > 1$, mps > aps, so that $p_i x_i/M$ rises as M rises and falls as M falls. Such goods are often termed *luxuries*.

The following illustrative numerical example may clarify this argument.

	Date 1 M = £80		Changes ΔM = £40		Date 2 M = £120		Budget-Elasticity
	(1)	(2)	(3)	(4)	(5)	(6)	(7)
	$p_i x_i$	$\frac{p_i x_i}{M}$	$p_i \Delta x_i$	$\frac{p_i \Delta x_i}{\Delta M}$	$p_i x_i$ (1)+(3)	$\frac{p_i x_i}{M}$	(4)÷(2)
Commodity 1	£20	0·25	£4	0·1	£24	0·2	0·4
Commodity 2	£60	0·75	£36	0·9	£96	0·8	1·2

Commodity 1 is a necessity ($\eta_{1,M} = 0{\cdot}4 < 1$); its share of the increasing budget has fallen from 0·25 to 0·2. Commodity 2 is a luxury ($\eta_{2,M} = 1{\cdot}2 > 1$); its share has risen from 0·75 to 0·8.

Note that the use in this table of $\Delta x_i/\Delta M$ rather than $\partial x_i/\partial M$ creates little difficulty (cf. the own-price elasticity of demand). It is true that if we measured backward from Date 2 to Date 1, the budget-elasticities would be (4)÷(6), or 0·5 for commodity 1 and 1·125 for commodity 2. The reason that this causes no concern is that if $\eta_{i,M} < 1$ when measured from Date 1 to Date 2, it will also be less than 1 when measured from Date 2 to Date 1. The same is true if it is equal to or greater than 1. Thus no matter in which direction we measure, there is no ambiguity as to whether a commodity is a necessity, or a luxury, or on the borderline between. And the reason for *this* is that when a change is made from one value of *any* independent variable to another, the marginal value (cost, propensity to spend, or whatever) is always either less than, or equal to, or greater than *both* average values (see Technical Appendix, section **T.2**).

Finally, we draw the reader's attention to a proposition which ties together the various sections of this chapter. There is an important mathematical theorem (Euler's theorem on homogeneous functions) which states that if a function such as $x_i = f_i(p_1,\dots, p_i,\dots, p_n, M)$ is homogeneous of degree r in $p_1,\dots, p_i,\dots, p_n, M$, then

$$p_1\frac{\partial x_i}{\partial p_1}+\dots+p_i\frac{\partial x_i}{\partial p_i}+\dots+p_n\frac{\partial x_i}{\partial p_n}+M\frac{\partial x_i}{\partial M} = rx_i.$$

Proof: If x_i is homogeneous of degree r, then

$f_i(kp_1,\dots, kM) = k^r f_i(p_1,\dots, M)$.

Differentiation of both sides with respect to k gives

$$\frac{\partial f_i}{\partial kp_1}\frac{dkp_1}{dk}+\dots+\frac{\partial f_i}{\partial kM}\frac{dkM}{dk} = p_1\frac{\partial f_i}{\partial kp_1}+\dots+M\frac{\partial f_i}{\partial kM}$$

$$= rk^{r-1}f_i(p_1,\dots, M).$$

Setting $k=1$, we get

$$p_1\frac{\partial f_i}{\partial p_1}+\dots+M\frac{\partial f_i}{\partial M} = rf_i(p_1,\dots, M) = rx_i,$$

as required.

As we saw in section **4.3**, demand functions are homogeneous of degree zero. If we take the equation above stating the conclusion of Euler's theorem, divide both sides by x_i and set r equal to zero, we get

$$\frac{p_1}{x_i}\frac{\partial x_i}{\partial p_1}+\dots+\frac{p_i}{x_i}\frac{\partial x_i}{\partial p_i}+\dots+\frac{p_n}{x_i}\frac{\partial x_i}{\partial p_n}+\frac{M}{x_i}\cdot\frac{\partial x_i}{\partial M} = 0.$$

This says that if, for any commodity, we add together the own-price elasticity of demand, all the cross-elasticities of demand, and the budget-elasticity of demand (or the income-elasticity of demand if $M = cY$), the sum must be zero!

Exercises

1. What would the budget line in Figure 13 look like if $p_1 = 0$ (i.e. if x_1 were given away)?

2. In the *production* function $q = f(v_1,\dots, v_m)$, if a p per cent increase in all inputs $v_1,\dots, v_m$ always leads to a p per cent increase in output q, is this function homogeneous? If so, of what degree?

3. (a) In Figure 17, draw the tangent to the demand curve at A, and let

it cut the p_i-axis at D and the x_i-axis at E. Prove geometrically that the elasticity of demand at the point A equals $-$AE/DA.

(b) Using the result of (a), show that:

(i) Any two straight-line demand curves with the same price-intercept have equal elasticities at the same price.

(ii) Any two straight-line demand curves with the same quantity-intercept have equal elasticities at the same quantity.

4. Recompute the table at the end of section **4.5**, replacing M by Y ($= 1{\cdot}25M$) throughout, and using the same expenditure figures. Verify that $\eta_{i,Y} = \eta_{i,M}$, and that from Date 1 to Date 2 $p_i x_i / Y$ falls for commodity 1 and rises for commodity 2.

Notes on the literature

Most of the material in this chapter is standard textbook fare, modified slightly by the assumption that the consumer is constrained by a budget rather than by income. The reader will find a very gentle introduction to derivatives in Baumol (*Economic Theory and Operations Analysis*, ch. 4).

4.3 Paul A. Samuelson (*Foundations of Economic Analysis*, Harvard University Press, 1947, p. 111) stressed three major results of demand theory, of which the existence and homogeneity of degree zero of demand functions are the first two. The third will be presented in the next chapter. On arc-elasticity and point-elasticity, see Baumol (*op. cit.*, pp. 174–8).

4.4 In drawing the demand curve, we have followed the economic convention of putting quantity (the dependent variable) on the horizontal axis and price (the independent variable) on the vertical axis, though mathematical orthodoxy would require us to reverse the axes and Chiang (*Fundamental Methods of Mathematical Economics*, p. 42) does reverse them. Now for Marshall, who thought of the demand curve as showing the maximum price that would be paid for a given quantity (see section **8.1**.), price was the dependent variable, so that to draw the demand curve as we have done was for him mathematically orthodox. In treating quantity as the dependent variable, economists follow Walras. Their analysis is Walrasian, but their geometry is Marshallian!

4.5 Our definition of an inferior good is all but universal, and is due to Hicks (*Value and Capital*, p. 28). But Chiang (*op. cit.*, p. 468) defines an inferior good as one which displays the Giffen Paradox (see the next chapter). So did Henderson and Quandt in the *first* edition of *Microeconomic Theory* (1958, p. 27); but in the *second* edition (1971, p. 34), their definition of an inferior good is that of Hicks.

Chapter 5
Effects of Price Changes

5.1 Substitution and income effects

The first two basic results of demand theory, derived in section **4.3**, are that if, from one period to the next, the budget and all prices either (i) remain unchanged or (ii) change in the same proportion, all quantities demanded will remain unchanged. In this chapter we consider the effect of a change in one price, say p_i, with the budget and all other prices unchanged.

The change in p_i has two types of effect. Firstly, all price-ratios p_i/p_j have changed. Secondly, the consumer is either better or worse off. If p_i has fallen, the point of contact of the budget area with the x_i-axis has moved outward, so that he can reach a higher indifference class than before, whereas if p_i has risen the budget area has contracted, and he is forced to a lower indifference class.

This may be illustrated, for the case of two commodities x_i and x_j, by Figure 18. The price of x_i falls, with M and the price of x_j unchanged. The initial choice is at x; the choice after the fall in price from p_i to p'_i is at x'. It is useful to divide the movement from x to x' into two parts, corresponding to the two effects of the fall in price, as follows.

(*a*) *The substitution effect*

Suppose that, after the fall in p_i, we counteract its effect in making the consumer better off by taking from his budget just enough money to keep him on the same indifference curve as before. We must draw in Figure 18 a third budget line, parallel to the new and flatter budget line, to touch the original indifference curve I at x''. The movement from x to x'' is called the *substitution effect* of the change in the price of x_i.

It is clear from the diagram that the substitution effect of a fall in p_i must increase x_i. As we shall see in section **5.3**, the substitution effect must always change the quantity of a commodity and its own price in opposite directions, no matter how many commodities there are.

When there are only two goods, x_i and x_j, the substitution effect must, as in Figure 18, change p_i and x_j in the same direction, so that $\partial x_j/\partial p_i > 0$ and (cf. p. 56 above) x_i and x_j are *net substitutes* (i.e.

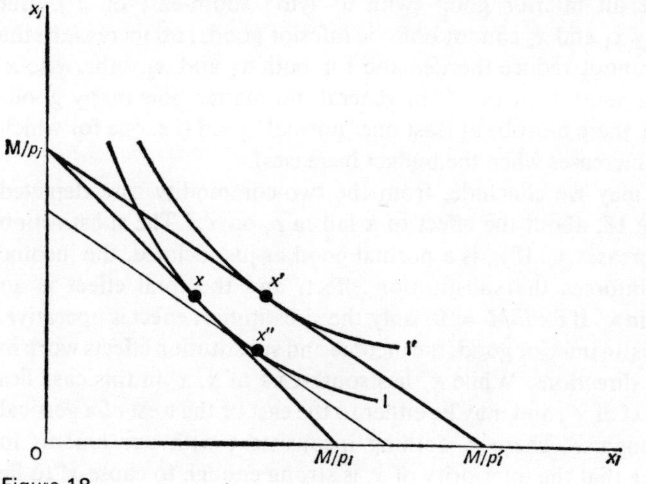

Figure 18

substitutes with respect to the substitution effect alone). But if there are more than two goods, x_i is not necessarily a net substitute for every other good. x_i must have at least *one* net substitute, for the substitution effect of a fall in p_i keeps the consumer in the same indifference class and (as we have stated) increases x_i; therefore, by Proposition **1** (p. 34) the quantity of at least one commodity must fall (i.e. move in the same direction as p_i). But the substitution effect may change the quantity of some goods in the opposite direction from p_i; such a good is a *net complement* to x_i.

(b) The income effect

The remainder of the effect of the change in price – the movement from x'' to x' – is termed the income effect.[10] It is the effect of restoring

10. I feel that it would be too much of a departure from standard usage to call this (as I ought for consistency) the 'budget effect'.

to the consumer the amount of his budget that was taken away from him to measure the substitution effect. Between x'' and x' the budget increases but no price changes.

As we have drawn Figure 18, both x_1 and x_2 increase as we move from x'' to x'. But this is not necessarily the case. x_1 could be (see section **4.5**) an inferior good (with x' lying north-west of x'') or x_2 could be an inferior good (with x' lying south-east of x''). But obviously x_1 and x_2 cannot both be inferior goods; an increase in the budget cannot reduce the demand for both x_1 and x_2, otherwise x' would be south-west of x''. In general, no matter how many goods there are, there must be at least one 'normal' good (i.e. one for which demand increases when the budget increases).

What may we conclude, from the two-commodity case depicted in Figure 18, about the effect of a fall in p_i on x_i? The substitution effect increases x_i. If x_i is a normal good as just defined, the income effect reinforces the substitution effect, and the total effect is an increase in x_i. If $\partial x_i/\partial M = 0$, only the substitution effect is operative. But if x_i is an inferior good, the income and substitution effects work in opposite directions. While x'' lies south-east of x, x' in this case lies north-west of x'', and may lie either to the east or the west of a vertical line through x. There is nothing inconsistent with our axioms in supposing that the inferiority of x_i is strong enough to cause x' to lie to the west of x, so that a fall in p_i reduces the quantity of x_i demanded. This phenomenon is known as the *Giffen paradox*, and is further discussed in section **5.3**.

Two final points on Figure 18. First, there is no reason why we should consider the substitution effect before the income effect. We could equally well first find the increase in the budget necessary to move the consumer to the higher indifference curve I′ with no change in prices. A budget line (which the reader is invited to supply) must be drawn parallel to the original (steeper) budget line to touch I′ at, say x'''. The movement from x to x''' is then the income effect, and the movement from x''' to x' is the substitution effect. The verbal argument of this section is unaffected (*mutatis mutandis*). Secondly, the effects of an *increase* in p_i can be traced by starting at x' and moving back to x, either via x'' or via x'''. (It would be a useful exercise for the reader to try to repeat the argument of this section for an increase in p_i).

5.2 The Slutzky equation

If we tried to record algebraically the results of the previous section, in which the effect of a change in the price of one commodity on its own quantity demanded, or on the quantity demanded of another commodity, was split up into a substitution effect and an income effect, the result might be as follows

$$\frac{\partial x_j}{\partial p_i} = \left[\frac{\partial x_j}{\partial p_i}\right]_S + \left[\frac{\partial x_j}{\partial p_i}\right]_M.$$

Since x_j is a function of $p_1, \ldots, p_n, M$, the expression on the left-hand side is the regular partial derivative of x_j with respect to p_i: the limit of $\Delta x_j/\Delta p_i$ as Δp_i approaches zero and all independent variables other than p_i are held constant. The two terms on the right-hand side stand for the substitution effect and the income effect respectively. The first of these is not really a partial derivative, since although all prices other than p_i are held constant, M is adjusted so as to keep the individual in the same indifference class as before the price change. But if we enclose $\partial x_j/\partial p_i$ in parentheses and append the letter S for 'substitution' it should be clear what we mean. The second term (the income effect), however, is something of a monstrosity. It is not really the effect of a price change at all, but rather of a change in the budget equivalent to the change in price in its effect on the consumer's well-being. It is desirable to replace the income effect term as quickly as possible.

What then is the change in the budget equivalent to the price change? In Figure 18 it could in fact be measured in several different ways. But we are interested in limits as Δp_i approaches zero, and fortunately in the limit all the measures approach the same value. We therefore concentrate on the one that appeals most to the intuition.

If p_i falls by £2 ($\Delta p_i = -$£2) and you have been buying 20 units of x_i, you can continue to buy the same amount of everything and have £40 left over; £40 is then the equivalent change in the budget. £40 $= -(-$£2$) \times 20$, and in general

$$\Delta M = -\Delta p_i x_i \quad \text{or} \quad \Delta p_i = -\frac{\Delta M}{x_i}.$$

Now the original expression $(\partial x_j/\partial p_i)_M$ is of course that part of the limit of $\Delta x_j/\Delta p_i$ that is attributable to the income effect. If Δp_i is replaced by $-\Delta M/x_i$, this part of $\Delta x_j/\Delta p_i$ becomes $-x_i\Delta x_j/\Delta M$. As Δp_i approaches zero, the limit of this expression is $-x_i\partial x_j/\partial M$, where, since x_j is a function of $p_1,\ldots,p_n$, M, $\partial x_j/\partial M$ is a normal partial derivative.

Thus in place of the original unsatisfactory formulation we have the *Slutzky equation*,

$$\frac{\partial x_j}{\partial p_i} = \left[\frac{\partial x_j}{\partial p_i}\right]_S - x_i\frac{\partial x_j}{\partial M}.$$

5.3 The 'fundamental theorem of consumption theory'

In this section we return to the relationship between the quantity of a commodity demanded and a change in its own price. In the Slutzky equation, x_i and x_j are then the same commodity, and we have

$$\frac{\partial x_i}{\partial p_i} = \left[\frac{\partial x_i}{\partial p_i}\right]_S - x_i\frac{\partial x_i}{\partial M}.$$

Let us interpret the verbal discussion on p. 64 above in the light of this equation. The usual demand curve (see Figure 17, p. 54) slopes downward to the right so that $\partial x_i/\partial p_i < 0$. It was shown on p. 62 that when there are only two commodities the substitution effect must always change x_i and p_i in opposite directions, so that $(\partial x_i/\partial p_i)_S < 0$. It follows from the Slutzky equation that so long as the term $-x_i(\partial x_i/\partial M)$ is not positive (i.e. so long as $\partial x_i/\partial M \geqq 0$), the income effect will reinforce, or at least not counteract, the substitution effect, and the demand curve will have the usual slope. But if x_i is an inferior good $\partial x_i/\partial M < 0$, $-x_i\,\partial x_i/\partial M > 0$, and the income term may be large enough to outweigh the substitution effect so that $\partial x_i/\partial p_i > 0$. In this case (the Giffen paradox) the demand curve (unlike Figure 17) slopes upward to the right; a rise in price increases the quantity demanded and a fall in price reduces it.

Now the argument in section **5.2** which led up to the replacement of $(\partial x_j/\partial p_i)_M$ in the Slutzky equation by $-x_i\,\partial x_j/\partial M$ in no way depended on an assumption that there were only two commodities; it was perfectly general. But the argument in section **5.1** that the substitution effect changes x_i and p_i in opposite directions was limited to two commodities. In fact, $(\partial x_i/\partial p_i)_S < 0$, no matter how many commodities there are. But before we can claim to have completed our analysis of the relationship between p_i and x_i, this result must be proved.

Consider a bundle of goods $x = (x_1, x_2, \ldots, x_n)$ chosen at prices $p = (p_1, p_2, \ldots, p_n)$, and another bundle x', *indifferent* to x, chosen at prices p'. The argument is illustrated by Figure 19, but is not confined to two commodities.

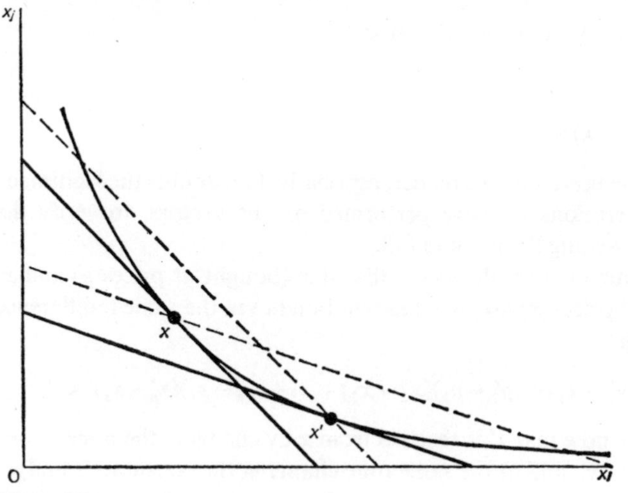

Figure 19

Now x is the unique best point when the consumer is restricted to the budget area touching the indifference class at x. Moreover, if the consumer were asked to find the point in that indifference class which was least expensive at the prices defining that budget area, his answer would be the unique point x. (This is because in Figure 19 any other budget line at the same prices p would be parallel to that through x; if it anywhere met the indifference class it would lie above the budget line through x and thus represent a higher expenditure.) It follows that any other point indifferent to x such as x' would, if bought at the prices at which x was bought, cost more than x. Thus

$$\sum_{i=1}^{n} p_i x_i < \sum_{i=1}^{n} p_i x_i' \quad \text{or} \quad p.x < p.x'.$$

Here we have used the inner product notation for vectors (see p. 46 above).

Similarly, at prices p', x' is the unique least expensive point in the indifference class, so that

$$p'.x' < p'.x.$$

Writing $x'-x$ and $p'-p$ for the vectors $(x'_1-x_1, x'_2-x_2, \ldots, x'_n-x_n)$ and $(p'_1-p_1, p'_2-p_2, \ldots, p'_n-p_n)$ respectively, we therefore have

$$p.(x'-x) > 0 \quad \text{and} \quad p'.(x'-x) < 0,$$

so that

$$(p'-p).(x'-x) < 0.$$

It would be useful for the reader, especially if he doubts the legitimacy of the operations we have performed on the vectors, to verify the results by writing them out in full.

What our final result says is that if x (bought at prices p) and x' (bought at prices p') are two different bundles in the same indifference class, then

$$(p'_1-p_1)(x'_1-x_1)+(p'_2-p_2)(x'_2-x_2)+\ldots+(p'_n-p_n)(x'_n-x_n) < 0.$$

Suppose now that x' is reached from x by changing the price of *one* commodity x_i, and at the same time changing the consumer's budget so that he remains in the same indifference class. By definition the movement from x to x' is the substitution effect of the change in p_i. Since only p_i has changed, for all commodities x_j other than x_i $p'_j-p_j = 0$. Thus in our last inequality the only term different from zero is that relating to x_i, and the inequality reduces to:

$$(p'_i-p_i)(x'_i-x_i) < 0.$$

Obviously $p'_i-p_i = \Delta p_i$ and $x'_i-x_i = \Delta x_i$, so that the inequality says: $\Delta p_i.\Delta x_i < 0$. Dividing by $(\Delta p_i)^2$, and recalling that the changes reflect the substitution effect only, we state the result as

$$\left[\frac{\Delta x_i}{\Delta p_i}\right]_S < 0,$$

and this holds whether we take the limit as Δp_i approaches zero or not.

We have therefore proved that the term $(\partial x_i/\partial p_i)_S$ in the Slutzky equation at the beginning of this section is negative irrespective of the number of commodities. We are now entitled, on the basis of the argument there given, to summarize our results on the relationship between any x_i and its price p_i in (a slightly modified version of) what Samuelson has called the *Fundamental Theorem of Consumption Theory: Any good that is known never to decrease in demand when the budget alone rises must definitely shrink in demand when its price alone rises.*

5.4 Substitutes and complements

In section **4.5** we said that x_i is a gross substitute for x_j if $\partial x_i/\partial p_j > 0$, and a gross complement for x_j if $\partial x_i/\partial p_j < 0$; $\partial x_i/\partial p_j$ is the total effect (income and substitution) of p_j on x_i. We said in section **5.1** that x_i and x_j are net (or Hicksian) substitutes if $(\partial x_i/\partial p_j)_S > 0$, net complements if $(\partial x_i/\partial p_j)_S < 0$: $(\partial x_i/\partial p_j)_S$ is of course only the substitution effect of p_j on x_i (the effect of changing p_j and adjusting the budget so as to keep the consumer in the same indifference class).

By using the Slutzky equation, modified from the form at the end of section **5.2** by interchanging $_i$ and $_j$ (which is of course perfectly legitimate since x_i and x_j are *any* two commodities),

$$\frac{\partial x_i}{\partial p_j} = \left[\frac{\partial x_i}{\partial p_j}\right]_S - x_j\frac{\partial x_i}{\partial M},$$

the reader can easily verify the following relationships between net and gross substitutes:

(a) if x_i and x_j are net substitutes, x_i is a gross substitute for x_j if x_i is an inferior good ($\partial x_i/\partial M < 0$); but if x_i is a normal good ($\partial x_i/\partial M > 0$), x_i may be either a gross substitute or a gross complement for x_j, since in this case the substitution and income effects work in opposite directions;

(b) if x_i and x_j are net complements, x_i is a gross complement for x_j if x_i is a normal good; but if x_i is an inferior good, x_i may be either a gross substitute or a gross complement for x_j.

The perceptive reader will have noticed a subtle difference in wording between 'x_i is a gross substitute (or complement) for x_j' and 'x_i and x_j are net substitutes (or complements)'. The reason is that if

x_i is a *net* substitute for x_j, x_j must be a net substitute for x_i, and similarly for net complements. Indeed, it can be shown that for all pairs of goods x_i and x_j

$$\left[\frac{\partial x_i}{\partial p_j}\right]_S = \left[\frac{\partial x_j}{\partial p_i}\right]_S.$$

I know of no short way to prove this; a proof will be found in the Technical Appendix (section **T.5**).

But even given this fact, it does not follow that if x_i is (for example) a *gross* substitute for x_j, x_j must be a gross substitute for x_i. If we consider the Slutzky equation in the form at the end of section **5.2** together with the form earlier in this section, we conclude that if x_i and x_j are net substitutes, and both are normal goods, then each may be either a gross substitute or a gross complement for the other.

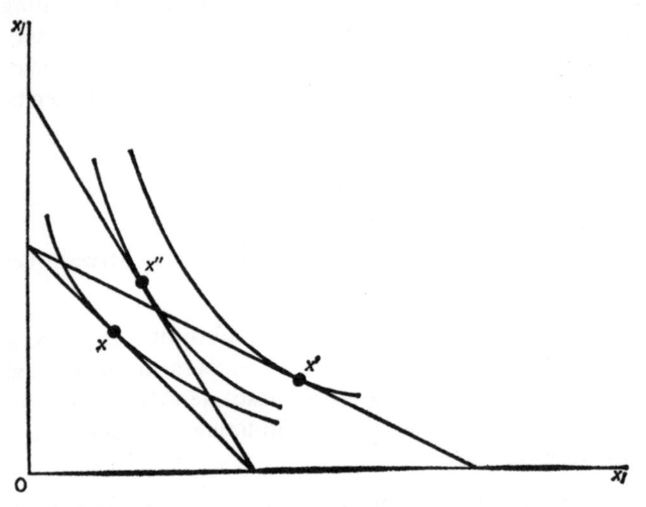

Figure 20

Figure 20 shows a perfectly possible case. Initially the consumer is at x. When p_i falls, he moves to x', where x_j has fallen, so that x_j is a gross *substitute* for x_i. But when p_j falls, he moves from x to x'', where x_i has risen, so that x_i is a gross *complement* for x_j.

5.5 An application: the supply of effort

The reader has now been introduced to many of the fundamental concepts of the theory of consumer behaviour. It will be necessary to acquire further analytical tools and to relax several assumptions before the theory can be usefully put to work. But there is one application that can be made with only minor modifications of our present assumptions: how much work is an individual willing to do? A discussion of this question (the 'supply of effort' problem) concludes this part of the book.

Suppose that a consumer is free to choose how many hours per week he will work. (If this appears artificial because of the prevalence of working weeks of standard length, at least the preferences of individuals are of interest because they presumably have some influence on the agreed length; and of course not everyone is tied to a standard week.) Then 168 less the number of hours worked may be defined as the number of hours of leisure; we represent leisure by x_0.

By working (i.e. giving up leisure) the consumer earns money. We assume for simplicity (many variations are possible) that the entire wage income is devoted to the purchase of non-durable current consumption goods, so that it equals the budget M of earlier sections. And we assume that it is legitimate to treat the bundle of consumption goods purchased as if it were a single good, consumption (x_1), measured in pounds per week. (This may be justified in various ways, to be considered later in the book; the easiest way is to assume that the money price of each individual consumption good remains unchanged throughout the analysis.) Finally, it is assumed that a weak preference ordering, satisfying all the axioms of earlier sections, exists for combinations of the two goods x_0 (leisure) and x_1 (consumption).

Let the wage rate received be initially £1 per hour, irrespective of the number of hours worked. (We thus ignore overtime rates and progressive income taxes, though it is not difficult to take them into account.) Then the consumer (see Figure 21) can choose 168 hours of leisure and no consumption, or £168 of consumption and no leisure, or any point on the straight line between these extremes. He will presumably not choose either extreme, since both leisure and consumption are necessary for survival; we assume that the wage rate is high enough to permit him to survive. Let his choice be at the point x, representing £48 of consumption and 120 hours of leisure.

If the wage-rate increases to £2 per hour, the budget line pivots about the point (£0, 168 hrs) on the x_0-axis and cuts the x_1-axis at (£336, 0 hrs). Let the choice now be at x' where $x_0 = 124$ hours and $x_1 = £88$. How can we distinguish the substitution and income effects of this change in the wage rate?

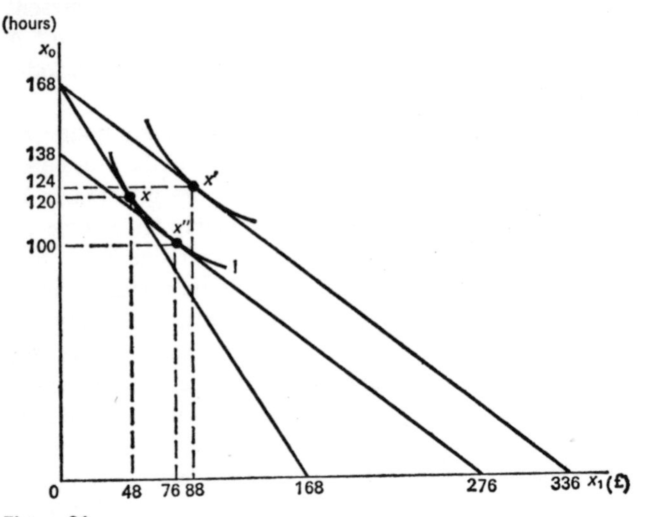

Figure 21

If we compare Figure 21 with Figure 18, it is just as if p_1 had fallen, with the budget and p_0 remained unchanged. But in Figure 21 what has remained unchanged on the vertical axis is not M/p_0, but the immutable number, 168, of hours in a week. We do not have two money prices, one for leisure and one for consumption; what has happened is that the amount of leisure that must be given up to get a pound's worth of consumption has fallen. At £1 per hour, the price of a pound's worth of consumption is 60 minutes of leisure; at £2 per hour it is 30 minutes. The increase in the wage rate must be thought of as a fall in p_1 – the price of a pound's worth of consumption in terms of leisure – if we are to use the analysis of the earlier sections of this chapter.

To measure the substitution effect we draw a line parallel to the flatter £2 budget line to touch the first indifference curve I at x'', where, say, $x_0 = 100$ hours and $x_1 = £76$. If these are the figures, this budget line goes from 138 hours on the x_0-axis to £276 on the x_1-axis.

In Figure 18 we moved from x to x'' by lowering the price of x_i and depriving the consumer of part of his budget. In Figure 21 we do it by raising the wage-rate from £1 to £2 per hour (i.e. reducing p_1 from 60 minutes to 30 minutes per pound) and depriving him of a number of hours of leisure corresponding to the vertical distance between the parallel budget lines through x'' and x'; with the illustrative numbers in the diagram this number is 30 hours ($= 168-138$). This could be done by telling him that he must work for that number of hours without pay. The 'income effect', from x'' to x', is obtained by shifting the budget line outward again.

The precise interpretation of this 'income effect' must be considered with care, since we wish to use the Slutzky equation and must therefore find the appropriate term to replace $-x_i\ \partial x_j/\partial M$. We wish to obtain an income effect and a substitution effect by splitting the partial derivative $\partial x_0/\partial p_1$, the effect on the demand for leisure of a change in the price of consumption goods in terms of leisure. The substitution term $(\partial x_0/\partial p_1)_S$ creates no difficulties. The 'income' term is the result of asking the consumer the following hypothetical question: If, starting from x'' (100 hours of leisure and £76 of consumption), you could have either 30 more hours of leisure and the same amount of consumption as at x'', or £60 more consumption and the same amount of leisure as at x'', or any combination of Δx_0 and Δx_1 such that

$$\Delta x_0 + \frac{\Delta x_1}{£2} = 30 \text{ hours},$$

what would be your choice? Since positive amounts of x_0 and x_1 are being consumed at x'', either Δx_0 or Δx_1 may of course be negative, provided that neither x_0 nor x_1 falls below a level necessary for survival. (The choice shown in the diagram is $\Delta x_0 = 124-100=24$, $\Delta x_1 = £88-£76 = £12$.)

Our way of measuring the increase in the 'budget' which gives rise to the 'income effect' is therefore as an increase of 30 hours of leisure. Let us call this ΔH (H for hours). The Slutzky equation may then be written as

$$\frac{\partial x_0}{\partial p_1} = \left[\frac{\partial x_0}{\partial p_1}\right]_S - x_1 \frac{\partial x_0}{\partial H}.$$

We are now in a position to draw on the analysis of section **5.4**. We seek the effect on the demand for leisure (x_0) of an increase in the wage rate – that is, of a fall in p_1 (the price of consumption in terms of leisure). Since there are only two goods they must be net substitutes (see p. 63), so that $(\partial x_0/\partial p_1)_S > 0$ and the substitution effect of the fall in p_1 (the rise in the wage rate) reduces the amount of leisure (and increases the amount of work done).

We may redefine 'inferiority' to mean that if the outward shift of the budget line (measured by $\Delta H = 30$ hours) reduces the demand for leisure ($\partial x_0/\partial H < 0$), then leisure is an inferior good. If this is the case, leisure is a gross substitute for consumption, and the total effect of the increased wage rate (the fall in p_1) is to reduce the demand for leisure and therefore to increase the 'supply of effort'.

But if leisure is a normal good ($\partial x_0/\partial H > 0$), the substitution and 'income' effects work in opposite directions, so that leisure may be either a gross substitute or a gross complement for consumption. As we have drawn Figure 21, leisure *is* a normal good, and the total effect of the fall in p_1 (the movement from x to x') is an increase in leisure from 120 to 124 hours. Thus in our diagram leisure is a gross complement for consumption, so that an increase in the wage rate reduces the number of hours worked. But if the consumer had chosen to take more of ΔH in the form of consumption, x' could have been at, say, (£104, 116 hrs), above x'' (so that leisure was still a normal good) but below x. In that case he would have chosen to consume less leisure and supply more labour than at x; leisure and consumption would then have been gross substitutes.

In conclusion, our analysis shows that a higher wage rate will tend to *increase* the number of hours worked if the consumer is inclined to respond to increased well-being (measured by $\Delta H = 30$ hours) by consuming more goods rather than by taking more leisure. And this is more likely to be the case if he is (a) on the threshold of a higher standard of living to which he aspires, or (b) living at a standard below that to which he is accustomed and which he wishes to regain, or (c) unable to put additional leisure to enjoyable use, or (d) in an agreeable occupation.

Exercises

In all three questions, x_i and x_j are the only two goods consumed.

1. p_i is reduced, and at the same time the budget is reduced so much that the consumer is forced to a *lower* indifference curve than before. Which of the statements (a) – (d) is or are true? As compared with the situation before these changes:

(a) x_i must increase if x_i is an inferior good;

(b) x_i must decrease if x_i is an inferior good;

(c) x_i must increase if x_i is not an inferior good;

(d) x_i must decrease if x_i is not an inferior good.

2. p_i is increased, with M and p_j unchanged. What can you deduce about the inferiority or normalcy of x_i and x_j from each of the following cases?

(a) x_i increases, x_j decreases;

(b) x_i and x_j both decrease;

(c) x_i decreases, x_j increases.

3. Indicate, for each of the cases (a) – (c) in question 2, whether x_j is a gross substitute or a gross complement for x_i.

Notes on the literature

The classic treatment of the subject-matter of this chapter is Hicks's *Value and Capital* (chs. 2 and 3). He is one of the most lucid of writers, and these chapters are strongly recommended. When he speaks of substitutes and complements, he means what we have called net or Hicksian substitutes and complements.

5.1 The Giffen paradox was named after Sir Robert Giffen by Marshall; the relevant passage is reproduced on p. 119 below.

5.2 The equation comes from E. Slutzky, 'Sulla teoria del bilancio del consumatore', *Giornale degli Economisti*, July 1915, pp. 1–26, translated in American Economic Association, *Readings in Price Theory* (Holt, Rinehart & Winston, 1952, pp. 27–56). Most textbook treatments of the equation use (like Slutzky) heavy mathematical methods (relegated in this book to the Technical Appendix, section **T.5.**). A notable and recommended exception is Milton Friedman, *Price Theory* (Cass, 1962, pp. 48–55). Newman (*Theory of Exchange*, p. 157) attempts a similar simple treatment, but seems to treat the formulation of the income effect as a problem in accounting rather than of measuring an equivalent budget (income) change; in consequence his statement of the Slutzky equation is wrong because his income term (our $-x_i\,\partial x_j/\partial M$) does not have a minus sign in front of it.

5.3 The technique of deriving interesting results from inequalities between expressions like $\sum p_i x_i (= p.x)$ is one which Samuelson frequently uses with great effect. The 'Fundamental Theorem . . .' was so named by him in an article which we discuss in detail in section **8.3**.

5.4 The third chapter of Hicks's *Value and Capital* still seems to me the best simple treatment of substitutes and complements. Hicks's *Revision of Demand Theory*, ch. 13, contains an elementary proof of the 'reciprocity theorem', $(\partial x_i/\partial p_j)_S = (\partial x_j/\partial p_i)_S$, as well as of other basic results. These proofs cannot be understood unless virtually the whole book is read; it is characteristically lucid and ingenious.

5.5 A very good discussion of the supply of effort is to be found in E. H. Phelps Brown, *A Course in Applied Economics* (Pitman, 1951, ch. 4) where the effects of taxation are also discussed.

An entirely new approach is that of G. S. Becker, 'A theory of the allocation of time' (*Econ. J.*, vol. 75, no. 299, pp. 493–517, 1965), reprinted in part in B. J. McCormick and E. O. Smith (eds), *The Labour Market: Selected Readings* (Penguin Books, 1968, pp. 75–102). Briefly, all activity (work, sleep, travel, entertainment) requires the expenditure of time. An increase in the wage-rate raises the 'price' of consumption activities which involve a lot of time. Thus the substitution effect of a higher wage rate increases the number of hours worked by reducing time-intensive consumption. Becker's provocative and wide-ranging article deserves careful study (but will be a little easier to follow when the reader has some familiarity with utility theory, to be taken up in Part Two).

Another classic application of the theory of Part One – direct versus indirect taxation – has been omitted because unless we bring in production, which is beyond the scope of this book, the results of the analysis are totally misleading. The interested reader will find a good treatment in Friedman (*op. cit.*, ch. 3), or in I. M. D. Little, *A Critique of Welfare Economics* (2nd edn, Oxford University Press, 1957, App. 4).

Part Two
Utility

Chapter 6
Utility and Preferences

6.1 Why utility?

In the first part of this book, a number of important results in demand theory were derived from axioms concerning the consumer's preference ordering. We now introduce the notion of a utility function, about which we shall make assumptions which are precisely equivalent to Axioms **1** to **7**. The reader is entitled to know why he is being asked to learn this new concept.

The reason is simply that it is easier, if one uses a utility function, (i) to derive useful additional consequences of Axioms **1** to **7**, (ii) to think of hypotheses with interesting behavioural implications, (iii) to discover what is implied about preferences by particular types of behaviour, than if one considers only the preference ordering defined in Chapters 2 and 3.

Now of course if our axioms about the preference ordering and the utility function are equivalent, anything that can be stated in terms of one can be stated in terms of the other, just as anything that can be stated in mathematical symbols can also be stated in words. The analogy goes further; just as it is always desirable to translate one's mathematical economics into words so that one is clear about what is being said, so it is desirable to translate, for example, a hypothesis about a utility function into one about the (more immediately comprehensible) preference ordering so that its plausibility may be examined. It is precisely because preference orderings are more easily comprehensible that they were introduced in this book before utility functions. But as we hope to show, the utility function is a more powerful tool.

6.2 Utility, rationality and non-saturation

Consider a consumer with a consumption set C and a weak preference ordering satisfying Axioms **1** to **7** of Chapters 2 and 3. Suppose that a function can be found which assigns to each bundle of goods x in C a unique real number u, so that

$$u = u(x) = u(x_1, x_2, \ldots, x_n),$$

and that for all x, x' in C

$$u(x) \geqq u(x') \quad \text{if and only if } xRx'.$$

In words, the 'utility derived from' x is greater than or equal to that derived from x' if and only if x is regarded by the consumer as at least as good as x'.

By the nature of real numbers, the relation defined by $u(x) \geqq u(x')$ satisfies Axioms **1** and **2** of Chapter 2. For of any two real numbers $u(x)$ and $u(x')$, the first must be either greater than, equal to or less than the second (Axiom **1**), and of any three real numbers $u(x)$, $u(x')$ and $u(x'')$, if $u(x) \geqq u(x')$ and $u(x') \geqq u(x'')$, clearly $u(x) \geqq u(x'')$ (Axiom **2**). If we make the following obvious definitions

$$u(x) = u(x') \quad \text{if and only if } xIx';$$
$$u(x) > u(x') \quad \text{if and only if } xPx';$$

all the corollaries on pages 23 and 24 follow at once.

The assumption that the consumer chooses, from any set of alternatives S, one which maximizes utility, is equivalent to Axiom **3**. For to say that x maximizes utility means that there is no x' in S such that $u(x') > u(x)$. That is, for all x' in S, $u(x) \geqq u(x')$, which is equivalent to xRx'.

If the utility function is differentiable everywhere in the consumption set C,[11] so that partial derivatives $\partial u/\partial x_i$ with respect to every commodity exist at all points, the following property is equivalent to Axiom **4** (non-saturation):

$$\text{At every point in C,} \quad \partial u/\partial x_i > 0 \quad (i = 1, 2, \ldots, n).$$

This says that the partial derivatives of u with respect to all commodities are positive. Hence if we start from a point x, holding constant

11. Axioms **1** to **7** imply that such a utility function exists, and is differentiable; this will be discussed in the next section.

the quantities of all commodities but one, and increase the quantity of the remaining commodity, u will increase. We may repeat the process as few or as many times as we like, until we reach a point x'. The point x' will contain more of some commodities than x and less of none, so that $x' \geqslant x$. At each step on the way from x to x' we increased u, so that $u(x') > u(x)$. Thus $x'Px$, which is Axiom **4**. Conversely, if the preference ordering is representable by a differentiable utility function, all partial derivatives must be positive; for if any were zero or negative one could find x and x' such that $x \geqslant x'$ without $u(x) > u(x')$, so that xPx' would be false in violation of Axiom **4**.

The partial derivative $\partial u/\partial x_i$ has a familiar name: it is the *marginal utility* of x_i. Thus Axiom **4** says that all marginal utilities are positive.

The counterparts in utility theory of Axioms **5** to **7** (continuity and smooth strict convexity) are more difficult to develop and will occupy the remainder of the chapter.

6.3 Existence of utility functions

In this section we discuss the relationship between Axioms **5** and **7** and the existence of a differentiable utility function. General readers may prefer to omit the section entirely, since it is of technical rather than of economic interest. Its results are summarized at the beginning of section **6.4**.

It may be surprising to learn that a preference ordering satisfying Axioms **1** to **4** alone may not be representable by a utility function. But an example is provided by the so-called 'lexicographic ordering'. Consider a two-commodity consumption set. Of any two points $x = (x_1, x_2)$ and $x' = (x_1', x_2')$, xPx' if $x_1 > x_1'$, irrespective of the values of x_2 and x_2'. But if $x_1 = x_1'$, xPx' if $x_2 > x_2'$.

Thus in Figure 22, $x''Px'$, $x'Px$, xPx'''. The term 'lexicographic' of course draws attention to the similarity of the ordering to the arrangement of the words in a dictionary: x_1 plays the role of the first letter in a word, x_2 that of the second.

Given this ordering, there is *no* set of real numbers such that $u(x) \geqq u(x')$ if and only if xRx'. This can be proved. It can also be proved that any preference ordering satisfying Axioms **1** to **4** and Axiom **5** (Continuity) can be represented by a utility function. The proofs of these results lie beyond the scope of this volume. We shall, however, prove an obvious corollary of these two results – that the lexicographic ordering violates Axiom **5**.

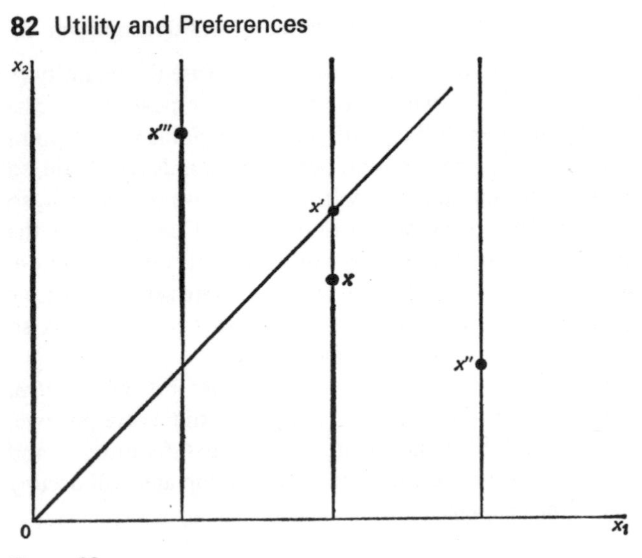

Figure 22

Consider the point x in Figure 22, and any other point x' on the vertical line through x. If we draw a ray from the origin through x', every point above x' on Ox' is preferred to x (since it contains more x_1 than x), and x is preferred to every point below x' on Ox'. Thus by definition of the 'boundary set' B(x) of x (see section **3.3** above), x' and indeed all points on the vertical line through x belong to B(x). By Axiom **5**, all points in B(x) are indifferent to x. But by the lexicographic ordering x' is preferred to x. Thus the lexicographic ordering violates Axiom **5**.

Axiom **5** in fact ensures not only that a utility function exists but that it is continuous. What this means, roughly, is that if one travels along any path in the consumption set, one does not ever come to a point at which the value of u abruptly breaks off and resumes at a higher or lower level.

Differentiability of the utility function, which is needed if we are to use its partial derivatives (marginal utilities) is implied by Axiom **7**, which says that at every point in the consumption set the marginal rate of substitution between any two goods has a unique value. Differentiability means, roughly, that as one travels along a path in the consumption set, the value of u not only does not break off, but also does not change direction sharply; the graph of the function is composed of smooth curves or straight lines, with no kinks or angles.[12]

12. Strictly speaking, Axiom **7** needs to be strengthened if the preference ordering is to be representable by a utility function which implies the symmetry

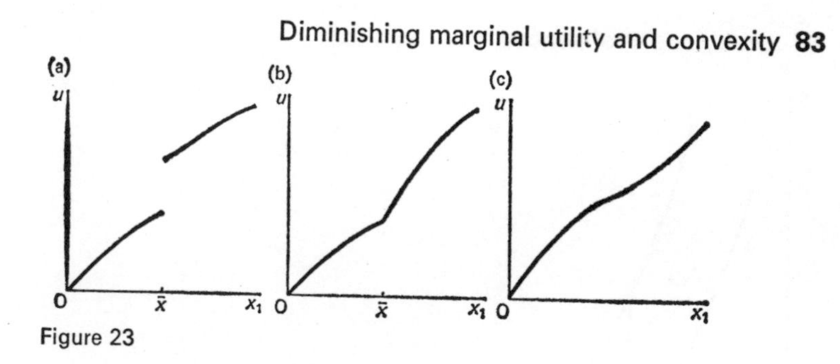

Figure 23

These distinctions are illustrated in Figure 23, in which the consumption set consists of quantities of the single commodity x_1. In Figure 23(a), $u(x_1)$ is not continuous at $\bar{x}$. In Figure 23(b) $u(x_1)$ is continuous but not differentiable at $\bar{x}$; there is a kink at which the slope is not uniquely determined. In Figure 23(c), $u(x_1)$ is continuous and differentiable everywhere.

6.4 Diminishing marginal utility and convexity

In section **6.3** it was argued (but not strictly proved) that Axioms **5** and **7** of Chapter 3, together with Axioms **1** to **4**, ensure the existence of a utility function with partial derivatives (marginal utilities) for all commodities, as was assumed in section **6.2**. The implications for the utility function of Axiom **6** (strict convexity), which implies convex-to-the-origin indifference curves, remain to be examined.

First of all, what corresponds in utility theory to the marginal rate of substitution between two commodities? Let us assume that, in Figure 24, x and x' lie on the same indifference curve, and that x' is reached from x by taking away 3 units of x_2 from the consumer and giving him 2 units of x_1 in compensation. (The quantities of all other commodities may be assumed constant throughout.) Then measuring the marginal rate of substitution for the moment along an arc of the indifference curve rather than at a point, we should say that the mrs of x_2 for x_1 (mrs_{21}) is 3/2.

of substitution effects – $(\partial x_i/\partial p_j)_S = (\partial x_j/\partial p_i)_S$ – mentioned in section **5.4**. For such a utility function all second-order partial derivatives are continuous (see sections **T.3** and **T.5** of the Technical Appendix). And this implies that the *slope* of the mrs_{ji} curve in Figure 11 of section **3.4** (given by the expression in small type on p. 90 below; see also section **T.3**) is continuous. If we drew in Figure 11 a third curve below the other two, showing the slope of the *tangent* to the mrs_{ji} at all points, that third curve would have to be a continuous curve.

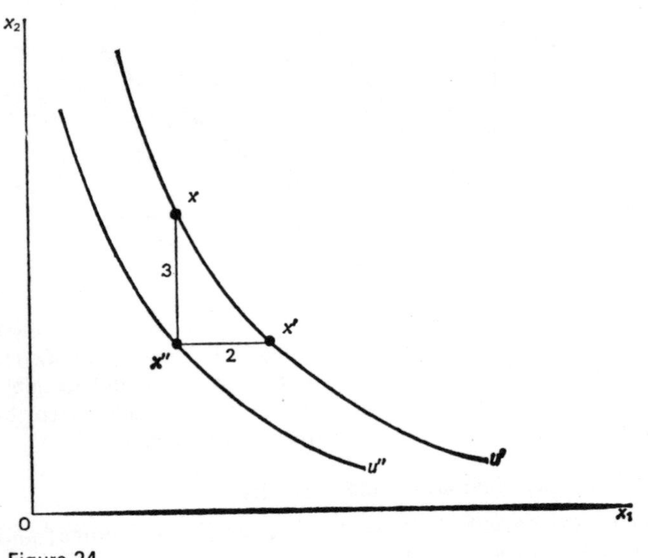

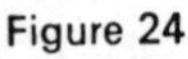
Figure 24

Let the utility level at x or x' be u'. After three units of x_2 have been taken from the consumer and before the compensating two units of x_1 have been given to him, he is at x'', on a lower indifference curve and therefore at a lower utility level (say $u'' < u'$) than at x or x'.

Defining the marginal utility of x_2 for the moment over the interval from x to x'' as $\Delta u/\Delta x_2$ with x_1 held constant (rather than as $\partial u/\partial x_2$ at a point), we have

$$\frac{\Delta u}{\Delta x_2} = \frac{u''-u'}{-3} = \frac{u'-u''}{3} = \text{marginal utility of } x_2.$$

And as we go from x'' to x' $\Delta u/\Delta x_1$ with x_2 held constant gives

$$\frac{\Delta u}{\Delta x_1} = \frac{u'-u''}{2} = \text{marginal utility of } x_1.$$

Therefore

$$\text{mrs}_{21} = \frac{3}{2} = \frac{u'-u''}{2} \div \frac{u'-u''}{3} = \frac{\text{marginal utility of } x_1}{\text{marginal utility of } x_2}.$$

And this is a commonsense result. If 3 units of x_2 are equivalent at the margin to 2 units of x_1, each unit of x_1 must be contributing one-and-a-half times as much 'utility' as a unit of x_2.

This equality continues to hold as all changes approach zero, so that for any pair of goods x_i and x_j,

$$\mathrm{mrs}_{ji} = \frac{\partial u/\partial x_i}{\partial u/\partial x_j}.$$

Writing the partial derivatives more compactly still as u_i and u_j, the result is

$$\mathrm{mrs}_{ji} = \frac{u_i}{u_j} \quad \text{for all } i, j.$$

Now Proposition **2** (p. 43 above), derived from Axiom **6** among others, implies that as we increase x_1 along the indifference curve in Figure 24, mrs_{21} steadily decreases. We can now also say that u_1/u_2 – the marginal utility of x_1 divided by the marginal utility of x_2 – steadily decreases.

One might be tempted to explain this by appealing to a general law of 'diminishing marginal utility' as follows. As a consumer consumes more of a commodity, the extra utility derived from each additional unit diminishes. Thus as x_1 increases along the indifference curve in Figure 24, u_1 falls. But at the same time x_2 is decreasing, so that by the same argument u_2 rises. Since the numerator of u_1/u_2 falls and its denominator rises, the ratio must fall.

There are two observations to be made about this argument. In the first place, there are other ways in which the ratio could fall. u_1/u_2 would also fall if u_1 *rose* and u_2 rose in a greater proportion, or if u_2 *fell* and u_1 fell in a greater proportion.

Secondly, any general law of diminishing marginal utility must be precisely stated. In general, unless special additional assumptions are made about the utility function, the behaviour of u_1 as x_1 increases depends on what is happening simultaneously to the quantities of other commodities. We have seen, for example, that if u_1 decreases, and u_2 increases, when x_1 increases *and* x_2 is reduced so as to keep the consumer on the same indifference curve, convex-to-the-origin indifference curves result.

Any general law of diminishing marginal utility must, therefore, specify what is assumed to be happening to the quantities of other commodities as, for example, x_1 increases. A natural specification would be that they do not change. The law would then say that for each commodity x_i, u_i decreases when x_i is increased and the quantities of all other commodities are held constant. That is, u_i and x_i move in opposite directions, so that $\Delta u_i/\Delta x_i < 0$. Again a compact notation is available. The limit of

$$\frac{\Delta u_i}{\Delta x_i} = \frac{\Delta(\partial u/\partial x_i)}{\Delta x_i}$$

as Δx_i approaches zero and all other independent variables in the utility function are held constant may be written in any of the following forms:

$$\frac{\partial(\partial u/\partial x_i)}{\partial x_i} = \frac{\partial^2 u}{\partial x_i^2} = u_{ii}.$$

It is the last of these forms that we shall use, so that the law may be stated as:

At all points in C

$u_{ii} < 0 \quad \text{for } i = 1, 2, \ldots, n.$

Note that we are not offering this as an axiom. Indeed, we intend to show that, whatever introspective or psychological plausibility the concept of diminishing marginal utility may have, it has no behavioural implications. In particular, it neither implies nor is implied by convex-to-the-origin indifference curves.

To show that convex indifference curves do not imply diminishing marginal utility in the sense of the above law, we shall exhibit three utility functions, each giving rise to the same convex indifference curves, in which marginal utility is (1) constant, (2) diminishing, (3) increasing.

1. Consider the utility function $u = x_1 x_2$. All points such that $x_1 x_2 = 100$ (e.g. (100, 1), (50, 2), (25, 4), (20, 5), . . .) lie on the indifference curve $u = 100$. This curve is shown in Figure 25. Technically it is a rectangular hyperbola asymptotic to the axes; clearly it is smoothly convex to the origin.

2. If $x_1 x_2 = 100$, $+\sqrt{(x_1 x_2)} = 10$. (We specify $+\sqrt{(x_1 x_2)}$, the *positive* square root, because $\sqrt{100} = +10$ or -10. $+\sqrt{(x_1 x_2)}$ *is* a function of x_1 and x_2; cf. Chapter 3, Exercise 4.) Thus if we take $u^* = +\sqrt{(x_1 x_2)}$ as our second utility function, the indifference curve $u^* = 10$ will pass through the same points as the curve $u = 100$ for utility function (1), and the two curves will be identical.

3. If $x_1 x_2 = 100$, $x_1^2 x_2^2 = 10{,}000$. Our third utility function is $u^{**} = x_1^2 x_2^2$ and the indifference curve $u^{**} = 10{,}000$ for this utility function is again the one shown in Figure 25.

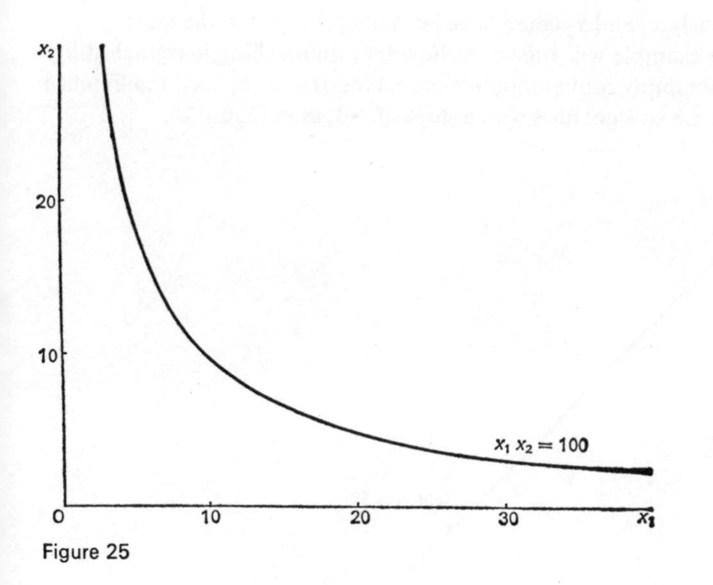

Figure 25

The following table shows what happens to the marginal utility of x_2, $\Delta(\text{utility})/\Delta x_2$, as x_2 is increased from 10 to 11 and 11 to 12 with x_1 held constant at 10, for each of the three functions. All indifference curves of all three functions are convex to the origin, but $\Delta u/\Delta x_2$ is constant for function (1), $\Delta u^*/\Delta x_2$ diminishes for function (2), and $\Delta u^{**}/\Delta x_2$ increases for function (3). (Note that $\Delta x_2 = 1$ in each case.)

		(1)		(2)		(3)	
		$u = x_1 x_2$		$u^* = +\sqrt{(x_1 x_2)}$		$u^{**} = x_1^2 x_2^2$	
x_1	x_2	u	$\Delta u/\Delta x_2$	u^*	$\Delta u^*/\Delta x_2$	u^{**}	$\Delta u^{**}/\Delta x_2$
10	10	100		10		10,000	
			10		0·488		2100
10	11	110		10·488		12,100	
			10		0·466		2300
10	12	120		10·954		14,400	

Obviously x_1 and x_2 could have been interchanged in the table.

One example will suffice to show that diminishing marginal utility does not imply convex indifference curves. If $u = x_1 + x_2$, indifference curves are straight lines with a slope of -1, as in Figure 26.

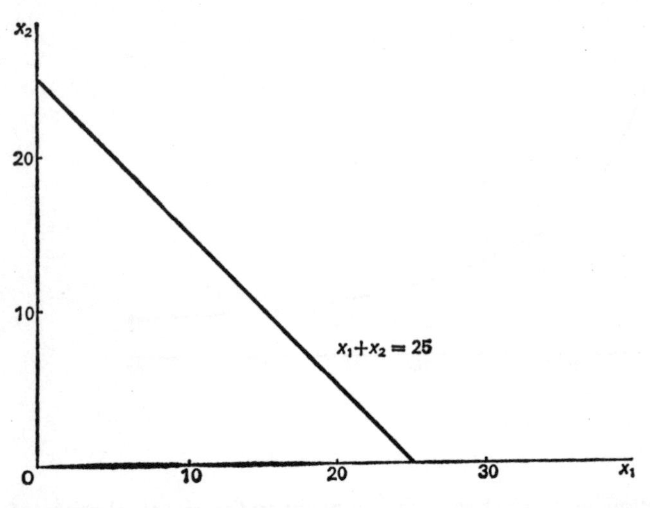

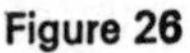
Figure 26

The indifference curve shown gives $u = 25$. For any pair of numbers such that $x_1 + x_2 = 25, +\sqrt{(x_1 + x_2)} = 5$. Thus if the utility function were $u^* = +\sqrt{(x_1 + x_2)}$, the indifference curve $u^* = 5$ would also be the one shown in Figure 26. But with x_1 held constant at 10, and x_2 going from 10 to 11 to 12, u^* goes from 4·472 to 4·583 to 4·690, so that

$\Delta u^*/\Delta x_2$ falls from 0·111 to 0·107, implying diminishing marginal utility. It is also possible to find utility functions with diminishing marginal utility but indifference curves concave to the origin.[13] But the point need not be further laboured.

Thus the assumptions of diminishing marginal utility and convex-to-the origin indifference curves are, in general, quite unrelated.

One final point before we leave this general discussion of the relationship between utility functions and preference orderings. A given preference ordering of the bundles of commodities in C which satisfies Axioms **1** to **7** can be represented by any number of utility functions (e.g. by $u = x_1 x_2$, $u^* = +\sqrt{(x_1 x_2)}$, $u^{**} = x_1^2 x_2^2$ as above) – indeed by an infinite number of functions. But any move from one bundle to another that increases, decreases or leaves unchanged the value of one utility function must respectively increase, decrease or leave unchanged the value of any other utility function that represents the same preference ordering. For if $u(x)$ and $u^*(x)$ represent the same preference ordering, and x and x' are any two bundles, $u(x) \geqq u(x')$ if and only if xRx', and $u^*(x) \geqq u^*(x')$ if and only if xRx'. Therefore $u(x) \geqq u(x')$ if and only if $u^*(x) \geqq u^*(x')$.

Two utility functions $u(x)$ and $u^*(x)$ both represent the same preference ordering, therefore, if and only if the real numbers u and u^* are related as in Figure 27. u^* is everywhere an increasing function of u and u is everywhere an increasing function of u^*.

This relationship among utility functions that represent the same preference ordering, and generate the same indifference classes and the same behaviour in the same circumstances, is sometimes expressed by saying that utility is *unique* (only) *up to an increasing* (or a 'monotonically' increasing) *transformation.*

6.5 A special hypothesis: independent utilities

The discussion in the preceding section of the relationship between strict convexity of the preference ordering (Axiom **6**) and the nature of the utility function is incomplete in two respects.

In the first place, while we showed that in general diminishing marginal utility and convexity were unrelated, we did *not* state what

13. If $u = (x_1^2+x_2^2)^n$ indifference curves are quarter-circles, and $u_{11} < 0$ if $(2n-1)x_1^2+x_2^2 < 0$. For this to be true, n must be less than $\frac{1}{2}$, and n must be positive if marginal utilities are to be positive.

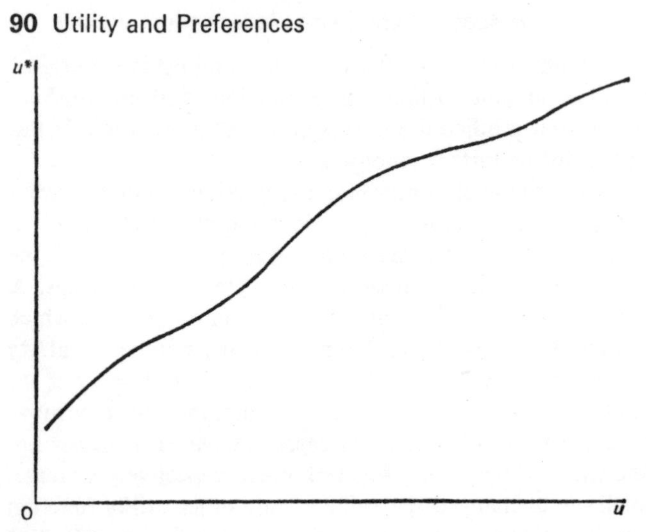

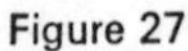
Figure 27

kind of utility function does imply convexity. We recall from section **4.2** that convexity is important because it ensures that tangency between an indifference curve and a budget line gives the best available point. It is possible, as we shall see in section **7.2**, to describe quite simply the kind of utility function that ensures this. But while such a simple description of the utility function suffices to identify optimal points, it needs to be developed if from utility analysis we are to derive testable hypotheses about the way people behave when budgets or prices change. For this purpose, unfortunately, the conditions for convexity have to be stated in quite a complex manner. The general conditions are developed in the Technical Appendix (section **T.3**); in the next two paragraphs, which the general reader may omit, we state them for the case of two commodities.

The indifference curves between x_i and x_j are strictly convex to the origin if and only if

$$u_{ii}(u_j)^2 - 2u_{ij}\, u_i\, u_j + u_{jj}(u_i)^2 < 0.$$

u_i and u_j are the marginal utilities $\partial u/\partial x_i$ and $\partial u/\partial x_j$; u_{ii} and u_{jj} are $\partial u_i/\partial x_i$ and $\partial u_j/\partial x_j$ (see p. 86 above), and are both negative if the law of diminishing marginal utility holds. $u_{ij} = \partial u_j/\partial x_i$, and measures the effect on u_j of a change in x_i. If Axiom 7 is strengthened as in the footnote on p. 82, u_{ij} always equals u_{ji}.

It is clear from the inequality that, as stated in section **6.4**, diminishing marginal utility is neither necessary nor sufficient for convexity. (Of course u_i^2, u_j^2 and $u_i u_j$ are positive). It is not sufficient because even if u_{ii} and u_{jj} are negative, u_{ij} may be sufficiently negative to make the above expression positive. It is not necessary because u_{ij} may be sufficiently positive to make the whole expression negative even if u_{ii} and u_{jj} are not negative.

In the second place, we mentioned in section **6.4** that on special assumptions diminishing marginal utility and convexity *were* related, without specifying those special assumptions. What we had in mind was the hypothesis of *independent utilities.* If we write the utility function in the additive form

$$u = f_1(x_1)+f_2(x_2)+\ldots+f_n(x_n)$$

we are saying that the utility derived from a batch of goods is the sum of the utilities derived from the individual goods; $f_1, f_2, \ldots, f_n$ are functional symbols. The utility of x_i, $f_i(x_i)$, and its marginal utility u_i $(= df_i/dx_i)$ are uniquely determined by the quantity of x_i alone, and independent of the quantity of any other goods.

With independent utilities, diminishing marginal utility *does* imply convex indifference curves. In Figure 28, assuming the quantities of all

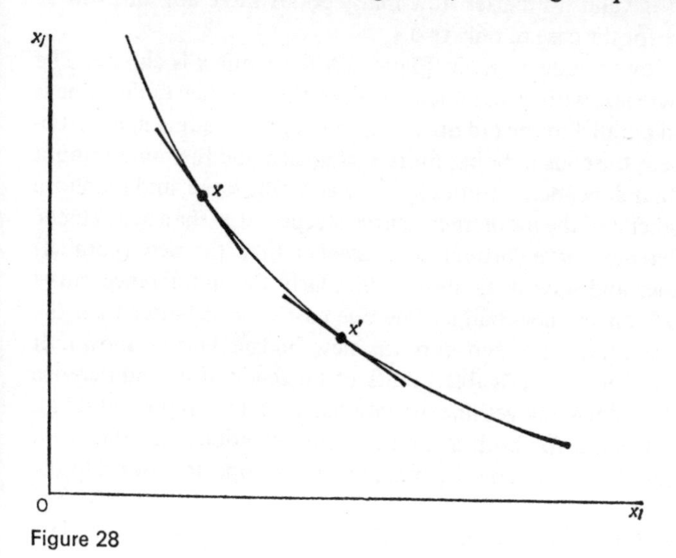

Figure 28

commodities other than x_i and x_j constant, consider a point x' south-east of x which is indifferent to x. The bundle x' contains more x_i and less x_j than x. If u_i depends only on x_i and u_j only on x_j, and marginal utility decreases for each commodity as its quantity increases, u_i must be lower and u_j higher at x' than at x: thus u_i/u_j is lower and the indifference curve is flatter, as shown. (A virtually identical argument was rejected on p. 85 above because it is not valid in general. but only when independent utilities are assumed.) Note however that we have shown only that diminishing and independent marginal utilities imply convexity. It is *not* true that independent utilities and convex indifference curves imply diminishing marginal utility of each good.

Independent utilities imply that $u_{ij} = 0$, since the marginal utility of each commodity is independent of the quantity of the other. Thus the inequality on p. 90 becomes $u_{ii}\, u_j^2 + u_{jj}\, u_i^2 < 0$. Obviously this is satisfied if u_{ii} and u_{jj} are both negative. But it *can* be satisfied even if one of them is not negative.

Moreover, independent utilities with diminishing marginal utilities have an interesting implication for behaviour, namely that the demand for every good must increase as the budget alone increases ($\partial x_i/\partial M > 0$, or all goods are normal; see section **4.5** above). The argument is valid no matter how many goods there are, but will be given here for the case of only two.

On the lower budget line in Figure 29, the point x is chosen. The budget increases with prices unchanged, so that the new budget line is above and parallel to the old one. At x' on the new budget line, vertically above x, the consumer has more x_j than at x and the same amount of x_i. With independent utilities u_j is lower, u_i the same, and therefore u_i/u_j is higher and the indifference curve steeper, at x' than at x. Hence the indifference curve through x' is steeper than the new (parallel) budget line, and cuts it as shown. Similarly the indifference curve through x'', on the new budget line due east of x, is flatter than the indifference curve at x and cuts the new budget line as shown. It follows that the only possible points of tangency of an indifference curve with the new budget line lie between x' and x'', representing an increased demand for both x_i and x_j. Inferior goods and therefore Giffen's paradox are ruled out; demand curves slope downward to the right.

Two important final points. Firstly, as was pointed out in the last section, if we take any utility function and replace it by any increasing function of itself, the underlying preference ordering is unaffected. Thus the preference ordering represented by $u = x_1 x_2$ (see p. 86 above) can also be represented not only by $u^* = +\sqrt{(x_1 x_2)}$ or $u^{**} = x_1^2 x_2^2$ but also by

$$u^{***} = \log u = \log (x_1 x_2) = \log x_1 + \log x_2.$$

This of course is an additive utility function. Moreover, the marginal

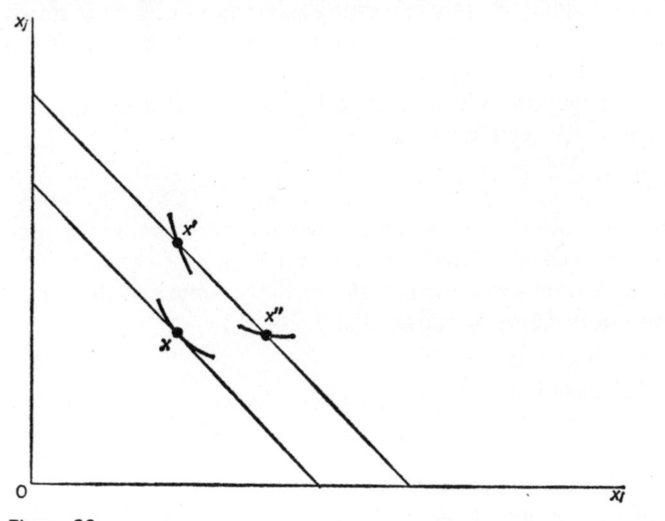

Figure 29

utilities of both x_1 and x_2 are diminishing in this function.[14]

We have just seen that the preference ordering represented by such a function implies that indifference curves are convex and all goods are normal. It follows that any utility function (such as $u = x_1 x_2$) that is an increasing function of such a function has convex indifference curves with all goods normal.

Secondly, it follows from this that independent utilities are in a sense illusory, since any preference ordering that can be presented by an additive utility function (such as $\log x_1 + \log x_2$) can also be

14. Those familiar with the rules of differentiation will know that $d(\log x_1)/dx_1 = 1/x_1$ and that $d^2(\log x_1)/dx_1^2 = -1/x_1^2$. Thus $u_{11} = -1/x_1^2 < 0$, and similarly $u_{22} = -1/x_2^2 < 0$.

represented by an infinite number of non-additive utility functions ($x_1 x_2$, $+\sqrt{(x_1 x_2)}$, $x_1^2 x_2^2$,...). To find out what independent utilities really mean it is desirable (see p. 79 above) to try to translate them into a property of the preference ordering. Independent utilities imply that u_i depends only on x_i and u_j only on x_j, so that $u_i/u_j = \text{mrs}_{ji}$ depends only on x_i and x_j. Hence the marginal rate of substitution between any two goods is independent of the quantity of any third good consumed.[15] We suggest to the reader (i) that it is much easier to understand, and judge the plausibility of, this interesting assumption when it is stated in terms of marginal rates of substitution rather than in the form of independent utilities, but (ii) that it would probably never have occurred to anyone as a hypothesis if it had not first been stated in the form of independent utilities.

Exercises

1. A movement along an indifference curve in a two-commodity consumption set *reduces* x_1 and *increases* x_2. Which of the following alternatives is (are) *inconsistent* with smoothly convex-to-the-origin indifference curves? (u_i = marginal utility of x_i.)

(a) u_1 and u_2 both rise;
(b) u_1 and u_2 both fall;
(c) u_1 rises, u_2 falls;
(d) u_1 falls, u_2 rises;
(e) u_1 rises, u_2 does not change;
(f) u_1 falls, u_2 does not change.

2. Which of the following utility functions represent(s) the same preference ordering as $u = x_1 x_2^2$?

(a) $10+17x_1 x_2^2$
(b) $10-17x_1 x_2^2$
(c) $+\sqrt{(x_1 x_2^2)}$

15. It can also be shown that if this condition holds for each pair of goods, the preference ordering can be represented by an additive utility function. If there are only *two* goods, the condition in the text holds for any utility function, additive or not, since there is then no third good. A utility function of the form $u = f_1(x_1)+f_2(x_2)$ must however have implications for the preference ordering, since not all two-commodity utility functions are increasing functions of an additive function – but these implications in the two-good case are not of great interest.

(d) $x_1 + x_2^2$
(e) $\log x_1 + 2 \log x_2$
(f) $10^{x_1 x_2^2}$

Notes on the literature

The reader may wish to consult again Chapter 2 of Newman's *Theory of Exchange* on some aspects of this chapter.

6.3 Proofs of the results on the lexicographic ordering and the existence of utility functions are to be found in G. Debreu, *Theory of Value* (Wiley, 1959, ch. 4); but it is not easy reading. Continuity and differentiability of functions are well treated in Chiang (*Fundamental Methods of Mathematical Economics*, ch. 6).

6.4 This section is based on Chapter 1 of Hicks's *Value and Capital* which the reader will now, I hope, be able to appreciate fully.

6.5 The reader who wishes to pursue further the implications of independent utilities, and who is familiar with the material of the Technical Appendix, sections **T.3** and **T.5**, may wish to consult my paper, 'Direct additivity and consumers' behaviour' (*Oxf. econ. Pap.*, vol. 13, no. 2, pp. 132–6, 1961). The implications of additivity in the case of only two goods are worked out by Samuelson in his *Foundations of Economic Analysis* (pp. 175–8).

Chapter 7
Utility and Choice

7.1 Utility maximization – the 'classical' case

If the consumer's budget constraint is as in section **3.1**, the problem he is assumed to face can be reformulated in terms of utility as follows:

$$\text{maximize} \quad u = u(x_1, x_2, \ldots, x_n)$$

$$\text{subject to} \quad \sum_{i=1}^{n} p_i x_i = M.$$

Now since, as we have been at pains to point out, our Axioms **1** to **7** on the consumer's preference ordering are equivalent to the assumptions we have made about the utility function,[16] it may appear otiose to go through the derivation of the implications of those assumptions with a new technique.

Indeed, we have had some success in deriving certain fundamental results of demand theory by elementary methods. But this becomes increasingly difficult as we seek (i) to obtain behavioural hypotheses more interesting than those we have so far derived (those of sections **4.3**, **5.2**, and **5.3**) by making additional assumptions (e.g. the 'independent utilities' hypothesis of section **6.5**), and (ii) to frame hypotheses about choice over time and choice under uncertainty, which we have hitherto ignored. Let us hasten to reassure the reader that technically difficult matters will continue to be relegated to the Technical Appendix (an example is the derivation of the Slutzky equation from the utility function: section **T.5**).

But since it will be repeatedly assumed henceforth that the consumer is seeking to maximize a utility function, it will be a great convenience if the reader is acquainted with at least the first steps in that

16. Except that our assumptions about the utility function imply a slight strengthening of Axiom 7: see p. 82. fn.

process. In this section we are concerned with what has been called the 'classical' case, in which the consumer (as is implied by our present assumptions) spends his whole budget and buys a positive amount of each commodity. To begin at the beginning, suppose for a moment that u is a function of the single variable x_1, and that the function is continuous and differentiable (which means roughly that its graph can be drawn without lifting pencil from paper and has no kinks in it, as in Figure 30).

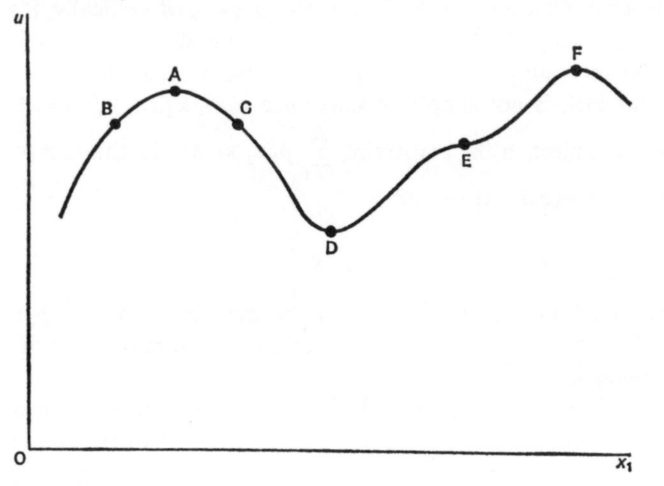

Figure 30

It is a *necessary* condition for u to reach a maximum at a particular value of x_1, say at A, that the derivative du/dx_1 (the slope of the tangent to the graph) be zero at that point. For *provided that* the value of x_1 is free to increase and decrease, the value of u can be increased by increasing x_1 if du/dx_1 is positive as at B, and the value of u can be increased by decreasing x_1 if du/dx_1 is negative as at C.

However, $du/dx_1 = 0$ is not a *sufficient* condition for a maximum. $du/dx_1 = 0$ also at D and E, but at D the value of u is at a minimum, and at E it is at what is called an inflexion point.

Moreover, even if we are satisfied that u reaches a maximum at A, this means only that it is a maximum in relation to points in its immediate vicinity (a *local* maximum). There may be other maxima (e.g. at F), and we cannot tell whether the value of u is higher at A than at F by considering the slopes of the graph at or near those two points.

If u is a function of $x_1, x_2, \ldots, x_n$, it is a *necessary* condition for a *local* maximum, *provided that* all variables are free to increase or decrease, that all *partial* derivatives be zero. For if $\partial u/\partial x_i > 0$ or < 0, u can be increased by increasing or decreasing x_i. But again we must investigate further to see whether, at a point where all partial derivatives are zero, u reaches a maximum, a minimum, or a *saddle point*. (The reader is asked to use his visual imagination to confirm that, in a three-dimensional diagram relating u, x_1 and x_2, with u measured vertically, if a point lies at the top of a hill as we increase x_1, and at the bottom of a valley as we increase x_2, the resulting surface resembles a saddle.)

Now our task is not simply to maximize $u(x_1, x_2, \ldots, x_n)$, but to maximize it subject to the constraint $\sum_{i=1}^{n} p_i x_i = M$. To this end we form the *Lagrangean* expression

$$L = u(x_1, x_2, \ldots, x_n) + \mu \left[M - \sum_{i=1}^{n} p_i x_i \right]$$

obtained by adding to $u(x_1, x_2, \ldots, x_n)$ the expression $M - \sum p_i x_i$ multiplied by the (for the moment) mysterious real number μ, known as a *Lagrange multiplier*.

We know from our previous analysis (section **4.1**) that the rational consumer will spend his whole budget, so that when utility is maximized the term $M - \sum p_i x_i$ vanishes, and $L = u$. The reason for setting up the Lagrangean is the convenient fact (which it is beyond the scope of this volume to establish) that it is a necessary condition for a maximum of u, subject to the constraint $\sum p_i x_i = M$, that the partial derivatives of L with respect to $x_1, x_2, \ldots, x_n$ be zero, provided that each x_i is free to increase or decrease. This proviso is met because (see section **4.2**) the consumer will on our present assumptions purchase a positive amount of each commodity.

The partial derivatives of L are obtained as follows. If the quantity of only one commodity, say x_i, changes,

$$\Delta L = \Delta u - \mu p_i \, \Delta x_i,$$

so that

$$\frac{\Delta L}{\Delta x_i} = \frac{\Delta u}{\Delta x_i} - \mu p_i.$$

As Δx_i approaches zero, and the quantities of all other commodities and μ) are held constant, $\Delta u/\Delta x_i$ approaches $\partial u/\partial x_i = u_i$, and μp_i does not change. Thus

$$\frac{\partial L}{\partial x_i} = u_i - \mu p_i.$$

Therefore it is necessary for a maximum of u subject to the budget constraint that

$$\begin{aligned} \frac{\partial L}{\partial x_1} &= u_1 - \mu p_1 = 0, \\ \frac{\partial L}{\partial x_2} &= u_2 - \mu p_2 = 0, \\ &\vdots \\ \frac{\partial L}{\partial x_n} &= u_n - \mu p_n = 0. \end{aligned}$$

The implications of this result, looked at in one way, are already familiar. For it follows that for all i and j

$$\frac{u_i}{u_j} = \frac{\mu p_i}{\mu p_j} = \frac{p_i}{p_j}.$$

That is, marginal utilities are proportional to prices. But u_i/u_j, as we saw in section **6.4**, is the marginal rate of substitution of x_j for x_i, so that we have the result of section **4.2**,

$$\text{mrs}_{ji} = \frac{p_i}{p_j}.$$

Looked at in another way, the necessary conditions for a maximum are less familiar. For they also imply

$$\frac{u_1}{p_1} = \frac{u_2}{p_2} = \ldots = \frac{u_n}{p_n} = \mu.$$

The first $n-1$ of these equations say that marginal utility divided by price must be the same for all commodities. Thus if $p_1 = £3$ and $p_2 = £1$, u_1 must equal $3u_2$. For suppose to the contrary that $u_1 = 4$ and $u_2 = 1$, then with the same budget, by spending £1 less on x_2 and

£1 more on x_1, one could have 1 unit less of x_2 (losing 1 'unit' of utility) and $\frac{1}{3}$ unit more of x_1 (gaining $\frac{4}{3}$ 'units' of utility) for a net gain of $\frac{1}{3}$ 'unit' of utility. Utility is maximized, in other words, only when the marginal utility per pound spent is the same for all commodities.

But the final equation says that the marginal utility per pound spent on each commodity is equal to μ. What is the significance of μ?

We can find out by asking what would happen to the value of L (and therefore to the value of u) if M were increased by £1, all prices remaining unchanged. A change in M will cause the consumer to change his purchases of $x_1, x_2, \ldots, x_n$, and this in turn will change u. Thus the total effect of a change in M on L is given by

$$\Delta L = \Delta u + \mu \left[\Delta M - \sum_{i=1}^{n} p_i \, \Delta x_i \right].$$

As the changes in $x_1, x_2, \ldots, x_n$ approach zero, the resulting change in u approaches $\partial u/\partial x_1$ times Δx_1 plus $\partial u/\partial x_2$ times $\Delta x_2 \ldots$ and so on. Thus

$$\Delta u \text{ approaches } u_1 \, \Delta x_1 + u_2 \, \Delta x_2 + \ldots + u_n \, \Delta x_n,$$

so that

$$\Delta L \text{ approaches } \sum_{i=1}^{n} u_i \, \Delta x_i + \mu \Delta M - \mu \sum_{i=1}^{n} p_i \, \Delta x_i.$$

Dividing through by ΔM, and taking the limit of $\Delta L/\Delta M$ as ΔM, and therefore $\Delta x_1, \Delta x_2, \ldots, \Delta x_n$ approach zero, we have

$$\frac{\partial L}{\partial M} = \sum_{i=1}^{n} (u_i - \mu p_i) \frac{\partial x_i}{\partial M} + \mu.$$

But as we have just seen, when utility is maximized $u_i - \mu p_i = 0$ for each i. In this case, $\partial L/\partial M = \mu$, and therefore, since L and u are equal when the whole budget is spent

$$\mu = \frac{\partial u}{\partial M}.$$

The mysterious symbol μ therefore measures the rate at which utility increases for each additional pound in the budget when the budget is spent in such a way as to maximize utility. This is why it is commonly called the *marginal utility of money*. And the conditions $u_i - \mu p_i = 0$ say that if utility is to be maximized subject to the budget constraint, the marginal utility of each commodity must be equal to its price multiplied by the marginal utility of money.

This is as far as we shall pursue utility maximization in the classical case. The conditions which ensure that the point chosen is a maximum (the utility-equivalent of convexity, cf. p. 50) are to be found in the Technical Appendix, section **T.3.**, or, for the case of two commodities, on p. 90.

We are, however, in a position to draw a further consequence of the assumption of independent utilities (section **6.5**) when the marginal utility of every commodity is diminishing. In this case all pairs of commodities must be net substitutes (section **5.1**).

For suppose that the price of x_i falls, and the consumer's budget is reduced so that he remains on the same indifference surface. The quantity of x_i must increase (section **5.3**), so that if he is to remain on the same indifference surface the quantity of at least one other commodity (say x_j) must fall.

With independent utilities and diminishing marginal utility, the reduction in the quantity of x_j must increase its marginal utility u_j. Both before and after the reduction in p_i and the compensating reduction in the budget, u_j must equal p_j multiplied by the marginal utility of money, as was shown earlier in this section. And since u_j has risen and p_j has remained unchanged, the marginal utility of money must have risen.

But since the prices of *all* commodities other than x_i have remained unchanged, the marginal utility of each of them must have risen to preserve its equality with the price multiplied by the higher marginal utility of money. And with independent utilities and diminishing marginal utilities, a higher marginal utility of every commodity other than x_i implies that the quantity of each of them must have fallen.

Hence the substitution effect of the fall in the price of x_i reduces not only the quantity of x_j but the quantities of all commodities other than x_i. Since x_i may be any commodity, it follows that all pairs of commodities are net substitutes when utilities are independent and all marginal utilities are diminishing.

7.2 Corner solutions and bliss

This section may be regarded as either an extension of, or a digression from, the main thread of analysis of this book. It is an extension in that it is designed to show that the theory of consumer behaviour does have something to say about cases in which the consumer's preference ordering (i) violates Axiom **4** of non-saturation, so that he does not necessarily spend all his budget (cf. p. 47 above), or (ii) violates Axiom **6** of strict convexity in that the consumption set includes parts of the commodity axes, so that not all commodities are bought or necessary for survival (cf. p. 49 below).

It is possible to develop, fairly briefly and painlessly, the utility maximization analysis of the last section to embrace (i) and (ii) above, and then to interpret the results in elementary terms. The reader who perseveres through the next few pages will be in a position both to see what difference the abandonment of Axioms **4** and **6** makes to the fundamental results of demand theory derived earlier, and to follow the discussion in the next section of consumer behaviour under rationing. As a bonus, he will have received an introduction to the important technique of non-linear programming, with its host of applications in economics and business; the 'classical' analysis of section **7.1**, and linear programming, are special cases.

We begin by rewriting the Lagrangean expression of p. 98 above as follows

$$L = u(x_1, x_2, \ldots, x_n) + \mu \left[M - \sum_{i=1}^{n} p_i x_i - S \right],$$

and add the constraints

$$x_1, x_2, \ldots, x_n, S \geqq 0.$$

The new variable S (for 'slack') is the amount of the budget that the consumer leaves unspent. The term in parentheses multiplied by μ is still zero, and obviously, since the budget must not be exceeded, $M - \sum p_i x_i = S \geqq 0$. By contrast with section **7.1**, S is now a variable whose value is to be determined, and is *not* assumed to be zero; and we state that $x_1, x_2, \ldots, x_n$ must be non-negative – we do *not* assume that they are all positive.

The necessary conditions for a maximum of u in these altered circumstances are

$$\frac{\partial L}{\partial x_i} = u_i - \mu p_i \leqq 0, \qquad x_i(u_i - \mu p_i) = 0 \quad (i = 1, 2, \ldots, n);$$

$$\frac{\partial L}{\partial S} = -\mu \leqq 0, \qquad \mu S = 0.$$

(When only S changes, $\Delta L = -\mu \Delta S$ or $\Delta L/\Delta S = -\mu$. This remains true as ΔS approaches zero, so that $\partial L/\partial S = -\mu$.)

The change in appearance of these conditions can be explained quite simply. When we said in section **7.1** that a function of several variables reached a maximum only when its partial derivatives (e.g. $\partial L/\partial x_i$) were all zero, we were careful to add the proviso that all the independent variables (e.g. $x_1, x_2, \ldots, x_n, S$) were free to increase or decrease.

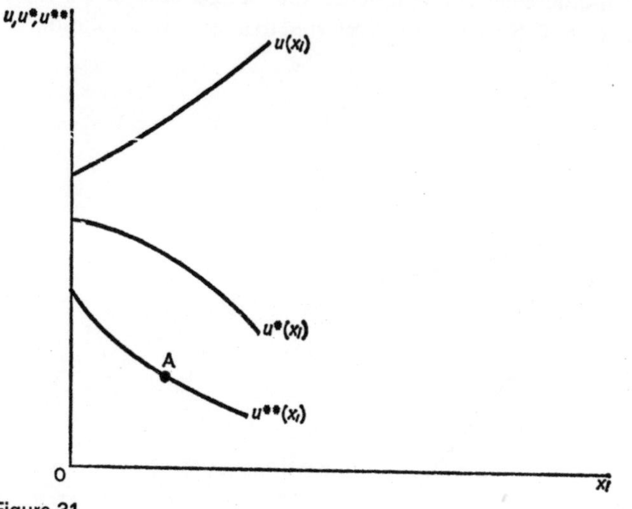

Figure 31

In Figure 31, where u, u^* and u^{**} are functions of the single variable x_i, u is clearly not maximized when $x_i = 0$, as u can be increased by increasing x_i. However, u^* has a maximum at $x_i = 0$ where $du^*/dx_i = 0$. But u^{**} also has a (local) maximum at $x_i = 0$ even though $du^{**}/dx_i < 0$. If x_i were positive (as at A), $du^{**}/dx_i < 0$ would be inconsistent with a maximum of u^{**}, since u^{**} could be increased by reducing x_i. But when $x_i = 0$, and we are operating under the constraint that x_i cannot be negative ($x_i \geqq 0$), it cannot be reduced, and $du^{**}/dx_i < 0$ is perfectly consistent with a maximum.

This is why the first n conditions for a maximum are

$$\frac{\partial L}{\partial x_i} = u_i - \mu p_i \leqq 0.$$

But of course $u_i - \mu p_i = 0$ remains a necessary condition if x_i is positive. Thus if $u_i - \mu p_i < 0$ at a maximum, x_i must be zero. The equation $x_i(u_i - \mu p_i) = 0$ is a convenient way of summarizing the last two sentences.

The implications of these conditions can be stated in terms which do not involve utility as follows. Suppose that in Figure 32, the highest attainable indifference curve touches the budget line at x, where $x_i = 0$ but $x_j > 0$. Such a point is referred to as a 'corner solution'.

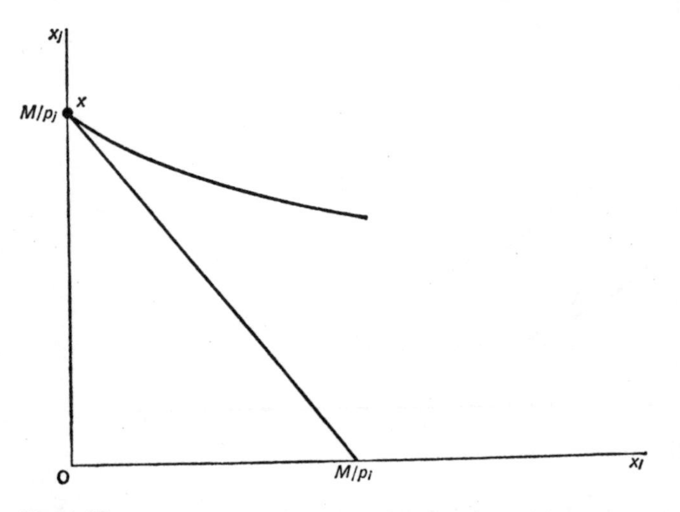

Figure 32

For this to be the case, the indifference curve must either be flatter than the budget line at x (as drawn) or tangent to it; it must not be steeper. This means that mrs_{ji} must be less than or equal to p_i/p_j. The marginal conditions say that $u_i - \mu p_i \leqq 0$, but since x_j is positive we must have $u_j - \mu p_j = 0$.

Hence $u_i \leqq \mu p_i$, $\quad u_j = \mu p_j$, and therefore

$$\frac{u_i}{u_j} \leqq \frac{p_i}{p_j}.$$

And of course u_i/u_j is simply mrs_{ji}.

The final marginal condition is that $\partial L/\partial S = -\mu \leqq 0$ (so that $\mu \geqq 0$), and that if $S > 0, \mu = 0$, while if $\mu > 0, S = 0$.

What is the economic significance of this?

The reader will recall that in section **7.1** it was shown that μ measured the marginal utility of money to the consumer– it was equal to $\partial u/\partial M$, the rate at which utility increased for each additional pound in the budget when it was spent in an optimal manner. This remains true in the present case.[18]

Now if the consumer chooses to leave some of his budget unspent ($S > 0$), no increase in it can make him better off; as our condition says, in this case $\mu = 0$. But if an increase in his budget *would* make him better off ($\mu > 0$), this can only imply, as the condition says, that he is now spending all of it ($S = 0$); if he had more, he would spend more.

Three loose ends remain to be tied. Firstly, we undertook to give a simple description of the type of utility function which ensured that satisfaction of the marginal conditions guaranteed a unique maximum of utility subject to the budget constraint. To allow for saturation and zero quantities of commodities, it is sufficient that Axiom **6** of strict convexity of the preference ordering is satisfied on a consumption set that (at least conceptually) extends beyond the axes.

This is illustrated in Figure 33 (where we have also drawn smooth curves, since marginal rates of substitution, and marginal utiiities, are assumed to be everywhere uniquely defined). A utility function generating such indifference classes is said to be everywhere *strictly quasi-concave*: we shall leave to the Technical Appendix (section **T.6**) the resolution of this terminological paradox.

18. If there were other constraints in addition to the budget constraint, $\partial u/\partial M$ could be less than – but not greater than – μ at a corner solution, i.e. at an optimal point where some quantities purchased were zero.

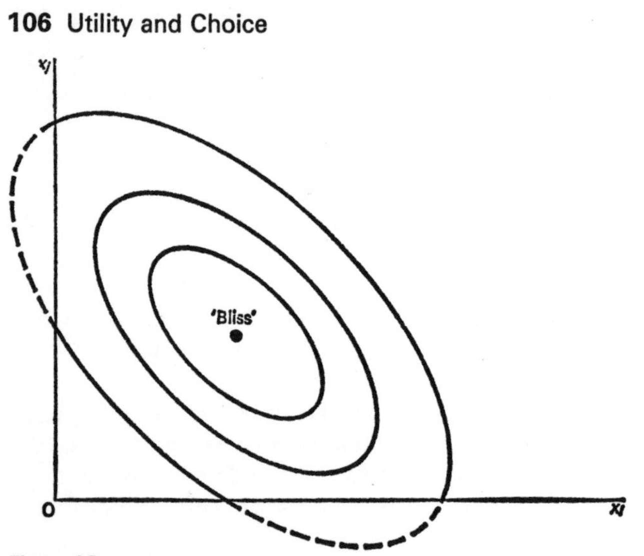

Figure 33

Secondly, we promised to show the implications of saturation and corner solutions for the fundamental results of demand theory derived in earlier chapters. It is clear that with a given (strictly quasi-concave) utility function the optimal bundle of goods does not change if prices and income do not change or all change in the same proportion, whether the consumer is at a corner solution as in Figure 32 or at the point of bliss shown in Figure 33. But what of the substitution effect on x_i of a change in p_i? It will be recalled that the 'Fundamental Theorem of Consumption Theory' of section **5.3** rested on the proposition that $(\partial x_i/\partial p_i)_S < 0$.

Suppose that a consumer is buying no x_i. A fall in its price, no matter what change is made in his budget, cannot reduce the quantity he buys. But if, in Figure 32, p_i alone falls, and the budget line remains steeper than the indifference curve at x, he will choose to remain at x. No adjustment of his budget is needed to keep him on the same indifference curve. But there has been no change in the quantity of x_i consumed: it remains at zero. Thus $(\partial x_i/\partial p_i)_S = 0$. (Of course, if the budget line becomes flatter than the indifference curve at x, a compensating reduction in the budget is necessary; x_i becomes positive, and $(\partial x_i/\partial p_i)_S < 0$.)

What if p_i rises? If $x_i = 0$ and $x_j > 0$, $u_i/u_j \leqslant p_i/p_j$. If the consumer, after a compensating increase in his budget, bought a positive amount of x_i and remained in the same indifference class, u_i/u_j would fall. But with x_i positive we must now have $u_i/u_j = p_i/p_j$. And yet p_i alone has risen, so that p_i/p_j has risen. Since initially $u_i/u_j \leqslant p_i/p_j$ it is not possible for u_i/u_j to fall, for p_i/p_j to rise, and for the two ratios to become equal. Thus when $x_i = 0$, the substitution effect of a rise in p_i must leave it at zero. Again $(\partial x_i/\partial p_i)_S = 0$.

If the consumer is completely saturated (as at the point marked 'bliss' in Figure 33) any change in price accompanied by a change in his budget which leaves him in the same indifference class (assumed to consist of a single point) will leave all quantities at their 'bliss' levels. Again $(\partial x_i/\partial p_i)_S = 0$.

Corner solutions and saturation therefore imply that we must replace the proposition $(\partial x_i/\partial p_i)_S < 0$ by

$$\left[\frac{\partial x_i}{\partial p_i}\right]_S \leqq 0.$$

In order to be sure that the demand curve for a commodity slopes downwards to the right it is now no longer sufficient that the commodity *not* be an *inferior* good. For in the Slutzky equation (which continues to hold as developed on pp. 65–6 above)

$$\frac{\partial x_i}{\partial p_i} = \left[\frac{\partial x_i}{\partial p_i}\right]_S - x_i \frac{\partial x_i}{\partial M},$$

if $\partial x_i/\partial M$ and $(\partial x_i/\partial p_i)_S$ are both zero, $\partial x_i/\partial p_i = 0$. To allow for the possibility that $(\partial x_i/\partial p_i)_S$ is zero, it is necessary that x_i be a normal good $(\partial x_i/\partial M > 0)$ if we are to be sure that $\partial x_i/\partial p_i < 0$. Thus the Fundamental Theorem must be restated as (cf. p. 69 above): *Any good that is known always to increase in demand when the budget alone rises must definitely shrink in demand when its price alone rises.*

Thirdly and finally, at the beginning of this section we described it as in a sense a digression. This is because in most applications of demand theory corner solutions and bliss are neglected. The neglect of bliss is not serious. To neglect corner solutions is not serious if, as in most attempts to measure demand functions a 'commodity' is not a detailed item but a *group* of goods (e.g. dairy products rather than Cheshire cheese), or if in the theory of choice over time, for example, the independent variables in the utility function are *total* consumption at different dates (though the justification for using such aggregates needs to be examined). And in any case we shall develop later, and make use of, Lancaster's 'goods-characteristics' analysis, which offers an alternative explanation of why some goods are not purchased.

7.3 An application: choice under rationing

The techniques of the preceding section find an interesting application in the problem of the consumer faced by rationing as well as a budget constraint. So as to keep the problem fairly simple, we shall revert to the assumptions that (i) a positive amount of each commodity is purchased and (ii) the whole of the budget M is spent; this makes sense because the size of the current budget is presumably determined, as part of the wider allocation process alluded to in section **4.1** above, in full knowledge of the rationing scheme.

Thus in the absence of rationing, the analysis would be that of section **7.1** rather than **7.2**. But if we introduce the simplest kind of rationing ('straight rationing'), in which the quantity of x_i purchased may not exceed R_i, we extend the Lagrangean expression of **7.1** as follows,

$$L = u(x_1, x_2, \ldots, x_n) + \mu\left[M - \sum_{i=1}^{n} p_i x_i\right] + \mu_i(R_i - x_i - S_i)$$

and add the condition $S_i \geqq 0$.

The constraint imposed by the rationing of x_i is represented by the term $R_i - x_i - S_i$ (where $S_i \geqq 0$ is the amount of the ration not taken up) multiplied by the new Lagrange multiplier μ_i. The first n necessary conditions for a maximum with all commodity quantities positive are obtained in the usual way as:

For the unrationed goods x_j $(j \neq i)$, $\dfrac{\partial L}{\partial x_j} = u_j - \mu p_j = 0;$

For the rationed good x_i, $\dfrac{\partial L}{\partial x_i} = u_i - \mu p_i - \mu_i = 0.$

But since the 'slack' variable S_i may be positive or zero we have (cf. p. 103 above)

$$\frac{\partial L}{\partial S_i} = -\mu_i \leqq 0, \qquad \mu_i S_i = 0.$$

These conditions say that the marginal utilities of the unrationed commodities must be equal to their prices multiplied by the marginal utility of money, as in section **7.1**. The marginal utility of the rationed good x_i must be equal to its price times the marginal utility of money *plus* μ_i. And μ_i can be interpreted as the marginal utility of the ration R_i, just as μ was interpreted as the marginal utility of M in section **7.1.** It is equal to $\partial u/\partial R_i$,[19] the rate at which the consumer's utility would increase if the ration were increased by one unit and he adjusted his purchases optimally. If he is not using his whole ration ($S_i > 0$), no increase in the ration will make him better off ($\mu_i = 0$). But if $\mu_i > 0$, he must be using his whole ration ($S_i = 0$).

An implication of these conditions is that, if x_j is any unrationed commodity,

$$\frac{u_i}{u_j} = \frac{\mu p_i + \mu_i}{\mu p_j}.$$

The significance of this is illustrated in Figure 34.

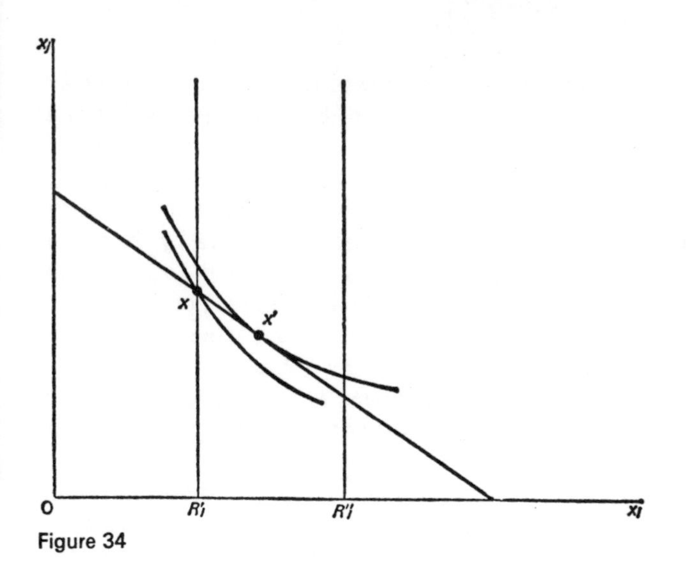

Figure 34

19. This is ensured (as are similar statements later in this section) by the assumption that all quantities bought are positive. Cf. p. 105, n. 18.

If $R_i = R_i'$, the consumer is constrained to the point x, while in the absence of rationing he would move to a higher indifference curve at x'. Clearly therefore $\mu_i > 0$, and the equation above implies that in this case $u_i/u_j > p_i/p_j$; correspondingly, in Figure 34 $\text{mrs}_{ji} = u_i/u_j > p_i/p_j$ at x. But if $R_i = R_i''$, the consumer would choose the point x', leaving part of his ration unused; $S_i > 0$, so that $\mu_i = 0$. Both algebra and geometry then give $\text{mrs}_{ji} = u_i/u_j = p_i/p_j$.

A more complex case is that of 'points rationing'. We shall indicate only the main lines of the analysis, since the algebra is very cumbersome. Some goods are unrationed, or subject to straight rationing as described above. The remainder are divided into categories, e.g. meat, clothing, tinned goods, etc. For each category of goods the consumer receives an allotment of 'points', and the 'points' price of each good in each category is specified.

Analytically, each such category of goods contributes to the Lagrangean an expression of the form

$$\mu^{(k)}\left[R^{(k)} - \sum_{i=1}^{n} p_i^{(k)} x_i^{(k)} - S^{(k)}\right],$$

where $R^{(k)}$ is the number of points the consumer receives for the kth category of goods, $p_i^{(k)}$ is the number of k-category points that must be given up for a unit of $x_i^{(k)}$, $S^{(k)} (\geqq 0)$ is the number of k-category points unspent, and $\mu^{(k)}$, the marginal utility of $R^{(k)}$, is zero if $S^{(k)} > 0$. It is not difficult to show, given Axioms **1** to **7**, that the demand for each commodity is uniquely determined by the money budget, the money prices, all the points allotments and all the points prices, and will not be changed by a doubling of the points allotment and of all the points prices in a given category. Moreover, it can be shown that a fall in any points price, say $p_i^{(k)}$, accompanied by a fall in the corresponding points allotment $R^{(k)}$ which leaves the consumer at the same utility level, will not reduce the quantity of $x_i^{(k)}$ purchased.

These results should not surprise the reader. A less obvious result, due to Samuelson, is that the demand for a good becomes less responsive to (small) compensated changes in its own money price as additional rationing constraints are imposed.

Finally, it is worth pointing out that Lagrange multipliers such as the μ, μ_i and $\mu^{(k)}$ introduced in sections **7.1–7.3** have, in other problems to which these methods of analysis may be applied, an interesting and important interpretation. They measure the effect on the maximand of relaxing a constraint, and are frequently termed the 'shadow prices' associated with the constraints. If it were discovered, for example, that an extra dollar of foreign exchange reserves would increase the maximum level of a country's national income by $2 (the 'shadow price' of foreign exchange), the policy implications would be significant.

7.4 The composite commodity theorem

We conclude this chapter by reverting to the 'classical' theory of section **7.1** and earlier, and discussing a result due to Hicks which permits a great simplification of parts of demand theory. This is the proposition that any group of commodities whose prices remain in fixed proportions may be 'treated as a single commodity'.

This implies that if there are n commodities, and the relative prices of $x_2, x_3, \ldots, x_n$ do not change, we can carry out our analysis as if there were only two commodites, x_1 and x_c. The latter commodity x_c is a 'composite commodity' whose quantity is defined as the total expenditure on $x_2, x_3, \ldots, x_n$ divided by the price of any one of these goods (or indeed by the value of any function homogeneous of degree one in $p_2, p_3, \ldots, p_n$), and whose price p_c is this divisor. Thus for example we might define the quantity of x_c as

$$x_c = x_2 + \frac{p_3}{p_2}x_3 + \ldots + \frac{p_n}{p_2}x_n$$

and its price as $p_c = p_2$. To say that x_c can be treated as a single commodity implies that if a preference ordering satisfying Axioms **1** to **7** exists on the consumption set of n commodities, such an ordering also exists on the two-commodity consumption set containing only x_1 and x_c.

Corresponding to given values of x_1 and x_c will be quantities of $x_2, \ldots, x_n$ chosen in such a way that their marginal utility ratios are equal to the given price ratios. Among vectors (x_1, x_c) there will be a preference ordering satisfying Axioms **1** and **2** of Chapter 2, since each such vector, given the price ratios $p_3/p_2, \ldots, p_n/p_2$, determines a unique vector of n commodities. From any feasible set of alternatives the consumer will choose the vector (x_1, x_c) highest in his preference ordering, thus satisfying Axiom **3**.

If x_1 were increased, given x_c, the consumer would be better off, by Axiom **4** of non-saturation, if he continued to consume the same quantities of $x_2,\ldots, x_n$; if he were to change his consumption of those goods, it would only be to bring him to a still more highly preferred position. If x_1 were held fixed and x_c were increased, it is as if his 'budget' to be spent on $x_2,\ldots, x_n$ had been increased, and clearly he would be better off. Thus if Axiom **4** holds for vectors $(x_1, x_2,\ldots, x_n)$, it holds for vectors (x_1, x_c).

The reader may perhaps be willing to believe without proof: (i) that if, as one travels along a path in the n–commodity consumption set, the value of u nowhere breaks off abruptly and resumes at a higher or lower level (Axiom **5** of Continuity), the same is true in the (x_1, x_c) consumption set; (ii) that *if* (x_1, x_c) indifference curves are strictly convex to the origin, they are smoothly curved with no kinks (Axiom 7).[20]

What appears very difficult to prove by elementary methods is that Axiom **6** of strict convexity (everywhere convex-to-the-origin indifference curves) in n commodities implies strict convexity in the (x_1, x_c) consumption set. It is because of the need to use utility theory to prove this result (see Technical Appendix, section **T.4**) that we have delayed until now the introduction of the composite commodity theorem.

The theorem could have been used (as Hicks uses it) to analyse fully the demand for a single commodity by means of a two-dimensional diagram (sections **5.1** and **5.3**), or to justify the treatment of consumption as a single commodity in our discussion of the supply of effort (section **5.5**). We shall find several further uses for it in later chapters.

Exercises

1. (a) If M and $p_1,\ldots, p_n$ all double in sections **7.1** and **7.2**, what happens to the marginal utility of money?

(b) Is μ a function of $M, p_1,\ldots, p_n$?

(c) If so, what kind of function?

20. And that the strengthened version of Axiom **7** holds for (x_1, x_c) if it holds for $(x_1,\ldots, x_n)$: see p. 82, fn. no. 12.

2. If, at an optimal point in section **7.2**, the marginal utility of x_i is *equal to* its price times the marginal utility of money, does it follow that x_i must be positive?

Notes on the literature

7.1 Chapter 4 of Baumol, *Economic Theory and Operations Analysis*, contains a useful and somewhat fuller elementary treatment of the techniques used in this section. For more detail (including techniques used in our Technical Appendix, sections **T.3** and **T.5**) Chiang, *Fundamental Methods of Mathematical Economics*, (ch. 12) may be consulted.

7.2 The techniques employed in this section are discussed (in order of increasing difficulty) by Baumol (*op. cit.*, ch. 7), R. Dorfman, P. A. Samuelson and R. Solow, *Linear Programming and Economic Analysis* (McGraw-Hill, 1958, ch. 8), K. Lancaster, *Mathematical Economics* (Collier, 1968, chs 4 and 5), and M. L. Balinski and W. J. Baumol, 'The dual in non-linear programming and its economic interpretation' (*Rev. econ. Stud.*, vol. 35, no. 3, pp. 237–56, 1968). The term 'classical' as used in our own discussion is Lancaster's. The basic source of the technique is H. W. Kuhn and A. W. Tucker, 'Non-linear programming', in J. Neyman (ed.), *Proceedings of the Second Berkeley Symposium on Mathematical Statistics and Probability* (University of California Press, 1951).

7.3 The classic references on rationing are P. A. Samuelson, *Foundations of Economic Analysis* (pp. 163–71) and J. Tobin, 'A survey of the theory of rationing' (*Econometrica*, vol. 20, no. 4, pp. 521–35, 1952). To appreciate these contributions fully (and to follow their proofs of the unsupported assertions towards the end of our own section), requires an understanding of sections **T.3** and **T.5** of the Technical Appendix. An interesting geometric treatment is that of M. McManus, 'The geometry of point rationing' (*Rev. econ. Stud.*, vol. 22, no. 1, pp. 1–14, 1954–5).

7.4 The composite commodity theorem is stated in Hicks, *Value and Capital* (p. 33). Proofs alternative to that of our Technical Appendix section **T.4**, but using similar methods, are in Hicks (*op. cit.*, p. 312) and in Samuelson (*op. cit.*, pp. 141–3).

Chapter 8
Two Alternative Approaches

8.1 Marshallian demand theory

It will be apparent to the reader by now that the demand theory we have been expounding in this volume is primarily an elaboration of the remarkably fertile first three chapters of Hicks's *Value and Capital*. Before we proceed with further applications – stating our general hypotheses in testable form, proposing special hypotheses, extending the analysis to the treatment of time and uncertainty – let us look briefly at two alternative approaches to demand theory, one earlier than Hicks and one later.

Our discussion of Alfred Marshall is not designed to do justice to the depth and breadth of his treatment of demand in his *Principles of Economics* (Book III) – the reader must discover these for himself. The next few pages are nothing but an interpretation of Marshall in the light of the analysis of our earlier chapters.

Firstly, Marshall assumed independent utilities. In speaking of two consumers with utility functions u and v consuming x (apples) and y (nuts), he says: 'Prof. Edgeworth's plan of representing u and v as general functions of x and y has great attractions to the mathematician; but it seems less adapted to express the everyday facts of economic life than that of regarding, as Jevons did, the marginal utilities of apples as functions of x simply' (p. 845).

Secondly, he assumed diminishing marginal utility: 'the marginal utility of a thing to anyone diminishes with every increase in the amount of it he already has' (p. 93).

As we saw in section **6.5**, these assumptions are sufficient to ensure that all goods are normal ($\partial x_i/\partial M > 0$) and therefore that demand curves slope downwards to the right. But this was not Marshall's line of argument. Instead, 'we assume that the marginal utility of money to the individual purchaser is the same throughout' (p. 842); this is justified 'on the assumption, which underlies our whole reasoning, that his expenditure on any one thing, as, for instance, tea, is only a small part of his whole expenditure' (*ibid.*; see also pp. 132, 334–5).

Given these assumptions, it follows that: 'The larger the amount of a thing that a person has the less, other things being equal (i.e. the purchasing power of money, and the amount of money at his command being equal), will be the price which he will pay for a little more of it' (p. 95). That is, the demand curve of section **4.4** slopes downwards to the right if his budget (and all other prices) and the purchasing power of money – by which he seems here to mean the marginal utility of money – are constant. (Note that Marshall treats price as the dependent variable and quantity as the independent variable; see p. 60 above.)

The proof (which Marshall does not give explicitly) is as follows. Draw a curve relating the marginal utility of x_1 to its quantity; u_1 is a function of x_1 alone by virtue of independent utilities.

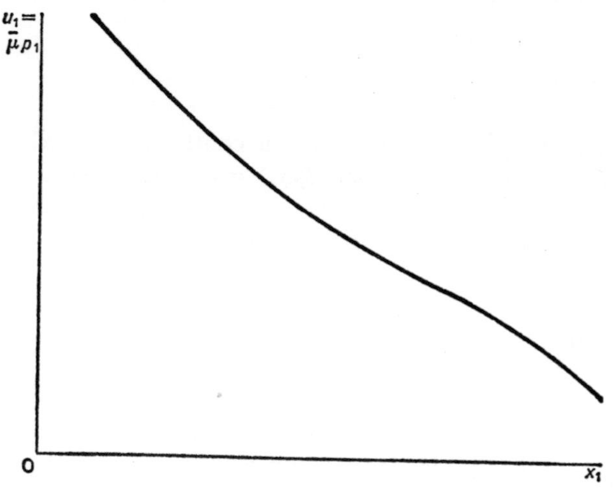

Figure 35

The consumer equates the marginal utility of x_1 to its price multiplied by the marginal utility of money, μ; see section **7.1**. But if μ is constant, u_1 and p_1 are in a fixed proportion. Thus the curve relating x_1 and u_1 has exactly the same shape as the demand curve relating x_1

and p_1; one becomes the other by a simple proportional transformation of the vertical scale. Thus if $u_{ii} = du_i/dx_i < 0$, $dp_i/dx_i < 0$.

How shall we interpret the constancy of the marginal utility of money in terms of our earlier analysis? We shall draw on the composite commodity theorem of section **7.4**. If the money prices of $x_2, \ldots, x_n$ do not change, let us define the quantity of x_c as simply the money expenditure on x_c divided by one pound, and its price p_c as one pound. The additive utility function is then $u = f_1(x_1) + f_c(x_c)$, and the Lagrangean (we are in the 'classical' case of section **7.1**) is

$$L = f_1(x_1) + f_c(x_c) + \mu[M - p_1 x_1 - x_c],$$

since by definition $p_c = 1$.

The necessary conditions for a maximum are

$$\frac{\partial L}{\partial x_1} = \frac{df_1}{dx_1} - \mu p_1 = 0,$$

$$\frac{\partial L}{\partial x_c} = \frac{df_c}{dx_c} - \mu = 0.$$

The constancy of μ implies that df_c/dx_c is constant. Since only a linear function has a constant slope, $f_c(x_c) = a + bx_c$. a and b are constants of which the first affects nothing and may be ignored; $b = df_c/dx_c = \mu$. Thus the utility function has the form

$$u = f_1(x_1) + \mu x_c,$$

$$\text{with} \quad u_1 = \frac{df_1}{dx_1} > 0, \qquad u_{11} = \frac{d^2 f_1}{dx_1^2} < 0.$$

In an indifference curve diagram, this implies that the slope of an indifference curve at any point depends only on x_1; $\text{mrs}_{c1} = u_1/u_c = u_1/\mu$, and μ is constant.

Therefore as long as x_1 is constant, the slope of indifference curves does not change; it is the same at x' as at x in Figure 36. And this has the important consequence that a change in the budget with prices constant does not change the demand for x_1. The income effect of a change in p_1 is zero because $\partial x_1/\partial M = 0$; only the substitution effect is operative.

8.2 How does the marginal utility of money behave?

It is clear that Marshall's assumption of a constant marginal utility of money, as just interpreted, cannot possibly hold exactly for all commodities. For it would then follow that an increase in the budget, with prices constant, would not increase the demand for any commodity. And Marshall was careful to point out that, even for commodities on which a small fraction of income is spent, the constancy of μ is only approximate (pp. 132, 842).

This suggests two difficulties: first, the marginal utility of money, unlike the marginal rate of substitution, is not an observable magnitude, nor does introspection shed light on how it behaves in different

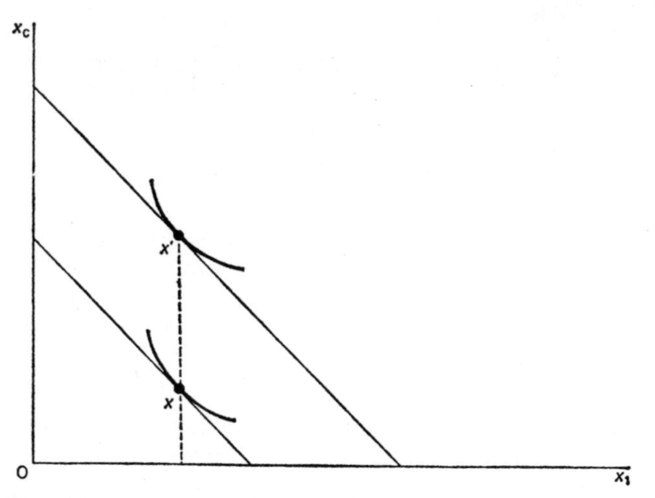

Figure 36

circumstances. Is it possible to interpret in terms of our earlier analysis the proposition that the marginal utility of money changes less with a change in the price of a commodity on which a small, rather than a large, fraction of the budget is spent? Secondly what becomes of Marshall's analysis when the fraction of the budget spent on a commodity is not 'small'?

1. When the marginal utility of money is constant on our interpretation, the income effect of a change in price is zero. If μ were not

constant, the slopes of the indifference curves in Figure 36 would depend on x_c as well as x_1 and the income effect would no longer be zero.

Now if the income effect is to be ignored in its effect on the slope of the demand curve, it is of course its size in relation to the substitution effect that is important. This suggests the following 'Marshallian' hypothesis: *The smaller the fraction of the budget spent on a commodity, the smaller is the income effect in relation to the substitution effect.*

The Slutzky equation will help us to determine whether this hypothesis can be deduced from our earlier analysis:

$$\frac{\partial x_i}{\partial p_i} = \left[\frac{\partial x_i}{\partial p_i}\right]_S - x_i \frac{\partial x_i}{\partial M}.$$

If we multiply both sides by p_i/x_i, and in addition multiply both numerator and denominator of the last term by M, we get

$$\frac{p_i}{x_i}\frac{\partial x_i}{\partial p_i} = \left[\frac{p_i}{x_i}\frac{\partial x_i}{\partial p_i}\right]_S - \frac{p_i x_i}{M}\left[\frac{M}{x_i}\frac{\partial x_i}{\partial M}\right].$$

On the left-hand side we have the own-price elasticity of demand for x_i, which is negative for a downward-sloping demand curve. The first term on the right-hand side is the elasticity of the demand curve obtained if, when p_i changes, the budget is adjusted so as to keep the consumer at the same utility level; this is called the *compensated demand curve.* Its elasticity is always negative since the substitution term $(\partial x_i/\partial p_i)_S < 0$. The last term is the fraction of the budget spent on x_i multiplied by the budget-elasticity of demand for x_i.

It follows that if there are two commodities for which the elasticity of the compensated demand curve and the budget-elasticity of demand are both equal, the influence of the income effect on the slope of the demand curve will be greater for the one on which the larger fraction of the budget is spent. If both are inferior goods, the one on which the larger fraction of the budget is spent is more likely to have an upward-sloping demand curve.

But of course the elasticities may be such that it does not work out in that way (see Exercise 1 at the end of the chapter). Little is known about how elasticities behave as fractions of the budget spent on commodities change; we limit ourselves to offering the last equation above as the evidence available in modern demand theory which is relevant to our 'Marshallian' hypothesis.

2. But what does Marshall have to say about cases in which the fraction of the budget spent on a commodity is not small? Consider the well-known passage:

... as Sir R. Giffen has pointed out, a rise in the price of bread makes so large a drain on the resources of the poorer labouring families and raises so much the marginal utility of money to them, that they are forced to curtail their consumption of meat and the more expensive farinaceous foods: and, bread being still the cheapest food which they can get and will take, they consume more, and not less of it (p. 132).

As we know from Chapter 5, this phenomenon can occur only if bread is an inferior good. And as we saw in section **6.5**, independent utilities and diminishing marginal utilities imply that all goods are normal ($\partial x_i/\partial M > 0$). Thus either the additive utility function or diminishing marginal utilities must go, and presumably Marshall would abandon the former.

But why does he assert with such confidence that the marginal utility of money rises? To be sure, when we have an additive utility function with diminishing marginal utilities, a reduction in the *budget* with all prices *constant* will increase the marginal utility of money; for in that case all goods are normal, all quantities will decrease, every u_i will increase, and $u_i = \mu p_i$ therefore implies that μ must increase. But in the present case of a rise in the price of bread (i) the utility function is not additive, (ii) after the rise in the price of bread a penny buys less bread than before, so that although the consumer is undoubtedly worse off, it is by no means clear that an extra *penny* would increase utility by more than before (see Exercise 2 at the end of the chapter).

What Marshall seems to be arguing is that the reduction in the quantities of meat and other farinaceous foods raises their marginal utilities and therefore (since their prices are unchanged) also raises μ. These reductions in quantity raise the marginal utility *curve* of bread (x_i) so much that, although μ and p_i have risen to μ' and p_i', it is still possible to have $u_i = \mu' p_i'$ at a higher quantity of x_i than before (see Figure 37).

This is not a satisfactory argument – it leaves too many questions unanswered. At the same time, it must be admitted that simply to say, as we should nowadays, that bread is an inferior good, is a little too easy: inferiority implies relationships between bread and other goods which are not made explicit. We submit only that if we were to pursue this matter, we should find speculation about what was happening to the marginal utility of money a hindrance rather than a help. (A promising line of approach is the goods-characteristics model; see the end of section **10.4.**)

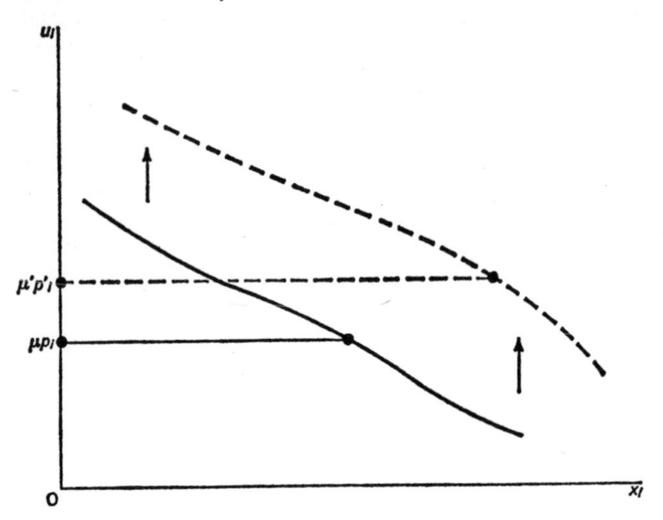

Figure 37

One final point. Friedman has claimed that the 'Marshallian demand curve' was intended by Marshall to be one along which 'real income', or the level of utility, remained constant as price changed (i.e. the compensated demand curve), in contrast to the 'current interpretation' according to which it is the budget and all other prices that remain constant. Now according to our interpretation at the end of the last section, if the marginal utility of money remains constant as we move along a demand curve, the level of utility does not remain constant, but nonetheless the income effect is zero; thus the resulting 'current interpretation' demand curve *coincides* with the compensated demand curve. Friedman admits that Marshall's passage on the Giffen paradox weakens his case; but it is precisely and only here that

Marshall abandons the assumption of a constant marginal utility of money, so that the compensated demand curve and the 'current interpretation' demand curve diverge. We conclude that the case for the 'current interpretation' of Marshall's demand curve is a strong one.

8.3 Revealed preference theory

The other approach to demand theory we shall consider in this chapter, associated primarily with the name of Samuelson, is in the sharpest possible contrast with that of Marshall. Not only does it eschew such unobservable magnitudes as the marginal utility of money – it does not even follow the course of earlier chapters of this book in deriving hypotheses about behaviour from assumptions about a preference ordering or a utility function. Though it is known as 'revealed preference theory', no assumptions are made about preferences as such. Its only axioms are about behaviour, and it is remarkable that the fundamental results of demand theory can be derived from only two such axioms:

Axiom **R1**: *From any set of alternatives, the consumer makes a choice.*

Axiom **R2** (Consistency): *If x is chosen from a set of alternatives that includes x' (which is different from x), then any set of alternatives from which x' is chosen must not contain x.*

A violation of Axiom **R2** would occur if x were chosen when x' could have been chosen (the consumer *revealed a preference* for x over x') *and* x' were chosen when x could have been chosen.

Note that nothing is said about non-saturation, continuity or convexity. Nevertheless the existence of demand functions, their homogeneity of degree zero, and the fundamental theorem of consumption theory (in its weaker form given on p. 107 above) can be derived from Axioms **R1** and **R2** alone. Lest the reader ask why, in this case, he has been asked to learn the techniques of earlier chapters, we hasten to repeat that utility theory is the best way of progressing beyond these three basic results.

Let the consumer then be faced with the usual budget constraint $p.x \leqq M$. This defines a set of alternatives from which the consumer, by Axiom **R1**, makes a choice x. If M and p remain unchanged, or change in the same proportion, the set of alternatives remains unchanged and continues to contain x. To choose any alternative other than x (and therefore a different quantity of any commodity) would violate the consistency Axiom **R2**.

The effect of a change in p_i on the quantity of x_i demanded will be analysed for three cases, proceeding from the special to the general. First we assume that there are only two commodities, and that the whole budget is spent (Figure 38).

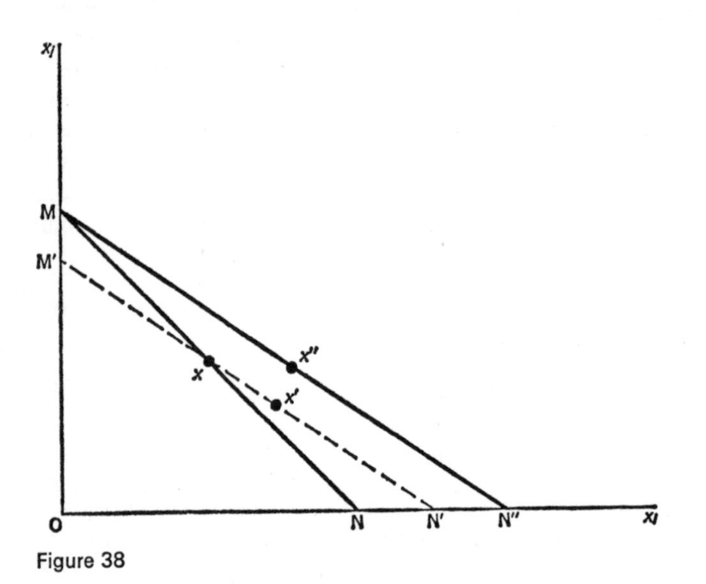

Figure 38

From the initial budget line MN the consumer chooses x. Then p_i falls, and the budget line becomes MN″. Since we are not assuming the existence of indifference curves, we cannot define a substitution effect as a movement along such a curve. Instead we define a *quasi-substitution effect* as follows. We reduce the consumer's budget so that he can just buy the same amount of each good as before the fall in p_i. Thus we draw a new budget line M′N′ passing through x and parallel to MN″. We then define the movement (if any) from x along M′N′ as the quasi-substitution effect.

Samuelson calls this the 'over-compensation effect'. But after the reduction in his budget the consumer – if there were indifference curves of the usual shape – would move to a higher indifference curve than at x, so that the fall in p_i appears to have been *under*-compensated. On the other hand, if p_i had risen – as in the article in which Samuelson coined the term – the quasi-substitution effect would require an increase in the budget which would put the consumer on a higher indifference curve than before, and the term over-compensation would be appropriate. It is because of this asymmetry that we propose the neutral term 'quasi-substitution effect'.

It is possible, from a knowledge of quantities and prices, to calculate precisely the change in the budget required for the quasi-substitution effect. (See Exercise 3 at the end of the chapter.) This is not possible, without a precise knowledge of the indifference map, for the substitution effect.

As to the direction of the quasi-substitution effect, note that x was chosen in preference to all other points in the triangle OMN. The new budget region is the triangle OM′N′. Since the quadrilateral OM′xN is common to both triangles, the axiom of consistency requires the consumer to choose *either* x again *or* a point in the triangle xNN′ above the line xN. The quasi-substitution effect of a fall in p_i cannot reduce x_i, but may leave it unchanged.

Now if the consumer moves, for example, to x', the remainder of the effect of the fall in p_i is that of an increase in the budget with no change in prices – for example from x' to x''. Without resorting to the Slutzky equation, we can see that since the quasi-substitution effect may be zero (the consumer may remain at x), it is necessary that x_i be a normal good ($\partial x_i/\partial M > 0$) if we are to be quite sure that a fall in p_i will increase the quantity demanded. Thus the weaker form of the fundamental theorem of consumption theory (above, p. 107) is appropriate.

For the second case of n commodities, in which we continue to assume that the whole budget is spent, we employ the technique of inequalities between inner products of vectors introduced in section 5.3. Let $x = (x_1, x_2, \ldots, x_n)$ be bought initially at prices $p = (p_1, p_2, \ldots, p_n)$, and let prices change to $p' = (p'_1, p'_2, \ldots, p'_n)$. In order to determine the quasi-substitution effect, we change the budget so that the initial quantities x can just be bought at the new prices p'. Thus $p'.x = \sum p'_i x_i$ is the money value of the initial quantities at the new prices. After the budget adjustment the consumer chooses the point x' and, since he spends the whole budget,

$$p'.x' = p'.x.$$

The movement from x to x' is the quasi-substitution effect of the change in the price vector from p to p'. Of course the consumer may choose not to move from x, in which case the quantity vectors x and x' are identical commodity by commodity. If this is the case, and the only difference between p and p' is in the price of the single commodity x_i, clearly the quasi-substitution effect on x_i of a change in p_i alone is zero.

But if $x \neq x'$, x' has been chosen in preference to x; when x' was chosen x could have been chosen, since their money values $p'.x$ and $p'.x'$ were equal. The consistency axiom then implies that when x was chosen the set of alternatives did not contain x'. That is to say that when the consumer bought x, he could not afford x'. Since x was bought at prices p, this means that

$$p.x' > p.x.$$

Thus when $x \neq x'$, $p'.x' = p'.x$ and $p.x' > p.x$, so that

$$(p'-p).(x'-x) = \sum_{i=1}^{n} (p'_i-p_i)(x'_i-x_i) < 0.$$ [20]

If only p_i changes, this inequality reduces to $(p'_i-p_i)(x'_i-x_i) < 0$.

In short, the quasi-substitution effect of a change in p_i alone either leaves x_i unchanged or changes it in the opposite direction.

Thirdly and finally, although the revealed preference axioms say nothing about non-saturation or convexity (let alone strict convexity), the corner solutions and bliss of section **7.2** do not upset the fundamental results of demand theory.

Let us assume first that the consumer does not necessarily spend his whole budget, so that in the initial position $p.x \leqq M$. Prices again change to p', and again we change the budget so that he can just buy x at the new prices. Thus the new budget is $M' = p'.x$. But he does not

20. The reader will have noticed that in this second case our definition of the quasi-substitution effect, and the results obtained, are more general than we need if we are interested in the effects of a change in a single price. This final inequality is valid for any number of simultaneous price changes, and the generality of the result was cheaply purchased. (A similar comment might be made about section **5.3**, and the third case immediately following.)

necessarily spend his whole quasi-substitution effect budget, so that $p'.x' \leqq M'$. As before, x and x' may be the same point, so that if only p_i has changed the quasi-substitution effect is zero. But if $x \neq x'$, as before he has revealed a preference for x' over x. Thus when he chose x he must have been unable to afford x'. When he chose x at prices p, his budget was M; therefore we must have $M < p.x'$.

Putting all the inequalities together, we have

$$p.x \leqq M < p.x' \quad \text{and} \quad p'.x' \leqq M' = p'.x,$$

from which it follows again that $(p'-p).(x'-x) < 0$, with the same consequences as in the second case.

Corner solutions cause no difficulty. When p_i alone changes, the foregoing analysis simply *rules out* a quasi-substitution effect in which $(p'_i-p_i)(x'_i-x_i) > 0$. If initially the consumer is at a point where $x_i = 0$ and therefore cannot decrease, it follows that if p_i rises $(p'_i > p_i)$ the quasi-substitution effect must leave x_i at zero, while if p_i falls x_i may either remain the same or increase.

8.4 Revealed preference and utility

It was shown in the last section that two purely behavioural axioms of revealed preference theory imply the three fundamental results of demand theory – existence and zero-degree homogeneity of demand functions, and the fundamental theorem of consumption theory in its weaker form – which were derived much more laboriously from the preference ordering and utility function of earlier chapters. Behavioural axioms are therefore a third source of hypotheses about consumer behaviour. And it is convenient to be able to translate a hypothesis about any one of the preference ordering, the utility function, or the consumer's behaviour into a hypothesis about the other two, so as to make it easier (a) to check the *prima facie* plausibility of the hypothesis, (b) to derive further hypotheses from it and (c) to test it, insofar as it is possible, against the behaviour of consumers in the market.

In saying this, we have implied that such translations are always possible. And it is desirable, in concluding our discussion of the three sources of hypotheses about consumer behaviour, to support what we have said by showing that it is possible to construct a set of purely behavioural axioms corresponding to Axioms **1** to **7** of Chapters 2 and 3. Clearly **R1** and **R2** are not sufficient, since they imply neither non-saturation, continuity nor convexity.

This is a difficult area, and we shall not attempt to give a full and rigorous treatment. It is clear, however, that the behavioural assumption that the consumer always spends his whole budget corresponds to Axiom **4** of non-saturation. And we shall briefly show that the assumption that each batch of goods is chosen in *one and only one* price-budget situation corresponds to Axioms **6** and **7** of smooth strict convexity.

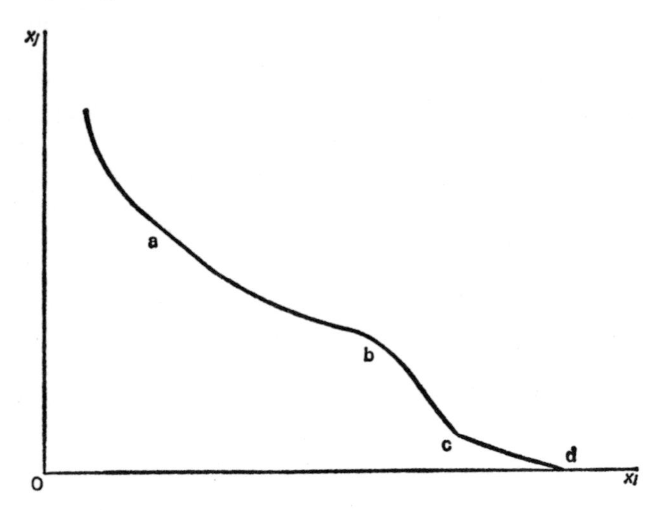

Figure 39

A 'price-budget situation' is a set of numbers M, $p_1,\dots, p_n$ corresponding to a given budget constraint, $\sum p_i\, x_i \leqq M$ or $\sum(kp_i)x_i \leqq kM$. In Figure 39 the possibility of straight stretches of indifference curve such as a is already implicitly ruled out by Axioms **R1** and **R2**; consistency requires the consumer to choose a unique point in any price-budget situation. If indifference curves were concave to the origin, there would be points in regions as at b which would be chosen in *no* price-budget situation. If they were kinked, a point such as c would be chosen in *more than one* price-budget situation. The same argument rules out indifference curves touching an axis as at d, and therefore excludes corner solutions.

There is a behavioural continuity assumption, corresponding to Axiom **5**, which we shall not pursue. The surprising thing is that, even with all these assumptions, unless we strengthen the consistency Axiom **R2**, Axiom **2** of *transitivity* may not hold. The development of this argument is primarily of technical interest, and the rest of this chapter (but not the exercises!) may be skipped with impunity.

Suppose that in the case of three commodities we discover at every point, by observing in what price-income situation the bundle of goods corresponding to that point is purchased, the marginal rate of substitution between each pair of goods. We can then, to use Samuelson's image, suspend (or insert) at each point in the three-dimensional space a thumb-tack (known to English readers as a drawing-pin) 'whose back or head lies in the budget plane and whose points tells us which is the "preferred" direction... Can we "join together" the little thumb-tacks to form bowl-like surfaces' which we can then, if we choose, identify with indifference surfaces or classes?

In general the answer is no. Unless we strengthen Axiom **R2**, we may be able to travel along a path of points which are 'indifferent' to each other and finish at a point x' which contains more of all goods than the starting point x. Thus $x'Px$, while transitivity of indifference requires that $x'Ix$.

Now Axiom **R2**, translated into price-quantity terms, says that if the consumer spends his whole budget on x at prices p and could have bought another bundle of goods x', $(p.x \geqq p.x')$, he has revealed a preference for x over x', and that when he buys x' at prices p' he must be unable to afford x $(p'.x > p'.x')$. We now call this the

Weak Axiom of Revealed Preference: If $p.x \geqq p.x'$, *and* $x \neq x'$, *then* $p'.x > p'.x'$.

The axiom that ensures that the thumb-tacks can be joined together into bowl-like surfaces (known technically as the 'integrability' of the equations defining the marginal rates of substitution) is the:

Strong Axiom of Revealed Preference: If $p.x \geqq p.x'$, $p'.x' \geqq p'.x''$,..., $p^{(s-1)}.\,x^{(s-1)} \geqq p^{(s-1)}.x^{(s)}$, *and at least two of the commodity bundles* x, x', ..., $x^{(s)}$ *are different, then* $p^{(s)}.x > p^{(s)}.x^{(s)}$ (i.e. it is *not* the case that $p^{(s)}.x^{(s)} \geqq p^{(s)}.x$).

This says that if there is a sequence of bundles of any length, of which at least one is revealed preferred to its successor, and of which each is either identical to or revealed preferred to its successor, the last bundle in the sequence must not be revealed preferred to the first (Houthakker). The Weak Axiom is obviously a special case of the Strong Axiom in which there are only two bundles in the sequence. If there are only two commodities, it can be shown that there is no integrability problem: the Weak Axiom implies the Strong Axiom. (This is not the case with more than two commodities unless one adds a further assumption of obscure economic import.)

Exercises

1. Calculate the own-price elasticities of demand for x_1 and x_2 from the following data,

	$\frac{p_i x_i}{M}$	$\left[\frac{p_i}{x_i}\frac{\partial x_i}{\partial p_i}\right]_S$	$\frac{M}{x_i}\frac{\partial x_i}{\partial M}$
x_1	0·3	−0·1	−0·5
x_2	0·4	−0·2	−0·4

2. Given the utility function $u = x_1 x_2$:

(a) Show that the marginal utilities are $u_1 = x_2, u_2 = x_1$.

(b) Given (a), show that the consumer will spend half his budget on each commodity.

(c) Express the marginal utility of money μ as a function of M, p_1 and p_2.

(d) Does μ increase or decrease as p_1 (or p_2) alone increases?

3. With $M = £100$, $p_1 = £2$, $p_2 = £5$, a consumer's choice is $x_1 = 25$, $x_2 = 10$. If p_1 falls to £1, what change must be made in his budget to determine the quasi-substitution effect?

Notes on the literature

References to A. Marshall, *Principles of Economics*, are to the eighth edition (Macmillan, 1920).

8.1 In an article by Samuelson, 'Constancy of the marginal utility of income', in O. Lange (ed.), *Studies in Mathematical Economics and Econometrics in Memory of Henry Schultz* (University of Chicago Press, 1942), reprinted in J. E. Stiglitz (ed.), *The Collected Scientific Papers of Paul A. Samuelson* (Massachusetts Institute of Technology Press, 1966, pp. 37–53), the constancy of μ is interpreted in a number of ways and found wanting. Although Samuelson refers to Hicks, he does not give our interpretation, which we believe to be faithful to Marshall and to Hicks's view of him (*Value and Capital*, pp. 26–33).

8.2 See Friedman, 'The Marshallian demand curve' (*J. Polit. Econ.*, vol. 57, no. 6, pp. 463–95, 1949; reprinted in part in W. Breit and H. M. Hochman (eds.), *Readings in Microeconomics*, Holt, Rinehart and Winston, 1968, pp. 104–14).

8.3 A standard source on revealed preference theory is Samuelson 'Consumption theorems in terms of overcompensation rather than indifference comparisons' (*Economica*, vol. 20, no. 77, pp. 1–9, 1953; reprinted in J. E. Stiglitz (ed.), *op. cit.*, pp. 106–14), foreshadowed in Samuelson (*Foundations of Economic Analysis*, chapter 5). Little (*A Critique of Welfare Economics*, ch. 2), should not be overlooked.

An alternative name for our 'quasi-substitution effect' might be the 'Slutzky substitution effect', since it is in accordance with his analysis. The usual substitution effect could then be called the 'Hicksian substitution effect'. Cf. Friedman (*Price Theory*, pp. 49ff.).

8.4 A difficult article by H. Uzawa, 'Preference and rational choice in the theory of consumption', in *Proceedings of a Symposium on Mathematical Methods in the Social Sciences* (Stanford University Press, 1960, pp. 129–48), provides the main reference for this section.

For the final paragraphs there is a good expository article by Samuelson, 'The problem of integrability in utility theory' (*Economica*, vol. 17, no. 68, pp. 355–85, 1950; reprinted in J. E. Stiglitz (ed.), *op. cit.*, pp. 175–205), from which the thumb-tacks quotation is taken. The Strong Axiom of revealed preference was discovered by H. S. Houthakker, 'Revealed preference and the utility function' (*Economica*, vol. 17, no. 66, pp. 159–74, 1950).

Part Three
From Pure Theory to Applied Theory

Chapter 9
Measured Demand Functions

9.1 Introduction

We referred several times in the last chapter to the testing of hypotheses of demand theory against actual behaviour. What we had in mind was the attempt to measure in the market-place the demand functions implied by theoretical relationships among quantities, prices and budgets. We shall not attempt to introduce the reader to techniques of estimation: such econometric problems as identification, multicollinearity, bias, time-series versus cross-section analysis, are beyond the scope of this volume.

But there are plenty of other difficulties. We remind the reader that the context within which the consumer in earlier chapters is assumed to be making his choices is extremely restricted. No stocks of goods are held, and price expectations and uncertainty are neglected. These limitations will be removed in parts Four and Five. Nevertheless, some success has been achieved in estimating demand functions which, despite these restrictions, conform to the behavioural hypotheses derived from the model of Parts One and Two.

Perhaps more serious is the fact that all our theory hitherto has been concerned with the individual consumer or household. What does this theory imply about the independent variables to be included in a demand function designed to explain the behaviour of the total demand for a commodity by all its purchasers, and its partial derivatives? This problem will be considered in later sections of this chapter.

Moreover, we have spoken lightly of 'n' commodities. The number of distinguishable commodities and brands is so enormous that it would be an impossible task to insert all their prices in a demand function, or to test our theory by estimating the demand functions for all of them. Commodities must obviously be grouped. We have already considered one aspect of this problem in section **7.4** on the composite commodity theorem. A further approach ('separability') will be discussed in the next chapter.

In the next section, to illustrate the interaction between demand theory and hypotheses about behaviour, we shall briefly exhibit a few specific demand functions and utility functions that have been used in estimation.

Before we do so, we must ask the reader to bear in mind certain important aspects of empirical work in economics as he reads the next few sections and when he comes across references to evidence relating to a particular hypothesis. No measured demand function ever fits price-quantity data exactly, since it is impossible to include among the independent variables all the forces that influence the dependent variable. Since every estimated demand function, when tested by making predictions which are compared with data, predicts imperfectly, the degree of imperfection must be measured and compared with that resulting from alternative hypotheses. (And if one tries to improve the predictions by adding more and more independent variables, such comparisons become less and less meaningful.)

One consequence of this is that when we say in sections **9.3** and **9.4**, for example, that in certain conditions market demand functions *can* be derived from individual demand functions, we must not be construed as implying that if these conditions are not exactly satisfied, the attempt to estimate market demand functions must be abandoned. What we imply, very roughly, is that, other things being equal, we should expect market demand functions to lead to smaller errors in prediction the more nearly the theoretical conditions for their existence are satisfied.

A second consequence is that there are so many changing variables to cause errors in our predictions that, at least at the present stage in the development of economics and econometrics, it is very seldom that a theoretical hypothesis can be decisively rejected on empirical grounds alone. (Consider, for example, the question of whether to accept the 'normal income' hypothesis or Clower's hypothesis relating to consumption in Chapter 12.)

9.2 Demand functions and utility functions: examples

Technical difficulties of estimation impose limitations on the type of demand function that can be used. By far the simplest is

$$x_i = b_i \frac{M}{p_i} \quad or \quad p_i x_i = b_i M \quad (i=1,\ldots,n), \tag{D1}$$

which says simply that expenditure on each commodity is a constant fraction of the budget. Obviously $b_i \geqslant 0$ and

$$\sum_{i=1}^{n} b_i = 1.$$

The budget-elasticity of demand for each commodity is unity (section **4.5**). The *Engel curves,* which join the points corresponding to the bundles $(x_1,\ldots, x_n)$ chosen by the consumer as his budget varies with prices constant, are therefore straight lines through the origin $(0,\ldots, 0)$. The function (D1), indeed, is inconsistent with *Engel's laws,* which are well established empirically and state that the proportions of the budget devoted to certain groups of commodities vary considerably as the budget changes; the best known of these is of course that the budget-elasticity of demand for food is less than unity.

Since expenditure on each commodity is constant given M, all own-price elasticities of demand are equal to -1. Clearly all cross-elasticities are zero. From the Slutzky equation,

$$\frac{\partial x_i}{\partial p_j} = \left[\frac{\partial x_i}{\partial p_j}\right]_S - x_j \frac{\partial x_i}{\partial M},$$

it follows that since $\partial x_i/\partial p_j = 0$ and $\partial x_i/\partial M > 0$, we must have $(\partial x_i/\partial p_j)_S > 0$, so that all pairs of commodities are net substitutes (section **5.1**).

The demand functions (D1) imply a utility function of the following form (or any increasing function of it: see section **6.4**):

$$u = x_1^{\beta_1} x_2^{\beta_2} \ldots x_n^{\beta_n} \tag{U1}$$

If $\beta_1 + \beta_2 + \ldots \beta_n \neq 1$, the expenditure shares b_i in (D1) are given by:

$$b_i = \frac{p_i x_i}{M} = \frac{\beta_i}{\sum_{j=1}^{n} \beta_j}.$$

Proof: The first-order conditions for the maximization of

$$L = x_1^{\beta_1} x_2^{\beta_2} \dots x_n^{\beta_n} + \mu\left(M - \sum_{i=1}^{n} p_i x_i\right) \text{ are (for } i = 1,\dots, n)$$

$$\frac{\partial L}{\partial x_i} - \mu p_i = \beta_i x_1^{\beta_1} \dots x_i^{\beta_i - 1} \dots x_n^{\beta_n} - \mu p_i = \frac{\beta_i u}{x_i} - \mu p_i = 0,$$

so that $p_i x_i = \dfrac{\beta_i u}{\mu}$,

and $M = \sum_{i=1}^{n} p_i x_i = \dfrac{u}{\mu} \sum_{i=1}^{n} \beta_i$,

and therefore, as stated above:

$$\frac{p_i x_i}{M} = \frac{\beta_i}{\sum_{i=1}^{n} \beta_i}$$

The function $u = x_1 x_2$ of section **6.4** is of the form (U1), with $\beta_1 = \beta_2 = 1$, $b_1 = b_2 = \frac{1}{2}$.

Exercise 2 of chapter 8 was a simple example of the derivation of demand functions from this utility function. One obtains the necessary conditions for a maximum of u as in section **7.1** and uses them, together with the budget constraint, to solve (though this is not always possible) for x_i in terms of $p_1, \dots, p_n, M$. To obtain the utility functions implied by a particular demand function (if they exist) is much more difficult, and we shall not attempt to show how it is done.

Apart from (D1), demand functions which are linear in $p_1, \dots, p_n, M$ (or can be changed into linear form) are the easiest to estimate. The most obvious is

$$x_i = a_{i1}\frac{p_1}{p_i} + \dots + a_{ii} + \dots + a_{in}\frac{p_n}{p_i} + b_i\frac{M}{p_i}. \tag{D2}$$

Sets of demand functions of this form have been important in empirical work (especially that of Richard Stone), and are known as 'linear expenditure systems'. It is remarkable that the theory of earlier chapters implies that there exist numbers $s_1,\ldots, s_n$ such that (D2) can be re-written as

$$x_i = s_i + \frac{b_i\left[M - \sum_{k=1}^{n} p_k s_k\right]}{p_i}. \tag{D2'}$$

(D2′) says that expenditure on x_i can be divided into two parts: the purchase of a fixed (survival?) quantity s_i, and a constant fraction b_i of what is left out of the budget after the quantities s_k of all commodities have been bought. If we interpret S $= (s_1,\ldots, s_n)$ as the 'bare survival set' of section **3.3**, this set has collapsed to a single point.

The great advantage to the econometrician of the replacement of (D2) by (D2′) is that he has to estimate only the $2n$ coefficients $s_1,\ldots, s_n, b_1,\ldots, b_n$, rather than (as appeared at first sight) the n^2+n coefficients $a_{11},\ldots, a_{nn}, b_1,\ldots, b_n$.

We relegate the proof that (D2) can be written as (D2′) to the Technical Appendix, section **T.7**, where it is also shown that if $M > \sum p_k s_k$, so that the consumer can buy more than the basic quantities of all goods, then all goods are normal ($b_i = p_i(\partial x_i/\partial M) > 0$), and all pairs of goods are net substitutes, i.e. $(\partial x_i/\partial p_j)_S > 0$, and that the demand for each commodity is inelastic with respect to its own price.

We can show more simply that the conflict of (D2′) with Engel's laws is less acute than that of (D1). For if the share, b_i, of x_i in the 'supernumerary' expenditure $M - \sum p_k s_k$ is greater (less) than its share in the 'basic' expenditure $\sum p_k s_k$, an increase in M will increase (decrease) $p_i x_i/M$. Although the Engel curves are straight lines, they pass through the point $(s_1,\ldots, s_n)$ rather than through the origin $(0,\ldots, 0)$ as in the case of (D1). Thus it is perfectly possible with (D2′) for the share of food in the budget to decrease as the budget increases.

The last result given in section **T.7** of the Technical Appendix is that one of the utility functions yielding the demand functions (D2) or (D2′) is

$$u = (x_1 - s_1)^{b_1} \ldots (x_n - s_n)^{b_n} \tag{U2}$$

Another form of demand function, more difficult to estimate than (D1), but no more difficult than (D2), is

$$x_i = C_i\, p_1^{a_{i1}} \ldots p_n^{a_{in}}\, M^{b_i}, \tag{D3}$$

because it can be written in the linear form

$$\log x_i = \log C_i + a_{i1} \log p_1 + \ldots + a_{in} \log p_n + b_i \log M \tag{D3'}$$

(by repeated application of the rules that $\log x^r = r \log x$ and $\log xy = \log x + \log y$).

The constants $a_{i1},\ldots, a_{in}, b_i$ are the *elasticities* of demand with respect to prices and the budget,[21] and with zero-degree homogeneity of the demand functions Euler's theorem (see section **4.5**, p. 59) implies that $a_{i1} + \ldots + a_{in} + b_i = 0$.

The difficulty with (D3) is that there is no utility function from which such demand functions can be derived for all commodities (unless of course $b_i = -a_{ii} = 1$, $a_{ij} = 0$ for $i \neq j$, which is (D1)). $\sum_{i=1}^{n} p_i x_i$ does not equal M when the x_i are obtained from functions like (D3).

Can alternative types of demand function then be derived from other specifications of the utility function? One possibility is

$$u = \sum_{i=1}^{n} a_i x_i^{b_i}. \tag{U3}$$

It appears very difficult to derive demand functions from (U3), though relationships among the budget and pairs of prices and quantities x_i, x_j, p_i, p_j can be estimated.

An interesting approach is to look at the utility function in a different way. Given the budget constraint, the consumer makes a unique choice and achieves a certain level of utility. The maximum utility attainable is therefore a function (given zero-degree homogeneity) of $p_1/M,\ldots, p_n/M$, and we can write

$$u_{\max} = u_{\max}\left[\frac{p_1}{M},\ldots, \frac{p_n}{M}\right].$$

This is called an *indirect* utility function, to distinguish it from the direct utility functions $u(x_1,\ldots, x_n)$.

21. For example in (D3), $\partial x_i/\partial p_1 = a_{i1}\, C_i\, p_1^{a_{i1}-1} \ldots p_n^{a_{in}}\, M^{b_i} = a_{i1}\, x_i/p_1$, so that $(p_1/x_i)(\partial x_i/\partial p_1) = a_{i1}$.

How do we obtain demand functions from an indirect utility function? The reader will recall that in section **5.3** we pointed out that the consumer's optimal choice could be thought of *either* as the most preferred way of spending a given budget *or* as the least expensive way, at given prices, of attaining a given indifference class (or level of utility). It is the second alternative that we now exploit. We find, by techniques similar to those of section **7.1**, the values of $x_1,\ldots, x_n$ which *minimize* $\sum p_i x_i$ subject to the constraint that u_{max} is at a given level.

Indirect utility functions analogous to (U1) and (U2) are:

$$u_{\max} = \left[\frac{b_1 M}{p_1}\right]^{b_1} \cdots \left[\frac{b_n M}{p_n}\right]^{b_n}$$

$$\text{and } u_{max} = \left[\frac{b_1(M - \Sigma\, p_k\, s_k)}{p_1}\right]^{b_1} \cdots \left[\frac{b_n(M - \Sigma\, p_k\, s_k)}{p_n}\right]^{b_n}.$$

But these indirect functions do not advance matters, since they give rise to precisely the same demand functions, (D1) and (D2) or (D2′), as (U1) and (U2).

But the indirect utility function analogous to (U3),

$$u_{\max} = \sum_{i=1}^{n} a_i \left[\frac{M}{p_i}\right]^{b_i} \qquad \text{(U4)}$$

implies demand functions different from those derivable from (U3). Though the demand functions from (U4) are neither linear in $p_1,\ldots, p_n$, M nor expressible in linear form, it is possible to estimate linear relationships from which their parameters may be obtained.

It is hoped that this section has given the reader some understanding of the relationship between the theory of consumer behaviour and the estimation of actual demand functions. In a similar vein, the implications of specific forms of the utility function for the consumer's choices over time and under uncertainty are considered in Parts Four and Five; see in particular sections **12.4**, **15.4** and **T.8**.

9.3 Individual demand and market demand

Of what assistance is the theory of earlier chapters in the estimation of the *total* demand for a commodity of a group of consumers? It tells us that for each of the m consumers in the group there is a demand function for each commodity

$$x_i^{(r)} = f_i^{(r)}(p_1,\dots, p_n, M^{(r)}) \quad (r = 1,\dots, m),$$

where $x_i^{(r)}$, $M^{(r)}$ are the rth household's demand for x_i and its budget. It follows that, if x_i is the total demand for the ith commodity,

$$x_i = \sum_{r=1}^{m} x_i^{(r)} = \sum_{r=1}^{m} f_i^{(r)}(p_1,\dots, p_n, M^{(r)}) = G_i(p_1,\dots, p_n, M^{(1)},\dots, M^{(m)}).$$

Obviously to collect data on the budgets of each individual purchaser of a commodity, as the last equation requires, would be an impossible task. It would be very convenient if there existed market demand functions with total demand uniquely determined by prices and the sum of all individual budgets $M = \sum_{r=1}^{m} M^{(r)}$, so that

$$x_i = F_i(p_1,\dots, p_n, M),$$

and if these demand functions had the properties deduced for individual demand functions from Axioms **1** to **7** of Chapters 2 and 3. Though it is not possible to give a complete set of necessary and sufficient conditions for this to be so, some of the important considerations will be discussed in this section and the next.

In the first place, it is obvious that if all m consumers have identical tastes and their budgets are always equal, the market demand function will have all the properties of the representative individual demand function $f_i^{(r)}(p_1,\dots, p_n, M^{(r)})$:

$$x_i = \sum_{r=1}^{m} x_i^{(r)} = mf_i^{(r)}(p_1,\dots, p_n, M^{(r)}) = mf_i^{(r)}(p_1,\dots, p_n, M/m)$$

$$= F_i(p_1,\dots, p_n, M).$$

It is as if, given the representative utility function $u_i^{(r)}(x_1,\dots, x_n)$, the market demand function had been derived from

$$u = u_i^{(r)}(mx_1,\dots, mx_n).$$

Without the assumption that all individual budgets are equal it is *not* sufficient, if total demand is to be independent of the distribution of M, that all consumers should have identical tastes. For suppose that at a certain set of prices the demands of two consumers for x_i would be as follows:

$M^{(r)}, M^{(s)}$	£100	£150	£200
$x_i^{(r)}, x_i^{(s)}$	10	14	16

If the sum of the two budgets $(M^{(r)}+M^{(s)})$ were £300, total demand would be 28 if each consumer's budget were £150, but only 26 if one budget were £100 and the other £200.

If we place no restrictions whatever on the distribution of a given total M (except that no individual budget may be negative), and require that demand functions $x_i = F_i(p_i, \ldots, p_n, M)$ exist for all commodities and all sets of prices, the tastes of all individuals must be not only identical but also 'homothetic with respect to the origin'. This means that a straight line from the origin must cut all indifference surfaces at points of equal slope, as in Figure 40.

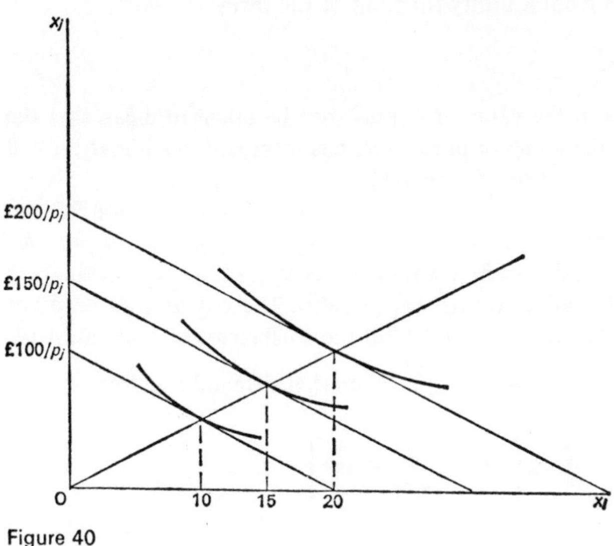

Figure 40

It is clear that if everyone's indifference curves were as in Figure 40, all Engel curves would be straight lines through the origin, so that a transfer of £y from the budget of individual r to that of individual s, leaving total M unchanged, would lead to an increase in demand for each commodity by s, and an exactly equal decrease in demand for each commodity by r, leaving total demand for each commodity unchanged.[22] In the numerical example given earlier indifference curves like those of Figure 40 would imply that if at a given set of prices each consumer demanded 10 units of x_i with a budget of £100, he would demand 15 and 20 with budgets of £150 and £200 respectively, so that with M = £300 total demand for x_i would be 30 irrespective of the distribution of the budgets.

The utility function (U1) of the previous section is homothetic with respect to the origin, and if everyone had that utility function, it would be as if a market demand function

$$x_i = b_i \frac{M}{p_i}$$

were derived from a utility function of the form

$$U = x_1^{b1} \dots x_n^{bn}.$$

(An increase in the value of U must not be taken to mean that the 'welfare' of the *group* of purchasers has increased; such matters will be discussed in section **16.4** below.)

Individual demand functions of the form (D2′) in section **9.2** can also give market functions involving only $p_1, \dots, p_n$ and M *provided that* the distribution of M always permits each of the m individuals to buy the 'survival' quantities $(s_1^{(r)}, \dots, s_n^{(r)})$. These quantities need not be the same for all individuals; but the coefficients $b_1, \dots, b_n$ must be. Then if we write $S_i = \sum_{r=1}^{m} s_i^{(r)}$, the market demand function is

$$x_i = \sum_{r=1}^{m} s_i^{(r)} + \frac{\sum_{r=1}^{m} b_i \left[M^{(r)} - \sum_{k=1}^{n} p_k \, s_k^{(r)} \right]}{p_i}$$

22. Market demand functions will also exist if the Engel curves for any given set of prices are all straight lines, with the same slope for all consumers, beginning at points on 'bare survival indifference curves', provided that the distribution of the total M permits all consumers to survive.

$$= S_i + \frac{b_i\left[M - \sum_{k=1}^{n} p_k S_k\right]}{p_i},$$

which could be derived from a utility function

$$U = (x_1 - S_1)^{b_1} \ldots (x_n - S_n)^{b_n}.$$

9.4 The consistency of market demand

In the cases described in the last section, market demand functions, being derivable from 'preference orderings' satisfying Axioms **1** to **7** of Chapters 2 and 3, have the properties which we derived from these axioms for individual demand functions. But they were based on the assumption that all consumers had the same preference ordering (which was subject to certain additional restrictions). An alternative approach is to assume that there are drastic restrictions on the distribution of M so that each $M^{(r)}$ is a function of (i.e. uniquely determined by) M. Then total demand would be a function of prices and M, for

$$x_i = \sum_{r=1}^{m} f_i^{(r)}[p_1, \ldots, p_n, M^{(r)}(M)]$$

$$= G_i[p_1, \ldots, p_n, M^{(1)}(M), \ldots, M^{(m)}(M)] = F_i(p_1, \ldots, p_n, M).$$

If each $M^{(r)}$ were a constant fraction of M, a doubling of M would double each $M^{(r)}$. In this case market demand functions F_i would exist and would be homogeneous of degree zero in $p_i, \ldots, p_n, M$, irrespective of individual preference orderings.

But it is *not* true in general that such market demand functions would have the usual properties. We shall show that even if M is distributed equally between two individuals, it is possible for their total demands to violate the revealed preference axiom **R2** of consistency (section **8.3**).

In Figure 41, two individuals r and s have equal budgets and therefore the same budget line, initially AB, from which r chooses $x^{(r)}$ and s chooses $x^{(s)}$. The total amounts of x_i and x_j chosen by the two consumers together are shown by the point x, reached by adding the coordinates of $x^{(r)}$ and $x^{(s)}$ (or by adding the vectors $Ox^{(r)}$ and $Ox^{(s)}$, or by completing the parallelogram two of whose sides are

$Ox^{(r)}$ and $Ox^{(s)}$). It is then as if the 'market' consisting of r and s had chosen the point x from the joint budget line CD, where OC = 2OA and OD = 2OB.

Now let there be a change in money budgets and prices such that the joint budget line pivots about the point x to become C′D′. The (common) individual line must therefore pivot about the point labelled $x/2$ (the midpoint of Ox) to become A′B′, where OA′ = $\frac{1}{2}$OC′ and OB′ = $\frac{1}{2}$OD′. Now r chooses $x^{(r)\prime}$ and s chooses $x^{(s)\prime}$. The new 'market' choice is x'.

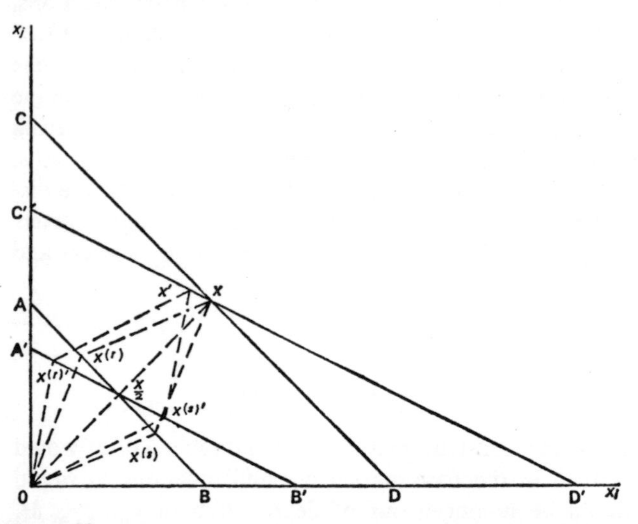

Figure 41

When x was chosen, x' was available, so that the 'market' revealed a 'preference' for x over x'. Now x' is chosen although x is available. This pair of choices violates the axiom of consistency, so that the market demand functions $F_i(p_1,\ldots, p_n, M)$ cannot be derived from a 'preference ordering' satisfying Axioms **1** to **7**. Yet neither individual has behaved inconsistently; indeed as Figure 41 is drawn, there is not even any evidence that either x_i or x_j is an inferior good for either individual. (For when the budget line shifts from AB to A′B′, p_j/p_i rises, r becomes worse off and buys less x_j; we could deduce that x_j was inferior for r only if he had bought more. Similarly, p_i/p_j falls, s is better off and buys more x_i).

This type of inconsistency cannot occur if the Engel curves (see p. 135 above) for each individual are straight lines through the origin, with different slopes for the different individuals, but the whole of M is distributed in fixed proportions between them. This can be illustrated in Figure 41. In that case $x^{(r)\prime}$ would lie to the right of the line $Ox^{(r)}$, $x^{(s)\prime}$ would lie to the right of the line $Ox^{(s)}$ and therefore x' would lie to the right of x on C′D′.

Even if the Engel curves are straight lines that do *not* go through the origin, the distribution of M may still be such as to give rise to consistent market behaviour. Consider, for example, the demand functions (D2′) of section **9.2.**

Let each household's budget consist of a sum sufficient to meet its basic needs $s^{(r)} = (s_1^{(r)}, \ldots, s_n^{(r)})$ plus a constant fraction $h^{(r)}$ of what is left out of the total M of all budgets after all households have met their basic needs. That is

$$M^{(r)} = \sum_{k=1}^{n} p_k s_k^{(r)} + h^{(r)} \left[M - \sum_{k=1}^{n} p_k S_k \right],$$

where, as before, $S_k = \sum_{r=1}^{m} s_k^{(r)}$. If we substitute this expression for $M^{(r)}$ in the individual demand functions (D2′), the market demand functions become

$$x_i = \sum_{r=1}^{m} \left[s_i^{(r)} + \frac{b_i^{(r)} \left[\sum_{k=1}^{n} p_k s_k^{(r)} + h^{(r)} \left(M - \sum_{k=1}^{n} p_k S_k \right) - \sum_{k=1}^{n} p_k s_k^{(r)} \right]}{p_i} \right]$$

$$= S_i + \frac{b_i \left[M - \sum_{k=1}^{n} p_k S_k \right]}{p_i};$$

where $b_i = \sum_{r=1}^{m} b_i^{(r)} h^{(r)}$. It is not difficult to show that $0 < b_i < 1$ and that $\sum_{i=1}^{n} b_i = 1$, [23]

23. One would use the facts that $\sum_{r=1}^{m} h^{(r)} = 1$, $\sum_{i=1}^{m} b_i^{(r)} = 1$ for each i, $0 < h^{(r)} < 1$ and $0 < b_i^{(r)} < 1$.

so that market demand functions have all the properties of the individual demand functions (D2′) in section **9.2**, and are derivable from a utility function of the form $U = (x_1 - S_1)^{b_1} \ldots (x_n - S_n)^{b_n}$.

Without attempting to be rigorous, we can conclude from the argument of this section and the last that market demand functions of the form $F_i(p_1, \ldots, p_n, M)$ are more likely to possess the usual properties of individual demand functions (i) the greater the similarity of individual preference orderings, (ii) the more nearly constant the shares of individual consumers in total expenditure M (or in some part of M) and (c) the closer the Engel curves are to linearity. These considerations should be borne in mind when we judge the results of attempts to test the hypotheses of demand theory by estimating market demand curves.

Three final points. Firstly, it may be desirable to estimate demand functions which include as *separate* variables the total budgets of a few different *groups* of consumers if it is believed that within each group the Engel curves of individuals are roughly parallel.

Secondly, a demand function $F_i(p_1, \ldots, p_n, M)$ will certainly not exist if, when the distribution of a given M changes, those whose budgets have increased all have (say) high values of $\partial x_i^{(r)}/\partial M^{(r)}$ and those whose budgets have decreased have low values of $\partial x_i^{(r)}/\partial M^{(r)}$, for the redistribution will increase x_i. But if both the gainers and the losers include consumers with both high and low values of $\partial x_i^{(r)}/\partial M^{(r)}$ (i.e. if the correlation between changes in the $M^{(r)}$ and values of $\partial x_i^{(r)}/\partial M^{(r)}$ is low) redistribution may result in little change in x_i. If the correlation is always strictly zero, a demand function $F_i(p_1, \ldots, p_n, M)$ will exist, but one can say little about its properties.

Finally, a pleasant fantasy whose relation to reality is for the reader to judge. Suppose that society has a consistent view as to the appropriate distribution of welfare among its members, which it implements by continual changes in personal taxes and subsidies. This matter will be further discussed in a later chapter (section **16.4**), but in such circumstances a 'social' utility function $U(x_1, \ldots, x_n)$ may exist satisfying Axioms **1** to **7** and generating market demand functions with the usual properties.

9.5 Market demand and interdependence

Before leaving the question of the relationship between individual and market demand functions, we must take up an important matter referred to in Section **2.4**. It was pointed out there that the dependence of one consumer's preferences on the choices of others had been largely disregarded in the theory of consumer behaviour, as had the information available to the consumer and other sources of changes in his preferences. (Estimators of demand functions do of course recognize that they can change over time, but typically allow for this only in a very general way). In this section we seek to make partial amends by enquiring briefly into the influence of the 'bandwagon effect' and the 'snob effect' of Section **2.4** on market demand functions.

Our model is very simple. We assume that all individuals have identical demand functions, which it is convenient in this case to express in Marshallian form, with the demand price (the price per unit the consumer is prepared to pay) as the dependent variable. The demand price p_i depends on the quantity bought by the individual consumer, x_i, and on his expectation of the total amount X_i bought by the relevant group of consumers. Thus

$$p_i = a - bx_i + cX_i.$$

We assume that $a > 0$, and that in the absence of interdependence demand curves (section **4.4**) would slope downwards to the right, so that $b > 0$. An increase in expected total purchases X_i may either increase the demand price ($c > 0$: the 'bandwagon' effect) or reduce it ($c < 0$: the 'snob' effect).

Equilibrium will be reached, in the sense that no consumer will wish to change his purchases, when the actual values of p_i, x_i and X_i are related as in the equation above. If there are m consumers, $X_i = mx_i$, so that

$$p_i = a + \left[c - \frac{b}{m}\right] X_i.$$

The equilibrium market demand curve will be downward-sloping if $c - b/m < 0$. Since b and m are positive, the snob effect ($c < 0$) will make the demand curve slope downwards more steeply than if it were absent. But clearly a strong bandwagon effect ($c > 0$) can turn $c - b/m$ positive. The condition for this to be the case can be explained in words as follows. With our simple model, if there are 100 consumers in the relevant group, the demand curve for x_i will slope upwards if an increase of y units in the total consumption of it would increase your demand price by more than one-hundredth as much as the amount by which an increase of y units in your own consumption would reduce your demand price.

We seek to do no more than to draw attention to this problem. It would be interesting to know how important the bandwagon and snob effects are in quantitative terms and their theoretical implications for the analysis of the last two sections. One point is that if expectations of the total demand for a commodity are based on total M, interdependence implies that M (as well as the individual $M^{(r)}$) should appear in the individual demand functions. Interdependence would then strengthen the argument for the existence of market demand functions $F_i(p_1,\ldots, p_n, M)$, but with at present unknown implications for their properties.

Exercises

1. For consumer r, $M^{(r)} = £100$, $p_1 = £1$, $p_2 = £2$. Find the quantities $x_1^{(r)}$ and $x_2^{(r)}$ demanded if:

(a) $u^{(r)} = (x_1^{(r)})^2(x_2^{(r)})^3$;

(b) $u^{(r)} = (x_1^{(r)}-10)^2(x_2^{(r)}-5)^3$.

2. With the utility function in 1(b), and $p_1 = £1$, $p_2 = £2$, determine whether the budget-elasticities of demand for $x_1^{(r)}$ and $x_2^{(r)}$ are greater or less than unity.

3. Market demand comes from only two consumers, r and s. r's utility function is as in Exercise 1(b). s's utility function is $u^{(s)} = (x_1^{(s)}-10)(x_2^{(s)}-10)$. The total M is always distributed in such a way that each consumer receives *half* of what is left after the basic needs of both r and s are satisfied (i.e. half of $M-\sum_k p_k S_k$). What are the values of b_1 and b_2 in the market demand functions

$$x_1 = S_1+\frac{b_1(M-\sum p_k S_k)}{p_1}, \qquad x_2 = S_2+\frac{b_2(M-\sum p_k S_k)}{p_2}?$$

Notes on the literature

A useful companion to this chapter, containing an elementary treatment of econometric problems, is Chapter 2 of L. R. Klein, *An Introduction to Econometrics* (Prentice-Hall, 1962). See also Baumol (*Economic Theory and Operations Analysis*, ch. 10).

9.1 Pioneering work on the estimation of demand functions was done by Henry Schultz in the 1920s and 1930s.

9.2 References on the subject-matter of this section are necessarily fairly technical. Demand functions of the form (D2) or (D2′) were used by R. Stone in his monumental work *The Measurement of Consumers' Expenditure and Behaviour in the United Kingdom, 1920–38* (Cambridge University Press, 1954), and in many others of his works. For earlier discussions see L. R. Klein and J. Rubin, 'A constant-utility index of the cost of living' and P. A. Samuelson, 'Some implications of linearity', both in *Rev. econ. Stud.* vol. 15, no. 2, pp. 84–90, 1947–48, the latter reprinted in J. E. Stiglitz (ed.), *The Collected Scientific Papers of Paul A. Samuelson* (pp. 61–3). On the functions (U3) and (U4) see H. S. Houthakker, 'Additive preferences' (*Econometrica*, vol. 28, no. 2, pp. 244–57, 1960). For a later theoretical development see P. A. Samuelson, 'Using full duality to show that simultaneously additive direct and indirect utilities imply unitary price elasticity of demand' (*Econometrica*, vol. 33, no. 4, pp. 781–96, 1965).

9.3 and **9.4** The argument in these sections is a much simplified version of parts of Chapters 5, 8 and 12 of my *Aggregation in Economic Analysis* (Princeton University Press, 1964). (See also R. G. D. Allen, *Mathematical Economics* (Macmillan, 1956, ch. 20)). The argument of T. J. Finn in 'Some properties of group demand' (*Int. econ. Rev.*, vol. 3, no. 2, pp. 189–205, 1962), that the type of inconsistency displayed in Figure 41 can occur only if 'inferiority' is present, clearly rests on an idiosyncratic definition of inferiority.

9.5 This section is based on the article by H. Leibenstein, 'Bandwagon, snob and Veblen Effects in the theory of consumers' demand' (*Q.J. Econ.*, vol. 64, no. 2, pp. 183–201, 1950, reprinted in W. Breit and H. M. Hochmann (eds), *Readings in Microeconomics*, pp. 123–39). For reasons given in section **2.4**, we have omitted the Veblen effect. It is strange that Leibenstein does not mention the possibility that the bandwagon effect may cause the demand curve to slope upwards.

Chapter 10
Related Goods and Characteristics

10.1 Grouping of commodities

As was pointed out in section **9.1**, actual measurement of demand functions necessitates a restriction of the number of distinct commodities recognized, so as to make estimation manageable. The quantities and prices x_i and p_i that appear in estimated demand functions are therefore inevitably almost all *aggregates* or *indices* of the prices and quantities of groups of commodities.

We know from the composite commodity theorem that if the relative prices of a group of commodities remain constant, a quantity index can be defined by dividing expenditure on the group by any price index homogeneous of degree one in the individual prices, and that these indices can be treated in all respects as if they were the quantity and price of a single good (section **7.4**). Moreover, if a group of goods has the property that they are always consumed in fixed proportions (e.g. $x_1 : x_2 : x_3 = 2 : 3 : 1$) we can define a unit of a new 'commodity' as the bundle $(x_1, x_2, x_3) = (2, 3, 1)$, and its price per unit as $2p_1 + 3p_2 + p_3$. The bundle (10, 15, 5) would then constitute 5 units of the new commodity, which could be treated in all respects as a single good.

One need not, however, limit oneself to price-proportionality or quantity-proportionality in seeking to justify the grouping of commodities. One can look for such justification in hypotheses about the form of the utility function. A number of hypotheses of this nature have been proposed, all of which have a common feature. If a particular set of commodities, say $x_1, x_2, \ldots, x_g$, is to be distinguishable as a group – to be (functionally) *separable* is the technical term – the following condition is necessary. Suppose that a consumer is indifferent between (*i*) a bundle of goods consisting of $(x_1', \ldots, x_g')$ of the goods $x_1, \ldots, x_g$ and $(x_h', \ldots, x_n')$ of the remaining goods $x_h, \ldots, x_n$, and

(ii) a bundle consisting of different quantities $(x_1'',\ldots, x_g'')$ of $x_1,\ldots,x_g$ and the same bundle $(x_h',\ldots, x_n')$ of the other goods. That is

$$(x_1',\ldots, x_g'; x_h',\ldots, x_n')I(x_1'',\ldots, x_g''; x_h',\ldots, x_n').$$

Then it must be true that for *any other* bundle, say $(x_h'',\ldots, x_n'')$ of the goods $x_h,\ldots, x_n$ outside the group,

$$(x_1',\ldots, x_g'; x_h'',\ldots, x_n'')I(x_1'',\ldots, x_g''; x_h'',\ldots, x_n'').$$

In other words, if the utilities derived from two bundles of the goods $x_1,\ldots, x_g$ are equal when each is consumed together with a particular bundle of the goods $x_h,\ldots, x_n$, the utilities derived from these two bundles of $x_1,\ldots, x_g$ must be equal when they are consumed together with any other bundle of $x_h,\ldots, x_n$. It is then possible to define a set of indifference curves or surfaces for the goods $x_1,\ldots, x_g$ alone, whose shape and position are independent of the quantities outside the group.

To illustrate, if there are three commodities, x_1, x_2, x_3 in the group and three, x_4, x_5, x_6 outside it, separability of the group implies that

if $\quad u(2, 3, 4; 1, 2, 2) = u(3, 1, 4; 1, 2, 2)$,

then $\quad u(2, 3, 4; 3, 3, 1) = u(3, 1, 4; 3, 3, 1)$.

This numerical example shows that the marginal rate of substitution (mrs) of x_2 for x_1 is 2, since the loss of 2 units of x_2 (a reduction from 3 to 1) is compensated by the gain of 1 unit of x_1 (an increase from 2 to 3): separability requires that this mrs over this range of quantities be 2 whether the quantities of x_4, x_5, x_6 are (1, 2, 2), (3, 3, 1) or anything else.

Thus another way of defining *weak separability* (so called to distinguish it from other types of separability that have been proposed) is that a group of commodities is weakly separable if and only if the mrs between any two commodities in the group is independent of the quantity of any commodity outside the group. This implies (and is implied by) the possibility of writing the utility function

$$u(x_1,\ldots, x_g, x_h,\ldots, x_n)$$

as $\quad u = u[f_a(x_1,\ldots, x_g), x_h,\ldots, x_n]$,

with $f_a(x_1,\ldots, x_g)$ as a sort of group utility function.

If the utility function has this form, the mrs of x_2 for x_1, which equals $\frac{\partial u/\partial x_1}{\partial u/\partial x_2}$, is equal by the chain rule of differentiation to

$$\frac{(\partial u/\partial f_a)(\partial f_a/\partial x_1)}{(\partial u/\partial f_a)(\partial f_a/\partial x_2)} = \frac{\partial f_a/\partial x_1}{\partial f_a/\partial x_2}.$$

Now $\partial f_a/\partial x_1$ and $\partial f_a/\partial x_2$ depend only on $x_1, x_2, \ldots, x_g$, and are thus independent of $x_h, \ldots, x_n$; so also therefore, is their ratio, which is equal to the mrs of x_2 for x_1. The proof that this independence of the mrs implies that the utility function can be written in this way would take considerable space and will not be given.

If the commodities $x_1, \ldots, x_n$ can be divided exhaustively into, say, three weakly separable groups, we have, for example,

$$u = u[f_a(x_1, \ldots, x_g), f_b(x_h, \ldots, x_j), f_c(x_k, \ldots, x_n)].$$

10.2 Types of separability and their implications

Weak separability alone does *not* imply that it is possible to define quantity and price indices $x_a, x_b, x_c, p_a, p_b, p_c$, for the utility function above, which can be treated just like the quantities and prices of single commodities. Nor indeed has this been the primary motivation of work that has been done on separability. Rather it has been regarded as a hypothesis on utility functions which has implications for the form of demand functions, like the hypotheses of section **9.2**. We can distinguish three types of separability, each of which assumes weak separability and something more, and has implications (which we shall not pursue) for the number of distinct coefficients to be estimated in the demand functions. The three types are:

(a) Pearce-separability (named after its author): the mrs between any two commodities in a given group is independent of the quantity of any commodity but those two. Pearce calls this 'neutral want-association'.

(b) Homogeneous separability: the indifference surfaces for a given group are all homothetic with respect to the origin (see section **9.3**, Figure 40). This means that the elasticity of demand for each commodity in the group with respect to expenditure on the group is unity; '. . . we must never group luxuries, near-luxuries and necessities together' (Gorman), (see section **4.5** pp. 57–8).

(c) Strong or additive separability: the mrs between any two commodities in any two distinct groups is independent of the quantity of any commodity in any third group; 'e.g. the marginal rate of substitution between blue jeans and steaks should be independent of the consumption of tents' (Gorman).

These three types of separability are by no means mutually exclusive. As an extreme illustration, in the utility function (U1) of section **9.2**, $u = x_1^{\beta_1} \ldots x_n^{\beta_n}$, the commodities can be divided into groups in any way one pleases, and all three types of separability will be present.[24]

Our interest in these types of separability is twofold. First, we seek in separability a possible justification for including in the estimated demand functions of chapter 9 price and quantity indices which are treated like the quantities and prices of single commodities.

But these estimated demand functions are based on the analysis of Parts One and Two, which was developed on the assumption that $x_1, \ldots, x_n$ were nondurable goods of current consumption. As was implied at the beginnings of chapters 2 and 9, a full treatment of the consumer's decisions would require us to include in his utility function all distinguishable commodities and services at all times, in all places and in all contingencies. His budget constraint should include the current and expected future prices of all such commodities and services, his current wealth and all expected future receipts. It would of course be absurd to proceed in this manner. What consumers in fact do is to set aside or commit sums of money for broad general purposes, and decide at the appropriate time on the detailed disposition of these sums.

Our second reason for being interested in separability, therefore, is as a further possible justification (in addition to price-proportionality or quantity-proportionality) for this budgeting procedure, in which the decision to commit a sum of money to a particular purpose is taken, not on the basis of detailed knowledge or prediction of the prices of the individual commodities on which it is to be spent, but rather on a notion of the general level of those prices.

24. The reader may care to confirm that this is the case by considering (U1) in the following form, and referring to section **6.5**,
$u^* = \log u = (\beta_1 \log x_1 + \ldots + \beta_g \log x_g) +$
$(\beta_h \log x_h + \ldots + \beta_j \log x_j) + (\beta_k \log x_k + \ldots + \beta_n \log x_n)$.

Thus whether we look backwards to the demand functions of Parts One and Two, or forward to the discussions of time and uncertainty in Parts Four and Five, we wish to ask whether any of the types of separability described earlier in this section justify the following analysis. One can define quantity-indices which are functions of the quantities in their groups, $x_a = x_a(x_1,\ldots, x_g)$, $x_b = x_b(x_h,\ldots, x_j)$, $x_c = x_c(x_k,\ldots, x_n)$, and insert their values in a utility function $u^* = v(x_a, x_b, x_c)$. This function represents exactly the same preference ordering of the bundles $(x_1,\ldots, x_n)$ as the utility function $u = u[f_a(x_1,\ldots, x_g), f_b(x_h,\ldots, x_j), f_c(x_k,\ldots, x_n)]$ at the end of section **10.1**. One can define price indices $p_a = p_a(p_1,\ldots, p_g), p_b = p_b(p_h,\ldots, p_j), p_c = p_c(p_k,\ldots, p_n)$, and find the values of x_a, x_b, x_c which maximize $v(x_a, x_b, x_c)$ subject to the constraint $p_a x_a + p_b x_b + p_c x_c = M$. This determines the expenditure $M_a = p_a x_a$, M_b and M_c on each group. The detailed disposition of, for example, M_a is then determined by maximizing $x_a(x_1,\ldots, x_g)$ subject to $p_1 x_1 + \ldots + p_g x_g = M_a$. And this two-stage budgeting procedure is *consistent* in the sense that it leads to the same optimal vector of quantities as if one had found directly the quantities $x_1,\ldots, x_n$ by maximizing $v[x_a(x_1,\ldots, x_g), x_b(x_h,\ldots, x_j), x_c(x_k,\ldots, x_n)]$ subject to

$$\sum_{i=1}^{n} p_i x_i = M.$$

Pearce-separability does not justify the foregoing analysis. Nor does strong or additive separability; though price-indices and quantity-indices appear in discussions of it, they do not have the properties we seek.

Only homogeneous separability meets the requirements. Suppose, by way of illustration, that the utility function for group a is of the type (U1) of section **9.2**, namely $f_a(x_1,\ldots, x_g) = x_1^{\beta_1}\ldots x_g^{\beta_g}$. Now this function is homogeneous of degree $\beta_1 + \ldots + \beta_g$ in $x_1,\ldots, x_g$, (since $f_a(kx_1,\ldots, kx_g) = (kx_1)^{\beta_1}\ldots(kx_g)^{\beta_g}$

$$= k^{\beta_1+\ldots+\beta_g} f_a(x_1,\ldots, x_g).$$ See p. 52 above.)

If the quantity-index x_a is to meet our requirements, it must be homogeneous of degree one in $x_1,\ldots, x_g$. To ensure this, we define the quantity index as

$$x_a = x_1^{b_1}\ldots x_g^{b_g}$$

where $b_i = \beta_i/(\beta_1+\ldots+\beta_g)$, so that

$$\sum_{i=1}^{g} b_i = 1,$$

and b_i, as was implied in section **9.2**, is the share of group expenditure M_a which will be devoted to x_i if the function $x_1^{b_1}\ldots x_g^{b_g}$ (or the function $x_1^{\beta_1}\ldots x_g^{\beta_g}$) is maximized subject to

$$\sum_{i=1}^{g} p_i x_i = M_a.$$

If we now define the group price index as

$$p_a = \left[\frac{p_1}{b_1}\right]^{b_1}\cdots\left[\frac{p_g}{b_g}\right]^{b_g}$$

then since $b_1 = p_1 x_1/M_a$, and so on, $p_a = (M_a/x_1)^{b_1}\ldots(M_a/x_g)^{b_g}$, so that as required
$p_a x_a = (M_a/x_1)^{b_1}\ldots(M_a/x_g)^{b_g}(x_1^{b_1}\ldots x_g^{b_g}) = M_a^{b_1}\ldots M_a^{b_g} = M_a.$
And it is not difficult to show that the two-stage budgeting procedure is consistent as defined above.

A typical condition for a maximum of the Lagrangean
$L = v(x_a, x_b, x_c)+\mu(M-p_a x_a-p_b x_b-p_c x_c)$ is that $\partial v/\partial x_a-\mu p_a = 0$. On the assumptions just made in the text, $p_1 x_1 = b_1 M_a = b_1 p_a x_a$, so that $p_a = p_1 x_1/b_1 x_a$. And since $x_a = x_1^{b_1}\ldots x_g^{b_g}$, $\partial x_a/\partial x_1 = b_1 x_a/x_1$, so that

$$p_a = \frac{p_1}{\partial x_a/\partial x_1}.$$

Thus $\partial v/\partial x_a-\mu p_a = 0$ implies that

$$\frac{\partial v}{\partial x_a}-\frac{\mu p_1}{\partial x_a/\partial x_1} = 0.$$

This in turn implies that $(\partial v/\partial x_a)(\partial x_a/\partial x_1)-\mu p_1 = 0$, which is a typical condition for a maximum of $v[x_a(x_1,\ldots, x_g), x_b(x_h,\ldots, x_j), x_c(x_k,\ldots, x_n)]$ subject to $\sum_{i=1}^{n} p_i x_i = M$.

If the implication of homogeneous separability, that the elasticities of $x_1,\ldots, x_g$ with respect to M_a are all unity, bothers the reader, we may resort, again as an illustration, to the assumption that each group utility function has the form (U2) of section **9.2**, which does not have this implication. If we define

$$x_a = (x_1 - s_1)^{b1} \ldots (x_g - s_g)^{bg}$$

and p_a exactly as above, it is easy to show, by replacing x_1 by $x_1 - s_1, \ldots, x_g$ by $x_g - s_g$, and M_a by $M_a - \sum_{i=1}^{g} p_i\, s_i$ in the argument just given, that

$$p_a\, x_a = M_a - (p_1\, s_1 + \ldots + p_g\, s_g).$$

The group quantity and price indices thus relate only to purchases in excess of the basic requirements $s_1, \ldots, s_n$, so that the consumer, at the first stage of the budgeting procedure, would be maximizing $v(x_a, x_b, x_c)$ subject to the budget constraint

$$p_a\, x_a + p_b\, x_b + p_c\, x_c = M - \sum_{i=1}^{n} p_i\, s_i.$$

In conclusion, therefore, when in future chapters we treat consumption at different dates and in different contingencies as if they were single commodities, we must be taken to assume either that the prices or the quantities of the different commodities consumed at each date and in each contingency are in fixed proportions, or that homogeneous separability obtains (which may require, to make it more plausible, an adjustment of the budget constraint in the manner just indicated).

10.3 Goods and 'characteristics'

To add a final tool to the kit we shall use in discussing time and uncertainty, we shall now give an elementary exposition of Lancaster's recent analysis of consumer behaviour. This analysis is also in part backward-looking, since Lancaster begins by expressing dissatisfaction with current theory of the type presented in earlier parts of this book. It does not, he argues, offer a satisfactory account of why some goods are more closely related in consumption than others (nor of why some goods are not purchased at all). And it must be conceded, despite our discussion of corner solutions in section **7.2** and of separability in earlier sections of this chapter, that if we were asked *why* some goods are not purchased and others can be grouped together, the only answer which emerges from our analysis hitherto is that this is the way the consumer's preference ordering is.

A further difficulty is that if a new commodity is introduced, or the quality of an existing commodity changes, the only response of current theory is to add a new commodity, x_{n+1}, to the list. This creates particular difficulties in the construction of cost-of-living index numbers. For if such an index number shows the change over time in the money cost of a representative bundle of goods (or, as in more sophisticated versions, of a bundle of goods that maintains a representative utility function at a specified level), what are we to do if in 1970 the representative consumer begins to buy a commodity which did not exist in 1969, or continues to buy a commodity which has significantly improved in quality since 1969?

Lancaster suggests that these difficulties can be lessened if we regard the elements of the set of alternatives C (see chapters 2 and 3), on which the consumer's preference ordering is defined, as bundles of *characteristics of goods*, rather than as bundles of goods.[25] Thus for example different brands of toothpaste constitute a closely related group of goods because they, and they alone, supply the characteristics: prevention of tooth decay, and whitening of teeth. This is an extreme example. One cannot strictly partition the set of all goods and the set of all characteristics in such a way that characteristics c_1 and c_2 are supplied by, and only by, goods $x_1, \ldots, x_4$, characteristics $c_3, \ldots, c_5$ are supplied by, and only by, $x_5, \ldots, x_8$, and so on. But clearly characteristics do provide a basis for relating goods, and the toothpaste example is convenient for expository purposes.

Let us assume therefore that there are five brands of toothpaste, supplying in different proportions the characteristics: decay prevention (d), and whitening (w). The strong assumption is made that the quantities of d and w in an ounce of each brand are objectively measurable and therefore agreed upon by all consumers. A consumer has decided (perhaps because of homogeneous separability of a utility function with characteristics as its independent variables – this need not detain us) to spend one pound per month on toothpaste. Then given the money prices of the various brands he knows how many

25. Lancaster also defines a third concept, the 'activity' (e.g. going on holiday), which involves the consumption of several goods.

units of *w* and *d* he will get by spending one pound on each brand. Suppose that the figures are as in the following table:

Brand	*w per pound's worth*	*d per pound's worth*
A	10	2
B	8	4
C	8	5
D	5	7
E	2	10

If our consumer accepts these figures, is rational in the sense of Chapter 2, and prefers more *w* and/or *d* to less, then he obviously will not buy brand B, for a pound spent on brand C gives more *d* and the same amount of *w*. Brand D will not be bought if toothpaste is homogeneously divisible,[26] either in the sense that it can be bought in any desired amount, or that one can alternate between brands in successive months.[27] For if by spending 50p on brand C one can obtain half the amounts shown in the table (i.e. $4w$ and $2\frac{1}{2}d$), and similarly $1w$ and $5d$ by spending 50p on brand E, one has in total $5w$ and $7\frac{1}{2}d$ – better than the $5w$ and $7d$ obtained by spending a pound on brand D.[28]

In Figure 42, each brand of toothpaste is represented by a ray through the origin, and the points A,..., E show the quantities of *d* and *w*

26. This intuitive term should be made precise. What we mean is that if $c = (w, d)$ and $c' = (w', d')$ are any two attainable vectors of quantities of characteristics, then any vector $kc+(1-k)c' = [kw+(1-k)w', kd+(1-k)d']$ with $0 \leqslant k \leqslant 1$ is also attainable. The numerical examples in the text illustrate this.

27. Such alternation creates difficulties with regard to the axiom of consistency if the consumer buys brand C one month and brand E the next. One would have to define consistency as relating to purchases in successive quarters: no doubt the reader can think of further difficulties raised by this procedure, but we shall not let them detain us.

28. Since February, 1971 the pound sterling has been divided into 100 " newpence ", written as £1 = 100p.

obtainable by spending a pound on each brand. Homogeneous divisibility implies that the consumer can spend his pound in such a way as to reach any point on a straight line joining any two of the points A,..., E. The line CE, for example, consists of all the points attainable by travelling along the ray or vector OC for a certain fraction k $(0 \leqslant k \leqslant 1)$ of its length, and then turning and travelling parallel to OE for the fraction $1-k$ of the length of OE. For example,

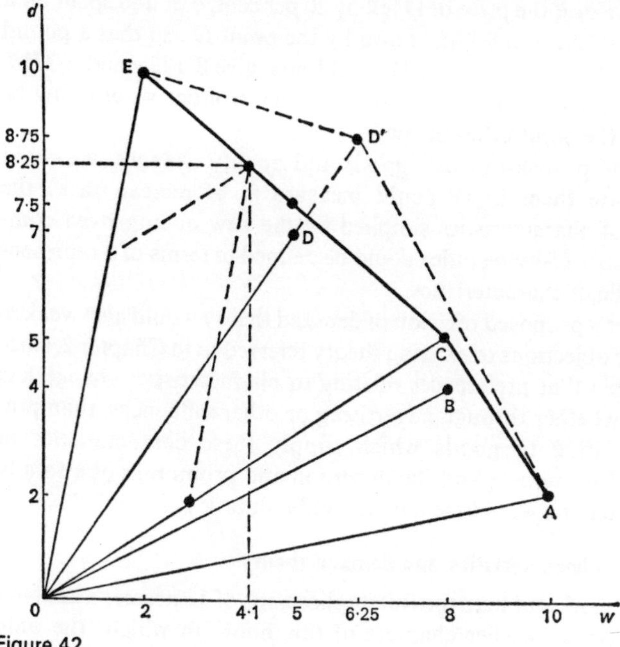

Figure 42

35p spent on C and 65p spent on E give $0{\cdot}35 \times 8 + 0{\cdot}65 \times 2 = 4{\cdot}1$ units of w and $0{\cdot}35 \times 5 + 0{\cdot}65 \times 10 = 8{\cdot}25$ units of d, and the point ($w = 4{\cdot}1$, $d = 8{\cdot}25$) lies on the straight line CE.

If all consumers agree that the quantities of d and w per pound's worth of the five brands are as in Figure 42, no one will buy B or D. The choice will be from an 'efficiency frontier' like ACE no matter how much is to be spent on toothpaste; the frontier for a consumer who spends two pounds a month on toothpaste will have exactly the same shape as ACE but be twice as far from the origin. This argument explains why some goods or brands are not bought at all. And it must be emphasized that the shape of the frontier ACE depends on the prices (e.g. per ounce) of the brands as well as on the quantities of *d* and *w* per ounce. If the price of brand D were to fall, the quantities of *d* and *w* per pound spent on it would increase, and the point D would move out along its ray. Some people might buy it when this point reached the line CE, and its price might fall so far that brand C was eliminated. For if the price of D fell by 20 per cent, a pound spent on it would give $6{\cdot}25w$ and $8{\cdot}75d$, shown by the point D′. so that a pound divided evenly between A and D would now give $8{\cdot}125w$ and $5{\cdot}375d$, which is better than brand C. The efficiency frontier would now be AD′E, and the point C lies below it.

As for the problem of new goods and quality changes, we could accommodate them if we could measure (a Herculean task) the quantities of characteristics supplied by the new or improved commodity. A cost-of-living index could be defined in terms of a representative bundle of characteristics.

Lancaster's proposed revision of demand theory would also weaken some of the objections to existing theory referred to in Chapter 2, since it is plausible that preferences relating to characteristics change less over time, whether through advertising or other influences, than preferences relating to goods which supply these characteristics in different proportions. (And the invention and promotion of a totally new characteristic would seem to be a difficult task.)

10.4 Goods, characteristics and demand theory

We cannot work out here the full implications of Lancaster's analysis for the theory of earlier chapters of this book, in which 'the only characteristic of an apple was appleness and the only source of appleness was an apple'. But a few fundamental points will be discussed briefly.

In arguing that the consumer's choice would be from the efficiency frontier ACE in Figure 42, we implicitly made certain assumptions about the consumer's preferences among bundles of characteristics. These were analogous to Axioms **1** to **4** of chapters 2 and 3 – that he has a complete and transitive weak preference ordering defined on a set of bundles of characteristics, that he is not saturated with any characteristic, and that he makes a rational choice in the sense of Axiom **3**. The analogues to Axioms **5** to **7** would imply that indifference curves in terms of characteristics were smoothly convex to the origin, so that the consumer might choose to buy only one brand, as at the 'corner solutions' A, C or E in Figure 42, or a combination of two brands, as at a point between A and C or between C and E.[29] In the latter case the marginal rate of substitution between characteristics equals the implicit price-ratio of characteristics, and of course this price-ratio changes as one moves from one pair of goods to another (from AC to CE).

If we now think of a multi-dimensional efficiency frontier like that of Figure 42, relating to all goods and all characteristics, can we show that demand functions for goods exist and are homogeneous of degree zero in M and the commodity prices $p_1,\ldots, p_n$? A doubling of M and p leaves the efficiency frontier, and therefore the optimal bundle of characteristics, unaffected. But does a given bundle of characteristics imply a unique bundle of goods? If the number of distinct goods does not exceed the number of characteristics, (e.g. if there were only one or two goods in Figure 42), the answer is yes. But if there are more goods than characteristics (which Lancaster believes to be the case in a complex consumption technology) we may be in a position where, for example, the price of brand D is such that the point D lies exactly on the line CE in Figure 42. Then a given bundle of characteristics lying between C and D on CE could be obtained by combining brand C with either brand D or brand E or both; the quantity of *none* of the brands would be uniquely determined.

One consequence of the goods–characteristics model, then, is that the commodity demand curves of section **4.4** may be perfectly elastic (i.e. horizontal) at a given price. This may not be very common among consumption goods, since it occurs only when the point D lies exactly on the line CE. (But, as we shall see in section **15.2**, there is good reason to regard it as the *rule* when the 'goods' are financial assets.) And it may be even less common than our model suggests because typically it costs more to buy small quantities of each of two brands than to buy a large quantity of a single brand (see Exercise 3 at the end of this chapter). The model could be improved if this type of 'cost' were taken into account.

29. It can be shown, as a consequence of the fundamental theorem of linear programming, that no point on an efficiency frontier requires the consumer to buy a number of distinct goods greater than the number of characteristics.

As to the substitution effect, an increase in the price of a commodity or brand may remove it from the 'efficiency frontier', so that everyone's consumption of it will fall to zero. The decision not to buy it is then a 'pure efficiency choice'. But short of this, what is the effect of a change in the price of a good accompanied by a change in the budget which leaves the consumer on the same characteristics-indifference curve?

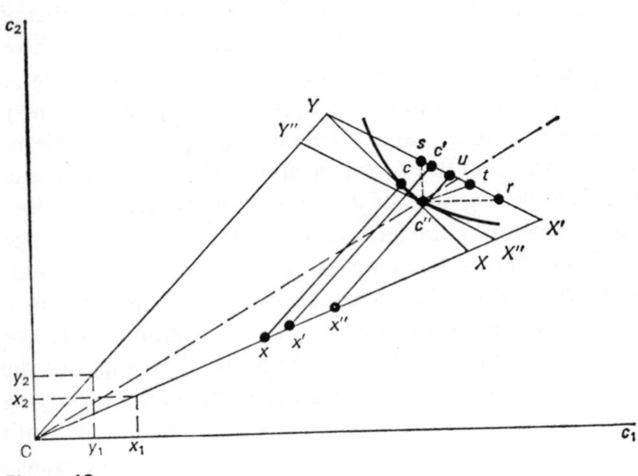

Figure 43

A single geometric illustration must suffice. Let there be only two goods, X and Y, possessing the characteristics c_1 and c_2 in the proportions represented by the slopes of the rays OX and OY in Figure 43. A unit of X is defined as the amount containing x_1 of characteristic c_1 and x_2 of characteristic c_2; a unit of Y contains y_1 of c_1 and y_2 of c_2.

Initially the prices of X and Y are such that the efficiency frontier is the line XY, and the consumer chooses the point c. If the price of the good X falls, the efficiency frontier becomes $X'Y$. To determine the substitution effect we must reduce the consumer's budget so that he can just attain the original indifference curve at the new prices. That is, we must draw the efficiency frontier $X''Y''$, parallel to $X'Y$, which touches the original indifference curve at c''. With smoothly convex-to-the-origin indifference curves, c'' must lie below and to the right of c.

Points like c and c'' are reached, as we saw in the last section, by travelling from O along OX or OY or lines parallel to them. Thus c is reached by travelling a distance Ox along OX and then turning and travelling the distance xc parallel to OY. And c'' is reached by travelling along Ox'' and $x''c''$. Now the number of units of X purchased (see the definition of a unit of X above) is proportional to the distance travelled along OX. Since c'' is below and to the right of c, it can be seen in Figure 43 that Ox'' > Ox, so that more X is purchased at c'' than at c, and the substitution effect of the fall in the price of X has increased the quantity of X purchased.

With regard to the income effect of the fall in the price of X – the movement from c'' to the line $X'Y$ resulting from the restoration of the amount of the budget taken away to measure the substitution effect – an interesting observation has recently been made. Let us assume that both characteristics are *normal*, in the sense (cf. section **5.1**) that an increase in the budget with prices unchanged increases the demand for both characteristics. This implies that the point chosen from $X'Y$ will lie between r and s, the points at which the horizontal and vertical dotted lines through c'' cut the line $X'Y$.

The remarkable thing is that *normal characteristics* are quite consistent with *inferior goods*. Draw two straight lines through c'', one parallel to OX to cut $X'Y$ at t, and the other parallel to OY to cut $X'Y$ at u. If the consumer moves from c'' to u, the whole of the increase in his budget will be spent on Y. But if he moves from c'' to c', between u and s, he will consume more of both *characteristics* at c' than at c'', but less of the *good* X. For the point c' is reached by travelling from O to x' along OX, and then along $x'c'$ parallel to OY. Since Ox' < Ox'', the movement from c'' to c', which is perfectly consistent with normal characteristics, implies that X is an inferior good.

Of course, the consumer could have moved from c'' to a point between t and u, in which case both goods would be normal. Indeed, if the characteristics-indifference curves are homothetic with reference to the origin, both goods must be normal. For then (see section **9.2**. Figure 40) the increased budget must move the consumer to a point on the ray from the origin through c'', and this ray must cut $X'Y$ between t and u.

As we have drawn Figure 43, Ox′ > Ox, so that the *total* effect of the fall in the price of *X* is to increase the quantity bought. But the inferiority of *X* *could* have made it a Giffen good. And our demonstration that normal characteristics are consistent with inferior goods leads one to wonder whether Giffen goods are as exceptional a phenomenon as they are usually thought to be.

At this point we leave our general analysis of the goods-characteristics approach to demand theory. As was implied earlier, its application to empirical work faces the formidable hurdle of objective measurement of the characteristics supplied by different goods. But Lancaster's work provides important insights, not only into the somewhat restricted world of earlier chapters, but also when we extend our analysis, as at last we do in the next chapter, to embrace time and uncertainty.

Exercises

1. A homogeneously separable group of two goods has the utility function $x_1^2 x_2^3$. Write down a quantity index and a price index for the group which meet the conditions of section **10.2.**

2. You are given the following data about the two objective characteristics of three homogeneously divisible products:

	Product		
	x_1	x_2	x_3
Units of characteristic 1 per lb.	30	30	70
Units of characteristic 2 per lb.	70	30	30
Price in newpence per lb.	30		30

What is the critical price of x_2 (i.e. the price at or below which some consumers may buy it, and above which no one will buy it)?

3. Suppose that, although the table in section **10.3** correctly shows the quantities of *w* and *d* per pound's worth of each brand, the price per ounce of each brand steadily declines as the number of ounces bought increases.

(a) What happens to the shape of the efficiency frontier?

(b) Might some consumers now buy brand B or brand D?

(c) Will a given bundle of characteristics now correspond to a unique efficient bundle of goods?

Notes on the literature

Separability is a difficult subject with a difficult literature, but K. J. Lancaster has provided a non-technical introduction to 'goods and characteristics' in his 'Change and innovation in the technology of consumption' (*Amer. econ. Rev.*, vol. 56, no. 2, pp. 14–23, 1966). A fuller treatment is to be found in his 'A new approach to consumer theory' (*J. polit. Econ.*, vol. 74, no. 2, pp. 132–57, 1966).

10.1–10.2 Most of the assertions made here are proved in Chapters 3 and 4 of my *Aggregation in Economic Analysis*. The key references are R. H. Strotz, 'The empirical implications of a utility tree' (*Econometrica*, vol. 25, no. 2, pp. 269–80, 1957), W. M. Gorman, 'Separable utility and aggregation' (*Econometrica*, vol. 27, no. 3, pp. 469–81, 1959) (whence the quotations about luxuries and blue jeans are taken), and I. F. Pearce, *A Contribution to Demand Analysis* (Oxford University Press, 1964). On the implications of different types of separability for demand functions, see S. M. Goldman and H. Uzawa 'A note on separability in demand analysis' (*Econometrica*, vol. 32, no. 3, pp. 387–98, 1964).

10.4 For the argument about normal characteristics and inferior goods see R. G. Lipsey and G. Rosenbluth, 'A contribution to the new theory of demand: a rehabilitation of the Giffen good' (*Canadian Journal of Economics*, vol. 4, no. 2, pp. 131–63, 1971).

Part Four
Time

Chapter 11
Short-Period Problems

11.1 Introduction

We now abandon the assumption that the consumer is concerned only with the allocation of a predetermined budget among goods of current consumption. We take into account his expected consumption of $x_1, \ldots, x_n$ in future periods $1, \ldots, T$. We continue to assume until Part Five, so as not to introduce too many complications at once, that if he plans at the beginning of the current period 0 to consume 10 units of x_i in period t he has no uncertainty as to what he will get.

What are the implications of specifying a terminal period T? If the consumer were an individual, T would indicate the expected date of his death. But at the beginning of Chapter 2 we suggested that a 'consumer' should be thought of as typically a household. Even if the head and sole (or chief) breadwinner of the household expects to die in period T, he may wish to make bequests to those who are now, or will become, members of the household. We may therefore assume that he is interested in their consumption after period T, so that their additional consumption in periods $T+1, \ldots$ made possible by his bequests should be included in his preference ordering. The weight he gives to such additional consumption by them may depend on his expectation of their earnings and therefore on expenditures (e.g. on their education) made by him before his death.

This is a complex matter, and we do not wish at this stage to attempt a formal treatment of it; consideration of the aggregations implied by the usual broad budgeting procedure, referred to several times in earlier chapters, is deferred until the next chapter. Suffice it to say, for the present, that we assume a preference ordering defined for bundles of goods to be consumed in periods $0, 1, \ldots, T$, and perhaps beyond T, which obeys Axioms **1** to **7** of Chapters 2 and 3.

How are the consumption plans to be financed? At the beginning of period 0 the consumer may be thought of as possessing wealth of two kinds, usually referred to as 'human' and 'non-human'. His human wealth $H(0)$ is measured by his current earnings from work $E(0)$ plus the present value (see below) of $E(1), \ldots, E(T)$, his expected earnings from work at the beginning of subsequent periods. We take these expectations as given, though it would be possible to show how they were determined by the work–leisure choices of section **5.5**. Non-human wealth at the beginning of period 0 is the present value of all other types of asset (e.g. cash, securities, houses, durable consumer goods, expected future receipts other than earnings from work) less the present value of all liabilities (e.g. debts, mortgages, expected future tax payments).

In this section and the next we continue to make no practical distinction between purchase and consumption; $x_i(t)$ is consumed in period t if and only if it is bought at the beginning of period t. But the consumer can adjust his pattern of consumption by borrowing or lending. He expects with certainty that if he lends (or borrows) £1 at the beginning of period t he will receive (or must repay) £$(1+r_t)$ at the beginning of period $t+1$. There is a single one-period rate of interest in each period which the consumer cannot affect no matter how much he lends or borrows. The money price of x_i at the beginning of period t is expected (with certainty) to be $p_i(t)$.

We are now in a position to write down the full 'budget constraint' as follows:

$$W(0) = V(0)+H(0)$$

$$= V(0)+E(0)+\frac{E(1)}{1+r_0}+\ldots+\frac{E(t)}{(1+r_0)\ldots(1+r_{t-1})}+$$

$$+\ldots+\frac{E(T)}{(1+r_0)\ldots(1+r_{T-1})}$$

$$= \sum_{i=1}^{n} p_i(0)x_i(0)+\frac{\sum_{i=1}^{n} p_i(1)x_i(1)}{1+r_0}+\ldots+\frac{\sum_{i=1}^{n} p_i(t)x_i(t)}{(1+r_0)\ldots(1+r_{t-1})}+$$

$$+\ldots+\frac{\sum_{i=1}^{n} p_i(T)x_i(T)}{(1+r_0)\ldots(1+r_{T-1})}+\ldots.$$

$E(t)/\{(1+r_0)\ldots(1+r_{t-1})\}$ and $p_i(t)/\{(1+r_0)\ldots(1+r_{t-1})\}$ are the *present values* or the *discounted* values, at the beginning of period 0, of the consumer's expected earnings and the expected price of x_i at the beginning of period t. The budget constraint is written as an equality on the assumption that Axiom **4** of non-saturation holds for the full inter-temporal preference ordering (see section **4.1**).

To confirm that this budget constraint represents the consumer's opportunities, consider any consumption plan which satisfies it. Such a plan would almost certainly involve spending in excess of earnings in some years (typically the early years of the earning span, and years of retirement when earnings are zero) and less in others (typically the later years of the earning span). Starting from such a plan, suppose that the consumer decides to spend £1 more in period 0, and to reduce his consumption below that originally planned in the single period t. By how much must his consumption in period t be reduced?

Given his assets and his expected earnings, and his planned consumption in all periods other than 0 and t, the budget constraint implies that

$$\sum p_i(0)x_i(0)+\frac{\sum p_i(t)x_i(t)}{(1+r_0)\ldots(1+r_{t-1})}$$

is fixed, so that

$$\Delta \sum p_i(t)x_i(t) = -(1+r_0)\ldots(1+r_{t-1})\Delta \sum p_i(0)x_i(0).$$

Thus if the money value of consumption in period 0 is £1 more than originally planned, expenditure in period t must be less than that originally planned by £$(1+r_0)\ldots(1+r_{t-1})$; the consumer must borrow £1 more (or lend £1 less) at the beginning of period 0, and repay at the beginning of period t an amount which is greater (or receive an amount which is less) by £1 plus accumulated interest. By a similar argument, if a consumption plan had been made, no change in it would be necessary if $E(0)$ fell by £1 and $E(t)$ rose by £$(1+r_0)\ldots(1+r_{t-1})$. The same pattern of expenditure could be financed by borrowing £1 more now and repaying it (with interest) out of the additional earnings of the beginning of period t.

We shall proceed as follows. In the next section we investigate the implications of the extension of our time-horizon for the existence and properties of demand functions of the type derived in earlier chapters.

In sections **11.3** and **11.4** we distinguish for the first time purchases from consumption in analysing two very simple problems – whether to store a commodity, and when to replace a durable good. Section **11.5** is concerned with a classic problem – the optimal holdings of cash balances for transactions. In the next chapter we take up in more detail the general problem of the consumer's allocation of his resources over time.

11.2 Current demand functions and time

A rational consumer, given the preference ordering and the budget constraint described in the previous section, will choose a unique bundle of goods $(x_1(0),..., x_n(T),...)$. The set of alternatives is determined by total current wealth $W(0)$, by the current prices $p_1(0),...,$ $p_n(0)$, and by the discounted values of expected future prices. Thus the demand function for a commodity x_i to be bought in the current period is

$$x_i(0) = f_i(0)\left[W(0), p_1(0),..., \frac{p_i(t)}{(1+r_0)...(1+r_{t-1})},..., \frac{p_n(T)}{(1+r_0)...(1+r_{T-1})},...\right].$$

A doubling of $W(0)$ and of all current and discounted future prices will leave the set of alternatives, and therefore the consumer's choice, unchanged. Thus demand functions of this kind exist and are homogeneous of degree zero.

What if $p_i(0)$ changes? It would appear at first sight that the answer is quite simple. One can divide the effect of a change in $p_i(0)$ on $x_i(0)$ into a substitution effect and a 'wealth' effect by means of a Slutzky equation similar to those of Chapter 5:

$$\frac{\partial x_i(0)}{\partial p_i(0)} = \left[\frac{\partial x_i(0)}{\partial p_i(0)}\right]_S - x_i(0)\frac{\partial x_i(0)}{\partial W(0)}$$

and an argument similar to that of Chapter 5 would establish that $\{\partial x_i(0)/\partial p_i(0)\}_S < 0$. If $\partial x_i(0)/\partial W(0)$ were non-negative, the demand curve for $x_i(0)$ would be downward-sloping.

But this should not be regarded as the end of the story. In the first place, is it plausible to assume that a change in $p_i(0)$ has no effect on expected future prices of x_i? A useful tool is available to measure such effects. The *elasticity of expectations* is defined as the percentage change in the expected value of a variable divided by the percentage change in its current value. If the current and expected values in question were $p_i(0)$ and $p_i(t)$, we could define:

$$\text{Elasticity of expectations} = \frac{\Delta p_i(t)}{p_i(t)} \div \frac{\Delta p_i(0)}{p_i(0)}.$$

For example, suppose that initially $p_i(0) = £1$ and $p_i(t) = £1{\cdot}20$. If the current price rises to £1·10. and the price now expected at the beginning of period t rises to £1·26. the elasticity of expectations is

$$\frac{£1{\cdot}26-£1{\cdot}20}{£1{\cdot}20} \div \frac{£1{\cdot}10-£1{\cdot}00}{£1{\cdot}00} = \frac{1}{20} \div \frac{1}{10} = \frac{1}{2}.$$

The elasticity of expectations can of course differ for different time-periods, and the number of possibilities is endless; its value was clearly assumed to be zero in the earlier analysis of this section, when *only* $p_i(0)$ changed. An interesting case is that in which the elasticity of expectations is always unity – a q per cent increase in $p_i(0)$ leads to a q per cent increase in all expected future prices $p_i(1),\ldots,p_i(t),\ldots,p_i(T),\ldots$ For then we can treat current and all future purchases of x_i as a composite commodity measured as

$$x_i = x_i(0) + \frac{p_i(1)x_i(1)}{p_i(0)(1+r_0)} + \ldots + \frac{p_i(T)x_i(T)}{p_i(0)(1+r_0)\ldots(1+r_{T-1})} + \ldots,$$

with its price p_i therefore equal to $p_i(0)$. We can derive the Slutzky equation,

$$\frac{\partial x_i}{\partial p_i} = \left[\frac{\partial x_i}{\partial p_i}\right]_S - x_i \frac{\partial x_i}{\partial W(0)},$$

with $(\partial x_i/\partial p_i)_S$ as usual negative. On the reasonable assumption that the components of x_i $(x_i(0), x_i(1),\ldots, x_i(T),\ldots)$ increase and decrease together, the substitution effect of an increase in $p_i(0)$ (together with equal proportional increases in the expected prices $p_i(1),\ldots, p_i(T),\ldots$) will reduce $x_i(0)$.

Thus whether the consumer's elasticity of expectations with regard to p_i is zero or unity, the substitution effect will (almost certainly) change $x_i(0)$ and $p_i(0)$ in opposite directions, so that intertemporal considerations do not upset the general presumption of downward-sloping demand curves.

So far, so good. But what implications does the extension of our time-horizon have for the procedure of earlier chapters, in which we developed demand functions which we now write, for clarity, as

$$x_i(0) = f_i(0)[p_1(0),\ldots, p_n(0), M(0)],$$

where $M(0) = \sum p_i(0)x_i(0)$, the budget allocated to current consumption? The first thing to be said is that if goods of current consumption are *weakly separable* (see section **10.1**), so that there is a set of indifference classes relating to current bundles $(x_i(0),\ldots, x_n(0))$ alone which do not change when consumption in other periods changes, then *given* values of $M(0), p_i(0),\ldots, p_n(0)$ determine a unique optimal bundle of goods. Hence weak separability implies the existence (and zero-degree homogeneity) of the demand functions of earlier chapters.

But unfortunately this is not all. In earlier chapters we investigated the effects of changes in $p_i(0)$ on $x_i(0)$ with a *given* current budget $M(0)$, neglecting any effect of changes in $p_i(0)$ on the allocation of $W(0)$ among periods which might have resulted in a change in the amount $M(0)$ allotted to the current period. Formally, the effect of a change in $p_i(0)$ on $x_i(0)$ (or on $x_j(0)$), may be of two kinds – the direct effect with a given budget $M(0)$, and the indirect effect of the change in $M(0)$ induced by the change in $p_i(0)$

$$\frac{dx_i(0)}{dp_i(0)} = \frac{\partial f_i(0)}{\partial p_i(0)} + \frac{\partial f_i(0)}{\partial M(0)}\frac{dM(0)}{dp_i(0)}.$$

$dx_i(0)/dp_i(0)$ and $dM(0)/dp_i(0)$ are the limits, as $\Delta p_i(0)$ approaches zero, of $\Delta x_i(0)/\Delta p_i(0)$ and $\Delta M(0)/\Delta p_i(0)$, after all other changes, like changes in price expectations and allocations to other periods, have been taken into account. We write $dx_i(0)/dp_i(0)$, rather than the partial derivative $\partial x_i(0)/\partial p_i(0)$, because we no longer assume that *only* $p_i(0)$ changes; $M(0)$ is allowed to change as well.

The argument of earlier chapters implicitly ignored the second term on the right-hand side by assuming that $dM(0)/dp_i(0) = 0$.

We must, I think, acknowledge that a chicken has come home to roost. The simplicity of the analysis of earlier chapters was purchased with the neglect of $dM(0)/dp_i(0)$. Separability alone will not dispose of this difficulty, though special assumptions about the preference ordering (e.g. assumptions which imply that a constant fraction of $W(0)$ is always spent on each period's consumption) can be made which ensure that $dM(0)/dp_i(0) = 0$.

But how serious is the problem? We argued earlier in this section that in general the substitution effect will change $x_i(0)$ and $p_i(0)$ in opposite directions. If we permit ourselves to assume weak separability we can go a little further. As we have just seen, demand functions like those of earlier chapters will then exist and can be estimated. The Slutzky equations of Chapter 5 must be amended, however. (Since it is clear that we are speaking of the current period, let us drop the '(0)'s.) In the last equation above, the term $\partial f_i(0)/\partial p_i(0) = \partial f_i/\partial p_i$ can be written, according to Chapter 5, as $(\partial x_i/\partial p_i)_S - x_i\,\partial x_i/\partial M$. If we take into account the possible effect of p_i on M, the equation becomes

$$\frac{dx_i}{dp_i} = \left[\frac{\partial x_i}{\partial p_i}\right]_S - x_i\frac{\partial x_i}{\partial M} + \frac{\partial x_i}{\partial M}\frac{dM}{dp_i}$$

$$= \left[\frac{\partial x_i}{\partial p_i}\right]_S - \left[x_i - \frac{dM}{dp_i}\right]\frac{\partial x_i}{\partial M}.$$

The substitution term $(\partial x_i/\partial p_i)_S$ is negative. Thus the fundamental theorem of demand theory – that $\partial x_i/\partial p_i < 0$ if $\partial x_i/\partial M \geqslant 0$ – is still valid provided that $x_i - dM/dp_i \geqslant 0$; that is, unless $\Delta M > x_i \Delta p_i$, which would mean that an increase in p_i leads to an increase in M large enough to allow the consumer to buy more of *everything* in the current period than before $p_i(0)$ increased. Since it is not even clear whether we should expect dM/dp_i normally to be positive or negative, this extraordinary case can be safely ruled out.

11.3 A problem of storage

Let us now move into less troubled waters, and assume that a consumer has decided at the beginning of period 0 to allocate a certain sum of money M_i to his total consumption of a commodity x_i in the current period 0 and the next period 1. The commodity is storable, so that we must distinguish quantities *purchased* at the beginning of the two periods, $x_i(0)$ and $x_i(1)$, from quantities *consumed* during the two periods, $C_i(0)$ and $C_i(1)$. If we assume for simplicity that the consumer has no stocks at the beginning of period 0 and intends to carry none over to period 2, and that the commodity does not depreciate in storage, we have the equality

$$C_i(0)+C_i(1) = x_i(0)+x_i(1),$$

with $C_i(0) \leqslant x_i(0)$. With no stocks, anything consumed in period 0 must have been bought at the beginning of period 0, but some or all of period 1's consumption may also be bought at the beginning of period 0.

The current price is $p_i(0)$, the price expected at the beginning of period 1 is $p_i(1)$, and the rate of interest on one-period money loans is r_0. Thus if the consumer does not store x_i, but plans to buy at the beginning of each period what he will consume in that period, his budget constraint expressed in terms of $C_i(0)$ and $C_i(1)$ is

$$p_i(0)C_i(0)+\frac{p_i(1)C_i(1)}{1+r_0} = M_i$$

This is represented by one of the budget lines in Figure 44.

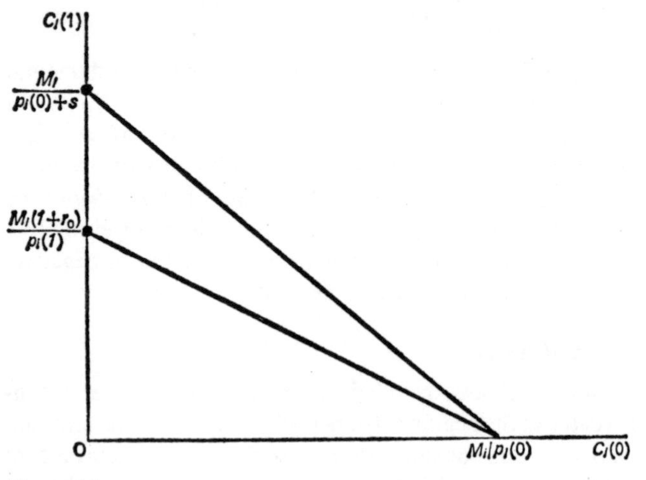

Figure 44

If on the other hand a purchase is made only at the beginning of period 0, $x_i(1) = 0$, and storage charges must be paid on the amount to be consumed in period 1, that is, on $C_i(1) = x_i(0)-C_i(0)$. If we assume that the storage charges are a certain sum of money s per unit stored, and are payable at the beginning of period 0 when the goods are bought and put into storage, the consumer's outlay is

$$\begin{aligned} p_i(0)x_i(0)+s[x_i(0)-C_i(0)] &= p_i(0)[C_i(0)+C_i(1)]+s\,C_i(1) \\ &= p_i(0)C_i(0)+\{p_i(0)+s\}C_i(1) \\ &= M_i. \end{aligned}$$

This budget line is also shown in Figure 44.

It is instructive to think of $C_i(0)$ and $C_i(1)$ as 'characteristics' in the sense of sections **10.3** and **10.4**, and of $x_i(0)$ and $x_i(1)$ as 'goods'. Whether to store is a simple 'efficiency choice'. As Figure 44 is drawn it is clearly more efficient to buy only $x_i(0)$, since the storage budget line lies everywhere outside the non-storage budget line. This is so because

$$p_i(0)+s < \frac{p_i(1)}{1+r_0}.$$

This implies that given the current price, the advantage in purchasing now for storage is greater (i) the lower the cost of storage, (ii) the higher the expected future price and (iii) the lower the rate of interest. The rate of interest is relevant in that by buying goods now and storing them one is forgoing interest that could be earned on the money so spent.

If one took into account storage charges which increased more than in proportion to the quantity stored, one might find that it was efficient to meet some of one's needs in period 1 through current purchase and storage and some by purchase at the beginning of period 1.

The example of this section is of course a very simple one, but it contains the elements of more complex problems, such as whether to buy a freezer. The consumer is more likely to do so (i) the lower the purchase price of the freezer and its running costs (corresponding to s in our example), (ii) the greater the saving by purchasing food in bulk when its price is low (corresponding to a low value of $p_i(0)$ in relation to $p_i(1)$), and (iii) the lower the rate of interest, which is relevant both because one must either borrow the purchase price of the freezer, or pay cash which one therefore can no longer invest, and because cash has to be paid for food earlier than would otherwise be the case.

11.4 A problem of replacement

In this section we consider, in a somewhat oversimplified manner, the problem of a consumer who owns a car, and must decide at the beginning of a particular year whether to replace it, and if he does, whether to replace it with a brand-new car or a car of a different age. We limit our attention to the current year on the assumption that his present decision will not affect the alternatives open to him in any subsequent year. It is only the temporal aspects of the problem that concern us; hence we do not consider alternative makes or types of car, nor the possibility of renting a car or of dispensing with a car and using taxis and public transport instead.

We assume that a car that is now t years old is expected to depreciate in value by £d_t during the current year, and that £d_t is also the difference between the current prices of a car t years old and a car $t+1$ years old.[30] (Of course $t = 0$ for a brand-new car, $t = 1$ for a car one year old, and so on.)

The consumer believes that he would have to make a current cash outlay of £m_t in order to make a car now t years old the equivalent in all respects which are significant to him of a car now $t-1$ years old. Obviously $m_0 = 0$ since, there *is* no car newer than a brand-new one. £m_1 is the current outlay needed to make a one-year-old car the equivalent (in terms of performance, running costs, repair costs, safety, accessories, style, etc., insofar as these are important to the consumer) of a brand-new car. The sums £m_1, £m_2,... may alternatively be regarded as the current money values set by the consumer on ownership of a brand-new car as compared with a car one year old, of a one-year-old car as compared with one two years old, and so on, whether they are fully spent or not. They therefore clearly depend on his tastes as well as on the expected size of repair bills. If we take tastes into account in this way, we can treat the replacement decision as a pure 'efficiency choice' in the sense of section **10.3**, though we shall suggest later how tastes may affect the values of $m_1, m_2, \ldots$.

This efficiency choice in fact becomes simply a matter of deciding how old a car to own. It makes no difference to this choice whether the

30. This is of course not quite true, since transactions costs (the dealer's expenses and profit) cause the price for which I can buy a car t years old to exceed the price for which I can sell one.

consumer now owns a car, as we shall see later. And since this is the case, it is convenient to assume that he does not, and to ask the following question. What is the current cost of (i) buying a car t years old, (ii) making the current outlay necessary to make it for a year the equivalent of a brand-new car, and (iii) the depreciation that will occur over the year? (The depreciation must be discounted at the current rate of interest per year, r.)

If the price of a new car is p, the price of a one-year-old car, a two-year-old car, ... is $p-d_0$, $p-d_0-d_1$, ... Our assumptions yield the following table.

Age of car in years	*Current year's cost in pounds*
0	$p+\frac{d_0}{1+r}$
1	$p-d_0+m_1+\frac{d_1}{1+r}$
2	$p-d_0-d_1+m_1+m_2+\frac{d_2}{1+r}$
.	
.	
.	
t	$p-d_0-...-d_{t-1}+m_1+...+m_t+\frac{d_t}{1+r}$
.	
.	
.	

The efficient choice is of course to buy a car of the age that gives the lowest cost. To show that this table is relevant also to the consumer who owns a car, suppose that he has a car two years old. If he were to trade it for a car one year old, he would have to make a cash outlay of £d_1 (the difference between the prices of one-year-old and two-year-old cars), and the newer car would depreciate by £d_1 over the year (this sum must be discounted). In considering the cost of keeping his two-year-old car, we must include, to make the comparison accurate, the cost £m_2 of making a two-year-old car the equivalent of a one-year-old car, and add the discounted value of depreciation, £$d_2/(1+r)$. Thus it is more efficient to trade his car for the newer one if

$$d_1+\frac{d_1}{1+r}-\left[m_2+\frac{d_2}{1+r}\right] < 0.$$

And this is precisely the expression we obtain if we subtract the cost of a two-year-old car from that of a one-year-old car in the table above.

It is well known that the rate of depreciation falls as the car becomes older, so that $d_0 > d_1 > d_2 \ldots$, and the final term in the lines of the table gets steadily smaller. For a consumer to whom the ownership of a very new car is important in itself, m_1 and m_2 are likely to be high in relation to d_0 and d_1 (especially if the latter are tax-deductible), so that he may well not keep a car that is two years old. But to one whose primary concerns are safety and the size of repair bills, m_1 and m_2 may be low in relation to d_0 and d_1, and he is quite likely to buy, or trade an older car for, one that is three, four or five years old. But when a car becomes very old (and warranties expire) considerations of safety and repair cause, say, m_9 and m_{10} to be large in relation to d_8 and d_9, and eventually it becomes efficient to replace the old car.

11.5 Optimal transactions balances

Money has hitherto received little attention in this volume. We assumed in earlier chapters that a sum of money was set aside for current purchases, and in the first section of the present chapter that that part of the consumer's wealth which was needed for current purchases was readily available in the form of money. It has also been assumed that current purchases are made at the beginning of period 0, so that a part of the consumer's wealth is spent at once and the remainder earns interest at the rate r_0 over the entire interval until the beginning of period 1.

We introduce the problem of cash balances by asking what the consumer would do if payment for current purchases were not concentrated at the beginning of period 0, but were spread evenly and continuously over the period, so that if total payments during the period were M, an amount kM would be due in each fraction k of the period. It is assumed that, if the interest rate on money lent for the whole period is r, one pound lent for any fraction k of the period will earn £rk in interest.

What alternatives are open to the consumer? He may, at the beginning of the period, hold the whole of M in cash, but by so doing he loses the interest he could have earned by lending part of M for part of the period. Then let him lend the whole of M at the beginning of the period, converting the loan into cash little by little as payments become due. But it is reasonable to assume that every time a loan is converted into cash, the transaction involves a cost or brokerage fee. This fee will be assumed to consist of two parts, one proportional to the size of the transaction T and one independent of it, so that the brokerage fee for each transaction is $aT+b$. (For the more humble consumer who does not have a broker, there are analogies to this brokerage fee in the trouble involved, or the petrol or bus-fare expended, in going to the bank to withdraw money from his interest-bearing savings account).

The problem to be solved is by now probably clear. The more transactions are made, the greater are the total brokerage fees, but at the same time the average cash balance and the total interest forgone are smaller. The consumer should minimize the sum: total brokerage fees plus total interest forgone.

Suppose that at the beginning of the period (say on 1 February, the first day of a month of exactly four weeks) he decides to lend $\frac{3}{4}M$ and keep $\frac{1}{4}M$ in cash to make payments during the first week. On 8 February he converts $\frac{1}{4}M$ into cash to make payments during the second week, and so on. What are the total brokerage fees?

As we shall discover, the solution of the general problem takes the form of a simple formula. But its simplicity depends on the following convention. A 'transaction' takes place when a loan is converted into cash, and the size of the transaction is the amount so converted. This creates no difficulties except at the very beginning of the period, when we must say that the decision to hold, as above, $\frac{1}{4}M$ in cash requires a transaction of $\frac{1}{4}M$. It is as if on 1 February the consumer had already made loans equal to M and was converting $\frac{1}{4}M$ into cash.

The subsequent analysis would not be greatly changed if we altered this convention, though it would be a shade more complex. If we adopt it, the number of transactions in the earlier example is 4 (1, 8, 15, 22 February) and the total brokerage fees are $4(aT+b)$, where T is the size of each transaction. T is equal to $\frac{1}{4}M$ in each case, so that

$4(aT+b) = aM+4b$. If there were n transactions the total brokerage fees would be $n(aM/n+b) = aM+nb$, so that the term $naT = aM$ is the same regardless of the number of transactions. Since our interest is only in finding that value of n which minimizes brokerage fees plus interest forgone, we can disregard this constant term, and take brokerage fees henceforth to consist only of bn.

Since in our example the consumer begins each week with a cash balance of $\frac{1}{4}M$, and spends it evenly through the week, his average cash balance is $\frac{1}{8}M$. In general the average cash balance is $M/2n$, where n is the number of transactions.

As to the interest forgone, if initially the consumer leaves the whole of M on loan, and converts it continuously into cash over the month (thus engaging, strictly speaking, in an infinite number of brokerage transactions!), the average amount of money on loan during the month is $\frac{1}{2}M$, and interest earned is $\frac{1}{2}rM$. This is a limiting case which sets a maximum on the interest that can be earned if all payments are to be made as they become due, and interest forgone is defined as the difference between $\frac{1}{2}rM$ and the interest actually earned.

Now if $n = 4$, the amounts of money earning interest during the first, second, third and fourth weeks are respectively $\frac{3}{4}M, \frac{1}{2}M, \frac{1}{4}M$ and zero. In each week interest is earned at the rate $\frac{1}{4}r$. Thus total interest earned is $M(\frac{3}{4}+\frac{1}{2}+\frac{1}{4})\frac{1}{4}r = \frac{3}{8}rM$. Interest forgone is therefore $\frac{1}{2}rM-\frac{3}{8}rM = \frac{1}{8}rM = rM/2n$. Indeed, $rM/2n$ is the general expression for interest forgone when there are n transactions.

The amounts earning interest at the rate of r/n during the 1st, 2nd,... $(n-1)$th, nth subperiods into which the 'month' is divided are $(n-1)M/n, (n-2)M/n, \ldots, M/n, 0$. Thus total interest earned is

$$\frac{rM}{n^2}\sum_{i=1}^{n} i-1 = \frac{rM}{n^2}\frac{n(n-1)}{2} = \frac{rM}{2}\left[1-\frac{1}{n}\right].$$

Interest forgone is then $\frac{rM}{2}-\frac{rM}{2}\left[1-\frac{1}{n}\right] = \frac{rM}{2n}$ as stated.

We conclude that if n is the number of transactions, the sum of brokerage fees (ignoring the constant term aM) and interest forgone is

$$C = bn+\frac{rM}{2n}.$$

We must find the value of n that minimizes C. It is easy to do this by means of the calculus, but an interesting alternative method is to show that C is minimized when brokerage cost bn and interest forgone are equal. For suppose that $bn = rM/2n$. Let n increase by (say)10 per cent. Then bn increases by $\frac{1}{10}$ and $rM/2n$ falls by $\frac{1}{11}$. Now let n fall by 10 per cent. Then bn falls by $\frac{1}{10}$ and $rM/2n$ increases by $\frac{1}{9}$. In each case, if they are initially equal their total must increase. And it is easy to show that if initially $bn \neq rM/2n$, *some* changes in n would decrease their sum.[31]

Therefore when C is minimized $bn = rM/2n$, so that $n^2 = rM/2b$.[32] Hence

$$\text{optimal number of transactions} = \sqrt{\frac{rM}{2b}}.$$

Since the average cash balance is equal to $M/2n$, we also have

$$\text{optimal average cash balance} = \sqrt{\frac{bM}{2r}}.$$

It follows that with given values of b and r, the optimal average transactions balance is proportional to the *square root* of the total value of payments to be made. If prices of all goods and services were changing in the same proportion, with r constant, b would change in the same proportion as M, and the optimal balance would be proportional to $\sqrt{(bM)}$, that is, proportional to M. But it would still increase in a smaller proportion than M, and might even decline absolutely, if, as in recent history, inflation is accompanied by an

31. Strictly speaking, this is true – and the calculus proof in the next footnote is valid – only if n is allowed to be any *real* number, and we are not confined to the case where the number of transactions per period is an *integer* (i.e. a whole number).

32. Since $C = bn+\frac{rM}{2n}$,

$$\frac{dC}{dn} = b-\frac{rM}{2n^2} = 0 \quad \text{when } n^2 = \frac{rM}{2b}.$$

$$\frac{d^2C}{dn^2} = \frac{rM}{n^3} > 0,$$

so that $dC/dn = 0$ gives a *minimum* of C.

increase in money interest rates. For example, if b and M both increase by 5 per cent, the numerator of $bM/2r$ rises by about 11 per cent. If r rises from 5 per cent to 6 per cent (an increase of 20 per cent in the denominator of $bM/2r$), the optimal transactions balance will *fall.*

In this section we have presented a third illustration of an efficiency choice. The characteristic of the good, money, on which we have concentrated is its immediate acceptability as a means of payment, and we have asked how much of the good it is efficient to hold to meet a given stream of payments. As we shall find in Part Five (section **14.2**), money has additional important characteristics when uncertainty is taken into account.

The reader will no doubt have noticed that in each of the last three sections *only* an efficiency choice was discussed, and the consumer's tastes played little or no part. In section **11.3** the storage budget line lay uniformly outside the non-storage budget line in Figure 44 (though it might not have done so if we had allowed s to vary with the quantity stored). In section **11.4** we absorbed the consumer's preferences among older and newer cars into the sums of money $m_1, m_2, \ldots$, and in this section we have assumed total payments M to be given independently of the cost of holding cash balances. So these examples are not intended as definitive analyses, but only as illustrations of a technique. In Parts Five and Six we shall encounter cases where both efficiency choices and tastes must be systematically taken into account.

Exercises

1. A consumer who has determined his consumption plan experiences a single change in his budget constraint: $E(1)$, his expected earnings at the beginning of period 1, increase by £2100. The rate of interest r_0 is 5 per cent. He decides to increase his consumption above that planned only in period 0 and period 1. If he increases current consumption, $\sum p_i(0)x_i(0)$, by £1100, by how much will consumption in period 1, $\sum p_i(1)x_i(1)$, be increased?

2. A consumer buys only two commodities x_1 and x_2, is interested in consumption only in periods 0 and 1, and expects no earnings after the beginning of period 1. Given that $V(0)+E(0) = £100$, $E(1) = £165$, $r_0 = 10$ per cent, $p_1(0) = £1$, $p_2(0) = £3$, $p_1(1) =$ £1·10, $p_2(1) =$ £5·50, write down the consumer's budget constraint.

(The only undetermined quantities in the budget constraint are $x_1(0)$, $x_2(0)$, $x_1(1)$, $x_2(1)$.)

3. If the utility function of the consumer in Exercise 2 is:

$$u = \{x_1(0)\}^{0\cdot3}\{x_2(0)\}^{0\cdot3}\{x_1(1)\}^{0\cdot2}\{x_2(1)\}^{0\cdot2}$$

what quantities of $x_1(0),\ldots, x_2(1)$ will he buy? (Hint: this utility function is of the form (U1) in section **9.2**).

Notes on the literature

The towering classic on the subject-matter of Part Four is Irving Fisher, *The Theory of Interest* (Kelley, 1930). Fisher was the first to recognize that the same commodity at different dates could be regarded as two different commodities, and that the standard theory of consumer behaviour could therefore be readily applied to choice over time. His book is a masterly piece of exposition; the reader may take his choice of verbal, geometric and mathematical treatments.

11.1 An analysis of the consumer's choice over time in the spirit of this section is to be found in Henderson and Quandt (*Microeconomic Theory*, ch. 8).

11.2 The problem discussed in this section has been raised by Pearce (*A contribution to Demand Analysis*, ch. 2).

11.5 This section follows closely the analysis of W. J. Baumol, 'The transactions demand for cash: an inventory-theoretic approach' (*Q. J. Econ.*, vol. 66, no. 265, pp. 545–56, 1952). See also Baumol (*Economic Theory and Operations Analysis*, pp. 5–10, 349–54). The 'square-root formula' is also applicable to a firm's holding of inventories (carrying costs and reorder costs playing the parts of r and b respectively).

Chapter 12
Long-Period Problems

12.1 The budget constraint

In the last chapter we were concerned with problems involving short periods of time and purchases or holdings of a single good. We now turn to the more difficult problem of the allocation of a consumer's resources over his lifetime. A great deal of work has been done in this area in the last twenty years, motivated by a wish to explain current consumption, and to go beyond Keynes's simple hypothesis that current consumption is a function of current income, with the marginal propensity to consume between zero and unity.

Let us first clear away some of the problems of aggregation. It is convenient to be able to regard the intertemporal preference ordering or utility function as relating to total consumption in each period, and not to be concerned with individual commodities. And it is convenient to be able to associate a discounted price with the consumption of each period. This procedure is legitimate if either (i) the prices of all goods in any period t are expected to remain in constant proportions (section **7.4**) or (ii) the goods of each period are homogeneously separable in the utility function (section **10.2**). Then consumption in period t, $C(t)$, can be treated as either (i) a composite commodity or (ii) a quantity index, with a price or price index $p(t)$, and in either case $p(t)C(t)$ will equal the expected money value of consumption in period t.

If it strikes the reader as odd that a consumer should be supposed to have definite expectations about prices and interest rates over the whole course of his life, it will no doubt seem even stranger to make this supposition concerning prices and interest rates after his death. In fact, as we shall see, only very general assumptions are made about expectations during a consumer's lifetime. And we shall now assume that we can form, by virtue of either (i) or (ii) above, a composite commodity or quantity index $C(T+1)$ of all consumption by the consumer's heirs, with its price or price index $p(T+1)$, so that $p(T+1)C(T+1)$ is the money value of his expected bequests.

Let us dispense with one more variable by defining our units in such a way that the known price or price index of current consumption goods $p(0)$ is equal to unity. Then $p(1)$ is the expected price level (this term will stand henceforth for 'price or price index') at the beginning of period 1 as a proportion of the current price level, and $p(1)-1$ measures the expected rate of inflation over the period.

The consumer's problem may now be formulated as follows (cf. section **11.1**):

Maximize $u[C(0), C(1),..., C(T), C(T+1)]$ subject to

$$W(0) = V(0)+E(0)+\frac{E(1)}{1+r_0}+...+\frac{E(T)}{(1+r_0)...(1+r_{T-1})}$$

$$= C(0)+\frac{p(1)C(1)}{1+r_0}+...+\frac{p(T)C(T)}{(1+r_0)...(1+r_{T-1})}+$$

$$+\frac{p(T+1)C(T+1)}{(1+r_0)...(1+r_T)}.$$

$C(0), C(1),...$ are to be thought of as consumption rather than purchases. One would not include in consumption the full purchase price of a house in the year in which it was bought.

The usual procedure is now to make special assumptions about the utility function, and about the expected behaviour of prices and interest rates, in order to derive hypotheses about the consumer's inter-temporal choices. But let us first, in the next section, stand back from the problem and look at this conventional method of analysis through the eyes of two critics of it.

12.2 Two critical views

The first criticism to be considered is that of Strotz. The analysis of the previous section implies that on a particular date the consumer determines his consumption in every period until the time of his death. But time does not stand still, and it must be assumed that as it passes the consumer has at each date a preference ordering relating to the pattern of consumption over the remainder of his life.

Leaving aside uncertainty as to the length of his life or future earnings, prices and interest rates (which can be met in part by insurance and judicious choice of assets – see Part Five), there remains doubt about his future *preferences.* How can the consumer be sure that ten years from now he will wish to allocate his wealth over the remainder of his life in the way that he is now planning?

Of course he cannot be sure. But does inconsistency of current preferences with past plans lessen the usefulness of the theory? Our hypothesis is simply that at each date the consumer's decisions are based on a view of his current and future wants. The contribution of Strotz's criticism is that it draws attention to the fact that the rational consumer will consider the extent to which he should provide for *future changes* in preferences.

How can such provision be made? Now on the assumptions of section **11.1**, where there was a single short-period rate of interest in each period, such questions did not arise. It was implicitly assumed that all assets earned the same rate of return and could be turned into cash without loss at any time. But in practice of course if one commits resources to a particular type of asset (e.g. a house) one may receive a low rate of return if one tries to turn it into cash after a short period of time (the agent has to be paid).

Hence with a given $W(0)$ one can purchase various types of asset leading to various alternative consumption streams. If one wishes to allow oneself the maximum freedom to change one's mind, one avoids assets which cannot be readily turned into cash, thereby usually earning a lower rate of return. But as Strotz points out, it may well be desirable, in a sober frame of mind, to *protect* oneself against changing one's mind lightly. One may wish, for example, to ensure that funds for retirement are not squandered, by investing in a pension plan in which the rate of return on funds withdrawn before retirement is so low as to deter one from doing so.

This 'strategy of precommitment', as Strotz calls it (examples of protecting oneself from oneself in other contexts are getting married and volunteering for the army!), is precisely what we should expect of a rational consumer making a lifetime allocation plan. It seems to me to constitute a valuable development of the analysis of the last section.

A criticism which leads to a quite different analysis is that of Clower and others. They think of consumers as essentially short-sighted, and as deriving satisfaction from the ownership of (non-human) wealth in itself, and not only from the future consumption which it permits. They do not totally deny that the consumer is concerned with lifetime allocation, but for the purpose of deriving strong and testable hypotheses they disregard all independent variables in the utility function other than current consumption and non-human wealth.

Referring to the budget constraint in section **12.1**, we note that non-human wealth at the beginning of period 1, $V(1)$, will be the result of investing $V(0)$ plus earnings $E(0)$ less consumption $C(0)$ at the rate of interest r_0. Thus $V(1) = [V(0)+E(0)-C(0)](1+r_0)$ or

$$C(0)+\frac{V(1)}{1+r_0} = V(0)+E(0).$$

Subject to this constraint, we are to maximize

$$f\left[C(0), \frac{V(1)}{1+r_0}\right].^{33}$$

If one makes the special assumptions that the rate of interest is constant and that $C(0)$ and $V(1)/1+r_0$ are always chosen in the proportions $(\alpha, 1-\alpha)$, and defines 'income' as the amount that can be consumed while leaving $V(1)$ equal to $V(0)$, some simple testable results follow. It can be shown that current consumption is equal to α times current income plus $1-\alpha$ times last period's consumption. And provided that α exceeds the rate of interest, it can be shown that if earnings are growing at the constant proportional rate g, wealth, income and consumption will also eventually grow at the rate g, with consumption a constant fraction (approximately[33] $\alpha/(g+\alpha)$) of income.

These are interesting hypotheses, and a comparison of statistical results with those of the approach of the next section are at present inconclusive. The distinguishing features of the theory are that the satisfaction derived from a given quantity of non-human wealth is assumed to be independent of both (i) future prices and interest rates, changes in which can affect substantially the flows of *consumption* permitted by $V(1)/(1+r_0)$, and (ii) the present value of future earnings, or the consumer's 'human wealth'.

33. These authors treat time as continuous, and do not divide it into discrete periods as we do. In consequence, their formulations are neater than ours.

Now it would be quite consistent with the usual analysis – though the case would be very special – to assume that the consumer behaved as if he were maximizing $g[C(0), W(1)/(1+r_0)]$ subject to

$$C(0)+\frac{W(1)}{1+r_0} = W(0).$$

For if his utility function were of the form (U1) in section **9.2** – $u = C(0)^{\alpha_0}C(1)^{\alpha_1}...C(T)^{\alpha_T}C(T+1)^{\alpha_{T+1}}$, with $\alpha_0+...+\alpha_{T+1} = 1$, he would spend a fraction α_0 of $W(0)$ on current consumption regardless of future prices and interest rates. But note that here it is *total* wealth that enters the utility function, not just non-human wealth.

Thus the fundamental difference between the two theories is that in one current consumption and non-human wealth are the only sources of satisfaction, while it is implicit in the other, even in the special case where future prices and interest rates do not affect current consumption, that only current and future flows of consumption provide satisfaction. In this second view, to which we turn in the next section, all assets are 'goods' and streams of consumption goods are their 'characteristics'.

12.3 Consumption and income

The demand for current consumption can be derived from the budget equation at the end of section **12.1** as follows,

$$C(0) = C(0)\left[W(0), \frac{p(1)}{1+r_0},..., \frac{p(T+1)}{(1+r_0)...(1+r_T)}\right].$$

Following the work of Friedman, we define what Farrell calls 'normal income' – that rate of receipts per period which, if maintained at a constant level over one's lifetime, would have a present value equal to that of one's total wealth (human and non-human) (Friedman's concept of 'permanent income' is less precise). Its value at the beginning of period 0 is determined by solving the following equation for $Y(0)$,

$$Y(0)+\frac{Y(0)}{1+r_0}+...+\frac{Y(0)}{(1+r_0)...(1+r_{T-1})} = W(0) = V(0)+H(0).$$

The 'normal income hypothesis' is that $C(0)$ is a function of $Y(0)$.

Friedman assumes that indifference surfaces relating to $C(0), C(1), \ldots, C(T+1)$ are homothetic with reference to the origin, so that given $p(1), \ldots, p(T+1), r_0, \ldots, r_T$, a 10 per cent increase in $W(0)$ will lead to a 10 per cent increase in $C(0)$ – and in $C(1), \ldots, C(T+1)$. On this assumption, $C(0)$ is a constant fraction of $Y(0)$, but this fraction depends on (i) expected future interest rates and prices, since different combinations of $W(0), p(1), \ldots, p(T+1), r_0, \ldots, r_T$ can give rise to the same value of $Y(0)$; (ii) the age of the consumer – when period t is reached, even if $Y(0) = Y(t)$ there is no reason to suppose that $C(0)/Y(0) = C(t)/Y(t)$; (iii) the ratio of non-human to human wealth – the greater that ratio, the greater $C(0)/Y(0)$, because human wealth is less secure, and it may be both difficult and unwise to borrow against it.

In discussions of the normal income hypothesis, considerable attention has been devoted to the effect on current consumption of changes in current earnings and changes in wealth.

As to the former, what is the effect on $Y(0)$ of a change in $E(0)$ alone? If we assume for simplicity that current and expected future interest rates are all equal to r, normal income is

$$Y(0) = \frac{r}{(1+r)\{1-[1/(1+r)]^{T+1}\}} W(0).$$[34]

If $r = 5$ per cent per annum and T (the number of years of life remaining) is between 20 and 40, it turns out that approximately

$$Y(0) = \frac{2}{T} W(0).$$

$$\left(\frac{Y(0)}{W(0)} \text{ is about } \frac{2}{27} \text{ when } T = 20, \frac{2}{33} \text{ when } T = 30, \frac{2}{37} \text{ when } T = 40.\right)$$

An increase in current earnings $E(0)$ of £100 will of course increase $W(0)$ by £100, but if $T = 25$, say, $Y(0)$ will increase by only about £8,

34. $(1+x+\ldots+x^T)(1-x) = 1-x^{T+1}$; thus $1+x+\ldots+x^T = \dfrac{1-x^{T+1}}{1-x}$.

Therefore $W(0) = Y(0)\left[1+\dfrac{1}{1+r}+\ldots+\left(\dfrac{1}{1+r}\right)^T\right]$

$$= Y(0)\left[\frac{1-\{1/(1+r)\}^{T+1}}{1-\{1/(1+r)\}}\right] = Y(0)\,\frac{1+r}{r}\left[1-\left(\frac{1}{1+r}\right)^{T+1}\right],$$

whence the result in the text.

and if $C(0)/Y(0)$ is, say, 0·75, current consumption will increase by only about £6.

But it is hoped that the reader will have spotted an analogy with a problem raised in section **11.2.** If an increase in $E(0)$ leaves expectations of future earnings unchanged, the foregoing analysis is valid: in that case the elasticity of expectations is zero. But suppose that a consumer's current earnings rise by 10 per cent, and his elasticity of expectations with respect to future earnings is unity. This means that all expected future earnings will also rise by 10 per cent, as therefore will the present value of his current and expected earnings (his human wealth) and that part of his normal income which is derived from human wealth.

In the special case, which implies unit elasticity of expectations, where earnings are expected always to be the same in the future as at present, an increase in current earnings (and therefore in expected future earnings) of £100 per period will increase normal income by £100. This is because if

$$\Delta Y(0)+\frac{\Delta Y(0)}{1+r_0}+\ldots+\frac{\Delta Y(0)}{(1+r_0)\ldots(1+r_{T-1})}$$

$$= 100+\frac{100}{1+r_0}+\ldots+\frac{100}{(1+r_0)\ldots(1+r_{T-1})}$$

obviously $\Delta Y(0) = 100$. If $C(0)/Y(0) = 0{\cdot}75$ as before, $C(0)$ will increase by £75, as compared with only about £6 when the elasticity of expectations was zero (though $C(0)/Y(0)$ may fall somewhat as a result of the reduction in the ratio of non-human to human wealth).

The argument suggests a test of the theory. It is reasonable to suppose that in occupations where earnings fluctuate widely over time the elasticity of expectations with respect to earnings is low, and is much higher where earnings are stable over time. One would expect, therefore, that for two groups of consumers with roughly equal ratios of $C(0)$ to $Y(0)$, the consumption of those with volatile earnings would respond less to changes in current earnings. The evidence is encouraging.

As to increases in wealth – if they are expected, the theory implies that they are already accounted for in normal income. But if they are unexpected ('windfalls') they will affect normal income by only about $2/T$ times their value. Friedman argues:

Will not a man who receives an unexpected windfall use at least some part of it in 'riotous living'? ... The offhand affirmative answer reflects in large measure, I believe, an implicit definition of consumption in terms of purchases, including durable goods, rather than in terms of the value of services.... Is not the windfall likely to be used for the purchase of durable goods? Or, to put it differently, is not the timing of the replacement of durable goods and of additions to the stock of such goods likely to some extent to be adjusted so as to coincide with windfalls?

Moreover, even if the ratio of consumption to normal income does increase after the windfall, this could be explained by the increase that has occurred in the ratio of non-human to human wealth.

Various tests of the normal income hypothesis have been devised, but one serious difficulty is that normal income, a large part of which is defined in terms of *expected* earnings, is virtually impossible to measure. Consumption functions fitted to national data involve in addition problems of aggregation over households and over age-groups.

Measured consumption functions do nowadays usually relate consumption in different ways to human and to non-human wealth, or to earnings and to property income, as the normal income hypothesis discussed above would suggest. If current earnings are assumed proportional to the human part of normal income, and expected future rates of interest and inflation are given, then the following simple equation is an example of a relationship consistent (problems of aggregation apart) with the normal income hypothesis:

$$C(0) = \alpha_1 E(0) + \alpha_2 V(0).$$

Its apparent success with United States data does not confirm the normal income hypothesis, but does not disprove it either.

12.4 Consumption, interest and inflation

We turn now to a further question, on which it must be admitted that there is little empirical evidence – the effect of changes in current and expected interest rates and price levels on the consumption plan. We make strong assumptions which lead to definite results. When these assumptions are not fully satisfied, the results may still be helpful in explaining the behaviour of consumers, and in the framing of an optimal savings policy for an economy.

Let us first look again at the budget constraint at the end of section 12.1. The coefficients of $C(0),\ldots, C(T+1)$ are $p(1)/(1+r_0),\ldots, p(T+1)/(1+r_0)\ldots(1+r_T)$, and they involve both prices and interest rates. If $p(1)$ is 1·03 and r_0 is 0·05, the coefficient of $C(1)$ is $1{\cdot}03/1{\cdot}05 = 1/1{\cdot}0194$. The budget constraint would be no different if the money rate of interest r_0 were 1·94 per cent and the price level were not expected to change over the current period. For if one lends someone £100 now in exchange for his promise to repay £105, and in the mean-time prices rise by 3 per cent, it will take £103 to buy what £100 buys now, leaving only £2 as real interest. One lends £100 and receives in real terms £100 × $\frac{105}{103}$ = £101·94, thus earning a *real* interest rate of only 1·94 per cent. When the money rate of interest r_0 and the expected rate of inflation $i(0)$ (3 per cent in this example) are both small, the real rate of interest R_0 is approximately equal to $r_0-i(0)$; in the present example this is $5-3 = 2$ per cent, which is very close to the true value of 1·94 per cent.

The real rate of interest R_1 from the beginning of period 1 to the beginning of period 2 is (approximately) equal to $r_1-i(1)$, where $i(1)$ is the expected rate of price increase over that interval, namely

$$i(1) = \frac{p(2)-p(1)}{p(1)} = \frac{p(2)}{p(1)}-1.$$

And in general R_t is (approximately) equal to $r_t-i(t) = r_t-\{[p(t+1)/p(t)]-1\}$. Thus the budget constraint can be written in terms of real rates of interest as follows

$$W(0) = C(0)+\frac{C(1)}{1+R_0}+\frac{C(2)}{(1+R_0)(1+R_1)}+\ldots+\frac{C(T+1)}{(1+R_0)\ldots(1+R_T)}.$$

The first of our special assumptions is that rates of inflation and money rates of interest are expected always to be the same in the future as in the present. This (like a similar assumption with regard to earnings in the last section) implies that the elasticity of expectations is unity with regard to prices and interest rates. It also implies (and this is the great convenience of the assumption) that we can work with a single real rate of interest $R = R_0 = R_1 = \ldots = R_T$, so that the budget constraint is further simplified to

$$W(0) = C(0)+\frac{C(1)}{1+R}+\frac{C(2)}{(1+R)^2}+\ldots+\frac{C(T+1)}{(1+R)^{T+1}}$$

$$= \sum_{t=0}^{T+1}\frac{C(t)}{(1+R)^t}.$$

Our remaining assumptions relate to the utility function $u = u[C(0), C(1),\ldots, C(T+1)]$. The first is the familiar one that it is additive

$$u = f_0[C(0)]+f_1[C(1)]+\ldots+f_{T+1}[C(T+1)].$$

We know from page 94 above that this implies that the marginal rate of substitution between consumption at any two dates (no matter how widely separated in time) is independent of consumption at any third date. What is rather surprising is that if we modify this assumption to the rather more palatable one that the marginal rate of substitution between consumption at any two *adjacent* dates is independent of consumption at any third date, it can be shown that we are still committed to full additivity as in the equation above.

Secondly, we assume that there is a single utility function $f(\ )$, with the usual properties, applicable to consumption at all dates, and that the functions $f_0(\ ), f_1(\ ),\ldots, f_{T+1}(\ )$ differ only that each is the function $f(\ )$ multiplied by a number applying to its time-period. Thus

$$u = \lambda_0 f[C(0)]+\lambda_1 f[C(1)]+\ldots+\lambda_{T+1} f[C(T+1)].$$

What this means is that if $C(0) = C(1), f[C(0)] = f[C(1)]$, so that their contributions to u are in the ratio λ_0/λ_1. It also means that if $C(0) = C(1)$, an increase of 1 unit in $C(0)$ accompanied by a decrease of λ_0/λ_1 units in $C(1)$ will leave u unchanged, so that λ_0/λ_1 is the marginal rate of substitution of $C(1)$ for $C(0)$.

The third assumption about the utility function is that the numbers $\lambda_0, \lambda_1,\ldots, \lambda_{T+1}$ are related in a special way, namely

$$\frac{\lambda_1}{\lambda_0} = \frac{\lambda_2}{\lambda_1} = \ldots = \frac{\lambda_{T+1}}{\lambda_T} < 1.$$

This implies that $\lambda_0 > \lambda_1 > \ldots > \lambda_T > \lambda_{T+1}$, so that roughly speaking the present satisfaction derived from expected future consumption declines the longer one has to wait for it. (Since $C(T+1)$, however, is consumption by the consumer's *heirs*, λ_{T+1} may have almost any value, and one may wish to exclude it from this assumption.) More precisely, if $C(0) = C(1) = \dots = C(T+1)$, the contribution to u of an extra unit of consumption will be less the later the date at which one expects to enjoy it. 'Impatience' is the usual name for this feature of the utility function u.

The assumption that the ratios λ_1/λ_0, $\lambda_2/\lambda_1, \dots$ are all equal is purely a matter of convenience. One can define

$$\frac{\lambda_1}{\lambda_0} = \frac{\lambda_2}{\lambda_1} = \dots = \frac{1}{1+p},$$

in which case $\lambda_1 = \lambda_0/(1+p)$, $\lambda_2 = \lambda_0/(1+p)^2, \dots, \lambda_t = \lambda_0/(1+p)^t$, and so on. We are also at liberty to assume that $\lambda_0 = 1$ (since to multiply or divide a utility function by any positive number is to subject it only to a monotonically increasing transformation, which in no way affects behaviour; see section **6.4**). In that case, $\lambda_1 = 1/(1+p)$, $\lambda_2 = 1/(1+p)^2, \dots$, and the utility function becomes

$$u = f[C(0)] + \frac{f[C(1)]}{1+p} + \frac{f[C(2)]}{(1+p)^2} + \dots + \frac{f[C(T+1)]}{(1+p)^{T+1}}$$

$$= \sum_{t=0}^{T+1} \frac{f[C(t)]}{(1+p)^t}.$$

(For reasons given above, one may wish to replace the term $(1+p)^{T+1}$ by some other number.)

This bears a striking resemblance to the final form of the budget constraint. Indeed, p can be thought of as a *subjective* rate of interest or *time-preference* at which future utilities are discounted, while R is a market rate of interest or time-preference at which future (real) values are discounted. Our assumptions permit us to represent subjective time-preference and real market interest by the single numbers p and R. We are now in a position to investigate the way in which a change in R affects the consumption plan, and how the result depends on p. These results can be modified in applications if there is reason to believe that p and R do not remain constant over time.

Given the budget constraint, which depends only on $W(0)$ and R, and the utility function, the optimal quantity of consumption at each date is determined. Since the utility function is additive, the mrs between consumption at any two dates, say in periods 0 and 1, depends only on $C(0)$ and $C(1)$, so that we can draw a set of indifference curves for $C(0)$ and $C(1)$ which stay put even if $C(2),\ldots, C(T+1)$ change.

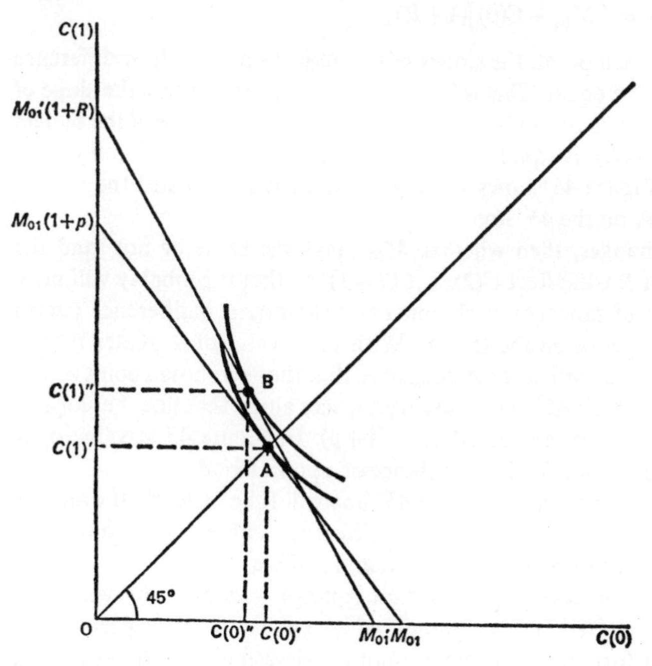

Figure 45

We saw earlier that when $C(0) = C(1)$, the mrs of $C(1)$ for $C(0)$ was λ_0/λ_1, which equals $1+p$. Thus on the 45° line in Figure 45, where $C(0) = C(1)$, all indifference curves have the slope $-(1+p)$. Let us begin our investigation by asking: At what real rate of interest R will the consumer choose equal quantities of $C(0)$ and $C(1)$? This can be determined only by considering the budget constraint.

With $C(2),\ldots, C(T+1)$ determined, let

$$M_{01} = W(0) - \frac{C(2)}{(1+R)^2} - \ldots - \frac{C(T+1)}{(1+R)^{T+1}}$$

be the amount of wealth allocated to $C(0)$ and $C(1)$. Then the budget constraint on $C(0)$ and $C(1)$ is

$$M_{01} = C(0)+\frac{C(1)}{1+R}$$

or $C(1) = [M_{01}-C(0)](1+R)$.

At the chosen point, the slopes of the budget line and the indifference curve will be equal. This will occur on the 45° line, where the slope of all indifference curves is $-(1+p)$, if and only if the slope of the budget line, $-(1+R)$, is equal to $-(1+p)$. Thus $C(0) = C(1)$ if and only if $R = p$. Figure 45 shows a budget line with $R = p$ and the chosen point at A on the 45° line.

If R changes, then whether M_{01} stays the same or not (and the change in R will affect $C(2),\ldots,C(T+1)$, so that it probably will not), the point of tangency with convex-to-the-origin indifference curves will no longer be on the 45° line. With a new value of R greater than p, the budget line will become steeper, so that the new chosen point will lie to the left of the 45° line, since everywhere along that line the slope of indifference curves is equal to $-(1+p)$. In Figure 45, a value of R greater than p will lead to the choice of a point like B.

But how far to the left of the 45° line will B lie? Clearly the answer depends on the shape of the indifference curves, and cannot be determined from a knowledge of R and p alone.

There is, however, an important concept – an elasticity which we have not yet used in this volume – which enables us (if we permit ourselves one further special assumption) to describe the optimal pattern of consumption over time in a very simple way. This is the *elasticity of substitution*, the most complex of elasticities. It measures the responsiveness of the *ratio* of two quantities to changes in the *ratio* of their prices. More precisely, when the quantities of two goods x_1 and x_2 alone change in such a way as to keep the individual on the same indifference curve, it is defined as

$$\eta = \frac{\Delta(x_1/x_2)}{x_1/x_2} \div \frac{\Delta[(\partial u/\partial x_2)\div(\partial u/\partial x_1)]}{(\partial u/\partial x_2)\div(\partial u/\partial x_1)},$$

the proportional change in the ratio of x_1 to x_2 divided by the proportional change in the ratio of the marginal utility of x_2 to that of x_1.

Three special cases are illustrated in Figure 12 on p. 44. In Figure 12(c) the ratio $(\partial u/\partial x_2)/(\partial u/\partial x_1)$, the mrs of x_1 for x_2, is not uniquely defined at the corner x. But it is clear that if the consumer were at x, the ratio of x_1 to x_2 would not change irrespective of what happened to the ratio of (positive) prices.[35] If we imagine smooth indifference curves for which the mrs is uniquely defined at x, it is clear that the more 'sharply bent' they are, and thus the more closely they approach the right-angled shape, the smaller is the change in the ratio x_1/x_2 corresponding to a given change in the mrs. As indifference curves approach the right-angled shape, this change in x_1/x_2, and therefore the elasticity of substitution, approaches zero, and it is conventional to say that $\eta = 0$ when they have the shape in figure 12(c).

In Figure 12(b) the mrs is constant as we move along the indifference curve. Thus changes occur in x_1/x_2 with no change in the MRS. To apply the definition of η in this case would necessitate division by

$$\Delta \frac{\partial u/\partial x_2}{\partial u/\partial x_1} = 0,$$

which is of course undefined. But we can say that as indifference curves approach linearity the elasticity of substitution approaches infinity, or loosely that for straight-line indifference curves $\eta = \infty$. In Figure 12(a), as x_1/x_2 *increases*, $(\partial u/\partial x_2)/(\partial u/\partial x_1)$ *decreases* so that η as we have defined it is negative. Negative elasticities of substitution are associated with concave-to-the-origin indifference curves.

The normal convex-to-the-origin indifference curve corresponds to a positive and finite value of η. Consider the following numerical example:

Period	x_1	x_2	$\frac{\partial u}{\partial x_1}$	$\frac{\partial u}{\partial x_2}$
0	20	50	2	4
1	30	40	1	5

35. This is of course true, for *some* changes in the price-ratio, whenever an indifference curve has a kink, as at x in Figure 10, p. 42.

Originally $x_1/x_2 = 20/50 = 0{\cdot}4$; it increases to $30/40 = 0{\cdot}75$, a proportional change of $(0{\cdot}75-0{\cdot}4)/0{\cdot}4 = +7/8$. Originally

$$\frac{\partial u/\partial x_2}{\partial u/\partial x_1} = \frac{4}{2} = 2;$$

it increases to 5, a proportional change of $(5-2)/2 = +3/2$. The elasticity of substitution is $7/8 \div 3/2 = 7/12$.

To return to $C(0)$ and $C(1)$. When the real rate of interest increases from p to R in Figure 45, the slope of the budget line changes from $-(1+p)$ to $-(1+R)$. In the budget constraint

$$C(1) = [M_{01}-C(0)](1+R),$$

$1+R$ can be thought of as the ratio of the price of a unit of $C(0)$ to the price of a unit of $C(1)$, by analogy with the budget constraint of section **4.1**,

$$M = p_1 x_1 + p_2 x_2, \qquad x_2 = \frac{M}{p_2} - \frac{p_1}{p_2} x_1.$$

Thus when the real rate of interest goes from p to R, the ratio of the price of $C(0)$ to that of $C(1)$ goes from $1+p$ to $1+R$, a proportional change of

$$\frac{(1+R)-(1+p)}{1+p} = \frac{R-p}{1+p}.$$

And since the price-ratio is equal to

$$\frac{\partial u/\partial C(0)}{\partial u/\partial C(1)}$$

before and after the change, $(R-p)/(1+p)$ is also the proportional change in the ratio of the marginal utilities.

When $C(0)$ and $C(1)$ change, in Figure 45, from $C(0)'$ and $C(1)'$ to $C(0)''$ and $C(1)''$, the proportional change in their ratio is

$$\frac{C(1)''/C(0)'' - C(1)'/C(0)'}{C(1)'/C(0)'}.$$

But since $C(1)'/C(0)' = 1$, this is equal to $C(1)''/C(0)''-1$. Thus if the points $[C(0)', C(1)']$ and $[C(0)'', C(1)'']$ were on the same indifference curve in figure 45, we could use the definition of the elasticity of substitution to deduce that

$$\eta = \frac{[C(1)''/C(0)''] - 1}{(R-p)/(1+p)}.$$

But if we assume (and this is our final assumption) that the elasticity of substitution between $C(0)$ and $C(1)$ is a constant of the utility function (like p), and is the same at all points on the $C(0)-(C1)$ indifference map (and on the indifference map between consumption at any two dates), the above expression for η is valid whether or not the two points are on the same indifference curve. (This, and other implications of this assumption, are shown in the Technical Appendix, Section **T.8**).

Finally, then, what does the expression for η above say? The term $C(1)''/C(0)''-1$ is equal to the proportional *rate of growth* of consumption from period 0 to period 1, since we define

$$g = \frac{C(1)'' - C(0)''}{C(0)''} = \frac{C(1)''}{C(0)''} - 1,$$

so that finally we obtain the (approximate) result

$$g = \frac{\eta(R-p)^{36}}{1+p}.$$

If, as we assume, η, R and p are constant over time, a similar argument can be made for any pair of adjacent periods, so that consumption will grow at a constant proportional rate over the consumer's lifetime. Alternatively, if η, R and p are 'social' rates assumed to hold indefinitely, g is the optimal social growth rate of consumption for ever. As may be seen by referring to Figure 45, g will be:

1. An increasing function of R; with given p and η, the greater R the greater will be the chosen ratio of $C(1)$ to $C(0)$.
2. An increasing function of η; with given R and p, a higher value of η leads to a higher ratio of C(1) to $C(0)$.

36. Since one is moving along an *arc* of an indifference curve, the formula is not always exact. It *is* exact, however, if $\eta = 1$, and if $\eta \neq 1$ it is very close if R and p are fairly small. For example, if $R = 5$ per cent and $p = 3$ per cent, the formula gives $g = 0{\cdot}97$ per cent if $\eta = \frac{1}{2}$ and 3·88 per cent if $\eta = 2$. The exact answers are 0·96 per cent and 3·92 per cent respectively.

3. A decreasing function of p; a higher value of p means that future consumption is (subjectively) discounted more heavily, so that with given R and η the consumer will wish consumption to grow less rapidly.

A brief final note on the ratio of consumption to 'normal income' in this model. Of course $Y(0)$ is defined by

$$\sum_{t=0}^{T} \frac{Y(0)}{(1+R)^t} = W(0).$$

As T becomes larger, the solution approaches more and more closely (if $R > 0$) to

$$Y(0) = \frac{R}{1+R} W(0).$$ [37]

Using the budget constraint, and the fact that consumption grows at the rate g from its initial value $C(0)$, we have

$$C(0) + C(0)\frac{1+g}{1+R} + \ldots + C(0)\left[\frac{1+g}{1+R}\right]^{T+1} = W(0).$$

If $R > g$ (and consumption certainly cannot grow indefinitely at the rate g unless this is the case, for if $R \leqslant g$, $W(0)$ would have to be infinite), then as T becomes larger the solution comes closer and closer (the proof is similar to that mentioned above) to

$$C(0) = \frac{R-g}{1+R} W(0).$$ [38]

Hence we have the approximate result

$$\frac{C(0)}{Y(0)} = \frac{R-g}{1+R} \div \frac{R}{1+R} = \frac{R-g}{R} = 1 - \frac{g}{R},$$

37. Refer to n.34 on p. 191 above, replacing r by R. If $R > 0$, then as $T \to \infty$,

$$\left(\frac{1}{1+R}\right)^{T+1} \to 0 \quad \text{and} \quad \left[1 - \left(\frac{1}{1+R}\right)^{T+1}\right] \to 1.$$

38. Again refer to n.34 on p. 191.

$$W(0) = C(0)\left[\frac{1-(1+g)/(1+R)^{T+1}}{1-(1+g)/(1+R)}\right],$$

and if $R > g$, the numerator of the expression multiplying $C(0) \to 1$ as $T \to \infty$. The denominator $= (R-g)/(1+R)$.

so that the ratio of savings $S(0) = Y(0) - C(0)$ to normal income is given by

$$\frac{S(0)}{Y(0)} = \frac{Y(0) - C(0)}{Y(0)} = 1 - \frac{C(0)}{Y(0)} = \frac{g}{R}.$$

Using the earlier (approximate) result that $g = \eta(R-p)/(1+p)$, we obtain

$$\frac{S(0)}{Y(0)} = \frac{\eta(R-p)}{R(1+p)} = \frac{\eta}{1+p}\left[1 - \frac{p}{R}\right]$$

The fraction of income saved is, like g, a decreasing function of p and an increasing function of η and R. This last implies that $S(0)/Y(0)$, like g, is an increasing function of the money rate of interest and a decreasing function of the rate of inflation.

In our survey of choice over time in this part of the book we have succeeded, for the most part, in keeping uncertainty out of the argument. In Part Five we recognize that the consumer does not hold expectations with certainty, and discuss how in these conditions his optimal choices are determined. But we cannot leave the discussion of time without digressing briefly to introduce the reader to Böhm-Bawerk's classic explanation of why (as we have assumed) rates of interest are normally positive.

12.5 Why is the rate of interest positive?

If this question is taken to refer to *money* rates of interest, the answer is fairly obvious. If the rate of interest on money were zero or negative, one would lend £100 at the beginning of one period and receive £100 or less in repayment at the beginning of the next. One could do as well or better by keeping the £100 and having it intact (apart from the risks of loss and theft) at the beginning of the next period. No one would lend money at a zero or negative rate of interest.

But the same argument cannot be used to show that the *real* rate of interest must be positive. If, for example, the money rate of interest is 3 per cent per annum and prices are expected to rise over the year by 5 per cent, the real rate of interest is (approximately) $3-5 = -2$ per cent. The only way in which one could earn a rate of return greater than this would be to buy goods now and store them, rather than to wait and buy them when their prices had risen by 5 per cent. But this cannot be done without cost – goods may spoil, and in any case it costs money to store them. Thus it may be that £100 spent now will buy, when storage costs and spoilage are allowed for, goods at the beginning of next period which are worth now only, say, £96: a real rate of return of −4 per cent.

Böhm-Bawerk argues, however, that there are three forces at work to make the real rate of interest positive. A simplified form of the argument is as follows. Consider a group of consumers who are identical in all respects. Each of them is interested only in his consumption in this period and the next, $C(0)$ and $C(1)$. No one has any assets other than his current earnings $E(0)$ and his earnings expected at the beginning of the next period, $E(1)$.

The key assumptions initially are (a) that for each individual, $E(0) = E(1)$; (b) that each individual's utility function is $u = f[C(0)]+f[C(1)]$, which is to say that $1/(1+p) = 1$ so that $p = 0$. Thus every consumer expects his earnings to remain constant, and the rate of time-preference is zero for everyone. (See Figure 46.)

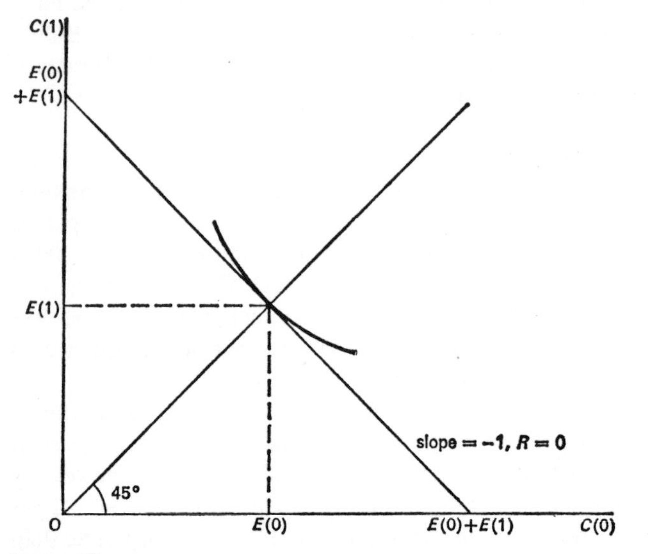

Figure 46

It follows that on the 45° line where $C(0) = C(1)$, the slope of all indifference curves is $-(1+p) = -1$. The budget line is given by

$$E(0)+\frac{E(1)}{1+R} = C(0)+\frac{C(1)}{1+R}.$$

What value of R will give *equilibrium*, which in this context means a position in which the total amount that would-be borrowers wish to borrow is equal to the total amount that would-be lenders wish to lend?

Suppose that $R > 0$. The budget line then has a slope of $-(1+R)$ and is therefore steeper than the indifference curves on the 45° line. Everyone will therefore wish to move to a point to the left of the 45° line where $C(0) < C(1)$. But since for each consumer $E(0) = E(1)$, he can do this only by saving a part of his current earnings equal to $E(0)-C(0)$, and lending it at the rate R. But since everyone in our model is alike, *everyone* will wish to lend and no one will wish to borrow. Thus there can be no equilibrium if $R > 0$.

Similarly if $R < 0$ everyone will wish to move to the right of the 45° line where $C(0) > C(1)$ by borrowing against his future earnings. But no one will wish to lend, so that there is no equilibrium where $R < 0$.

Thus, if there *is* an equilibrium, it must occur when $R = 0$. When $R = 0$, the slope of the budget line is equal to -1 and therefore touches an indifference curve on the 45° line where $C(0) = C(1)$. In this case, since $E(0) = E(1)$, the budget constraint implies that $C(0) = E(0)$ and $C(1) = E(1)$. Everyone wishes to consume exactly his earnings in each period, so that no one wishes to lend or borrow. Thus the total amounts which people wish to lend and borrow are equal because they are both zero. And therefore in this case $R = 0$ in equilibrium.

Now let us abandon our initial assumption (a), and assume that everyone expects his earnings to grow over time, so that $E(0) < E(1)$ We continue to assume that $p = 0$.

If $R = 0$ in this case, everyone will wish as before to consume equal amounts in the two periods. But since $E(0) < E(1)$ for everyone, this can be done only if everyone borrows against $E(1)$. (See figure 47.) Thus $R = 0$ cannot be an equilibrium. Equilibrium can be reached only if R rises from zero until everyone consumes $E(0)$ in the current period and $E(1)$ in the next period, so that the total amounts people wish to borrow and lend are, as before, both equal to zero and therefore to each other. This will occur only when the budget line is tangent to the indifference curve through the point $[E(0), E(1)]$. With convex indifference curves, if the slope is -1 when $C(0) = C(1)$, it must be steeper when $C(0) = E(0) < E(1) = C(1)$. This means that $1+R > 1$, so that $R > 0$.

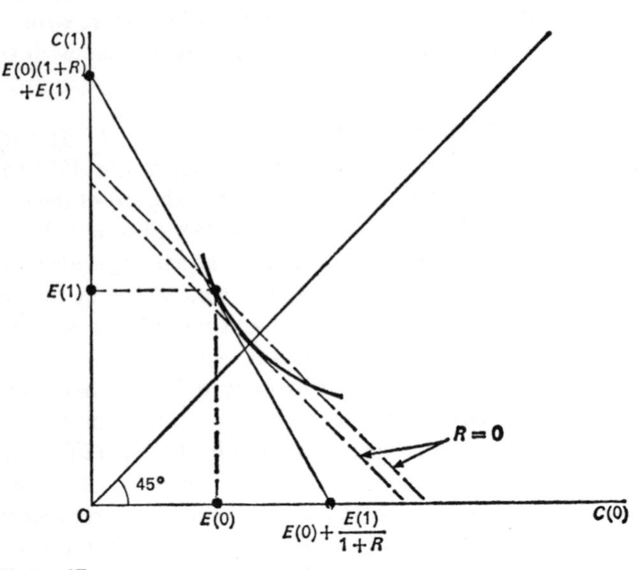

Figure 47

The expectation of earnings growing through time is the first of Böhm-Bawerk's three *Gründe* (reasons) for a positive rate of interest. Note that it is valid even when p (the rate of time-preference) is zero. His second reason is 'impatience' – the assumption that $p > 0$. To show that this reason operates independently of the first, let us abandon assumption (b) by assuming that $p > 0$, but restore assumption (a) – that $E(0) = E(1)$.

If $p > 0$, the slope of indifference curves on the 45° line, $-(1+p)$, is steeper than when $p = 0$ and the slope is -1. (See Figure 48.) Thus if $R = 0$, so that the budget line has the slope -1, everyone will wish to move to the right of the 45° line where $C(0) > C(1)$, and since $E(0) = E(1)$, everyone will have to borrow to make $C(0) > C(1)$.

Equilibrium can be reached only if R rises from 0 to a value at which everyone wishes to have $C(0) = E(0) = E(1) = C(1)$. In this case everyone will be on the 45° line, and the slope of the budget line $-(1+R)$ must equal the slope of indifference curves on the budget line, $-(1+p)$, that is, we must have $R = p > 0$.

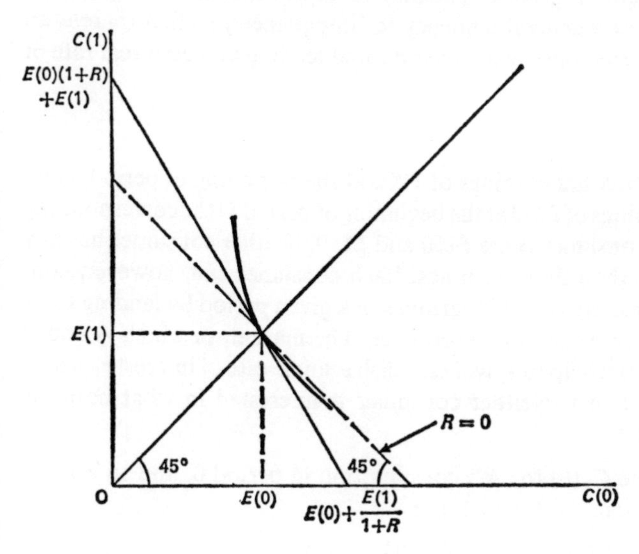

Figure 48

Clearly R will be greater than zero *a fortiori* if both of Böhm-Bawerk's first two reasons, $E(0) < E(1)$ and $p > 0$, are in effect. (His third reason involves production, and is based on the 'technical superiority of present over future goods'. If one can withdraw resources from the production of current consumption goods, reducing their output by one unit, and use the resources so released to increase the output of consumption goods next period by $1+c$ units, no one to whom this investment opportunity is open will lend money at a real rate of interest below c. If $c > 0$, present goods are 'technically superior' in the sense that one unit of current consumption goods can be transformed, as it were, into more than one unit of future consumption goods.)

It may seem strange to the reader that in the equilibria described in this section, desired borrowing and desired lending were both zero. This resulted from our assumption that consumers were alike in all respects. Differences in either tastes or endowments are necessary if mutually beneficial exchanges are to take place. But this homogeneity of consumers is not necessary for Böhm-Bawerk's argument. One needs only a general tendency to expect higher earnings in the future, and/or a general tendency to 'impatience', so that there is an excess of desired borrowing over desired lending at a zero real rate of interest.

Exercises

1. Consumer A has earnings of £200 at the beginning of period 0 and expects earnings of £250 at the beginning of period 1; the corresponding figures for consumer B are £150 and £150. Neither consumer has any assets other than these earnings. Each consumer can, however, consume less or more than his earnings in a given period by lending to or borrowing from the other consumer. The market, in which A and B are the only participants, will establish a single rate of interest r_0 which neither can affect. Neither consumer is interested in what happens after period 1.

If we write $C_A(0)$ for A's consumption in period 0, and so on, the utility functions of A and B are

$$u_A = C_A(0)\, C_A(1); \quad u_B = [C_B(0)]^2\, C_B(1).$$

(a) Write down the present value of each individual's wealth.

(Hint: In your answers to (a), (b) and (c), r_0 will appear as an unknown number.)

(b) Write down the budget constraint for each individual.

(c) Write down each individual's demand function for consumption in period 0.

(d) In order to *calculate* the equilibrium rate of interest, is it necessary to equate the demand for and supply of consumption in *each* year? Why or why not?

(e) Calculate the equilibrium rate of interest.

(f) In equilibrium, who borrows how much from whom?

2. (a) A consumer buys only x_1 and x_2. When p_1/p_2 falls, and his budget

is adjusted so that he remains on the same indifference curve, his demands change in such a way that $p_1 x_1/p_2 x_2$ is higher than before. Is the elasticity of substitution between x_1 and x_2 greater than, equal to or less than unity?

(b) What is the elasticity of substitution between x_1 and x_2 if the utility function is $u = x_1^2 x_2$?

Notes on the literature

A good survey of post-war consumption theories is M. J. Farrell, 'The new theories of the consumption function' (*Econ. J.*, vol. 69, no. 276, pp. 678–96, 1959).

12.2 The first critical view is to be found in R. H. Strotz, 'Myopia and inconsistency in dynamic utility maximization' (*Rev. econ. Stud.*, vol. 23, no. 3, pp. 165–80, 1955–56). Clower's latest contribution is R. W. Clower and M. Bruce Johnson, 'Income, wealth and the theory of consumption', in J. N. Wolfe (ed.), *Value, Capital and Growth: Papers in honour of Sir John Hicks* (Edinburgh University Press, 1968, pp. 45–96). A paper written from the same viewpoint is R. J. Ball and Pamela Drake, 'The relationship between aggregate consumption and wealth' (*Int. econ. Rev.*, vol. 5, no. 1, pp. 63–81, 1964). The results cited on p. 189 are to be found in these two papers.

12.3 Perhaps the most influential contribution has been the book by Milton Friedman, *Theory of the Consumption Function* (Princeton University Press, 1957); the quotation on p. 193 is from p. 28 of this work. Modigliani has been working with a similar model; see Albert Ando and Franco Modigliani, 'The life-cycle hypothesis of saving' (*Amer. econ. Rev.*, vol. 53, no. 1, pp. 55–74, 1963); the final equation in this section is a translation into our notation of one of the equations they test empirically.

12.4 I know of no full treatment of this subject which does not presuppose a knowledge of integral calculus and exponential functions. Readers so equipped will find a lucid treatment in Chapter 20 of J. R. Hicks, *Capital and Growth* (Oxford University Press, 1965); I would ask them to read in conjunction with this chapter my own 'Intertemporal utility and consumption' (*Oxf. econ. Pap.*, vol. 19, no. 1, pp. 111–15, 1963).

The proof that one cannot escape full additivity of the utility function by making an apparently weak independence assumption (see p. 195 of the text) is due to W. M. Gorman, 'Conditions for additive separability' (*Econometrica*, vol. 36, no. 3–4, pp. 605–9, 1968).

The geometric derivation of the rate of growth of consumption is based on pp. 75–8 of J. E. Meade, 'Life-cycle savings, inheritance and economic growth' (*Rev. econ. Stud.*, vol. 33, no. 1, pp. 61–78) (Meade assumes that $p = 0$).

12.5 Böhm-Bawerk's 'drei Gründe' are given in *The Positive Theory of Capital* (translated by G. D. Huncke as vol. 2 of Eugen von Böhm-Bawerk, *Capital and Interest*, Libertarian, 1959; see especially pp. 259–89).

Part Five
Uncertainty

Chapter 13
Uncertainty and Utility

13.1 Introduction

Many years ago Professor Knight made a distinction between 'uncertainty' and 'risk'. One is faced with a decision which will have one of a number of alternative outcomes. If there is sufficient experience of similar decisions for the 'probabilities' of the outcomes to be 'measurable', the situation is one of risk; if not, it is one of uncertainty.

Now probability, as many readers will be aware, is an extremely difficult concept, which we do not intend to examine in any depth. At this point we shall only remind the reader that, by convention, the probability of an event is a (real) number not less than zero nor greater than unity, and that given a set of events of which one (and only one) will occur, the sum of the probabilities of these events is equal to unity.

'Measurable' probability is not a well-defined notion, though it may be argued that the probability that a man aged 35 in good health living in Toronto will die before he is 40 is in some sense more 'measurable' than the probability that intelligent life exists on Mars. One test of 'measurability' is the ability to find someone who will set odds on the events in question, as life insurance companies do when they determine the relationship between premiums and benefits. The willingness of Lloyd's of London to insure virtually any well-defined 'risk' blurs this distinction somewhat – though of course there are many life insurance companies and only one Lloyd's.

The distinction between risk and uncertainty appears therefore to be a matter of degree only, and in most modern writings the terms are used interchangeably. There are, however, some economists (notably Shackle) who argue that the typical economic decision (e.g. the investment decision) has elements of uniqueness, or non-comparability with previous decisions, which make the concept of probability totally inapplicable. The great majority, while agreeing that the probabilities involved in most economic decisions are far removed from those implicit in life-tables, nonetheless find it useful to distinguish two types of determinant of a decision under uncertainty. First, there are the individual's preferences among the alternative outcomes (e.g. the alternative net rates of return in the case of an investment decision). Secondly, there are his beliefs, treated formally as *subjective* probabilities, as to how likely it is that each outcome will occur. It is this approach that we shall follow. (Though it appears difficult to measure an individual's subjective probabilities by observation or experiment, it is at least possible to formulate meaningful hypotheses about the influence on them of evidence available to him.)

This subject, and our approach to it, has a long history. Early in the eighteenth century Nicolas Bernoulli posed the following paradox (known as the *St Petersburg paradox* because of the long association of the Bernoulli family with that city):

> A tosses a coin in the air and B commits himself to give A one ducat if, at the first throw, the coin falls with its cross upward; 2 if it falls thus only at the second throw, 4 if at the third throw, 8 if at the fourth throw, etc.

As soon as the coin falls with the cross upward, the game is over. How much should A be prepared to pay in order to play the game? 'The paradox lies in the infinite sum which calculation yields as the equivalent which A must pay to B. This seems absurd since no reasonable man would be willing to pay 20 ducats as equivalent.'

The 'infinite sum' is the expected *money* value of the game, obtained by adding together the sums of money 1, 2, 4, 8,... ducats after each has been multiplied by the probability of receiving it. The probabilities that the first cross will appear at the first, second, third ... throw are easily seen to be $\frac{1}{2}$, $\frac{1}{4}$, $\frac{1}{8}$, ..., so that the expected money value of the game to A in ducats is

$$\tfrac{1}{2}\times 1+\tfrac{1}{4}\times 2+\tfrac{1}{8}\times 4+\tfrac{1}{16}\times 8+\ldots = \tfrac{1}{2}+\tfrac{1}{2}+\tfrac{1}{2}+\tfrac{1}{2}+\ldots,$$

which is infinite.

Of the many resolutions of this paradox which were proposed, the one which has had the greatest influence is that of Cramer: '*in their theory*, mathematicians evaluate money in proportion to its quantity while, *in practice*, people with common sense evaluate money in proportion to the utility they can gain from it.'

As we should now express it, Cramer is arguing that A must calculate the *expected utility* he will enjoy if he plays the game, i.e. (if $\overline{W}$ is his present wealth)

$$\tfrac{1}{2}u(\overline{W}+1)+\tfrac{1}{4}u(\overline{W}+2)+\tfrac{1}{8}u(\overline{W}+4)+\ldots.$$

Provided that the utility function is *bounded from above*, so that utility never exceeds a certain finite value no matter how large wealth becomes, the expected utility derived from this or any similar game will be finite. In that case expected utility will be equal to $u(\overline{W}+x)$, where x is some finite number of ducats, and x is therefore the maximum amount A should pay in order to play the game.

Daniel Bernoulli, Nicolas's cousin, proposed that utility be regarded as proportional to the *logarithm* of wealth, which increases without limit as wealth increases. While the expected utility is then finite for the original game with prizes 1, 2, 4, 8,..., it can be shown that a game can be constructed, with prizes increasing more rapidly, for which expected *utility* is infinite.

This is because, if utility is not bounded from above, one can find for any value of n, a sum of money x_n such that $u(\overline{W}+x_n) \geqslant 2^n$. If x_n is specified as the sum of money to be paid if the first cross appears at the $(n-1)$th throw, expected *utility* is (at least) $\frac{1}{2}\times1+\frac{1}{4}\times2+\frac{1}{8}\times4+\frac{1}{16}\times8+\ldots$, identical with the infinite *money* value of the original game in the text.

It may equally well be argued that utility is bounded from *below*, i.e. that it does not approach minus infinity as wealth approaches zero. For otherwise, consider a wealthy prisoner threatened with a form of torture which would deprive him of larger and larger fractions of his wealth (but never of his whole wealth) if the first cross did not appear until the second, third, ... throw of the coin. It his utility function were not bounded from below, an argument similar to that given earlier in this footnote would show that one could devise a torture with an expected utility of minus infinity. This would have the absurd implication that a multi-millionaire would rather surrender all but one penny of his wealth than be subject to such a torture. For further discussion of boundedness of the utility function see the Technical Appendix, section **T.8**.

13.2 The expected utility hypothesis: postulates

In introducing a utility-of-wealth function into the discussion of the St Petersburg paradox, we begged a number of questions. It will be recalled that in Chapter 6 we discussed the relationship between preference orderings and utility functions in the absence of uncertainty. When uncertainty is present, this relationship must be examined afresh.

The set of alternatives from which a choice must now be made, and on which a preference ordering is defined, is a set of *prospects*. Each prospect $(y, y', y'', \ldots)$ is defined by a number of *objects* $(x, x', x'', \ldots)$ – which may be sums of money, batches of goods, flows of consumption over time, etc., with the crucial feature that they are to be had with *certainty* – and associated *probabilities* $(\pi, \pi', \pi'', \ldots)$.

An example of a simple prospect is a bet with a probability of $\frac{1}{3}(=\pi)$ of winning £10 and a probability of $\frac{2}{3}(=1-\pi)$ of losing £5, i.e. of receiving $-$£5. Formally, we write this prospect as

$$y = (x, x'; \pi, 1-\pi) = (\overline{W}+£10, \overline{W}-£5; \tfrac{1}{3}, \tfrac{2}{3}),$$

with the objects written before the semi-colon and the probabilities after it in the same order as the objects with which they are associated.

A more complex prospect would be one with given probabilities of receiving the prospects y, y', each of which was of the type illustrated in the last paragraph, e.g.

$$\begin{aligned} y'' &= (y, y'; \pi'', 1-\pi'') \\ &= [(x, x'; \pi, 1-\pi), (x'', x'''; \pi', 1-\pi'); \pi'', 1-\pi'']. \end{aligned}$$

And obviously other prospects, both more and less complex, can be devised. Indeed, the expectation of receiving the object x with certainty can be regarded as a 'prospect', though one of a degenerate kind, $y = x = (x; 1)$.

The *expected utility hypothesis* may be stated as follows. For a given individual and any prospect – for example, $y''' = (y, y', y''; \pi, \pi', 1-\pi-\pi')$ – one can associate with each of the component prospects y, y', y'' a real number, $f(y), f(y'), f(y'')$. The *expected utility* of the prospect y''' can be obtained by adding together these numbers, after multiplying each by the probability associated with it, that is

$$\pi f(y) + \pi' f(y') + (1-\pi-\pi') f(y'').$$

Of any two prospects, the one with the higher expected utility as defined will stand higher in the preference ordering of the individual in question. (It is important to warn the reader that, as we shall see in the next section, this is not the *only* way in which expected utility may be defined.)

As we have stated the hypothesis, it clearly implies – since any of the prospects y, y', y'' may in fact be an object – the existence of what we shall call a *utility function* $u(x)$ defined on the objects $x, x', x'', \ldots$. And since every prospect involves objects, the reader can probably foresee that to calculate the expected utility of a very complex prospect it is necessary to take the utilities of the objects involved and to perform the operations of multiplication by probabilities and addition. But we shall not pause at this stage to explain all the details – they will, it is hoped, become clear as the argument proceeds.

Now economists have typically not been content simply to accept the expected utility hypothesis. They have asked a question similar to that raised in Chapter 6: what kind of preference ordering of prospects will ensure the existence of a utility function of objects such that the expected utility of prospects represents the preference ordering? The work of a number of mathematicians and economists – notably von Neumann and Morgenstern and Samuelson – has led to general agreement on a set of postulates which are sufficient (and seem also to be necessary) for the expected utility hypothesis to hold. We shall state and examine these postulates one by one.

The first two postulates arouse little controversy. The first is that the individual has a complete and transitive weak preference ordering on the set of prospects, and chooses rationally, as these terms were defined in Chapter 2 above. The second is that he will prefer a higher probability of a preferred prospect to a lower probability. Thus if he prefers the prospect y to the prospect y' (yPy'), and he is faced with the two complex prospects

$$y'' = (y, y'; \pi'', 1 - \pi'') \text{ and } y''' = (y, y'; \pi''', 1 - \pi''')$$

he will prefer y'' to y''' if and only if $\pi'' > \pi'''$ (i.e. if and only if the probability of receiving the preferred prospect y is higher in y'' than in y''').

The third postulate is one of continuity. Consider three prospects

y, y', y'' such that $yRy'Ry''$ (R and I have the meanings given to them in Chapter 2). Then there exists some probability π such that

$$(y, y''; \pi, 1-\pi)Iy'.$$

This simply says that if $yPy'Py''$, there is some probability-mix of the best and the worst of the three prospects that is indifferent to the one in the middle. We leave it to the reader to satisfy himself that in the other cases permitted by $yRy'Ry''$, the postulate is reasonable. If $yIy'Py''$, it is satisfied by $\pi = 1$, if $yPy'Iy''$, by $\pi = 0$, and if $yIy'Iy''$, by any value of π.

The following objection has been raised against this postulate by Alchian. If you prefer two candy bars (2c) to one candy bar (1c), and one candy bar to being shot in the head (S), is there any positive probability π of being shot in the head such that

$$(\mathrm{S}, 2c; \pi, 1-\pi)I(1c)?$$

I should answer that I should regard the second candy bar as compensation for the (positive) probability that someone in the middle of the Sahara desert firing a revolver in the direction of my head in Toronto would hit his target (if I were certain that no one but myself would be hurt thereby).

The remaining two postulates will be introduced in a moment. But first let us assume (this scarcely has the status of a postulate) that among the objects x, x', x'',... there is a best object $x^{(b)}$ (b for 'best' or 'bliss') and a worst object $x^{(w)}$ (w for 'worst' or 'woe'), and plenty of objects in between such that $x^{(b)}PxPx^{(w)}$, $x^{(b)}Px'Px^{(w)}$ and so on. By our third postulate there exist probabilities π_x, $\pi_{x'}$ such that

$$xI(x^{(b)}, x^{(w)}; \pi_x, 1-\pi_x) \quad \text{and} \quad x'I(x^{(b)}, x^{(w)}; \pi_{x'}, 1-\pi_{x'}).$$

Now consider the prospect

$$y = (x, x'; \pi, 1-\pi).$$

The fourth postulate (the 'strong independence' postulate) is that in any prospect (e.g. y), any component object or prospect (e.g. x) can be replaced by an object or prospect indifferent to it (e.g. $(x^{(b)}, x^{(w)}; \pi_x, 1-\pi_x)$), and the resulting prospect is indifferent to the prospect as it was before the replacement was made.

In our example, this implies that

$$y = (x, x'; \pi, 1-\pi) I [(x^{(b)}, x^{(w)}; \pi_x, 1-\pi_x), x'; \pi, 1-\pi]$$

and further that if we make a similar replacement for x'

$$y I [(x^{(b)}, x^{(w)}; \pi_x, 1-\pi_x), (x^{(b)}, x^{(w)}; \pi_{x'}, 1-\pi_{x'}); \pi, 1-\pi].$$

An objection to this postulate is illustrated by the following example. An individual may be indifferent between £200 for certain and a 50–50 chance of £0 and £500. Now consider two prospects y and y' (e.g. two lottery tickets) which are identical in all respects except that £200, with probability $\frac{1}{5}$, is a prize in y, and a 50–50 chance of £0 or £500, with probability $\frac{1}{5}$, is a prize in y'. The fourth postulate implies that the individual will be indifferent between y and y'. But some have been uneasy about this, arguing that since in y £200 is no longer certain, but a prize in a lottery, the former indifference between £200 and a 50–50 chance of £0 and £500 may be upset (Baumol).

In an attempt to cure this malaise, one should remind oneself that, with equal probabilities of $\frac{4}{5}$, the prospects y and y' will give the *same* prize. With equal probabilities of $\frac{1}{5}$, one will give £200 and the other (£0, £500; $\frac{1}{2}, \frac{1}{2}$), which we know to be indifferent. (£0, £500; $\frac{1}{2}, \frac{1}{2}$) remains more 'uncertain' than £200, as it was when the indifference between them was established. Is it reasonable to permit the presence of other prizes to upset this indifference?

The fifth postulate is that any complex prospect y involving the objects $x, x', x'', \ldots$ is indifferent to one of the form $(x, x', x'', \ldots; \pi, \pi', \pi'', \ldots)$, when the probabilities π, π', π'' are calculated by the usual rules for combining probabilities. The complex prospect which emerged from our earlier discussion will serve as an illustration,

$$y = [(x^{(b)}, x^{(w)}; \pi_x, 1-\pi_x), (x^{(b)}, x^{(w)}; \pi_{x'}, 1-\pi_{x'}); \pi, 1-\pi].$$

The only objects involved are $x^{(b)}$ and $x^{(w)}$. What is the probability of $x^{(b)}$ in y? It is the probability π of $(x^{(b)}, x^{(w)}; \pi_x, 1-\pi_x)$ times the probability π_x of $x^{(b)}$ in $(x^{(b)}, x^{(w)}; \pi_x, 1-\pi_x)$, plus the probability $1-\pi$ of $(x^{(b)}, x^{(w)}; \pi_{x'}, 1-\pi_{x'})$ times the probability $\pi_{x'}$ of $x^{(b)}$ in $(x^{(b)}, x^{(w)}; \pi_{x'}, 1-\pi_{x'})$. That is, the probability of $x^{(b)}$ is $\pi\pi_x + (1-\pi)\pi_{x'}$. Similarly, the probability of $x^{(w)}$ is $\pi(1-\pi_x)+(1-\pi)(1-\pi_{x'})$. The fifth postulate therefore implies that

$$y I [x^{(b)}, x^{(w)}; \pi\pi_x + (1-\pi)\pi_{x'}, \pi(1-\pi_x)+(1-\pi)(1-\pi_{x'})].$$

An awkward question relating to the fifth postulate is: why do slot machines have three spinning wheels? Why are the wheels not covered so that one simply pulls the handle and waits to see what comes out of the machine? 'Does seeing the wheels go round, or seeing how close one comes to winning, affect the desirability?' (Alchian) It is impossible to avoid an affirmative answer. But here the context is one of what has been called 'pleasure-oriented' gambling. It seems likely than in more strictly 'wealth-oriented' decisions, considerations analogous to the excitement of seeing the wheels spin would be relatively less important. (We shall meet this distinction again in section **14.1** below.)

The objections which have been raised against the fourth and fifth postulates raise an interesting question. Are they to be regarded as prescriptions as to how one *should* behave, or descriptions of how one *does* behave? It seems to me that violations of the fourth postulate are apt to be the result of insufficient reflection, and violations of the fifth result from attaching weight to certain aspects of the *process* whereby the final outcome is determined. In important 'wealth-oriented' activities, one would expect that violations of these postulates would be relatively uncommon.

This view is implicit, at least, in the work of those who have taken the expected utility hypothesis as the basis of their work on choice under uncertainty. The proof that our five postulates imply the expected utility hypothesis is lengthy and of technical interest only, and is relegated to the Technical Appendix, Section **T.9**. The result is that for any individual who obeys the five postulates, there exists a set of real numbers $u(x), u(x'), u(x''),\ldots$ such that given any two prospects, e.g. $y = (x, x'; \pi, 1-\pi)$ and $y' = (x'', x'''; \pi', 1-\pi'){:}\,yRy'$ if and only if $\pi u(x)+(1-\pi)u(x') \geqslant \pi' u(x'')+(1-\pi')u(x''')$.

13.3 Cardinal and ordinal utility

In section **6.4** we found that if a particular utility function $u(x_1, x_2,\ldots, x_n)$ represented a preference ordering of batches of goods from which a choice was to be made in conditions of *certainty*, *any* increasing function of the function $u(\;)$ would represent the same preference ordering. Is it true that the utility function $u(x)$, where the x are *objects*, referred to at the end of section **13.2**, can similarly be replaced by *any* increasing function of itself, and that expected utilities of prospects calculated from this new function, say $u^*(x)$, will represent the same preference ordering of *uncertain* prospects as $u(x)$?

It can easily be shown that the answer is no. Consider any three objects x, x' and x'' such that in a particular preference ordering $xPx'Px''$. Then by the third postulate there is a probability π such that $(x, x''; \pi, 1-\pi)Ix'$. Then if u, u^* are any two utility functions, defined on objects, which can be used to calculate expected utilities which will rank prospects according to the preference ordering, it must be the case that both

$$\pi u(x)+(1-\pi)u(x'') = u(x')$$

and $\pi u^*(x)+(1-\pi)u^*(x'') = u^*(x')$,

so that

$$u(x')-u(x'') = \pi[u(x)-u(x'')]$$

and $u^*(x')-u^*(x'') = \pi[u^*(x)-u^*(x'')]$,

and therefore

$$\frac{u(x')-u(x'')}{u^*(x')-u^*(x'')} = \frac{u(x)-u(x'')}{u^*(x)-u^*(x'')}.$$

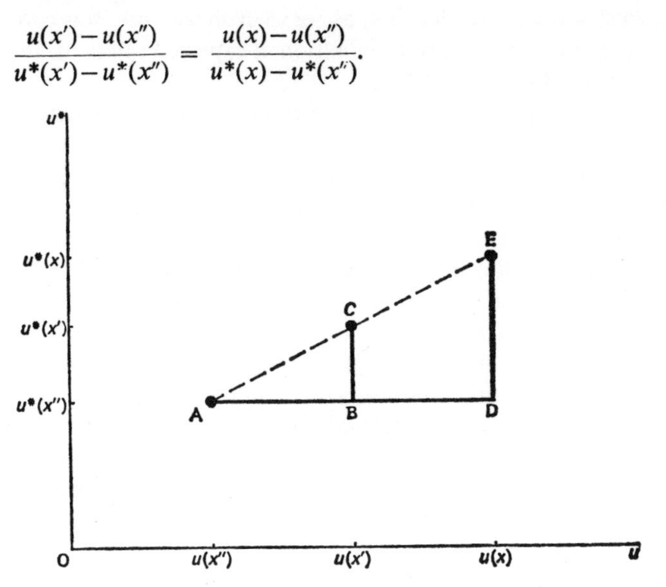

Figure 49

In Figure 49 we plot values of the function u on the horizontal axis and values of u^* on the vertical axis. It may be easily seen that if the condition at the end of the last paragraph is to be satisfied, the three points $[u(x), u^*(x)]$, $[u(x'), u^*(x')]$ and $[u(x''), u^*(x'')]$ must lie on a *straight line*. For only then can

$$\frac{u(x')-u(x'')}{u^*(x')-u^*(x'')} = \frac{\text{AB}}{\text{BC}}$$

be equal to

$$\frac{u(x)-u(x'')}{u^*(x)-u^*(x'')} = \frac{\text{AD}}{\text{DE}}.$$

We have shown that u^* must be not only an increasing function of u, but an *increasing linear* function of u; any two such utility functions of objects leading to expected utilities of prospects which rank them in the same way must be related as follows,

$$u^* = a+bu \quad (b > 0).$$

(But we must warn the reader that, as we shall shortly see, this conclusion depends on the (additive) definition of expected utility as, for example, $\pi u(x)+(1-\pi)u(x'')$.)

Now in the case of choice under certainty, where any strictly increasing function of a given utility function preserves the same preference ordering of bundles of goods, utility is said to be *ordinal*; the utility numbers attached to the bundles of goods are required only to keep them in the same *order*. The term *cardinal utility* is commonly (though not universally) used for cases like that just described, in which any acceptable utility function must preserve not only the preference ordering of objects, but also the *ratios* of *differences* between the utilities of objects; in the example above, the utility of x' minus that of x'' must equal π times the utility of x minus that of x''.

This restriction on the set of acceptable alternative utility functions which implies, as we have seen, that any two utility functions must be increasing linear transformations of each other, makes 'cardinal utility' a measure like that of temperature. Given a centigrade temperature scale, only an increasing linear function of centigrade temperatures (e.g. Fahrenheit, defined by $F = 32+\frac{9}{5}C$ or Réaumur, defined by $R = 0+\frac{4}{5}C$) is acceptable. In such a linear transformation (e.g. $u^* = a+bu$) the origin a and the scale b can be chosen arbitrarily (provided that $b > 0$).

Some authors appear to interpret cardinal utility as meaning that the utility of a particular object or bundle of goods is, say, 10, no more and no less, with no nonsense about 'transformations'. Others think of it as a measure with a well-defined zero, so that in the transformation $u^* = a+bu$ the origin $a = 0$, and we have an increasing *proportional* transformation. On this view if $u(x) = 4$ and $u^*(x) = 8 = 2u(x)$, then if $u(x') = 10$ we must have $u^*(x') = 2u(x') = 20$; in this example $b = 2$. Cardinal utility on this interpretation would be like weight (weight in kilogrammes = 2·2 times weight in pounds) or distance (distance in inches = 39·37 times distance in metres). But the definition of cardinal utility given in this book is by far the most common.

It is very important to be clear at this point what cardinal utility does *not* mean. Let us suppose that in the example of the earlier part of this section x is £8, x' is £4, x'' is £2 and $\pi = \frac{1}{2}$. Then

$$\tfrac{1}{2}u(£8)+\tfrac{1}{2}u(£2) = u(£4),$$

$$\tfrac{1}{2}u(£8)-\tfrac{1}{2}u(£4) = \tfrac{1}{2}u(£4)-\tfrac{1}{2}u(£2)$$

and therefore $u(£8)-\mathrm{u}(£4) = u(£4)-u(£2)$

This says that u increases by exactly as much when wealth goes from £4 to £8 as when it goes from £2 to £4. We have deduced from observing a consumer's preferences between alternative prospects that two utility differences, $u(£8)-u(£4)$ and $u(£4)-u(£2)$ are equal, and indeed that the marginal utility of wealth for this consumer diminishes as his wealth increases, since clearly if $u(£8)-u(£4) = u(£4)-u(£2)$, then

$$\frac{u(£8)-u(£4)}{£8-£4} = \frac{u(£8)-u(£4)}{£4} < \frac{u(£4)-u(£2)}{£4-£2} = \frac{u(£4)-u(£2)}{£2}.$$

Does this mean that observation of choices under uncertainty permits us to look into the consumer's mind and *compare changes* in the amounts of satisfaction he enjoys, as observation of his choices under certainty did not? The answer to this is a resounding 'no'.

We have argued that by observing a consumer's choices under uncertainty, on the assumption that he obeys the five postulates of section **13.2**, we can represent his preference ordering of prospects by a set of expected utility numbers $E(y)$, where if, for example, $y = (x, x''; \pi, 1-\pi)$

$$E(y) = \pi u(x)+(1-\pi)u(x'').$$

Now it is true that when expected utility is defined in this way, diminishing marginal utility of wealth has observable implications. But the behaviour of the marginal utility of wealth is deduced purely from the observation of behaviour and is *not* derived from a direct comparison of the consumer's mental states; nor is it to be taken as an indication that a pound adds less to the individual's subjective satisfaction when he is rich than when he is poor.

I know that many readers will find this argument difficult to accept, and an attempt must be made to convince them. It will be recalled that in section **6.4** it was shown that in conditions of certainty, the same preference ordering of bundles of goods could be represented by any one of three utility functions, $+\sqrt{(x_1 x_2)}$, $x_1 x_2$ and $x_2^2 x_2^2$, and that the marginal utility of each good was decreasing for the first function, constant for the second, and increasing for the third. We concluded that the behaviour of marginal utility was, *in general*, quite irrelevant to the nature of the preference ordering or therefore to the consumer's behaviour. But in section **6.5** we showed that if we made the *special* assumption that the utility function was *additive*, e.g. $u = f_1(x_1)+f_2(x_2)$, then diminishing marginal utility of each good had observable implications, namely that indifference curves were convex to the origin and all goods were normal.

Now if the reader looks at the definition of expected utility, $E(y) = \pi\, u(x)+(1-\pi)u(x'')$, he will notice that this is in additive form. And if, with expected utility defined in this way, we find that the consumer is indifferent between £4 and the prospect (£8, £2; $\frac{1}{2}$, $\frac{1}{2}$) we conclude, as above, that the marginal utility of wealth is diminishing to him.

But the fact that we *can* use expected utility, defined in this additive manner, to represent the preference ordering of prospects, does not imply that we *must* define expected utility in this additive way. We are interested only in preserving the preference ordering of prospects, and for this purpose *any increasing function* of the *expected* utility function $E(y)$ is acceptable.

Let us replace the expected utility function $E(y)$ above, for example, by the function

$$E^*(y) = 10^{E(y)} = 10^{\pi u(x)+(1-\pi)u(x'')},$$

which is a strictly increasing function of $E(y)$. Then by the familiar rules of exponents

$$E^*(y) = [10^{u(x)}]^{\pi}[10^{u(x'')}]^{1-\pi}.$$

There is no reason in the world why we should not use the function $E^*(y)$ to rank prospects, since it will rank them in exactly the same way as $E(y)$. And there is also no reason why we should not define a corresponding new utility function $v(x)$ for objects, namely

$$v(x) = 10^{u(x)}.$$

Though $v(x)$ is clearly not a *linear* function of $u(x)$, this does not matter because we are no longer defining expected utility additively. Our earlier argument that u^* must equal $a+bu$ was based on the definition of $E(y)$ as $\pi u(x)+(1-\pi)u(x'')$. With our new definition, however, expected utility is

$$E^*(y) = [v(x)]^{\pi}[v(x'')]^{1-\pi}.$$

Expected utility is no longer obtained by *multiplying* utilities by their probabilities and *adding*, but by raising each utility to a *power* equal to its probability and *multiplying*. To repeat, this procedure gives precisely the same preference ordering of prospects as the additive definition of $E(y)$.

Now, to revert to our earlier numerical example, let us see what becomes of our conclusion that if

$$y = (x, x''; \pi, 1-\pi) = (£8, £2; \tfrac{1}{2}, \tfrac{1}{2})$$

is indifferent to £4 for certain, the marginal utility of wealth must be diminishing. Suppose that in that example $u(x) = \log_{10}x$. This fits the case, since

$$E(y) = \tfrac{1}{2}\log_{10} 8+\tfrac{1}{2}\log_{10} 2 = \tfrac{1}{2}\log_{10} 16 = \log_{10} 4.$$

In calculating $E^*(y)$, we note first that $v(8) = 10^{u(8)} = 10^{\log_{10} 8}$ which, by the definition of a logarithm, is equal to 8. Similarly $v(4) = 4$ and $v(2) = 2$. Thus

$$E^*(y) = 8^{1/2}\times 2^{1/2} = 4 = v(4).$$

This simply confirms that (£8, £2; $\frac{1}{2}$, $\frac{1}{2}$), which gives an expected utility $E(y)$ equal to $u(4)$, also gives an expected utility defined as $E^*(y)$ equal to $v(4)$.

But if we use the utility function of objects $v(x)$ which is appropriate to expected utility defined as $E^*(y)$, we find that

$$\frac{v(8)-v(4)}{8-4} = \frac{8-4}{8-4} = 1 = \frac{4-2}{4-2} = \frac{v(4)-v(2)}{4-2},$$

and the marginal utility of wealth remains *constant* as wealth goes from 2 to 4 and from 4 to 8.

Let us summarize this argument. A preference ordering of prospects can, given the postulates of section **13.2**, be represented by a set of numbers called the expected utilities of those prospects. It is usual and convenient to define expected utility additively, that is, as $E(y) = \pi u(x)+(1-\pi)u(x'')$. But it is also possible to define expected utility in other ways, for example as $E^*(y) = [v(x)]^{\pi}[v(x'')]^{1-\pi}$, provided that $E^*(y)$ is any strictly increasing function of $E(y)$. Since, as we have shown, a given set of preferences or choices can imply diminishing marginal utility of wealth when the utility of objects is measured by $u(x)$, but a constant marginal utility of wealth in terms of $v(x)$, it follows that no observation of choices under uncertainty can justify the conclusion that changes in a consumer's level of subjective satisfaction can be compared. If satisfaction appears to be increasing at a decreasing rate as wealth increases, this is only because of a purely arbitrary decision as to how expected utility is to be defined.

13.4 Risk-aversion and risk-preference

Despite our argument in the last section that the additive definition of expected utility is not the only acceptable definition, it is by far the most convenient definition, and the one we shall use henceforth. In applying the expected utility hypothesis, as it has been most commonly applied, to cases in which the objects x, x', x'' are quantities of wealth, we shall write the utility of wealth as $u(W)$, and assume that more wealth is preferred to less, so that the marginal utility of wealth to the consumer is positive: $du/dW = u'(W) > 0$. We shall discover that, with the additive definition of expected utility, the distinction between increasing and diminishing marginal utility of wealth has important implications for behaviour under uncertainty.

Let us begin by distinguishing three kinds of *bet* or *gamble*. In a betting situation a consumer is faced with a choice between a certain quantity of wealth $\overline{W}$ if he does not bet and an uncertain prospect $(W', W''; \pi, 1-\pi)$ if he does. The bet is said to be *favourable*, *fair* or *unfavourable* as the expected money value of the uncertain prospect is greater than, equal to or less than $\overline{W}$. That is, the bet is

$$\left.\begin{matrix}\text{favourable}\\ \text{fair}\\ \text{unfavourable}\end{matrix}\right\} \text{if } \pi W' + (1-\pi)W'' \begin{Bmatrix} > \\ = \\ < \end{Bmatrix} \overline{W}.$$

The reader can easily verify, for example, that if $\overline{W} = 10$ and $W' = 11$, the bet is fair if $\pi = \frac{1}{2}$ and $W'' = 9$, favourable if $\pi = \frac{3}{4}$ and $W'' = 8$, unfavourable if $\pi = \frac{2}{3}$ and $W'' = 7$.

A consumer is said to display *risk-aversion* if he rejects a fair bet and to display *risk-preference* if he accepts a fair bet.

Given these two sets of definitions, it is not difficult to relate risk-aversion and risk-preference to the shape of the utility-of-wealth function $u(W)$. Suppose that a consumer with wealth of £10 is invited to toss a fair coin: if it comes down heads, he wins £1, if tails, he loses £1. The uncertain prospect is $(£11, £9; \frac{1}{2}, \frac{1}{2})$ and clearly the bet is fair. Will he accept the bet?

In a utility-of-wealth diagram (Figure 50), plot the points $u(9)$ and $u(11)$. The fact that utility is cardinal as defined in the last section, so that the origin and scale of the utility function can be selected arbitrarily, also implies that the utilities of *any two* objects (in this case, any two quantities of wealth) can be selected arbitrarily. Thus we can make $u(9)$ and $u(11)$ what we like (so long as $u(11) > u(9)$, since the marginal utility of wealth is positive). But once we have selected $u(9)$ and $u(11)$, the utility of every other amount of wealth is uniquely determined by the consumer's preference ordering of prospects.

Given $u(9)$ and $u(11)$, and that $\pi = 1-\pi = \frac{1}{2}$, we can plot the expected utility of the prospect the consumer faces if he accepts the bet. It equals $\frac{1}{2}u(9)+\frac{1}{2}u(11)$, the height above the W-axis of the midpoint E of the straight line joining the points D and F. The point E lies directly above the point on the W-axis representing $\overline{W} = 10$, the amount of wealth that the consumer will have for certain if he rejects the bet; this is because the bet is a fair one. (If the choice were between $(11, 9; \frac{1}{2}, \frac{1}{2})$ and $\overline{W} = 9\frac{1}{2}$, the bet would be favourable, while if $\overline{W} = 10\frac{1}{2}$ it would be unfavourable, and a vertical line through E would cut the W-axis to the right or to the left of W respectively.)

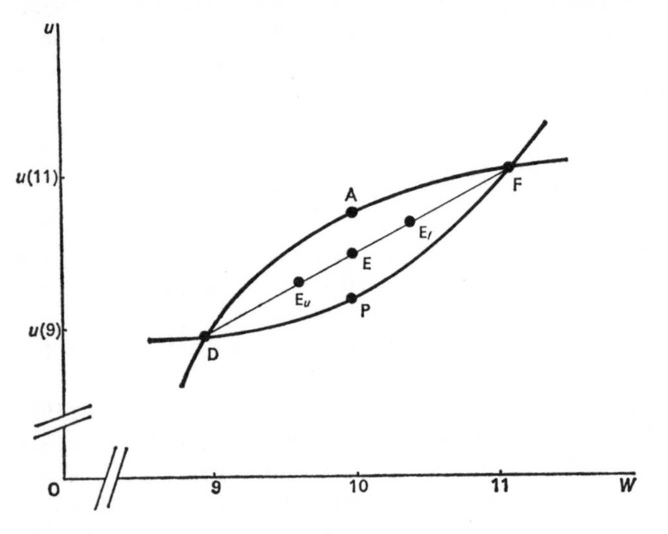

Figure 50

He will accept the bet, thus displaying risk-preference, if the utility of 10 units of wealth is represented by a point like P which lies below E, so that $u(10) < \frac{1}{2}u(9)+\frac{1}{2}u(11)$. He will reject the bet, displaying risk-aversion, if the utility of 10 units of wealth is represented by A, which lies above E. It is clear from the diagram that he will accept the bet if

$u(11)-u(10) > u(10)-u(9)$

and reject it if

$u(11)-u(10) < u(10)-u(9)$.

If we draw a smooth curve through the points D, P and F, its slope $u'(W)$ increases as wealth increases; the slope of DAF decreases as wealth increases. Thus increasing marginal utility of wealth implies the acceptance of fair bets and risk-preference; diminishing marginal utility of wealth implies the rejection of fair bets and risk-aversion.

What if the utility-of-wealth curve passes through the point E itself?

The consumer is then indifferent between acceptance and rejection of the bet. But will he accept it or reject it? The expected utility hypothesis gives no answer; his choice must be explained in some other way. This small but troublesome point can perhaps be resolved as follows. We distinguish three types of action when a consumer is offered a bet; he accepts it, he rejects it, or he adopts some procedure (e.g. tossing a coin) to determine his choice in the sole case where $\frac{1}{2}u(9)+\frac{1}{2}u(11) = u(10)$, i.e. when the utility of wealth curve passes through E. If we reserve the terms 'accept' and 'reject' for the first two cases, we can say that increasing marginal utility not only implies but is also implied by the acceptance of a fair bet, so that increasing marginal utility is equivalent to risk-preference, and similarly decreasing marginal utility is equivalent to risk-aversion.

In Figure 50, any bet resulting in a prospect $(11, 9; \pi, 1-\pi)$ in which $\pi < \frac{1}{2}$ would be unfavourable, and its expected utility would be represented by a point like E_u on DEF to the left of E. It is clear that a risk-averter will reject an unfavourable bet (since A lies above E, it must lie above E_u) while anyone who accepts an unfavourable bet displays risk-preference (since acceptance would mean that P lay below E_u and therefore below E). Similarly the expected utility of a favourable bet ($\pi > \frac{1}{2}$) would be represented by a point like E_f; a consumer who displays risk-preference will accept a favourable bet (P lies below E and therefore below E_f), and a consumer who rejects it must be a risk-averter (A then lies above E_f and therefore above E).

The foregoing argument has been concerned only with very simple bets. What if the choice is between $\overline{W}$ if the consumer does not bet and $(W', W'', W''', W''''; \pi', \pi'', \pi''', 1-\pi'-\pi''-\pi''')$ if he does? It is shown in the Technical Appendix (section **T.10**) that most of the relationships established above between the behaviour of the marginal utility of wealth and attitudes to risk continue to hold in more complex cases.

Exercises

1. Consider the following gamble. You draw a card from a pack (deck). If the card is a spade, a coin is tossed, and you win £1 if it comes down heads and lose £1 if it comes down tails. If the card is a heart, a diamond or a club, a die is rolled, and you win £1 if it lands with 5 or 6 uppermost and lose £1 if it lands with 1, 2, 3 or 4 uppermost.

Your present wealth is £$\overline{W}$. Write down the simplest prospect indifferent to the one you face if you accept the gamble, assuming that you obey all the postulates of section **13.2**.

2. Is the gamble in question 1 favourable, fair or unfavourable?

3. If in your utility function $u(\overline{W}-1) = 10, u(\overline{W}) = 12, u(\overline{W}+1) = 15$, do you display risk-aversion or risk-preference over this range of wealth? (Assume in this question and the next two that expected utility is defined in the usual additive way.)

4. If an alternative utility function which gave the same ranking of prospects as that in question 3 had $u^*(\overline{W}) = 5, u^*(\overline{W}+1) = 20$, what would be $u^*(\overline{W}-1)$?

5. If your utility function is as in question 3 or 4, will you accept or reject the gamble in question 1?

Notes on the literature

The most useful general readings on the subject-matter of this chapter are Baumol (*Economic Theory and Operations Analysis*, ch. 22), and A. A. Alchian, 'The meaning of utility measurement' (*Amer. econ. Rev.*, vol. 43, no. 1, pp. 26–50, 1953), reprinted in W. Breit and H. M. Hochman (eds.), *Readings in Microeconomics* (pp. 69–88). For this chapter and the next, read also the first six chapters of K. H. Borch, *The Economics of Uncertainty*, (Princeton University Press, 1968).

13.1 *Risk, Uncertainty and Profit* by Frank H. Knight, (Harper & Row, 1921), is the classic work on this topic. A representative work by G. L. S. Shackle is his *Expectation in Economics* (Cambridge University Press, 1949). A good discussion of probability, related to choice under uncertainty, is to be found in Chapter 2 of S. A. Ozga, *Expectations in Economic Theory* (Weidenfeld & Nicolson, 1965). The source of the St. Petersburg Paradox is a paper in Latin by Daniel Bernoulli, translated by Louise Sommer as 'Exposition of a new theory on the measurement of risk' (*Econometrica*, vol. 22, no. 1, pp. 23–36, 1954) quoted on pp. 214–15. A good survey of early work in this area is K. J. Arrow, 'Alternative approaches to the theory of choice in risk-taking situations' (*Econometrica*, vol. 19, no. 4, pp. 404–37, 1951). He attributes (p. 421) to Karl Menger the argument (in small type on p. 215 above) that utility must be bounded from *above*.

13.2 The postulates proposed by J. von Neumann and O. Morgenstern in their *Theory of Games and Economic Behaviour* (Wiley, 2nd edn, 1947, pp. 26–9, 617–32), were completed by Samuelson's 'strong independence' postulate (our fourth postulate). See his two papers 'Utility, preference and probability' and 'Probability, utility, and the independence axiom' (the latter is in *Econometrica*, Oct. 1952, pp. 670–78), reprinted in J. E. Stiglitz (ed.), *The Collected Scientific Papers of Paul A. Samuelson*, (pp. 127–45). The objections in the text to our third and fifth postulates are from Alchian (*op. cit.*, pp. 77–8) and to our fourth from Baumol (*op. cit.*, p. 522).

13.3 Support for our argument that 'diminishing marginal utility' under uncertainty has nothing to do with diminishing increments of subjective satisfaction will be found in Baumol (*op. cit.*, pp. 523–4) and in D. Ellsberg, 'Classic and current notions of measurable utility' (*Econ. J.*, vol. 64, no. 255, pp. 528–56). Neither of them, however, argues in terms of our non-additive definition $E^*(y)$ of expected utility, which I think is quite conclusive.

Chapter 14
Uncertainty and the Consumer

14.1 Insurance and lotteries

One of the earliest applications of the theory discussed in Chapter 13 to the behaviour of consumers was the attempt by Friedman and Savage to deduce the shape of the typical utility-of-wealth curve from the observed behaviour of consumers. They made use of three pieces of evidence.

First, it was observed that most people with moderately low levels of income and wealth insure their property against the risk of fire and other disasters. To take a simple illustrative example, suppose that each of 100 people owns property worth £1000, and that it is known with certainty that one of these pieces of property will be completely destroyed by fire in the course of a year, but not which one. If each of the 100 property owners contributes £10 a year to an insurance fund, the fund will amount to £1000, enough to compensate fully the one unfortunate owner. But in fact the administration of such an insurance fund will involve costs, and if the operation is performed by an insurance company the premium charged will exceed £10; it will be, say, £10+ c, where c is the cost charged to each person by the company to cover its expenses.

If the current wealth of the property owner is $\overline{W}$, the alternatives he faces are as follows:

If he insures his property, he will have his current wealth less the insurance premium, namely $\overline{W}-10-c$. If he does not insure, there is a probability of 1/100 that his wealth will be reduced by £1000 through destruction of his property. Thus the prospect he faces is: $(\overline{W}, \overline{W}-1000; 99/100, 1/100)$. Its expected money value is

$$\tfrac{99}{100}\overline{W}+\tfrac{1}{100}(\overline{W}-1000) = \overline{W}-10.$$

According to the definitions in section **13.4**, *not* to insure his property is a gamble. The expected money value of his wealth if he accepts the gamble, $\overline{W}-10$, is greater than the certain amount of wealth he will have if he insures his property, $\overline{W}-10-c$. The gamble is therefore a favourable one. If he insures his property, he is therefore rejecting a favourable gamble. And this, as was pointed out at the end of section **13.4**, implies risk-aversion and decreasing marginal utility of wealth.

Second, it was observed that most people (of moderately low income and wealth) buy lottery tickets. If each of 100 people pays £10 for a ticket in a lottery with a single prize of £1000, the proceeds of ticket sales are sufficient to award the prize. But the administration of a lottery involves costs, so that the price of a ticket will exceed £10; it will be, say £10+c. In considering whether to buy a lottery ticket, each individual faces the following alternatives:

If he does not buy a ticket, he retains his current wealth $\overline{W}$. If he buys a ticket and knows that 100 tickets will be sold his probability of winning is 1/100, and the prospect is

$$(\overline{W}-10-c,\ \overline{W}-10-c+1000;\ 99/100,\ 1/100),$$

with expected money value

$$\tfrac{99}{100}(\overline{W}-10-c)+\tfrac{1}{100}(\overline{W}-10-c+1000) = \overline{W}-c.$$

Since the expected money value of the individual's wealth if he accepts the gamble, $\overline{W}-c$, is less than $\overline{W}$, the gamble is unfavourable. To buy a lottery ticket is therefore to accept an unfavourable bet, which implies (see section **13.4**) risk-preference and increasing marginal utility of wealth.

Thus the purchase of insurance implies risk-aversion while the purchase of lottery tickets implies risk-preference. These two types of behaviour can be reconciled in a single utility-of-wealth function if we bear in mind that in the insurance decision the consumer is contemplating a substantial *reduction* in his wealth if his property is destroyed, while in the lottery decision he contemplates a substantial *increase* in his wealth if he holds the winning ticket. It is quite consistent, therefore, that the marginal utility of wealth should be diminishing for levels of wealth below $\overline{W}$ and increasing (at least for some distance) for levels of wealth above $\overline{W}$. This is depicted in Figure 51.

Now Friedman and Savage do *not* say that, since most people buy both insurance and lottery tickets, the typical utility-of-wealth curve has an inflexion point (in this case, a point where the slope of the curve stops decreasing and starts increasing) at the consumer's current level of wealth, $\overline{W}$. The foregoing analysis applies 'solely to the behaviour of relatively low-income consumer units'. What they seek is a utility-of-wealth curve of which one can say that poor consumers are at the left and rich consumers are at the right. But they deduce the shape of the remainder of the curve to the right not from the behaviour of wealthy consumers (because of the difficulty of obtaining reliable information) but from the third of the pieces of evidence alluded to at the beginning of this section.

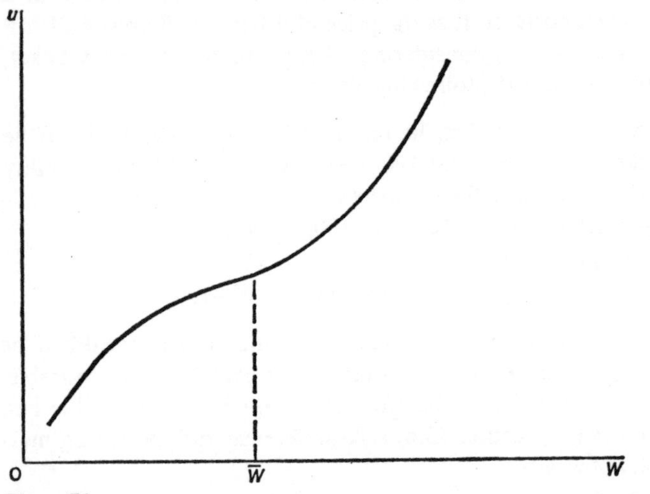

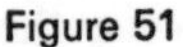
Figure 51

The third observation is that lotteries above a certain size typically have more than one prize. To deduce the implications of this for the shape of the utility-of-wealth function requires a fairly long chain of reasoning. Managers of lotteries, it is argued, seek to maximize the excess of receipts from ticket sales over payments (i.e. prizes plus expenses) and determine the number of prizes with this in mind. If they believe that, in a 100-ticket lottery with total prizes of £1000, the typical consumer will pay more for a ticket if the lottery has one prize than if it has two – or, which comes to the same thing, that he will prefer to buy a ticket at any given price in a one-prize rather than a two-prize lottery – then only one prize will be offered. It follows that if in fact they offer two prizes rather than one, they must believe that the typical consumer will prefer, at a given price, a ticket in a two-prize rather than a one-prize lottery. If we take the final step of assuming that what lottery managers believe about the typical consumer's preferences is true, we can draw inferences about the shape of the utility-of-wealth curve.

The reader may well object at this point that in a £1000 lottery one prize is in fact more likely than two. And he may well be right; we have chosen the figures of 100 tickets and £1000 for arithmetical simplicity and uniformity within this section. All the reader is asked to accept is the proposition that when the total of prizes reaches a certain size (£20,000?, £50,000?,...) two prizes become more likely than one. If he likes to supply for himself illustrative numbers more plausible than ours, and do the corresponding arithmetic, he will reach exactly the same conclusion about the general *shape* of the utility curve as we reach in the next paragraph.

With this understanding, our illustrative hypothesis is that the typical consumer prefers to pay £$10+c$ for a ticket in a 100-ticket lottery with two prizes of £500 each than in a 100-ticket lottery with one prize of £1000. In the two-prize lottery the probability of winning £500 is of course 2/100, and the prospect is therefore

$(\overline{W}-10-c,\ \overline{W}-10-c+500;\ 98/100,\ 2/100)$,

as compared with the prospect written down above,

$(\overline{W}-10-c,\ \overline{W}-10-c+1000;\ 99/100,\ 1/100)$,

if there is a single prize. The hypothesis that the former prospect is preferred to the latter implies that

$$\tfrac{98}{100}u(\overline{W}-10-c)+\tfrac{2}{100}u(\overline{W}-10-c+500)$$
$$>\tfrac{99}{100}u(\overline{W}-10-c)+\tfrac{1}{100}u(\overline{W}-10-c+1000).$$

If we multiply both sides by 100, and then subtract $u(\overline{W}-10-c+500)$ and $99u(\overline{W}-10-c)$ from both sides, we get

$$u(\overline{W}-10-c+500)-u(\overline{W}-10-c)$$
$$>u(\overline{W}-10-c+1000)-u(\overline{W}-10-c+500).$$

This implies that u increases by more when wealth increases by £500 from $(\overline{W}-10-c)$ to $(\overline{W}-10-c+500)$ than when it increases by £500 from $(\overline{W}-10-c+500)$ to $(\overline{W}-10-c+1000)$.

(In general, in a lottery with n tickets, total prizes of T and a price of $T/n+c$ per ticket, preference for two prizes of $\frac{1}{2}T$ rather than one prize of T can be easily shown to imply that

$$u(\overline{W}-T/n-c+\tfrac{1}{2}T)-u(\overline{W}-T/n-c) > u(\overline{W}-T/n-c+T)-u(\overline{W}-T/n-c+\tfrac{1}{2}T)$$

with consequences identical, *mutatis mutandis*, to those given above.)

Thus beyond a certain level of wealth the marginal utility of wealth begins to decrease again. When this feature is added to Figure 51, the final shape of the utility-of-wealth curve is as in Figure 52.

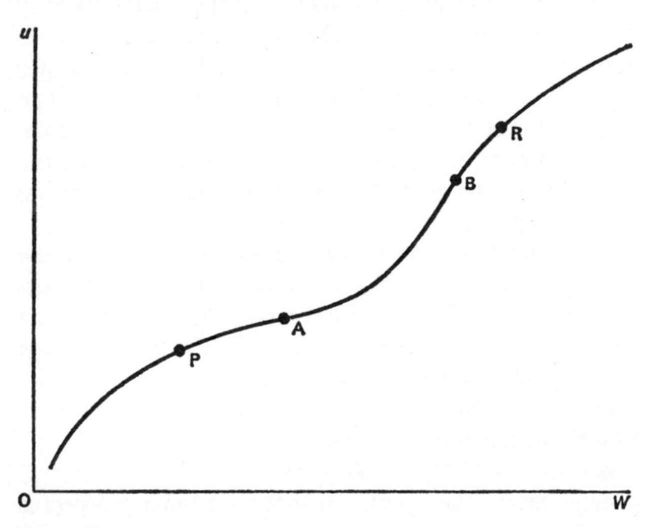

Figure 52

From a methodological point of view this analysis by Friedman and Savage is admirable. They begin with the expected utility hypothesis, which is simply that a utility-of-wealth function *exists*, and deduce its *shape* from certain observations. The next step is to test the hypothesis that the curve has this shape by deducing from it *further* implications concerning the behaviour of consumers at various levels of wealth, and seeing whether these are consistent with observation.

Unfortunately, as Hirshleifer has pointed out, the results of such a test are not encouraging. Some of the most telling discrepancies between hypothesis and observation are as follows.

A poor person, say someone at P in Figure 52, would display risk-aversion in relation to decreases or small increases in wealth. He would therefore insure his property and reject small fair bets. He would display risk-preference only in contemplating large increases in his wealth, so that he would accept a fair or unfavourable bet only if it were a 'long shot', i.e. a bet with a very small probability of raising his wealth to a level between A and B or beyond B. But poor people typically do not insure, and accept bets which are not long shots. One explanation, which is not inconsistent with risk-aversion in the vicinity of P, is that when a poor person 'bets' by not buying insurance or by accepting small gambles, in a sense he is not betting only his own money. Welfare payments provide a floor below which his wealth will not fall even if he is very unlucky.

A rich person, say someone at R in Figure 52, would display risk-aversion in relation to increases and small decreases in wealth. He would insure against small losses and have no interest in long-shot bets. He would display risk-preference only in contemplating large decreases in his wealth which would bring him down between A and B or below A. He would be more likely, therefore, to leave his major sources of wealth than his minor sources of wealth uninsured. And if he were to accept a fair or unfavourable bet, it would *only* be a 'short shot', i.e. one with a large probability of a small gain and a small probability of a large loss. These implications of Figure 52 scarcely conform to observation.

The implied behaviour of the middle group – say those between A and B in Figure 52 – is even less credible. They would display risk-preference with regard to substantial increases and decreases in their wealth, and 'would stand ready, at any moment, to accept at fair odds a gamble of such a scale as to thrust them out of [AB] and into (depending on the outcome) the poor-man or rich-man class'. Not only is this not consistent with observation, but it would imply that the segment AB would become rapidly depopulated, the result being a distribution of wealth with many poor and many rich and very few in the middle!

'Thus, the model would have us believe, the solid risk-avoiders of our society are only the poorer poor, and the richer rich', i.e. those well below P or well above R, to whom gambles that would bring them into the region AB are not available. The segment AB, with increasing marginal utility, causes all the trouble, and one wishes one could get rid of it. But how to explain gambling without it?

The proposed solution is to argue that most gambling is 'pleasure-oriented'; much of the satisfaction is derived from the act of gambling and its circumstances (see p. 220 above). One would expect such gambling to be repetitive and for small stakes, as at Las Vegas, at the race-track or on the football pools. 'Wealth-oriented' gambling, seriously designed to affect significantly one's level of wealth, would be infrequent and for stakes that were large in relation to one's wealth.

The hypothesis proposed as an alternative to that of Friedman and Savage is that risk-aversion with regard to serious 'wealth-oriented'

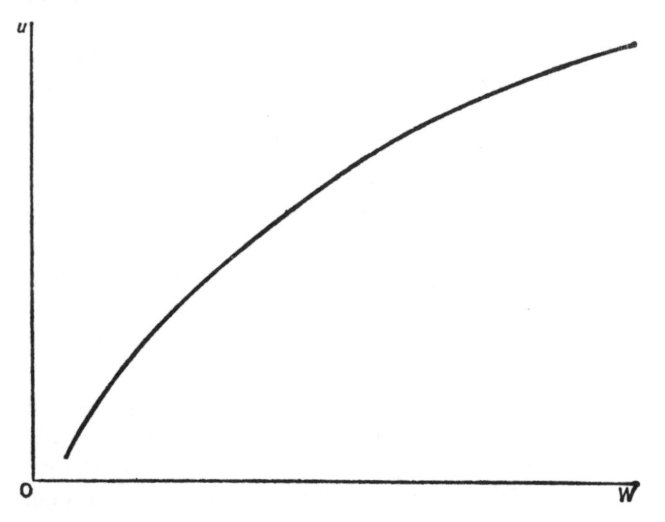

Figure 53

activities is displayed at all levels of wealth. The pleasure derived from gambling is not represented in the utility-of-wealth curve, though it is present at all levels of wealth. This curve therefore shows diminishing marginal utility of wealth throughout, as in Figure 53.

This hypothesis is consistent with the purchase of insurance at all levels of wealth, except perhaps for the very poor who are, as it were, insured by the floor of welfare payments and the very rich whose assets may be sufficiently diversified to permit self-insurance. Pleasure-oriented gambling would be present, on this hypothesis, at all levels of wealth also, but wealth-oriented gambling would be confined to the very poor, who (again because of the welfare floor) are not betting entirely their own money.

But finally, wealth-oriented gambling is perfectly consistent with risk-aversion as depicted in Figure 53 if the gamble is *believed* to be a favourable one, whether this belief is 'justified' (e.g. based on inside information or 'fixing') or not (e.g. a simple hunch). The distinction between 'subjective' and 'objective' probabilities implied here, and not discussed by Friedman and Savage, can be conveniently made within the framework of the 'state preference' approach to choice under uncertainty to be introduced in Chapter 15. For the moment, we close this section with the judgement that general risk-aversion as shown in Figure 53 represents the utility-of-wealth function relevant to wealth-oriented activities better than the shape of Figure 52.

14.2 Household portfolio decisions

We now attempt to pick up some of the threads of Part Four on choice over time. The crucial difference which the introduction of uncertainty makes is that the household must now decide on the *form* in which its wealth is to be held, as well as the *quantity* of wealth to hold.

This problem was not wholly neglected in Part Four. We asked in section **11.3**: given a certain sum to be spent on consumption of a good in this period and the next, should the consumer buy *goods* now and store them, or retain *cash* now and buy goods in the next period? And in section **11.5** we asked: given a certain steady flow of expenditure over a period, how large a transactions balance should be held at any given time? But the determining factor was not uncertainty but the *cost of transactions*, i.e. storage charges and brokerage fees. In Chapter 12, however, the problem was *only* how to distribute consumption over time, and therefore *how much* wealth to hold at a given time, in order to maximize intertemporal utility. It was assumed (except briefly in the discussion of Strotz's contribution in section **12.2**) that all assets bore the same perfectly safe rate of return.

There are of course innumerable forms in which wealth can be held, differing widely in the flows of receipts they yield while they are held, in the costs of holding them, and in the prices for which one can expect to sell them at various times in the future. But as is usually the case, the essence of the problem can be grasped if we consider a simple example.

Let us assume, therefore, that a consumer with current wealth $W(0)$ has a utility function of such a kind that he always spends the same fraction of his wealth on current consumption $C(0)$, regardless of future prospects. Neglecting the problem of transactions balances analysed in section **11.5**, he has wealth $W(0)-C(0)$ after providing for current consumption. Part of the original $W(0)$ consisted of expected future earnings and he may have borrowed against these to finance part of $C(0)$. The remainder of his human wealth is in the form of promises to pay wages or salary at future dates and there is nothing he can do at present to alter that form (though he may purchase life insurance to protect his dependants from its loss). There remains a sum of non-human wealth, say £100, which he can invest in various ways. We assume that it will remain invested from now until the beginning of period 1, and that the consumer invests it in such a way as to maximize the expected utility derived from its value at the beginning of period 1.[39]

We assume that the portfolio of £100 may be held in 'money', in 'bonds', or in some mixture of the two. If it is held in money it earns a safe positive rate of interest r (say 5 per cent), and the reader deserves a careful explanation of this startling supposition.

'Money' has two characteristics which are of interest in the theory of consumer behaviour. Firstly, it is a means of payment in current transactions. It is in this sense that in section **11.5** we contrasted it with 'short-term bonds' which are not a means of payment. 'Cash' in section **11.5** meant currency or deposits in current (checking) accounts. In that section 'bonds' could equally well have meant deposits in deposit (savings) accounts on which cheques can not be drawn. Secondly, 'money' is a form of wealth in which there is no uncertainty as to the future capital value in terms of money. No one would hold currency or deposits in a non-interest-bearing current account except for the purpose of making transactions. Thus when we speak of 'money' as a form in which *wealth* is to be held, we mean not a means

39. This is a usual and convenient simplifying assumption, but it may call for some justification. It is entirely in keeping with Clower's model (section **12.2**), in which utility depends only on current consumption and non-human wealth. But the intertemporal utility function of chapter 12 *may* be reducible to a function of current consumption and total human and non-human wealth in a special case (p. 190). Then with $C(0)$ and human wealth determined, non-human wealth at the beginning of period 1 is the only remaining determinant of utility.

of payment but any asset whose capital value in terms of money is certain. In *this* section, therefore, 'money' means very short-term bonds or deposits in savings accounts, both of which earn interest.

The distinguishing feature of money for our present purpose is the safety (or certainty) of the return on it. On the assumption that it is *real* present and future consumption that enters the utility function, it is the real rate of return on money that is relevant; a safe real rate of return of 5 per cent, for example, could be made up of a money rate of interest of 7 per cent and a rate of inflation expected with certainty to be 2 per cent (section **12.4**). Money ceases to be a safe asset if there is uncertainty about the rate of inflation. This case is considered in section **15.5**; until then we ignore inflation entirely, assuming that the money and real rates of interest are the same.

Bonds also earn a safe rate of interest r, but in addition their capital value may increase or decrease. We assume that there are just two possibilities. £1 invested now in bonds will either increase in capital value to £$1+g$ (with subjective probability π) or decrease in capital value to £$1-l$ (with subjective probability $1-\pi$). Thus, taking interest into account, the prospect associated with holding £1 in bonds is $(1+r+g, 1+r-l; \pi, 1-\pi)$. £1 held in money will, of course, increase to £$1+r$.

There is therefore a wide range of prospects, depending on the division of the £100 portfolio between money (M) and bonds (B). Since $M = 100-B$, the prospects can be written in terms of B as follows

$$[(100-B)(1+r)+B(1+r+g), (100-B)(1+r)+B(1+r-l); \pi, 1-\pi]$$
$$= [100(1+r)+Bg, 100(1+r)-Bl; \pi, 1-\pi].$$

Now if we assume that $\pi g-(1-\pi)l < 0$, it follows that $\pi(1+r+g)+(1-\pi)(1+r+l) < 1+r$, so that the expected rate of return on holding a bond is less than that on holding cash. Thus to hold bonds is to accept an unfavourable bet. If our consumer is a risk-averter, he will therefore hold no bonds, and his whole portfolio will be in money.

We may in fact wish to go further, and permit him to sell bonds short, so that his current cash holdings exceed £100 and his bond holdings are negative. Alternatively, if he is very optimistic and $\pi g-(1-\pi)l$ is greatly in excess of zero, he may wish to borrow money and buy bonds to a value of more than £100. But let us defer these possibilities to the next chapter, where they can be much more neatly explained in the geometry of state-preference theory. For the moment we forbid borrowing and short selling, so that the consumer is constrained by $0 \leqq B \leqq 100$.

In terms of expected utility theory, the problem is now very simple. Expected utility, given r, g, l and π, is the following function of B:

$$\pi u[100(1+r)+Bg]+(1-\pi)u[100(1+r)-Bl],$$

and we must select the value of B which maximizes this expression. If the consumer is a risk-averter and $\pi g-(1-\pi)l < 0$, he will choose to hold all his portfolio in cash, as we have seen, and we shall then have a 'corner solution' (section 7.2) with $B = 0$. We may have a corner solution with $B = 100$ if $\pi g-(1-\pi)l$ is sufficiently in excess of zero.

We can progress beyond this result, and tie the analysis of choice under uncertainty more closely to choice over time, if we regard this problem in the light of state-preference theory, which will concern us in the next chapter. But first we must consider briefly an alternative approach to portfolio selection which is widely used – the 'mean-variance' approach. This is related to, but not identical with, the expected utility approach, and the two can be reconciled only on special assumptions.

14.3 Mean-variance analysis

The idea underlying the mean-variance approach is that the determinants of an investor's choice among alternative portfolios can be reduced to two: expected return and risk. The expected return, or the mean of the 'probability distribution' of returns, is identical with what we have called the expected money value of the portfolio. It is obtained by adding together the possible money returns after each has been multiplied by the associated probability. Thus in the example above, for a given value of B we define

$$\begin{aligned}\mu &= \pi[100(1+r)+Bg]+(1-\pi)[100(1+r)-Bl]\\ &= 100(1+r)+B[\pi g-(1-\pi)l].\end{aligned}$$ [40]

40. In general, if the money return can take n discrete values x_i, with probabilities $\pi_i (0 \leqq \pi_i \leqq 1, \sum_i^n \pi_i = 1)$, $\mu = \sum_i \pi_i x_i$. If the money return is a continuous variable x, with probability function $\pi(x) (0 \leqq \pi(x) \leqq 1, \int \pi(x)\, dx = 1)$, $\mu = \int x\, \pi(x)\, dx$.

The variance of the probability distribution is usually adopted as the measure of risk. The variance measures the dispersion of the possible money returns about their mean μ, and is obtained by adding together the squares of the differences between the possible money returns and μ, after multiplying each square by its probability.[41]

In our example:

$$\sigma^2 = \pi[100(1+r)+Bg-\mu]^2+(1-\pi)[100(1+r)-Bl-\mu]^2.$$

By substituting for μ in this expression, the reader is asked to verify for himself that

$$\sigma^2 = \pi(1-\pi)B^2(g+l)^2.$$

It is convenient to work with the (positive) square root of the variance, known as the *standard deviation*

$$\sigma = +\sqrt{\{\pi(1-\pi)\}}\ B(g+l).$$

In order to discover the various combinations of the critical variables μ and σ which are available to the investor, we rewrite the last expression as

$$B = \frac{\sigma}{(g+l)\sqrt{\{\pi(1-\pi)\}}}$$

and substitute this in the expression for μ to obtain

$$\mu = 100(1+r)+\frac{\pi g-(1-\pi)l}{(g+l)\sqrt{\{\pi(1-\pi)\}}}\sigma.$$

The alternative combinations of μ and σ open to the investor can now be shown in Figure 54.

When $B = 0$, and the whole portfolio is held in cash, there is no risk ($\sigma = 0$) and the certain expected money return μ is $100(1+r)$. As B becomes positive, so does σ, but what happens to μ depends crucially on the expression $\pi g-(1-\pi)l$. As we saw earlier, if $\pi g-(1-\pi)l < 0$, to hold bonds would be to accept an unfavourable bet. In terms of Figure 54, it would mean that since the coefficient of σ in the expression for μ was negative, the opportunity line or budget line would slope downwards to the right, so that expected money return would decrease as risk increased. If $\pi g-(1-\pi)l = 0$, to hold

41. In the notation used in fn., 40. $\sigma^2 = \Sigma\, \pi_i(x_i-\mu)^2$ or $\sigma^2 = \int(x-\mu)^2\, \pi(x)\, dx$.

bonds is to accept a fair bet, and the bet is favourable if $\pi g-(1-\pi)l > 0$; the straight line relating μ and σ is horizontal in the former case and slopes upwards to the right in the latter.

In mean-variance theory the investor is assumed to have a complete and transitive preference ordering of the combinations of μ and σ

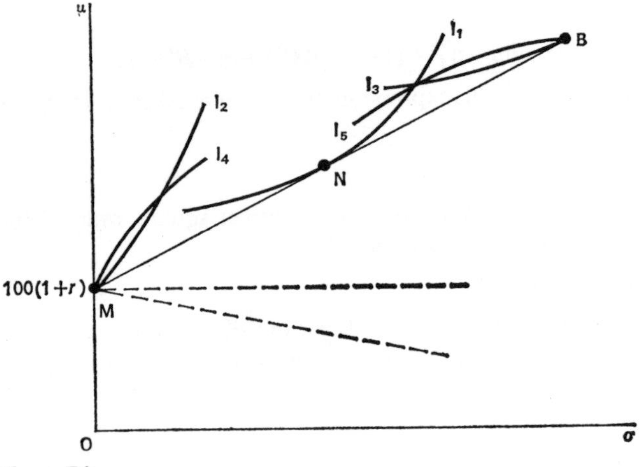

Figure 54

depicted in Figure 54, and to choose rationally. Of any two prospects of equal risk (equal values of σ) he prefers the one with the higher value of μ. One would hope that 'risk-aversion' would mean that of any two prospects with equal values of μ, he would choose the one with the *smaller* value of σ, so that the indifference curves of a risk-averter in Figure 54 would slope upwards to the right, and higher indifference curves would be preferred to lower ones.

And indeed this identification of risk-aversion with upward-sloping indifference curves is entirely consistent with our definition of risk-aversion in section **13.4**. As we saw above, to hold bonds is to accept a fair bet if the line relating μ and σ in Figure 54 is horizontal. The investor will reject this fair bet by holding only money, thus selecting the point M, if and only if his (μ, σ) indifference curves slope upwards to the right.

If to hold bonds is a favourable bet, so that the opportunity line MB slopes upwards to the right, terminating at the values of μ and σ

corresponding to $B = 100$, what choice will a risk averter make? Clearly the answer depends on the steepness and curvature of his upward sloping indifference curves. It is *only* if his indifference curves become steeper as σ increases that he will hold positive amounts of both money and bonds, since only then is it possible for the highest indifference curve, e.g. I_1 to touch MB at a point such as N between M and B. In a sense, such indifference curves imply 'increasing risk-aversion', since equal increments in σ require increasing increments in μ if the investor is to remain on the same indifference curve. An investor with indifference curves of this shape has been called a 'diversifier'. But this term is not entirely apt, since he may choose to hold his whole portfolio in money if his indifference curve (I_2) is steeper than MB at M, or in bonds if it is flatter than MB at B (I_3).

It is clear, however, that if the slope of the indifference curves decreases as σ increases ('decreasing risk-aversion'?), the investor must choose either M (I_4) or B (I_5). For such an investor the term 'plunger' is quite appropriate.

14.4 Mean-variance and expected utility

Enough has been said in section **14.3** to convey the flavour of mean-variance analysis. It would be possible, though complicated and not very conclusive, to consider the effects on the investor's portfolio of changes in r, π, g and l. We prefer, however, to consider the important question of the exact relationship between the mean-variance approach and the expected-utility approach to portfolio selection. In what conditions will an expected-utility maximizer be able to neglect all features of the expected returns on his portfolio other than the mean and variance of their probability distribution? To put it another way, in what conditions would any two prospects yielding equal values of expected utility, defined in section **14.2** as

$$\pi\, u[100(1+r)+Bg]+(1-\pi)u[100(1+r)-Bl]$$

always lie on the same mean-variance indifference curve in Figure 45?

It is now agreed (though we shall not attempt to prove it in this volume) that one (or both) of two conditions must be satisfied if the mean-variance and expected-utility approaches are to be reconciled. The first condition concerns the probability distribution of expected returns. If (and only if) this distribution is 'normal', the expected utility of the portfolio is a function of the mean and variance of the expected returns only, regardless of the form of the utility-of-wealth function. (Students of statistics will be familiar with the normal distribution, which gives rise to a symmetrical bell-shaped probability curve. It applies to a continuous variable which can take any value from plus infinity to minus infinity.) Many writers on the subject find it difficult to accept this pattern as even approximately valid for the returns on a typical portfolio.

The second condition has to do with the utility-of-wealth function $u(W)$. The expected utility maximizer will be indifferent between any two prospects with equal means and equal variances (whether the probability distributions are normal, lognormal, binomial, rectangular or whatever) if, and only if, his utility of wealth function is *quadratic*, i.e. if and only if:

$$u(W) = a+bW-cW^2.$$

But a quadratic utility function, together with risk-aversion, has two implications which make it quite unacceptable. If the marginal utility of wealth is to be positive and (because of risk-aversion) diminishing, we must have $b > 0$, $c > 0$ and $W < b/2c$.[42] This restricts the range of quantities of wealth over which the function may be used. More serious is the fact that, even over the range of W where the function can be used, in a problem like that discussed in sections **14.2–3** with a safe asset ('money') and a risky asset ('bonds'), the risky asset is an *inferior good*. That is to say that if, with given values of r, π, g and l, the investor with a portfolio of £100 chooses to put £60 into bonds, then with a larger portfolio (say £200) he will put *less than* £60 into bonds. (See Technical Appendix, section **T.11**.)

If one rejects both conditions necessary to reconcile the mean-variance and expected-utility approaches to portfolio selection, one must make a choice between them. The mean-variance approach is

42. $\dfrac{du}{dW} = b-2cW, \quad \dfrac{d^2u}{dW^2} = -2c.$

Since $d^2u/dW^2 < 0$, $c > 0$. If $du/dW = b-2cW$ is to be positive for some positive W, b must be positive; but du/dW will be positive only so long as $b-2cW > 0$, i.e. $W < b/2c$.

simpler, requiring knowledge or estimation of only two standard parameters of the probability distribution. A number of writers have chosen to assume that the investor's utility function has in it only the two variables μ and σ, disregarding entirely the possibility of deriving such a utility function from an underlying utility-of-wealth function.

In so doing, these writers have, as it were, departed from the 'main line' of analysis developed in this volume. The variables in their utility function are data which are (or may be) readily available, regardless of whether it is plausible that the consumer's preferences can be represented by such a function. These remarks are not intended to be critical – the theory of choice under uncertainty is in its infancy, and only time will tell which is the most fruitful approach. But there is a recent alternative approach to choice under uncertainty which is in the mainstream of economic analysis and which seems extremely promising. This is the so-called 'state-preference' theory, to which we turn in the next chapter.

Exercises

Consider the two prospects:

$y = (6, 1; 4/5, 1/5)$ and $y' = (9, 4; 1/5, 4/5)$

1, 4, 6 and 9 are quantities of wealth.

1. Which prospect will be preferred by a consumer whose utility is a function only of the mean and variance of prospects?

2. Which prospect will be preferred by an expected-utility maximizer whose utility-of-wealth function is $u = \sqrt{W}$? ($\sqrt{6} = 2{\cdot}45$)

Notes on the literature

14.1 The article on which this section is based is M. Friedman and L. J. Savage, 'The utility analysis of choices involving risk' (*J. polit. Econ.*, vol. 56, no. 4, pp. 279–304, 1948), reprinted in American Economic Association, *Readings in Price Theory* (Irwin, 1952, pp. 57–96). The criticisms of its implications at the end of the section are taken from J. Hirshleifer, 'Investment decision under uncertainty: applications of the state-preference approach' (*Q. J. Econ.* vol. 80, no. 2, pp. 252–77, 1966).

14.2 The pioneer in the analysis of portfolio problems of the type discussed in the remainder of this chapter and part of the next is James Tobin. See his 'Liquidity preference as behaviour towards risk' (*Rev. econ. Stud.*, vol. 25, no. 2, pp. 65–86, 1958).

14.3 An excellent discussion of mean-variance analysis, and of many other matters discussed in this chapter and the previous one, is to be found in H. M. Markowitz, *Portfolio Selection* (Wiley, 1959). The terms 'diversifier' and 'plunger' are used by Tobin (*op. cit.*).

14.4 The proof that a quadratic utility function is necessary, if an expected-utility maximizer is to be able to disregard *all* features of the probability distribution of returns (including its form) except μ and σ, is due to Markowitz (*op. cit.*, pp. 286–7). The discovery that, if the utility function is not quadratic, expected-utility and mean-variance can be reconciled in portfolio analysis only if the probability distribution of returns is normal, is quite recent. See M. S. Feldstein, 'Mean-variance analysis in the theory of liquidity preference and portfolio selection' and J. Tobin, 'Comment on Borch and Feldstein' (*Rev. econ. Stud.*, vol. 36, no. 1, pp. 5–12 and 13–14, 1969).

Sir John Hicks is one of those who have chosen to abandon expected-utility for mean-variance. See his 'Liquidity' (*Econ. J.*, vol. 72, no. 288, pp. 787–802, 1962). In his 'Pure theory of portfolio selection', the sixth of his *Critical Essays in Monetary Theory* (Oxford University Press, 1967), he finds it useful to introduce the third moment of the probability distribution ($Q^3 = \sum_i \pi_i(x_i - \mu)^3$), so that the utility function is $u = u(\mu, \sigma, Q)$, and suggests that for some purposes it may be desirable to use even higher moments.

Chapter 15
State-Preference Theory

15.1 Introduction

In the state-preference approach to choice under uncertainty it is assumed that during a period of time (say between now and the beginning of period one) one and only one of a number of well-defined events will occur and that therefore, at the beginning of period one, one and only one of a number of well-defined 'states of the world' will obtain. If there were only two such states, they might be war–peace, prosperity–depression, a Conservative–Labour government, a Democratic–Republican president and so on.

The fundamental objects (or 'characteristics' in Lancaster's sense) with which the consumer is concerned are 'pure' claims to wealth. Such a claim promises now to pay at the beginning of period one a certain sum of money if a particular state of the world then obtains. If there are two states *a* and *b*, one type of pure claim will be redeemed if state *a* obtains but worthless in state *b*, another will be redeemed if state *b* obtains but worthless in state *a*.

A perfect example of such a situation is to be found at the racetrack. In a two-horse race, a ticket on horse *a*, redeemed if horse *a* wins but worthless if horse *b* wins, is precisely the type of pure claim we have in mind. (Unfortunately, this illustration cannot be pursued in detail because of our concern with 'wealth-oriented' rather than 'pleasure-oriented' activity. See section **14.1**.)

A further critical feature of state-preference theory is that there is no uncertainty as to whether a pure claim will be redeemed if the state of the world with which that claim is associated obtains. The *only* uncertainty is: which state of the world will obtain? You are not certain whether horse *a* or horse *b* will win the race, but you *are* certain that if you hold a ticket on the winning horse, you will be paid at the stated odds.

We have spoken of pure claims as the 'characteristics' with which the consumer is ultimately concerned. But typically one does not purchase pure claims directly. Rather one purchases assets which contain the pure claims in fixed proportions, and these assets can therefore be thought of as 'goods' in Lancaster's sense. The portfolio selection example of sections **14.2–4** will serve as an illustration.

15.2 State-preference and household portfolios

It will be recalled that £1 now held in money grows to £$(1+r)$ at the beginning of period one, while £1 held in bonds grows either to £$(1+r+g)$ or to £$(1+r-l)$. Suppose that the capital gain g is associated with event a and the capital loss l with event b, and that one and only one of the events a and b will occur. We can then translate the alternative divisions of the investor's portfolio between money and bonds into alternative combinations of claims to wealth if state a obtains (W_a) and if state b obtains (W_b) at the beginning of period one.

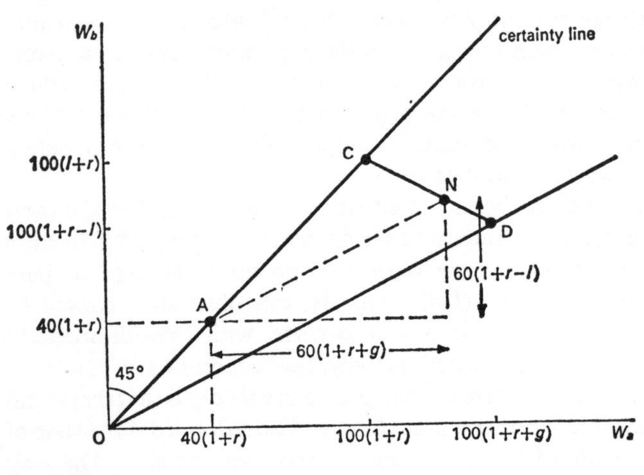

Figure 55

If the investor holds his entire portfolio in money, he is assured wealth of $100(1+r)$. This means that wealth will be $100(1+r)$ whether state a or state b obtains, so that $W_a = W_b = 100(1+r)$. The corresponding point C is plotted in figure 55, and lies on the 45° line through the origin, which for obvious reasons is called the 'certainty line'.

If the entire portfolio is held in bonds, the investor holds claims to $100(1+r+g)$ if a capital gain is enjoyed, as it will be in event a, and to $100(1+r-l)$ with the capital loss of event b. The corresponding point D is therefore placed where $W_a = 100(1+r+g)$, $W_b = 100(1+r-l)$.

Any division of the portfolio between money and bonds is represented by a combination of claims W_a and W_b lying on the straight line CD. The slope of CD is easily seen to be equal to $-l/g$, and any holding of bonds B corresponds to claims of $100(1+r)+Bg$ in event a and $100(1+r)-Bl$ in event b. If £40 is held in money and £60 in bonds, for example, the corresponding point in Figure 55 is N.

Geometrically, the point N can be reached by travelling along two 'vectors', the money vector and the bonds vector. By holding £40 in money, the investor acquires claims $W_a = W_b = 40(1+r)$, corresponding to the point A on the money vector OC. By holding £60 in bonds, he acquires in addition claims $W_a = 60(1+r+g)$, $W_b = 60(1+r-l)$. If we start from A and move, in a direction parallel to the bond vector OD, $60(1+r+g)$ to the right and $60(1+r-l)$ upward, we end at the point N at which

$$W_a = 40(1+r)+60(1+r+g) = 100(1+r)+60g$$
$$\text{and} \quad W_b = 40(1+r)+60(1+r-l) = 100(1+r)-60l.$$

(We could just as well have travelled first along the bond vector OD, and then turned and travelled along a line parallel to the money vector OC; the reader is invited to draw the appropriate lines in Figure 55.)

But is the investor confined to combinations of W_a and W_b lying on the line CD? If we extend CD to the axes in both directions, as in Figure 56, are points above C and below D attainable? The answer is yes, provided that we remove the ban on borrowing and short selling of bonds which we imposed in section **14.2.**[43]

43. Students of linear algebra will know that any point in two-dimensional space can be reached from the origin O by travelling along a path made up of lines parallel to two linearly independent vectors like OC and OD. But this is true only so long as one is free to move in either a positive or a negative direction. If one can move only upwards (holding only non-negative amounts of money and bonds), one is confined to the 'cone' enclosed by the extensions of the lines OC and OD. Downward movements are possible only if one permits borrowing or short selling of bonds, as the text goes on to show.

Suppose that the investor borrows £50 at the interest rate r and uses it, together with his own £100, to buy £150 worth of bonds. What will be his position at the beginning of period 1? In event a, his bonds are worth £$150(1+r+g)$, but he must repay £$50(1+r)$, the amount of his loan plus interest. Thus

$$W_a = 150(1+r+g)-50(1+r) = 100(1+r)+150g.$$

In event b his bonds will be worth $150(1+r-l)$, and after repaying his loan he will have

$$W_b = 150(1+r-l)-50(1+r) = 100(1+r)-150l.$$

The corresponding point B clearly lies on CD produced. Geometrically, the point B is reached by travelling along the bond vector OD to the point $W_a = 150(1+r+g)$, $W_b = 150(1+r-l)$, and then *back* along a line parallel to the money vector OC for a distance $W_a = W_b = -50(1+r)$.

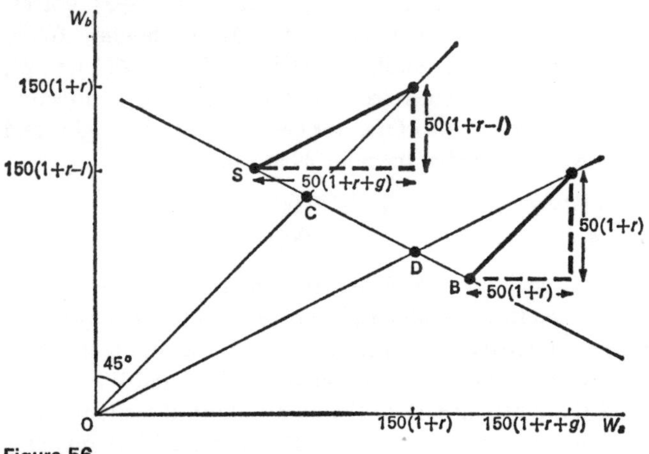

Figure 56

Is there any limit to the amount the investor can borrow? It is not difficult to see that if one travels sufficiently far along OD and then back along a line parallel to OC, one may end at a point which, to be sure, lies on the extension of the straight line CD, but *below* the W_a-axis. This means that W_b is negative, so that if event b occurs the capital loss he suffers on his bonds will leave him with insufficient funds to repay his loan, and he will be bankrupt. Presumably no one will lend him so large a sum.

Combinations of W_a and W_b above C may be reached by short selling of bonds. The investor undertakes, in exchange for, say, £50 in money received now, to deliver at the beginning of period one a quantity of bonds now worth £50. Whether event *a* or event *b* occurs, his own £100, plus the £50 received from the short sale, will be worth £150$(1+r)$ at the beginning of period one. In event *a*, it will cost him £50$(1+r+g)$ to buy the bonds he is pledged to deliver, so that

$$W_a = 150(1+r)-50(1+r+g) = 100(1+r)-50g.$$

In event *b*, the bonds will cost him only £50$(1+r-l)$, so that

$$W_b = 150(1+r)-50(1+r-l) = 100(1+r)+50l.$$

The corresponding point *S* lies on CD produced above C. It may be reached by travelling along the money vector OC to the point $W_a = W_b = 150(1+r)$, and then *back* along a line parallel to the bond vector OD for a distance corresponding to

$$W_a = -50(1+r+g), \quad W_b = -50(1+r-l).$$

The investor would presumably find no takers if he offered to sell short so many bonds that he would be bankrupt ($W_a < 0$) if event *a* occurred.

What we have now accomplished is the derivation from the 'goods', money and bonds, a budget line expressed in terms of the 'characteristics' W_a and W_b. But there are two important differences between the budget lines obtained in section **10.3** for consumer goods and those obtained here for assets when borrowing and short selling are permitted.

In the first place, if the vectors OC and OD in Figures 55 and 56 corresponded to the only two consumer goods available, the consumer would be confined to the triangle OCD, because it is assumed in section **10.3** that he cannot buy negative quantities of them. But in this section we assume that the investor can hold a 'negative' quantity of money (by borrowing) or a negative quantity of bonds (by selling short). Thus in Figure 56 the characteristic budget line extends from axis to axis.

Secondly, what happens if, with only the two 'characteristics' W_a and W_b, there are more than two 'goods' (say, money and two types of bond)? Suppose that in Figure 57 the combinations of W_a and W_b attainable if one holds one entire portfolio in the three assets A_1, A_2, and A_3 are represented by the points A_1, A_2, and A_3 respectively.

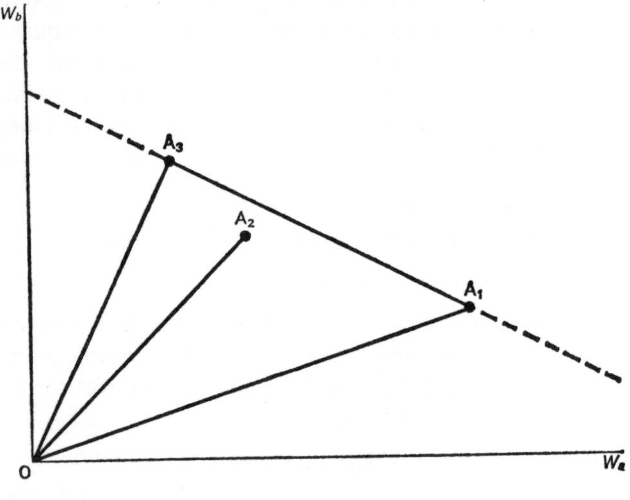

Figure 57

The analysis is identical with that of section **10.3** (Figure 42). No one will hold A_2, since the portfolio can be divided between A_1 and A_3 in such a way as to obtain greater quantities of both W_a and W_b than if A_2 is held. With borrowing and short selling, the budget line is the straight line A_1 A_3 extended to the axes.

A significant departure from section **10.3**, however, is that a budget line like A_1 A_2 A_3 in Figure 58, which is the typical shape when we are concerned with consumer goods of which only positive quantities can be bought (cf. Figure 42) is not possible for assets when borrowing and short selling are permitted.

No one will hold A_1, because it is possible, by selling A_3 short and using the proceeds to hold an amount of A_2 in excess of one's portfolio, to reach a point like B_1 on the line A_3 A_2 produced (as in Figure 58), where it intersects OA_1 above A_1; B_1 of course contains more W_a and W_b than A_1. Similarly B_3, above A_3 on OA_3, can be reached by selling A_1 short and holding an amount of A_2 in excess of one's portfolio. But if no one will hold A_1, to whom can it be sold short (and similarly for A_3)?

Clearly the assets A_1, A_2 and A_3 will all be held only if the prices of the combinations of claims W_a and W_b which they represent are adjusted. The price of A_1 or A_3 must fall, or the price of A_2 must rise, so that the point A_1 or A_3 moves outwards along OA_1 or OA_3, or A_2 moves inwards along OA_2. But of course these adjustments must not go too far, or we shall be back in Figure 57 where no one will hold A_2.

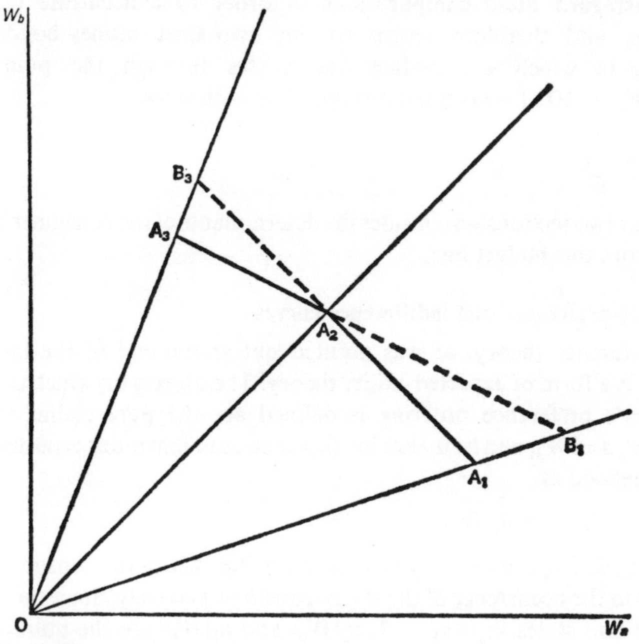

Figure 58

If we ignore the 'transactions costs' of various kinds which can, as in section 10.4, upset the tidiness of the foregoing argument, its obvious conclusion is that 'efficiency' choices by investors will ensure that the efficiency budget line in terms of the characteristics W_a and W_b is a *straight line.*[44]

44. It would not be difficult to show that a budget line with *more* than three assets which was bowed outwards like that of Figure 58 could not be maintained. And I feel reasonably confident that if there are three states of the world, and therefore three types of pure state-claims W_a, W_b, W_c, the budget region is bounded by a plane, and in general by an $(n-1)$ - dimensional hyperplane if there are n states of the world.

This being the case, if there are more than two assets and only two states, the demand for each asset is perfectly elastic at the relevant price, (cf. section **10.4**, p. 161). But if we introduce brokerage fees, the budget line ceases to be a straight line (see Exercise 1 at the end of this chapter.)

We disregard these complications in order to concentrate on essentials, and therefore return to our two-asset money-bonds example, in which the budget line passes through the point $W_a = W_b = 100(1+r)$ on the certainty line with slope

$$\frac{\Delta W_b}{\Delta W_a} = -\frac{l}{g}.$$

In the next two sections we consider the determinants of the consumer's choice from this budget line.

15.3 State-preference and indifference curves

State-preference theory, as was pointed out at the end of the last chapter, is a form of expected-utility theory. The objects on which the consumer's preference ordering is defined are the pure claims to wealth W_a and W_b, and he makes his choice so as to maximize expected utility, defined as

$$E = \pi_a u_a(W_a) + \pi_b u_b(W_b).$$

Here π_a and π_b are the subjective probabilities which the consumer attaches to the occurrence of the states a and b respectively. Since there are only two states, $\pi_a + \pi_b = 1$. $u_a(W_a)$ and $u_b(W_b)$ are the utilities derived now from holding claims to W_a if state a obtains at the beginning of period one and claims to W_b if state b obtains. Note that the functions $u_a(\ )$ and $u_b(\ )$ are *different*; this allows for the possibility that the utility derived from a *given* quantity of wealth may depend on the state of the world in which it is received. A bachelor, for example, may feel quite differently about £1000 received by himself if he is alive (state a) and £1000 in his estate if he is dead (state b). On the other hand, few players of roulette would care whether they won £10 on red if red came up (state a) or £10 on black if black came up (state b). State-preference theory, unlike the standard expected-utility theory of the last two chapters, does permit one to make a distinction between the utility functions $u_a(\ )$ and $u_b(\ )$ if the context requires it. We shall, however, neglect this distinction for the sake of simplicity, assuming that there is a single utility-of-wealth function $u(\ )$ independent of the state in which the wealth is enjoyed. The expression to be maximized is therefore specialized to

$$E = \pi_a u(W_a) + \pi_b u(W_b).$$

Indifference curves will join combinations of W_a and W_b yielding equal values of expected utility, E. What will these indifference curves be like? The argument is formally identical to that used in deriving indifference curves from the inter-temporal utility function $f[C(0)] + \{f[C(1)]\}/(1+p)$ in section **12.4**. The only difference is that the 'states' a and b have replaced the 'dates' 0 and 1.

Consider first the 45° or certainty line (OC in Figures 55 and 56), at all points on which $W_a = W_b$. We saw in section **12.4** (p. 195) that when $u = \lambda_0 f[C(0)] + \lambda_1 f[C(1)] + \ldots$, the mrs of $C(1)$ for $C(0)$ was λ_0/λ_1 at all points where $C(0) = C(1)$. By exactly the same argument, when $E = \pi_a u(W_a) + \pi_b u(W_b)$, the mrs of W_b for W_a is π_a/π_b when $W_a = W_b$. Thus the slope of an indifference curve on the certainty line is

$$\frac{\Delta W_b}{\Delta W_a} = -\frac{\pi_a}{\pi_b}.$$

The slope of the indifference curves away from the 45° line depends partly on the subjective probabilities π_a and π_b, and also on the consumer's attitude to risk. It is comforting to discover that risk-aversion, which we earlier decided to treat as typical in wealth-oriented activities, implies convex-to-the-origin indifference curves between W_a and W_b.

To demonstrate this requires a two-stage argument. Recall first from section **13.4** that risk-aversion implies diminishing marginal utility of wealth. It follows that for a risk-averter maximizing expected utility defined as $E = \pi_a u(W_a) + \pi_b u(W_b)$, the marginal utility of wealth, $u'(W_a)$, $u'(W_b)$, must be diminishing. If this is so, any fair bet will be rejected (but note that 'fairness' is defined here in terms of the *subjective* probabilities π_a and π_b; in a comparison between a certain quantity of wealth $\overline{W}$ and the bet $(W_a, W_b; \pi_a, \pi_b)$, the bet is fair, favourable or unfavourable as $\pi_a W_a + \pi_b W_b$ is respectively equal to, greater than or less than $\overline{W}$.)

The second stage of the argument draws on a result established in section **6.5**. In any additive utility function – the example used there was $f_1(x_1)+f_2(x_2)$ – if the marginal utility of each 'commodity' is positive and diminishing, the indifference curves are convex to the origin. The expected utility function $E = \pi_a u(W_a)+\pi_b u(W_b)$ is additive, and the marginal utilities of W_a and W_b are both positive and have just been shown to be diminishing. They are still positive and diminishing when $u(W_a)$ and $u(W_b)$ are multiplied by the positive subjective probabilities π_a and π_b respectively. (The cases where π_a or $\pi_b = 0$, which would give respectively horizontal and vertical indifference curves, are disregarded.) We conclude that with risk-aversion the indifference curves between W_a and W_b are convex to the origin.[45]

15.4 The determination of portfolio choice

Let us now put the budget line of section **15.2** and the indifference curves of section **15.3** together in figure 59. Consider first the very special case in which the slope of the budget line ECF, on which $\Delta W_b/\Delta W_a = -l/g$, happens to coincide with the slope of the indifference curve I_1 at C on the certainty line; this slope, as we saw in the last section, is equal to $-\pi_a/\pi_b$. In this case, with the convex-to-the-origin indifference curves implied by risk-aversion, the consumer will choose to remain at C, where $W_a = W_b = 100(1+r)$, and his whole portfolio will be in money.

To choose any point on ECF other than the perfectly safe C would be to accept a bet. And it is not difficult to see that in the present case where $l/g = \pi_a/\pi_b$, any such bet would be (in terms of the subjective probabilities π_a and π_b) a *fair* bet, which a risk-averter will by definition reject. A fair bet is one whose expected money value $\pi_a W_a+\pi_b W_b$ is the same as at C, so that when one moves from C to the prospect represented by such a bet, the changes in W_a and W_b are such that $\pi_a \Delta W_a+\pi_b \Delta W_b = 0$, or $\Delta W_b/\Delta W_a = -\pi_a/\pi_b$. Indeed, the set of all fair bets is represented by the straight line drawn *tangent* to the

45. It was pointed out in section **6.5** that convex-to-the-origin indifference curves do *not*, however, imply that the marginal utility of each commodity is diminishing. But it can be shown (though we shall not pause to do so) that if we require indifference curves to be convex to the origin for *all* positive values of π_a and π_b, the marginal utility of wealth must be everywhere diminishing.

indifference curve at C. When the budget line is ECF, it coincides with this tangent, since along ECF $\Delta W_b/\Delta W_a = -l/g = -\pi_a/\pi_b$; thus, as stated, all points other than C on ECF represent fair bets.

But of course there is no reason why the budget line should be tangent to an indifference curve on the certainty line. The slope of the

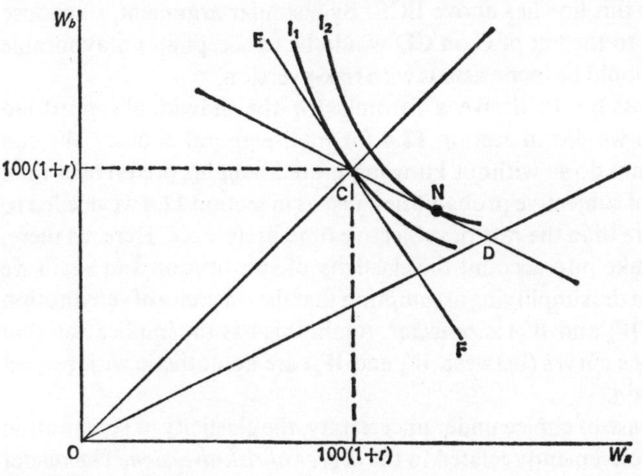

Figure 59

budget line is the result of numerous transactions among individuals with differing sizes of portfolio, subjective probabilities, and degrees of risk-aversion (to be defined in a moment) in the bond and money markets. It represents an equilibrium in which all transactors are content with the quantities of money and bonds (and therefore of claims to W_a and W_b) that they hold. To draw an analogy with the intertemporal problem of section **12.4**, the relationship there between the subjective rate of time-preference p and the market rate of interest R corresponds exactly to the relationship between the ratio of subjective probabilities π_a/π_b and the slope of the budget line l/g; l/g might almost be called the ratio of 'market' probabilities.

Let us suppose then that in Figure 59 the budget line shifts from ECF to CD, where now $l/g < \pi_a/\pi_b$. The highest indifference curve, I_2, touches CD to the right of C, say at N, and the consumer will now hold some bonds. He is accepting a bet by choosing N, but it is not difficult to see that any point on CD to the right of C represents, in terms of subjective probabilities, a *favourable* bet, which a risk-averter can consistently accept. For clearly the value of $\pi_a W_a + \pi_b W_b$ is higher at N than at C. The set of all points with an expected money value equal to that of N is found by drawing through N a straight line with slope $\Delta W_b / \Delta W_a = -\pi_a / \pi_b$, that is, a line parallel to ECF, and obviously this line lies above ECF. By a similar argument, to choose any point to the left of C on CD would be to accept an unfavourable bet, and would be inconsistent with risk-aversion.

Is it possible to derive a formula for the individual's portfolio choice, as we did in section **12.4** for intertemporal choice? We can certainly not do so without knowing more about his preferences than the ratio of subjective probabilities, just as in section **12.4** we needed to know more than the rate of subjective time-preference. Here, as there, we shall take into account the elasticity of substitution and again we shall make the simplifying assumption that the elasticity of substitution (between W_a and W_b) is *constant*. Again this has the implication that indifference curves (between W_a and W_b) are homothetic with respect to the origin.

In the case of choice under uncertainty, the elasticity of substitution η can be conveniently related to the *degree of risk-aversion*. The reader may wish to refresh his memory by referring to section **12.4**, pp. 198 ff, and to Figure 60. The case where $\eta = 0$, and the indifference curves have right angles on the certainty line, is one in which the consumer will not take a bet at any (positive) price for W_a or W_b; the term 'absolute risk-aversion' seems appropriate. When $\eta = \infty$, the indifference curves are straight lines with slope $\Delta W_b / \Delta W_a = -\pi_a / \pi_b$, so that $\pi_a W_a + \pi_b W_b$ is constant along an indifference curve; the consumer is indifferent between any two points with equal expected money values irrespective of their distances from the certainty line. We term this 'zero risk-aversion'. Negative values of η correspond to concave-to-the-origin indifference curves. If one draws the tangent at the certainty line to the indifference curve with this shape in Figure 60, and imagines other indifference curves with the same shape, one sees that, of any two points on the same side of the certainty line with equal expected money values, the one *further* from the certainty line will be chosen. This is a clear case of 'risk-preference'.

Normal convex-to-the-origin indifference curves represent risk-aversion and positive and finite elasticities of substitution. But since *higher* values of η correspond to *smaller* degrees of risk-aversion (consider the cases $\eta = 0$ and $\eta = \infty$), we shall define the degree of risk-aversion ρ as the reciprocal of η[46]

$$\rho = \frac{1}{\eta}.$$

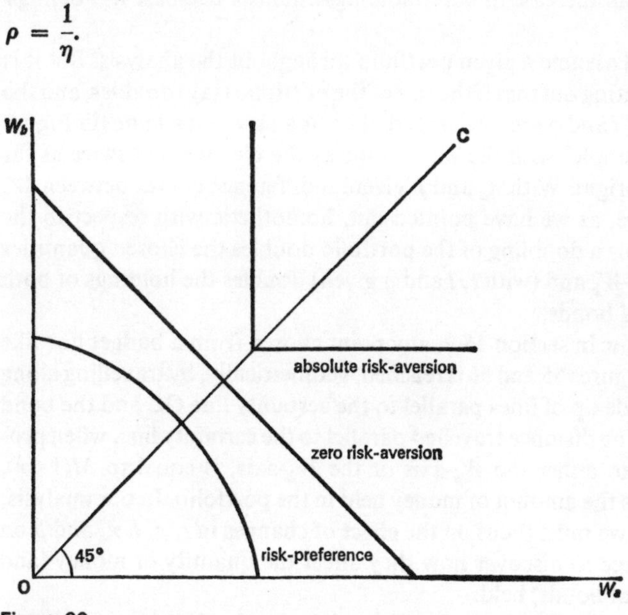

Figure 60

The question then is: what effect do the values of r, l, g, π_a and ρ have on the choice of portfolio? (π_b need not be considered separately, since $\pi_b = 1-\pi_a$.) This is a more difficult question than that tackled in section **12.4**. There we were interested only in the quantities of the 'characteristics' $C(0)$ and $C(1)$ consumed. Here our concern is with the quantities of the 'goods' or 'assets', bonds and money, that will be held.

To make the question precise, let us recall that the consumer is assumed to set aside £100 *now*, and must decide how to divide it between money and bonds. His choice is determined by his desire to

46. ρ is equivalent to Arrow's 'relative risk-aversion'; see Technical Appendix, section T.8.

maximize the expected utility of his claims to wealth at the beginning of period 1. But when we speak of an increase in bond-holdings we shall mean an increase in the number of pounds in the current portfolio of £100 that are held in the form of bonds. Thus with a given portfolio, an increase in bond-holdings entails a decrease in holdings of money.

We shall assume a given portfolio throughout the analysis. But it is worth pointing out that if the size of the portfolio (say) doubles, and the values of r, l and g are unchanged, there is a new budget line (in Figure 60, for example) with the same slope as the old one and twice as far from the origin. With π_a and ρ given, indifference curves between W_a and W_b are, as we have pointed out, homothetic with respect to the origin. Thus a doubling of the portfolio doubles the chosen quantities of W_a and W_b and (with r, l and g given) doubles the holdings of both money and bonds.

As we saw in section **15.2**, any point chosen from a budget line like those in Figures 55 and 56 is reached, geometrically, by travelling along a path made up of lines parallel to the certainty line OC and the bond line OD. The distance travelled parallel to the certainty line, when projected on to either the W_a-axis or the W_b-axis, is equal to $M(1+r)$, where M is the amount of money held in the portfolio. In our analysis, therefore, we must focus on the effect of changes in r, g, l, π_a and ρ on this distance to discover how they affect the quantity of money (and therefore of bonds) held.

In Figure 61, the effect of a change in the *rate of interest* r is to shift the budget line outwards. The points C and D, representing the combinations of W_a and W_b held when the whole portfolio is held in money and bonds respectively, become C′ and D′. C′ is obtained from C, and D′ from D, by adding $100(r'-r)$ to the quantities of W_a and W_b (here we are letting r and r' stand for the old and new values of the rate of interest respectively). But while the movement from C to C′ is simply a movement out along the 45° certainty line, we have added to OD, which is flatter than the certainty line, a movement DD′ parallel to the certainty line. The new bond 'ray' OD′ is therefore steeper than the old ray OD. It is closer to the 45° line, so that bonds have become a 'safer' asset. This is because, with l and g given, the safe interest component has become larger in relation to the uncertain capital gain and capital loss components in the return on a bond. (It might be argued that a change in r unaccompanied by a change in l and g is unlikely; indeed, a Keynesian might argue that an increase in r would be accompanied by a larger expected g and a smaller expected l. We are deliberately considering changes in the determinants of portfolio choice one at a time, but of course once this has been done the reader may combine them in any way he chooses.)

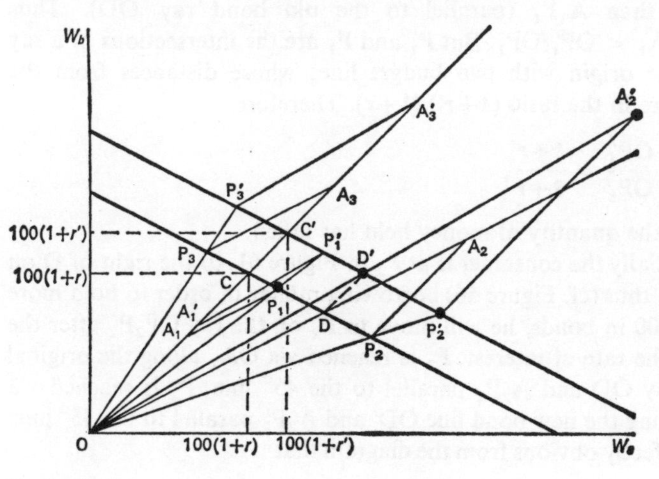

Figure 61

Consider the effect of an increase in the rate of interest on an investor initially at P_1, holding positive quantities of money ($M(1+r)$ is represented by OA_1) and bonds (represented by A_1P_1 parallel to OD). After the increase in r he moves to P'_1; since his indifference curves are homothetic with reference to the origin and the relative 'prices' of W_a and W_b have not changed (C′D′ is parallel to CD), he will continue to buy W_a and W_b in the same proportions as at P_1. Thus P'_1 will lie on the same ray through the origin as P_1. The point P'_1 is reached via OA'_1 (representing $M'(1+r')$) and $A'_1P'_1$, parallel to the new bond ray OD′.

We wish to discover whether the quantity of money held has risen or fallen. The distance OA_1 is proportional to the original quantity of money multiplied by $1+r$. The distance OA'_1 represents the new quantity of money multiplied by $1+r'$. It is clear, therefore, that

$$M \text{ has} \begin{Bmatrix} \text{risen} \\ \text{stayed the same} \\ \text{fallen} \end{Bmatrix} \text{as } \frac{OA_1'}{OA_1} \begin{Bmatrix} > \\ = \\ < \end{Bmatrix} \frac{1+r'}{1+r}.$$

It is not difficult to discover which alternative holds. *If* $A_1'P_1'$ were parallel to A_1P_1, by similar triangles OA_1'/OA_1 would be equal to OP_1'/OP_1. But in fact $A_1'P_1'$ (parallel to the new bond ray OD′) is steeper than A_1P_1 (parallel to the old bond ray OD). Thus $OA_1'/OA_1 < OP_1'/OP_1$. But P_1' and P_1 are the intersections of a ray from the origin with two budget lines whose distances from the origin are in the ratio $(1+r')/(1+r)$. Therefore

$$\frac{OA_1'}{OA_1} < \frac{OP_1'}{OP_1} = \frac{1+r'}{1+r},$$

so that the quantity of money held has fallen.

If initially the consumer is at P_2 in Figure 61, to the right of D on CD and thus (cf. Figure 56) borrowing money in order to hold more than £100 in bonds, he will move to P_2' on the ray OP_2P_2' after the rise in the rate of interest. P_2 is reached via OA_2 along the original bond ray OD and A_2P_2 parallel to the 45° line; P_2' is reached via OA_2' along the new bond line OD′ and $A_2'P_2'$ parallel to the 45° line. It is perfectly obvious from the diagram that

$$\frac{A_2'P_2'}{A_2P_2} > \frac{OP_2'}{OP_2} = \frac{1+r'}{1+r},$$

so that the amount of money *borrowed*, and therefore the quantity of bonds held, has increased.

Finally, if the consumer is initially at P_3 (reached via OA_3 and A_3P_3) to the left of C, selling bonds short and holding more than £100 in money, he will move to P_3' (reached via OA_3' and $A_3'P_3'$) after the rise in the rate of interest. Since $A_3'P_3'$ (parallel to OD′) is steeper than A_3P_3 (parallel to OD),

$$\frac{OA_3'}{OA_3} > \frac{OP_3'}{OP_3} = \frac{1+r'}{1+r},$$

and he will hold *more* money, and sell *more* bonds short, after the rise in the rate of interest.

Thus with g and l given, an increase in the rate of interest will increase the consumer's bond holdings and cause him to hold less money (or to borrow more) if his initial bond holdings are positive. But if he is selling bonds short, an increase in r will increase both his short sales and his holdings of money.

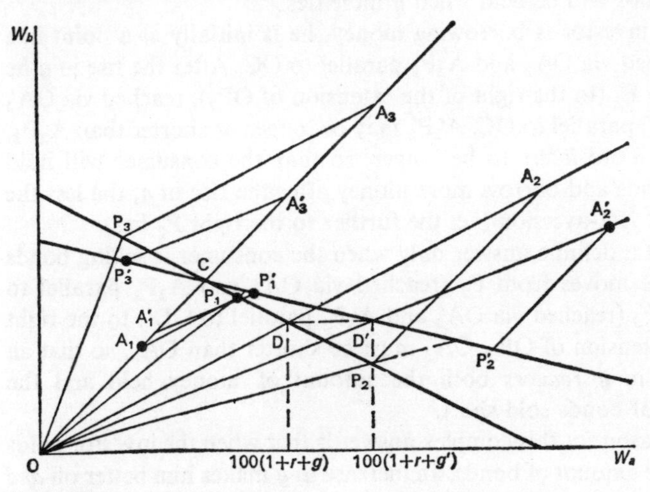

Figure 62

One can, unfortunately, not obtain such definite results for the effects of changes in the expected *capital gain* or *capital loss* on the consumer's portfolio choice. In Figure 62, an increase in the expected capital gain from g to g' in event a is represented by a shift of the point D horizontally to the right to D′; the new bond ray is OD′, flatter than OD.

If the point chosen from CD was P_1, the point chosen from the flatter budget line CD′ will lie (with homothetic convex-to-the-origin indifference curves) to the right of the intersection of OP_1 produced with CD′. P_1 is reached via OA_1 and A_1P_1 parallel to OD, P'_1 via OA'_1 and $A'_1P'_1$ parallel to OD′. Since the rate of interest r is the same in each case, we need compare only the distances OA_1 and OA'_1, representing respectively the old and new quantities of money multiplied by $1+r$. But it is obvious from Figure 62 that A'_1 may lie above A_1 or below it. The greater the elasticity of substitution (i.e. the lower the degree of risk-aversion), the greater the proportional change in W_a/W_b corresponding to the given change in their relative 'prices', and the further to the right will P_1' lie. And the further to the right P_1' lies, the more likely is it that A_1' will lie below A_1. Thus the smaller the value of ρ, the more likely it is that less money and more bonds will be held when g increases.

If the investor is borrowing money, he is initially at a point like P_2, reached via OA_2 and A_2P_2 parallel to OC. After the rise in g he moves to P_2' (to the right of the extension of OP_2), reached via OA_2' and $A_2'P_2'$ parallel to OC. $A_2'P_2'$ may be longer or shorter than A_2P_2, but it is more *likely* to be longer, so that the consumer will hold more bonds and borrow more money after the rise in g, the less the degree of risk-aversion (i.e. the further to the right P_2' lies).

We get a definite answer only when the consumer is selling bonds short. He moves from P_3 (reached via OA_3 and A_3P_3 parallel to OD) to P_3' (reached via OA_3' and $A_3'P_3'$ parallel to OD′) to the right of the extension of OP_3. OA_3' must be shorter than OA_3, so that an increase in g *reduces* both the amount of money held and the number of bonds sold short.

The reason for this complex answer is that when the investor holds a positive amount of bonds, an increase in g makes him better off *and* shifts his optimal point further from the certainty line; whether he then holds more of the risky asset, bonds, depends on his degree of risk-aversion. But when he is selling bonds short an increase in g makes him worse off and shifts his optimal point closer to the certainty line; he draws in his horns and reduces his short sales. It is left to the reader to work out the effects of a change in the expected capital *loss*.

It is somewhat easier to determine the effects on portfolio choice of changes in the parameters of the utility function, π_a and ρ. An increase in π_a is an increase in the *subjective probability* associated with the event, a, in which bond-holders will enjoy a capital gain; the higher π_a, the more 'bullish' the investor may be said to be. (If there were n states, some associated with capital gains and some with capital losses, greater 'bullishness' would mean a larger value of an expression like $\pi_a g_a + \pi_b g_b + \ldots - \pi_m l_m - \pi_n l_n$. This suggests that 'bullishness' may be interpreted as having to do with the magnitudes of expected gains and losses, as well as with subjective probabilities.) When π_a increases, the slope of an indifference curve on the certainty line becomes steeper.

In Figure 63, consider the two indifference curves I_1 and I_2, belonging to two families of curves for which the elasticity of substitution is the same, but with π_a higher for the I_2-family than for the I_1-family. Then $\pi_a/(1-\pi_a)$ is higher for I_2 than for I_1, and so therefore is the mrs of W_b for W_a on the certainty line. Suppose that there is an indifference curve belonging to the I_1-family that touches the budget line in Figure 63 at P_1. For the mrs to change from the slope of I_1 on the certainty line to that of the budget line requires a change in the ratio W_a/W_b from 1 on the certainty line to that represented by the slope of the line OP_1. With the same elasticity of substitution, the

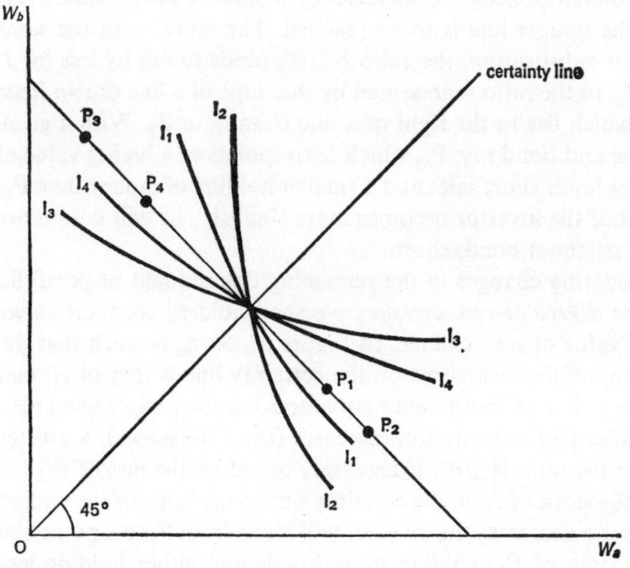

Figure 63

larger proportional change in the mrs from the slope of I_2 (steeper than I_1) on the certainty line to the slope of the budget line necessitates a larger proportional change in the ratio W_a/W_b; thus the point P_2 (the point of tangency of an indifference curve from the I_2-family with the budget line) must lie to the right of P_1, so that the ratio W_a/W_b is higher than at P_1. With a given budget line and bond ray, P_2, which corresponds to a higher value of π_a, requires a greater holding of bonds and a smaller holding of money (or a greater amount of money borrowed) than P_1.

Consider now the indifference curves I_3 and I_4, again from two families of curves with equal values of ρ, but with π_a higher for the I_4-family than for the I_3-family. Tangency of an indifference curve from the I_3-family with the budget line now requires an *increase* in the mrs of W_b for W_a from that represented by the slope of I_3 on the certainty line to the slope of the budget line, and therefore a *reduction* in the ratio W_a/W_b from unity on the certainty line to that represented by the slope of OP_3. When π_a is greater, as with the I_4-family of indifference curves, the mrs of W_b for W_a is greater on the certainty line, and therefore needs to increase by a smaller proportion if the slope of the budget line is to be reached. Therefore, with the same elasticity of substitution, the ratio W_a/W_b needs to fall by less for I_4 than for I_3, to the ratio represented by the slope of a line drawn from O to P_4, which lies to the right of a line from O to P_3. With a given budget line and bond ray, P_4, which corresponds to a higher value of π_a, requires fewer short sales and a smaller holding of money than P_3.

In short, if the investor becomes more 'bullish', he will hold more bonds, or sell fewer bonds short.

In considering changes in the remaining determinant of portfolio choice, the *degree of risk-aversion*, we shall hold π_a constant as we allow the value of ρ to change. In Figure 63, let π_a be such that the slope of an indifference curve on the certainty line is that of I_1, and let ρ be such that an indifference curve touches the budget line at P_1. If the elasticity of substitution increases (i.e. ρ decreases), a greater increase in the ratio W_a/W_b is necessary to reduce the mrs of W_b for W_a from the slope of I_1 on the certainty line to the slope of the budget line. Thus if ρ decreases the investor will move from P_1 to a point like P_2 to the right of P_1, holding more bonds and either holding less money or borrowing more.

But if the slope of an indifference curve on the certainty line is that of I_4, a decrease in ρ requires a greater *decrease* in the ratio W_a/W_b if the mrs of W_b for W_a is to change from the slope of I_4 on the certainty line to the slope of the budget line. The consumer will move, say, from P_4 to P_3, selling more bonds short.

A decrease in the degree of risk-aversion, in short, will move the investor's optimal point *away* from the certainty line. If he is holding the risky asset (bonds) he will hold more of it; if he is selling it short, he will sell more short.

To conclude this long section, we present a simple formula for a very special case of the problem discussed – that in which the elasticity of substitution η (and therefore the degree of risk-aversion ρ) is equal to unity. In this case

$$B = 100(1+r)\left[\frac{\pi_a}{l} - \frac{1-\pi_a}{g}\right].$$[47]

There are some results which follow from this formula and also for any other value of ρ:

1. If $\pi_a/(1-\pi_a) > l/g$, bonds will be held ($B > 0$); if $\pi_a/(1-\pi_a) < l/g$ they will be sold short ($B < 0$). (We discovered that this was so for a risk-averter in section **14.2**.)

(b) If the size of the portfolio or the rate of interest increases, more bonds will be held or *more* will be sold short.

(c) If the investor becomes more bullish (π_a increases) more bonds will be held or *fewer* will be sold short.

But there are some problems for which the formula is of little use:

(d) The formula implies that an increase in the expected capital gain, g, or a decrease in the expected capital loss, l, will increase the number of bonds held, or reduce the number sold short. As we saw earlier in the section, this is not true for all degrees of risk-aversion. We give in a footnote, but shall not derive or discuss, the general formula for any degree of risk-aversion p.[48]

(e) Obviously we cannot derive from the formula in the text the effects of a change in the degree of risk-aversion, which we discussed above in relation to figure 63.

47. When $\eta = \rho = 1$. the utility function (see Technical Appendix, section T.8.) is $u = \log W$. Thus (see section **14.2**)
$E = \pi_a \log[100(1+r)+Bg]+(1-\pi_a)\log[100(1+r)-Bl]$.
By setting the partial derivative $\partial E/\partial B$ equal to zero and solving for B, the required expression is obtained.

48. $$B = 100(1+r)\left[\frac{(\pi_a g)^{1/\rho}-\{(1-\pi_a)l\}^{1/\rho}}{(\pi_a g)^{1/\rho}l+\{(1-\pi_a)l\}^{1/\rho}g}\right].$$

15.5 Further applications and evaluation

The portfolio example just discussed by no means exhausts the possible applications of state-preference theory.

Consider, for example, the storage problem of section **11.3**. A certain sum was set aside to provide for consumption of x_i in periods 0 and 1, and we found that it was better to provide for future consumption $C_i(1)$ by buying at the current price $p_i(0)$, and storing at a cost of s per unit, than to wait and buy at next period's price $p_i(1)$, if $p_i(0)+s < p_i(1)/(1+r)$, where r was the rate of interest.

If we assume that the sum of money, $p_i(0)C_i(0)$, devoted to current consumption, is independent of s, r and current and future prices, we can concentrate on period 1. Uncertainty can be introduced by supposing that either state a or state b will obtain at the beginning of period 1, and that the price of x_i will then be $p_i(a)$ in state a and $p_i(b)$ in state b, with $p_i(a) < p_i(b)$. The earlier result clearly implies that if $p_i(0)+s < p_i(a)/(1+r) < p_i(b)/(1+r)$ it is better to store whichever state obtains, while if $p_i(0)+s > p_i(b)/(1+r) > p_i(a)/(1+r)$, it is better to wait in either event.

The interesting case is therefore that in which

$$\frac{p_i(a)}{1+r} < p_i(0)+s < \frac{p_i(b)}{1+r}.$$

If A is the sum of money the consumer has left after providing for $C_i(0)$, the alternatives are as shown in figure 64.

If the consumer buys now and stores, his consumption in each state will be $A/\{p_i(0)+s\} = C_i(a) = C_i(b)$. If he waits, A will grow to $A(1+r)$, which will buy $C_i(a) = A(1+r)/p_i(a)$ in state a and $C_i(b) = A(1+r)/p_i(b)$ in state b. His choice will be from the line SW (S for 'store', W for 'wait'), since borrowing and short selling do not arise in this context.

But there may be a further option if a forward market in x_i exists. The consumer may be able to avoid uncertainty, without buying now and storing, by entering now into a forward contract to buy x_i at the beginning of period 1 at an agreed price $p_i(\mathrm{F})$, regardless of whether the actual price is then $p_i(a)$ or $p_i(b)$. If $p_i(0)+s > p_i(\mathrm{F})/(1+r)$, he may choose to take advantage of this opportunity. As his indifference curve is drawn in figure 64, he will choose to wait (W) rather than to store

(S) if no forward contract can be made, but he will choose F rather than W if it can.

As another example, let us introduce into the earlier portfolio problem the uncertainty about the rate of inflation alluded to in section

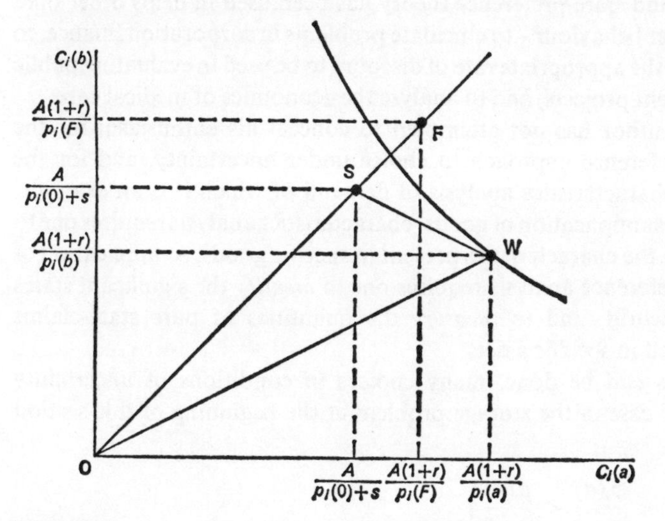

Figure 64

14.2. If prices are expected to rise during period 0 by 1 per cent in event a and 4 per cent in event b, a certain money rate of interest of 5 per cent becomes a real rate of only $(5-1) = 4$ per cent in event a and $(5-4) = 1$ per cent in event b, and in real terms money is no longer a perfectly safe asset. Indeed, it may well be that some asset other than money is *safer*, in the sense that its 'vector' or ray lies closer to the certainty line than the money vector and on the same side. For example, an asset which now sells for £1·00 and promises to pay £0·05 in interest, and is expected to suffer a capital *loss* of £0·01 in event a and to enjoy a capital *gain* of £0·01 in event b, will be worth in terms of current purchasing power £1·00+(£0·05−£0·01)−£0·01 = £1·03 in event a and £1·00+(£0·05−£0·04)+£0·01 = £1·02 in event b. Thus £100 held in money represents real claims W_a = £104, W_b = £101, while £100 held in the other asset yields W_a = £103, W_b = £102. It can easily be confirmed by drawing a diagram that the non-money asset is 'safer' (in real terms) in the sense defined above.

Finally, consideration of more than one future period is possible, though very complicated unless drastic simplifying assumptions are made. And state-preference theory has been used in fields other than consumer behaviour – to elucidate problems in corporation finance, to indicate the appropriate rate of discount to be used in evaluating public investment projects, and to analyse the economics of medical care.

The author has not attempted to conceal his enthusiasm for the state-preference approach to choice under uncertainty, and for the goods–characteristics analysis of demand of which it is an example. But just as application of goods–characteristics analysis requires one to measure the characteristics present in specific goods, so application of state-preference analysis requires one to *identify* the significant states of the world, and to *measure* the quantities of pure state-claims embodied in specific assets.

If this can be done, many choices in conditions of uncertainty (e.g. the case in the storage problem at the beginning of this section where

$$p_i(0)+s < \frac{p_i(a)}{1+r} < \frac{p_i(b)}{1+r}\Bigg)$$

become pure *efficiency* choices, and are therefore *independent* of the particular theory of ordering of uncertain prospects that one favours.

State-preference theory is an elegant and promising form of analysis, but a great deal of empirical work needs to be done before it can be said to have proved itself.

Exercises

1. In the portfolio problem of this chapter, let $r = 5$ per cent, $g = 10$ per cent and $l = 10$ per cent, so that in state-preference geometry the budget line, for a portfolio of £100, passes through the point where $W_a = W_b =$ £105 with a slope of $-l/g = -1$. The investor will hold some bonds if $\pi_a > \frac{1}{2}$ and sell some short if $\pi_a < \frac{1}{2}$.

Now suppose that at the beginning of period 0 his portfolio is initially entirely in money, and that in order to buy bonds or sell them short he must pay now out of his £100 a brokerage fee of 2 per cent of the current value of any bonds in which he trades.

(a) What now is the budget line in terms of W_a and W_b?

(b) What value of π_a is now necessary in order to induce the investor to hold any bonds?

(c) What value of π_a is now necessary in order to induce the investor to sell any bonds short?

2. In the portfolio problem of section **15.4**, with a portfolio of 100, $r = 5$ per cent, $l = 10$ per cent, $\pi_a = \frac{1}{3}$ and $\rho = 1$, what will be the chosen values of M and B if (a) $g = 15$ per cent, (*b*) $g = 25$ per cent? Assume that there are no transactions costs, and use the formula on p. 269.

Notes on the literature

This chapter draws very heavily upon the excellent article by J. Hirshleifer which brought state-preference theory within reach of the average economist: 'Investment decision under uncertainty: choice-theoretic approaches' (*Q. J. Econ.*, vol. 79, no. 4, pp. 509–36, 1965). A preliminary version is his 'Efficient allocation of capital in an uncertain world' (*Amer. econ. Rev.*, vol. 54, no. 3, pp. 77–85, 1964). Both papers are highly recommended to the reader.

15.1 The pioneers of state-preference theory are K. J. Arrow, 'The role of securities in the optimal allocation of risk-bearing' (*Rev. econ. Stud.*, vol. 31, no. 2, pp. 91–6, 1964, originally published in French in 1953), and G. Debreu (*Theory of Value*, Wiley, 1959, ch. 7).

15.2 The assertions in the footnote on p. 255 are, I believe, warranted by Arrow, *op. cit.*

15.4 The degree of relative risk-aversion was defined by K. J. Arrow in *Aspects of the Theory of Risk-Bearing*, Helsinki 1965, p. 33. This book also contains an interesting analysis of a portfolio problem (pp. 38–43) and a (very difficult) proof of the existence of utility functions (pp. 14–27) alternative to that in section **13.2** above.

15.5 An interesting paper on the relationship between the relative 'safety' of various assets and the household's intertemporal consumption plan is by R. C. O. Matthews, 'Expenditure plans and the uncertainty motive for holding money' (*J. polit. Econ.*, 1963, pp.

201–18). This paper does not explicitly adopt a state-preference approach, but can easily be translated into such a form.

The applications referred to in the fields of corporation finance and public investment are to be found in Hirshleifer ('Investment decisions under uncertainty: applications of the state-preference approach' (*Q. J. Econ.*, vol. 80, no. 2, 1966)). And Arrow's 'Uncertainty and the welfare economics of medical care' (*Amer. econ. Rev.*, vol. 53, no. 5, pp. 941–73, 1963), is highly recommended.

Part Six
Society

Chapter 16
Consumption and Welfare

16.1 Welfare economics

Hitherto our attention has been confined primarily to the preferences and behaviour of a single consumer or household. When we have considered the behaviour of a group of consumers, it has been for the purpose of determining the nature of the total demand for a single commodity (as in parts of chapter 9) or of the demand for aggregate consumption (as in parts of chapter 12), or for the purpose of inferring the nature of efficiency budget lines, or the value of the rate of interest, from the behaviour of the participants in a market (as in parts of chapters 10, 12 and 15).

Nowhere have we attempted to *evaluate*, from the point of view of *social welfare*, the arrangements whereby goods are distributed to consumers. As was pointed out in section **2.3**, evaluation and recommendation are the subject of *welfare economics*, while *positive economics*, concerned with explanation and prediction, has occupied us to this point.

Now evaluation requires the formulation of a criterion whereby social welfare may be measured, and the device traditionally used by welfare economists for this purpose is the *social welfare function* (SWF). Alternative situations are judged by the values of

$$W = W(u^{(A)}, u^{(B)}, \ldots, u^{(M)})$$

to which they give rise. $u^{(A)}, u^{(B)}, \ldots, u^{(M)}$ are the utility levels attained by the M individuals or households in the society.

Before we ask the obvious question – who is to decide the weights to be assigned to the preferences of different individuals or households? – there are two logically prior points to be made. The first is that the SWF as written is *individualistic*; social welfare is uniquely determined by the preferences of individuals or households – only these preferences count. Secondly, by listing the individuals A, B, ..., M, we imply that we know whom to include and therefore whom to *exclude*. In a given society, do we include the preferences of criminals and the insane? And what about the preferences of future generations?

We confine ourselves to pointing out these implications, henceforth accepting the individualistic nature of the SWF criterion and assuming that a decision (by its very nature, an arbitrary one) has been made as to *whose* preferences are to count.

As to the *weighting* of the utility levels of A, B,..., M, it is remarkable how much can be said about the relative merits of alternative situations without facing this problem at all! The only assumption we shall make about the form of the SWF is that W rises if one individual becomes better off and no one becomes worse off. This assumption, known as the *Pareto criterion* for an increase in social welfare (after the Italian economist and sociologist Vilfredo Pareto who first enunciated it) may be expressed compactly as

$$\frac{\partial W}{\partial u^{(J)}} > 0 \quad (\text{for all } J = A, B, \ldots, M).$$

Given this criterion, one can define the very useful concept of a *Pareto optimum*. Let S be a set of social situations whose elements are s, s', s'',.... For s to be a Pareto optimum there must be no alternative s' in S which is better than s by the Pareto criterion for an increase in social welfare.

To see what this definition implies, note that if there *were* an alternative s' that was better than s by the Pareto criterion, someone would be better off, and no one worse off, in s' than in s. When we say that in a Pareto optimum no such alternative s' exists, our definition therefore amounts to the following:

A Pareto optimum s is a situation with the property that one individual can be made better off than at s only by making someone else worse off than at s.

As we shall soon see, in a given set S of social situations there will be numerous Pareto optima. Our uncontroversial Pareto criterion permits us to *identify* Pareto optima, but to choose among them requires precisely the weighting of individual preferences referred to earlier. Pareto optima are *efficient* in the sense that one cannot move from a

Pareto optimum so as to make everyone better off (just as in section **10.3** one cannot move from a point on an 'efficiency' *budget* frontier so as to obtain more of both characteristics). But whether a Pareto optimum is also *equitable* is another matter.

In the next section we relate these abstractions to the problems of consumers discussed in earlier chapters.

16.2 Prices and efficiency: the simple case

Since this is a book about consumer behaviour, we do not concern ourselves with the way in which goods are produced. In this section and the next we simply assume that certain total quantities of goods are available to be distributed among consumers, without asking how the goods come to be available. We then consider the social desirability of the distribution of these goods which results from the operation of the price system implicit in the analysis of earlier chapters. In section **16.4** we introduce the problem of the significance of measurements of the level of 'real national income' at different times (though without taking production into account we cannot carry the analysis very far).

In this section, the goods to be distributed may be interpreted as the 'non-durable goods of current consumption' of chapters 2–9. Time, uncertainty and the distinction between goods and characteristics may be disregarded for the time being. If there are only two goods, the given totals $\bar{x}_1$ and $\bar{x}_2$ can be measured along the sides of the rectangle (known as the 'Edgeworth–Bowley box') in Figure 65.

If there are also only two consumers, A and B, the quantities they consume can be measured as follows. Measure $x_1^{(A)}$, the amount of x_1 received by A, to the right from A's origin, $O^{(A)}$, at the bottom left-hand corner of the box, and measure $x_2^{(A)}$ upwards from $O^{(A)}$. $x_1^{(B)}$ and $x_2^{(B)}$ are measured respectively to the *left* and *downwards* from B's origin $O^{(B)}$ at the top right-hand corner of the box.

If the quantities $x_1^{(A)}$, $x_2^{(A)}$, $x_1^{(B)}$ and $x_2^{(B)}$ put A at the point $x^{(A)}$ and B at the point $x^{(B)}$ as shown, there are amounts $x^{(A)}C$ of x_1 and $x^{(A)}D$ of x_2 which remain unused. Clearly if the totals $\bar{x}_1$ and $\bar{x}_2$ are fully distributed, $x^{(A)}$ and $x^{(B)}$ coincide in a single point. For example, if A were to consume the whole of $\bar{x}_1$ and B the whole of $\bar{x}_2$, the points $x^{(A)}$ and $x^{(B)}$ would coincide at the bottom right-hand corner of the box.

The only possible distributions are those in which *either* $\bar{x}_1$ and $\bar{x}_2$ are fully distributed *or* $x^{(A)}$ lies (roughly) south-west (as shown) or due south or due west of $x^{(B)}$. It would not be possible, for example, for A to be at $x^{(A)\prime}$ and B at $x^{(B)\prime}$ in Figure 65; although the amount $x^{(A)\prime}C'$ of x_1 would remain undistributed, the total amount of x_2 consumed would exceed by $x^{(A)\prime}D'$ the total $\bar{x}_2$ which was available.

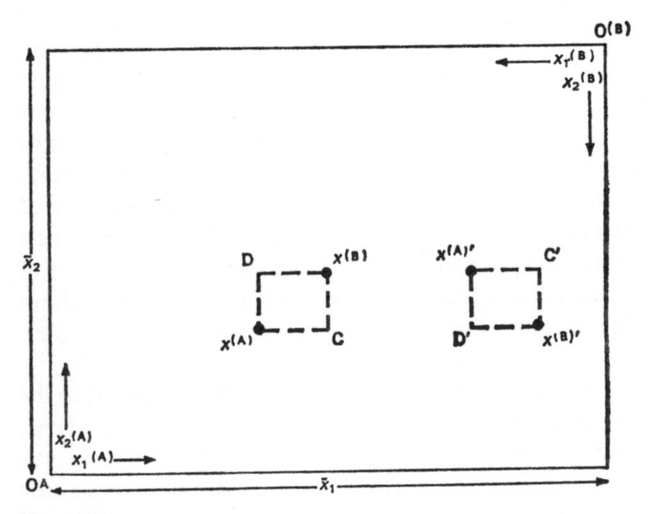

Figure 65

So much for availability. In this section we base our evaluation of the price mechanism on the strong assumption that the utilities $u^{(A)}$ and $u^{(B)}$ which appear in the SWF $W = W(u^{(A)}, u^{(B)})$ are the values of utility functions $u^{(A)}(x_1^{(A)}, x_2^{(A)})$, $u^{(B)}(x_1^{(B)}, x_2^{(B)})$ which represent preference orderings with all the usual properties of chapters 2 and 3.

Let us pause to consider what this implies. As was pointed out in section 2.3, the evaluations we make in our individualistic welfare economics are dependent on the assumption of individual rationality, which we retain throughout this chapter. By omitting from the utility functions $u^{(A)}$ and $u^{(B)}$ any sources of changes in preferences, we are disregarding, among other things, the effects of promotional advertising discussed in Section 2.4. It is for the reader to judge how far the relevance of the subsequent analysis is lessened by these assumptions.

To the extent, however, that advertising informs consumers of the characteristics present in goods, thus changing preferences among goods but not among characteristics, our demonstration in the next section that the argument of the present section can be applied to a goods-characteristics model reinforces the analysis.

The assumption of strict convexity (which rules out 'corner solutions') is also relaxed with little difficulty in the next section, as is (with more difficulty) the assumption that $u^{(A)}$ depends only on what A consumes (and similarly $u^{(B)}$ for B).

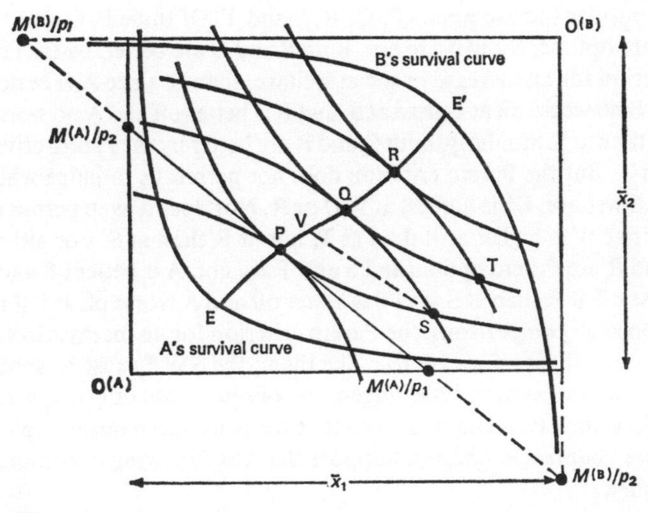

Figure 66

We return, then, to the simple case where $u^{(A)} = u^{(A)}(x_1^{(A)}, x_2^{(A)})$ and $u^{(B)} = u^{(B)}(x_1^{(B)}, x_2^{(B)})$. In Figure 66, we insert A's indifference curves with reference to $O^{(A)}$ as origin in the usual way. But since $x_1^{(B)}$ and $x_2^{(B)}$ are measured respectively to the left and downwards from B's origin $O^{(B)}$, his indifference curves must be turned through an angle of 180° from their normal position, as shown. A north-easterly movement in Figure 66 makes A better off but B *worse off*.

The assumption of smooth, strict convexity (so that no indifference curve ever touches an axis) implies that there is an infinite number of points of tangency of A's and B's indifference curves (e.g. P, Q and R), all of which lie in the interior of the box. If we include in the diagram the 'survival' indifference curve of each individual, below which no preference ordering exists, the points of tangency will all lie in the region enclosed by the 'survival' curves. The line EE′ joining the points of tangency is known as the *contract curve.*

Now every point, like P, on the contract curve is a Pareto optimum as defined in section **16.1**. For it can easily be seen that one cannot move from P so as to place A on a higher indifference curve without moving B to a lower indifference curve, or place B on a higher indifference curve without moving A to a lower indifference curve.

Consider the five points P, Q, R, S and T. Of these P, Q and R are Pareto optima, S and T are not. Both P and Q are better, by the Pareto criterion for an increase in social welfare, than S, since A is better off and B no worse off at Q than at S, and B is better off and A no worse off at P than at S. Similarly, both Q and R are better by the Pareto criterion than T. But the Pareto criterion does not permit us to judge whether social welfare, W, is highest at P, Q or R. Nor does it even permit us to say that W is higher at P than at T, nor at R than at S. For although P and R are Pareto optima and S and T are not, A is better off and B is worse off at R than at S, and B is better off and A worse off at P than at T. On such comparisons, the Pareto criterion for an increase in social welfare is silent; if we are to make them, the SWF must be specified more fully so as to include judgements of *equity*, not only of *efficiency.*

Nevertheless, it can be shown that the price mechanism implicit in earlier chapters is *efficient*. Suppose that the following conditions are satisfied:

(a) the price p_1 paid for x_1 is the same for A as for B, and the same is true of p_2;

(b) each consumer takes the prices p_1 and p_2 as *given*, so that their budget lines are the usual straight lines, defined by

$$M^{(A)} = p_1 x_1^{(A)} + p_2 x_2^{(A)}, \qquad M^{(B)} = p_1 x_1^{(B)} + p_2 x_2^{(B)};$$

(c) each consumer chooses the bundle of goods he most prefers from those permitted by his budget constraint;

(d) the choices made under (c) are such that the total amount of each commodity chosen equals the total available, i.e. $x_1^{(A)} + x_1^{(B)} = \bar{x}_1$, $x_2^{(A)} + x_2^{(B)} = \bar{x}_2$.

Conditions (a)–(d) define a *competitive equilibrium.* We shall now show that the resulting distribution $(x_1^{(A)}, x_2^{(A)}, x_1^{(B)}, x_2^{(B)})$ is a Pareto optimum lying on the contract curve EE′ (provided that the prices and budgets permit each consumer to survive).

For the distribution to lie on EE′ it is sufficient (and necessary) that (i) $x_1^{(A)}+x_1^{(B)} = \bar{x}_1, x_2^{(A)}+x_2^{(B)} = \bar{x}_2$, so that the points $x^{(A)}$ and $x^{(B)}$ in Figure 66 coincide in a single point – this is condition (d) for a competitive equilibrium; (ii) the indifference curves of A and B are tangent to each other, so that (in terms of marginal rates of substitution)

$$\text{mrs}_{21}^{(A)} = \text{mrs}_{21}^{(B)}.$$

Now when each individual chooses his optimal point from his straight budget line, $\text{mrs}_{21}^{(A)} = p_1/p_2$ and $\text{mrs}_{21}^{(B)} = p_1/p_2$, so that

$$\text{mrs}_{21}^{(A)} = \frac{p_1}{p_2} = \text{mrs}_{21}^{(B)}.$$

Geometrically, the budget lines for A and B both pass through the same point P in Figure 66, and since their slopes are the same $(-p_1/p_2)$ they must therefore coincide, at least over the range where they both lie within the box. A's budget line goes from $M^{(A)}/p_2$ to $M^{(A)}/p_1$ and B's budget line, which extends outside the box, goes from $M^{(B)}/p_2$ to $M^{(B)}/p_1$. At the point P, A's indifference curve and B's indifference curve are both tangent to the common budget line, and therefore tangent to each other.

This result, the most elementary theorem on the efficiency of the price mechanism, requires a few supplementary notes. Firstly, while it is important that each consumer takes prices as given, so that his budget line is a *straight* line, it is not necessary that A pay the same money price as B for each good. All that is needed is that the *ratio* of the prices paid for x_1 and x_2 be the same for each consumer, for if $p_1^{(A)}/p_2^{(A)} = p_1^{(B)}/p_2^{(B)}$, then $\text{mrs}_{21}^{(A)} = p_1^{(A)}/p_2^{(A)} = p_1^{(B)}/p_2^{(B)} = \text{mrs}_{21}^{(B)}$.

Secondly, the efficiency of the price mechanism can be similarly demonstrated if, instead of assigning to each consumer a money budget, we assign him a certain quantity of each of the two goods, making for example a preliminary distribution at the point S in Figure 66. If A and B then trade with each other, establishing an agreed exchange-ratio between x_1 and x_2 which each then treats as given, they will move from S along a straight line like SV, making a 'contract' which will bring them to a Pareto-optimal point like V on the contract curve. The initial allocation at S, or the ratio of money budgets $M^{(A)}$ and $M^{(B)}$ assigned to A and B, must of course be judged on grounds of equity.

Thirdly, we simply assert without proof that on our assumptions, given the budgets $M^{(A)}$ and $M^{(B)}$ a pair of prices p_1 and p_2 can be found to give a competitive equilibrium at which $x_1^{(A)}+x_1^{(B)} = \bar{x}_1$ and $x_2^{(A)}+x_2^{(B)} = \bar{x}_2$, and that given an initial distribution at S an exchange-ratio can be found leading to a point like V.[49]

Finally, our result has an important corollary. If it were thought that A was being unfairly treated at the point P in Figure 66, it might be proposed that A's consumption of, say, x_1 should be subsidized. That is, the price of x_2 should be the same to A as to B, but A should pay less than B for x_1 ($p_1^{(A)} < p_1^{(B)}$). It is not difficult to see that in this case

$$\text{mrs}_{21}^{(A)} = \frac{p_1^{(A)}}{p_2} < \frac{p_1^{(B)}}{p_2} = \text{mrs}_{21}^{(B)}.$$

If equilibrium prices $p_1^{(A)}$, $p_1^{(B)}$ and p_2 were found under this arrangement at which total demands exhausted $\bar{x}_1$ and $\bar{x}_2$, the result would be a point like T in Figure 66 where two indifference curves intersect, because A's budget line would be flatter than B's. A point on the contract curve, better for both A and B than T, could be attained by transferring money from B to A and letting the price of x_1 be the same for each consumer. There is a case for charging different prices for the same good to different consumers only if the transfer of money is not possible, or if one takes the paternalistic attitude that A *should* consume more x_1 and may not unless he is specifically encouraged to do so, or if there exists between the utility functions of A and B interdependence of a type to be discussed in the next section.

16.3 Prices and efficiency: extensions of the argument

It is straightforward to extend the results of the last section to any number of goods and consumers. In a competitive equilibrium as there

49. There may in fact be more than one such competitive equilibrium. We do not consider here the process whereby A and B search for and approach such an equilibrium.

defined, in which each consumer buys a positive amount of each commodity, the mrs between each pair of commodities is the same for each pair of consumers. It should then be intuitively obvious that it is not possible for one consumer to move to a higher indifference curve unless some other consumer moves to a lower one, so that the result is a Pareto optimum.

But what if some goods are not bought by some consumers because indifference curves touch the axes (i.e. the sets $R(x)$ of section 3.4 are not strictly convex)? A single illustration will suffice to show that a competitive equilibrium is still a Pareto optimum.

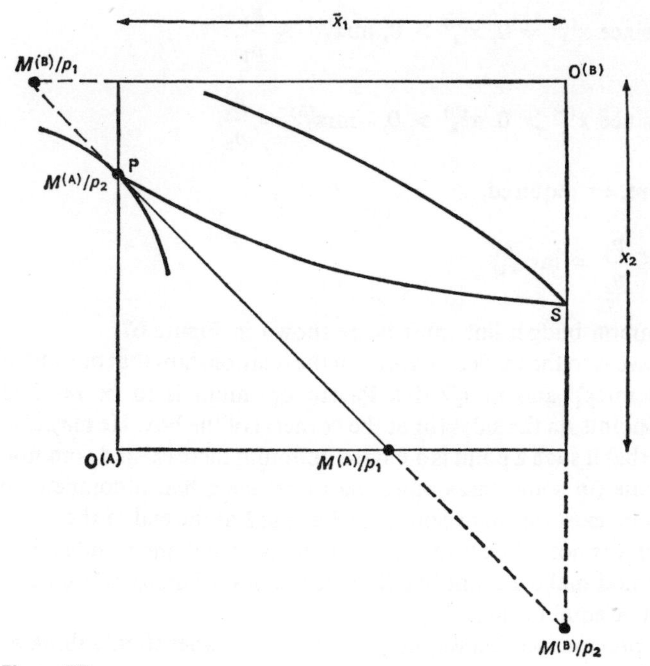

Figure 67

Consider the point P in Figure 67. At P, $x_1^{(A)} = 0$, while $x_2^{(A)}$, $x_1^{(B)}$ and $x_2^{(B)}$ are all positive. Although $\text{mrs}_{21}^{(A)} \neq \text{mrs}_{21}^{(B)}$ at P, this is clearly a Pareto optimum, because A cannot move to a higher indifference curve unless B moves to a lower one, and vice versa. S is another point at which $\text{mrs}_{21}^{(A)} \neq \text{mrs}_{21}^{(B)}$, but this is clearly *not* a Pareto optimum, since both consumers can become better off by moving to a point within the area enclosed by the indifference curves through S.

For a Pareto optimum at a point like P, where $x_1^{(A)} = 0$ and $x_2^{(A)}$, $x_1^{(B)}$ and $x_2^{(B)}$ are all positive it is sufficient (and necessary) that A's indifference curve be no steeper than that of B, i.e. that

$$\text{mrs}_{21}^{(A)} \leqq \text{mrs}_{21}^{(B)}.$$

In a competitive equilibrium at P, the points chosen by A and B (recall the analysis of section 7.2) will be such that:

For A, since $x_1^{(A)} = 0$, $x_2^{(A)} > 0$, $\text{mrs}_{21}^{(A)} \leqq \dfrac{p_1}{p_2}$.

For B, since $x_1^{(B)} > 0$, $x_2^{(B)} > 0$, $\text{mrs}_{21}^{(B)} = \dfrac{p_1}{p_2}$.

Therefore, as required,

$$\text{mrs}_{21}^{(A)} \leqq \frac{p_1}{p_2} = \text{mrs}_{21}^{(B)}.$$

The common budget line must be as shown in Figure 67.

We leave it to the reader to work out the relationships that must hold between $\text{mrs}_{21}^{(A)}$ and $\text{mrs}_{21}^{(B)}$ if a Pareto optimum is to be reached at other points on the sides (or at the corners) of the box. He may also confirm that if such a point is a Pareto optimum there exists a common budget line (in some cases more than one) such that a competitive equilibrium exists at that point. (See Exercise 2 at the end of the chapter.) And it is not difficult to see that there is no common budget line which would make a point like S, which is not a Pareto optimum, a competitive equilibrium.

In the previous section we suggested that the reader should think of the goods x_1 and x_2 as the 'non-durable goods of current consumption' of chapters 2–9. We shall not attempt to show that a competitive equilibrium is a Pareto optimum for each of the examples of choice over time and choice under uncertainty of chapters 11–15. But we shall be in a strong position to argue that this is in fact the case if we can show that a competitive equilibrium is a Pareto optimum in the goods–characteristics model of sections **10.3** and **10.4**, which played so large a part in Chapters 11–15.

Suppose, then, that each of the consumers A and B has a preference ordering, defined on bundles of the *characteristics* c_1 and c_2, $(c_1^{(A)}, c_2^{(A)})$ and $(c_1^{(B)}, c_2^{(B)})$, which obeys all the axioms of Chapters 2 and 3. And let there be fixed amounts, $\bar{x}_1$, $\bar{x}_2$, $\bar{x}_3$ of the three *goods* x_1, x_2 and x_3, of which x_1 has the highest, and x_3 the lowest, of the characteristics-ratios c_1/c_2. (See Figure 68.)

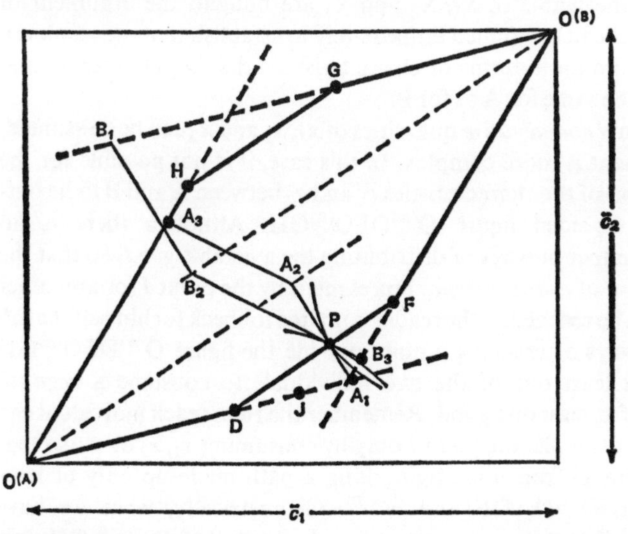

Figure 68

The total amounts of c_1 and c_2 available can be found by starting from A's origin $O^{(A)}$, travelling along the vector $O^{(A)}D$ representing the quantities of c_1 and c_2 present in the given amount of x_1, then along the vector DF representing the given amount of x_2, and finally along $FO^{(B)}$ representing the given amount of x_3. Alternatively, one could have started with the quantities of c_1 and c_2 in the given amount of x_3, going from $O^{(A)}$ to H (where $O^{(A)}H$ is equal and parallel to $FO^{(B)}$), then from H to G for x_2 (HG is equal and parallel to DF), and finally from G to $O^{(B)}$ for x_1 ($GO^{(B)}$ is equal and parallel to $O^{(A)}D$).

The total amounts of characteristics c_1 and c_2 available are now represented by the lengths of the sides of the rectangle whose corners are $O^{(A)}$ and $O^{(B)}$: an Edgeworth-Bowley box in the space of characteristics rather than of goods. Now if x_1, x_2 and x_3 are goods of which *negative* quantities can be bought, like the financial assets of section **15.2** when borrowing and short selling are possible, the argument of that section shows that the market prices of the *goods* (assets) will adjust themselves so that the budget line in terms of *characteristics* is a straight line extending from axis to axis for each consumer. In that case, if competitive equilibrium prices of x_1, x_2 and x_3 are established at which the whole of $\bar{x}_1$, $\bar{x}_2$ and $\bar{x}_3$ are bought, the argument of section **16.2** can be applied immediately to establish that the result is a Pareto optimum in terms of characteristics: the mrs between c_1 and c_2 will be the same for A as for B.

But if only *non-negative* quantities of x_1, x_2 and x_3 can be consumed, the argument is more complex. In this case, it is not possible for the distribution of the characteristics c_1 and c_2 between A and B to lie outside the six-sided figure $O^{(A)}DFO^{(B)}GH$. Although there is an infinite number of ways of distributing the available *goods* so that the distribution of *characteristics* represented by the point J (or any other point) can be reached,[50] the reader is invited to check for himself that *all* possible ways of reaching a point outside the figure $O^{(A)}DFO^{(B)}GH$ require at least one of the two individuals to consume a *negative* amount of at least one good. Remember the rules: each individual can reach, for example, the point J only by consuming x_1, x_2 or x_3, so that he must travel from his origin along a path made up only of lines parallel to $O^{(A)}D$, DF and $FO^{(B)}$. Geometrically, what we have asserted is that, to reach a point like J outside $O^{(A)}DFO^{(B)}GH$, it is necessary for a part of the path of at least one of the two individuals to be directed *towards* his origin (implying negative consumption of a good) rather than away from it. For example, in Figure 68 A may travel straight from $O^{(A)}$ to J, and B then goes from $O^{(B)}$ to F, from F to D, and then *back* from D to J.

Now if in competitive equilibrium either consumer is buying positive amounts of *both* x_1 and x_3, and at the same time the price of x_2 is such that the total of x_2 available is bought, each budget line in terms of characteristics must be a straight line. For if the budget lines had the shape of $C_1C_2C_3$ in Figure 69, no one would buy *both* x_1 and x_3, while

50. Students of linear algebra will recognize that we are in effect solving two independent equations in three unknown quantities.

if they had the shape of $C_1C_2'C_3$, no one would buy x_2. And if the characteristics budget line is a straight line, a competitive equilibrium is, as we have seen, a Pareto optimum in terms of characteristics.

The only difficulty arises, therefore, if neither consumer buys *both* x_1 *and* x_3. Either one buys only x_1 and the other only x_2 and x_3, or one buys only x_1 and x_2 and the other only x_2 and x_3, or one buys only x_1 and x_2 and the other only x_3. If the totals $\bar{x}_1$, $\bar{x}_2$ and $\bar{x}_3$ are to be fully consumed, all these distributions must lie either on the line DF or on the line GH in Figure 68.

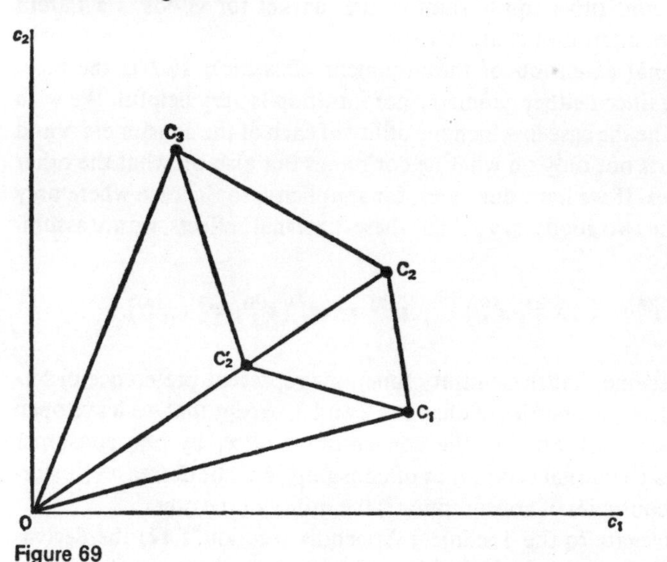

Figure 69

Consider such a point P on DF, where A is consuming x_1 and x_2 and B is consuming x_2 and x_3. It is probable that a competitive equilibrium at P will be one in which the budget lines in terms of characteristics are not straight lines. If they are not, they must (see section **10.3**) have the general shape of $C_1C_2C_3$ in Figure 69. A's budget line may be $A_1A_2A_3$ and B's budget line $B_1B_2B_3$. Since in competitive equilibrium the prices of x_1, x_2 and x_3 are the same for A as for B, A_1A_2 must be parallel to B_2B_1 and A_2A_3 must be parallel to B_3B_2.

It is true that at the point P the mrs between c_1 and c_2 is not the same for A as for B. The indifference curves through P enclose an area 'south-east' of P in which both A and B would be better off than at P. But they could enter this area only by moving *outside* the six-sided figure $O^{(A)}DFO^{(B)}GH$. And as we saw, they are confined to $O^{(A)}DFO^{(B)}GH$ by the restriction that only non-negative quantities of x_1, x_2 and x_3 can be bought. Thus a competitive equilibrium at P is, after all, a Pareto optimum – a 'corner solution' analogous to the point P in Figure 67.

This completes the argument (which it would not be difficult to generalize to the case of more goods, characteristics and consumers) that a competitive equilibrium in the market for goods is a Pareto optimum in terms of characteristics.

The final extension of the argument of section **16.2** is the most difficult, since neither geometry nor intuition is very helpful. We wish to examine the case in which the utility of each of the consumers A and B depends not only on what he consumes but also on what the other consumes. If we limit ourselves, for simplicity, to the case where only one of the two goods (say x_1) has these 'external' effects, we are assuming that

$$u^{(A)} = u^{(A)}(x_1^{(A)}, x_2^{(A)}, x_1^{(B)}), \qquad u^{(B)} = u^{(B)}(x_1^{(B)}, x_2^{(B)}, x_1^{(A)}).$$

We assume that these utility functions represent preference orderings with the properties of chapters 2 and 3, except that we leave open the question of whether the consumption of x_1 by one consumer increases ('external economies of consumption') or decreases ('external diseconomies of consumption') the utility of the other.

We relegate to the Technical Appendix (section **T.12**) the derivation of the conditions for a Pareto optimum in these circumstances, and state here only the answer to the following question. If A and B pay the same price for x_2 but may pay different prices ($p_1^{(A)}$, $p_1^{(B)}$) for x_1, and if each consumer equates the ratio of the prices he pays to the ratio of the marginal utilities of the commodities *he* consumes,

$$\left(\text{so that} \quad \frac{p_1^{(A)}}{p_2} = \frac{\partial u^{(A)}/\partial x_1^{(A)}}{\partial u^{(A)}/\partial x_2^{(A)}}, \qquad \frac{p_1^{(B)}}{p_2} = \frac{\partial u^{(B)}/\partial x_1^{(B)}}{\partial u^{(B)}/\partial x_2^{(B)}}\right),$$

what ratio of $p_1^{(A)}$ to $p_1^{(B)}$ is necessary to achieve a Pareto optimum? (Note that there is no question of subsidies or taxes to encourage or discourage *production*; we are interested only in a Pareto-optimal distribution of given totals $\bar{x}_1$ and $\bar{x}_2$). The answer is

$$\frac{p_1^{(A)}}{p_1^{(B)}} = \left[1 - \frac{\partial u^{(B)}/\partial x_1^{(A)}}{\partial u^{(B)}/\partial x_1^{(B)}}\right] \div \left[1 - \frac{\partial u^{(A)}/\partial x_1^{(B)}}{\partial u^{(A)}/\partial x_1^{(A)}}\right].$$

Though this result could scarcely be said to be intuitively obvious, it has certain implications which conform to one's intuition:

(a) If there is no interdependence, i.e. $\partial u^{(B)}/\partial x_1^{(A)} = \partial u^{(A)}/\partial x_1^{(B)} = 0$, then $p_1^{(A)}/p_1^{(B)} = 1$, so that one should let $p_1^{(A)} = p_1^{(B)}$ as in section 16.2.

(b) If an increase in $x_1^{(A)}$ *benefits* B, but by less than an equal increase in $x_1^{(B)}$, then $0 < \partial u^{(B)}/\partial x_1^{(A)} < \partial u^{(B)}/\partial x_1^{(B)}$, and the numerator of the expression for $p_1^{(A)}/p_1^{(B)}$ is positive and less than unity. If an increase in $x_1^{(B)}$ *harms* A, $\partial u^{(A)}/\partial x_1^{(B)} < 0$, and the denominator is greater than unity. In this case $p_1^{(A)}/p_1^{(B)} < 1$, and A should pay less for x_1 than B. This is clearly reasonable, since A's consumption of x_1 should be encouraged and B's should be discouraged.

(c) If the consumption of x_1 by each consumer benefits the other, both numerator and denominator are less than unity (and, let us assume for the moment, positive). If the consumption of x_1 by each consumer harms the other, both numerator and denominator are greater than unity. In each case the optimal price-ratio may require that $p_1^{(A)} \gtreqless p_1^{(B)}$; the answer depends on the relative magnitudes.

(d) Finally, there is a very intriguing set of cases. Suppose that an increase in $x_1^{(A)}$ benefits B by *more* than an equal increase in his own consumption $x_1^{(B)}$. Then

$$\frac{\partial u^{(B)}/\partial x_1^{(A)}}{\partial u^{(B)}/\partial x_1^{(B)}} > 1,$$

and the numerator of the expression for $p_1^{(A)}/p_1^{(B)}$ becomes negative. If the denominator remains positive, a Pareto optimum seems to require that $p_1^{(A)}/p_1^{(B)} < 0$, so that either $p_1^{(A)}$ or $p_1^{(B)}$ should be negative. A full analysis of such cases has not, to my knowledge, been made, and will not be attempted here. But one can imagine the following situation. x_1 is bread, and B knows A to be so poor that he would rather see A consume an extra loaf than consume it himself.

It might then be Pareto-optimal to charge A a negative price for bread ($p_1^{(A)} < 0$) so that in effect B is paying him to consume it. (This would hold, of course, only up to a point; when A had what B thought to be enough bread, the normal situation with $\partial u^{(B)}/\partial x_1^{(A)} < \partial u^{(B)}/\partial x_1^{(B)}$ would be restored, and the optimal value of $p_1^{(A)}$ would become positive.)

16.4 Index numbers of social consumption

Suppose that in a particular year (to be called the *base* year) a consumer bought the quantities $x = (x_1, x_2, \ldots, x_n)$ at the prices $p = (p_1, p_2, \ldots, p_n)$, and that in the current year he buys a different set of quantities x' at prices p'. Suppose that these are quantities of non-durable goods of current consumption and that the consumer obeys the assumptions of chapters 2 and 3.

We recall from section **8.3** that if the consumer can afford, with the budget and prices of the current year, to buy the goods of the base year, i.e. $\sum p_i' x_i' = p'.x' \geqq \sum p_i' x_i = p'.x$, then he reveals a preference for x' over x. Another way of putting this is to calculate the *ratio* of the values of the current year quantities to that of the base year quantities, when both are valued at the *current* year's prices, i.e. $p'.x'/p'.x$, and say that x' is revealed preferred to x if $p'.x'/p'.x \geqq 1$. The ratio $p'.x'/p'.x$ is the *Paasche quantity index*; the name Paasche indicates that the current year's prices are used in the valuation.

We may also measure the ratio of the values of the quantities x and x' when the *base* year prices are used in the valuation. The ratio $p.x'/p.x$ is the *Laspeyres quantity index*, the name Laspeyres indicating the use of base year prices. We should conclude that x is preferred to x' if $p.x'/p.x \leqq 1$.

Parallel to these quantity indices is a pair of price indices, measuring the change in the cost of a given set of quantities as prices have changed from the base year to the current year. When it is the change in the cost of the *base* year quantities that is measured, the ratio $p'.x/p.x$ is the *Laspeyres price index*. When the *current* year quantities are used, the ratio $p'.x'/p.x'$ is the *Paasche price index*.

Evidence on an individual's preferences derivable from price-quantity data can now be reformulated as follows. Recall that if $x \neq x'$ and $p'.x' \geqq p'.x$, a preference is revealed for x' over x, and consistency requires that $p.x' > p.x$. Similarly, if $p.x \geqq p.x'$, consistency requires that $p'.x > p'.x'$. Using the quantity indices defined above, we can construct the following table:

		Paasche quantity index $\frac{p'.x'}{p'.x}$		
		> 1	$= 1$	< 1
Laspeyres quantity index $\frac{p.x'}{p.x}$	> 1	$x'Px$	$x'Px$	no conclusion
	$= 1$	inconsistent	inconsistent (if $x \neq x'$)*	xPx'
	< 1	inconsistent	inconsistent	xPx'

* We can have $p'.x' = p'.x$ and $p.x' = p.x$ but $x \neq x'$ only if there are more than two goods.

How are these index numbers related to official statements of the form: gross national product in real terms has risen by 3 per cent? Such calculations are made by measuring first the percentage increase from a base year to the current year in the *money value* of final goods and services produced; suppose this is 5 per cent. Then (using q, q' for the very different quantities being measured, rather than x, x'), this means that $p'.q'/p.q = 1{\cdot}05$. This figure is then *deflated* by a price index, usually of the Laspeyres variety, i.e. $p'.q/p.q$. If this index shows an increase of 2 per cent from the base year, then $p'.q/p.q = 1{\cdot}02$.

Division of the ratio of money values by the Laspeyres price index gives

$$\frac{p'.q'}{p.q} \div \frac{p'.q}{p.q} = \frac{p'.q'}{p'.q} = \frac{1{\cdot}05}{1{\cdot}02} \simeq 1{\cdot}03.$$

The resulting ratio $p'.q'/p'.q$ is of course a Paasche quantity index. Is there any way in which we can go from the proposition: if $p'.x' \geqq p'.x$ for a single consumer, he reveals a preference for x' over x, to the proposition: if $p'.q' \geqq p'.q$ for an economy, its welfare has in some sense increased?

Now the quantities q and q' measure public goods and investment goods, as well as consumption goods, *produced*, so that there is an immense gulf between the two propositions. But we can make a small contribution to the bridging of the gulf if we limit ourselves to the following question. If a given number of consumers, satisfying all the conditions of the 'simple case' of section **16.2**, were in competitive equilibrium buying the total quantities x at prices p in the base year, and are in competitive equilibrium buying the total quantities x' at prices p' in the current year, and $p'.x' \geqq p'.x$, what conclusions can we draw about their 'welfare' in the two years?

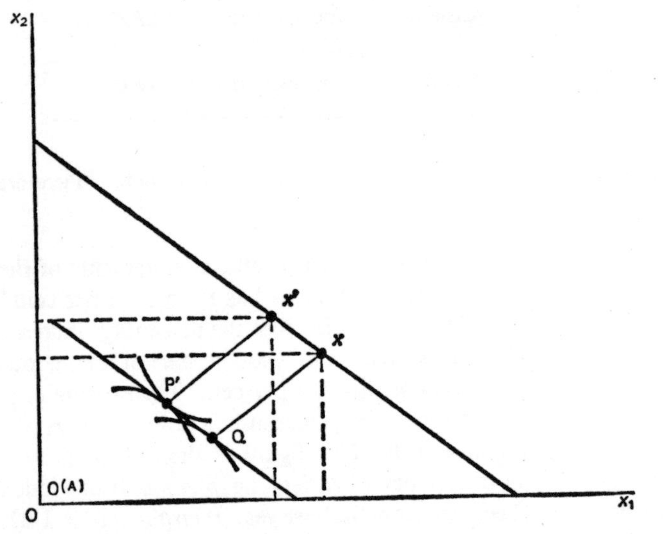

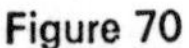
Figure 70

We shall limit ourselves, as we may without loss of generality, to the case of two goods and two consumers. In Figure 70, let the total quantities of x_1 and x_2 in the *current* year be represented by the point x', and draw through x' a 'budget line' with a slope determined by the current year's prices $p' = (p'_1, p'_2)$. We can regard the rectangle with corners at O and x' as an Edgeworth-Bowley box. Let A's origin $O^{(A)}$ coincide with O and B's origin with x'. Let the competitive equilibrium be at P′, with the common budget line through P′ of course parallel to the 'budget line' through x'.

Let the total quantities consumed in the *base* year be represented by the point x, which happens to lie on the 'budget line' through x'. This implies that at the prices p', x and x' cost the same amount, so that $p'.x' = p'.x$ and the Paasche quantity index $p'.x'/p'.x = 1$ (or 100 per cent).

Consider now the Edgeworth–Bowley box corresponding to the base year quantities x, with its corners at O and x. A's origin $O^{(A)}$ continues to coincide with O, but B's origin is now at x rather than at x'. Now it would clearly not have been possible for A and B both to consume in the base year exactly the same quantities of x_1 and x_2 as in the current year, since there was in total more x_1 and less x_2 in the base year than in the current year. The quantities of x_1 and x_2 consumed by B in the current year would be measured, with reference to x rather than x' as B's origin, by the point Q, reached by moving down the common budget line from P′ for a distance equal (and of course parallel) to $x'x$.

Now if it were possible (which it is not) for A to be at P′ and B at Q in the base year box with corners at O and x, then each would be on the same indifference curve as at P′ in the current year box with corners at O and x'. Is it possible to find a distribution of the base year quantities which puts each consumer on as high an indifference curve as at P′ in the current year?

Inspection of the diagram reveals that the answer is no. A's indifference curve through P′ has not moved. B is on the same indifference curve at Q with reference to x as his origin as he is at P′ with reference to x' as his origin, and this indifference curve is tangent at Q to the common budget line through P′. There is no distribution, within the base year box with corners at O and x, which can keep A on the indifference curve through P′ without putting B on a lower indifference curve than that through Q, and vice versa.

If the point x lay *below* the 'budget line' through x', so that $p'.x' > p'.x$, the comparison would be even less favourable to the base year. For then B's base-year origin would lie below the 'budget line' through x', the point Q would lie *below* the common budget line through P′, and *a fortiori* no distribution of the goods of the base year could make everyone as well off as at P′ in the current year.

Let us define a new relation H between bundles x and x' of goods consumed by a group of individuals:

$x'Hx$ if it is not possible to distribute x in such a way as to make each consumer as well off as in the observed competitive equilibrium distribution of x'.

Then what we have shown is that, given the assumptions of section **16.2**, if $x \neq x'$, and $p'.x' \geqq p'.x$, then $x'Hx$.

Two further points. Firstly, if x lies *above* the 'budget line' through x' ($p'.x' < p'.x$), the point Q lies above the common budget line through P′, and it *may or may not* be possible, with the goods x, to make everyone as well off as at P′. Secondly, we could have reversed x and x', and shown by an exactly similar argument that if $p.x \geqq p.x'$, then xHx', while if $p.x < p.x'$, no conclusion can be drawn.

We are now in a position to draw up for a group of individuals a table similar to that relevant for an individual earlier in this section:

		Paasche quantity index $\frac{p'.x'}{p'.x}$		
		> 1	$= 1$	< 1
Laspeyres quantity index $\frac{p.x'}{p.x}$	> 1	$x'Hx$	$x'Hx$	no conclusion
	$= 1$	$x'Hx$ and xHx'	$x'Hx$ and xHx' (if $x \neq x'$)	xHx'
	< 1	$x'Hx$ and xHx'	$x'Hx$ and xHx'	xHx'

The similarity between the two tables is interesting. Clearly the cases where both xHx' and $x'Hx$ are analogous to the cases of individual inconsistency.

But anyone who accepts $x'Hx$ as a criterion for an increase in the 'welfare' of a group of consumers is rather easy to please. For one thing, even if $p'.x' \geqq p'.x$ and $p.x' > p.x$, so that we know that $x'Hx$ but do not *know* whether xHx', it is perfectly possible in general that xHx', so that the criterion is a shaky one.

But let us not end this chapter on quite so negative a note. Our iconoclastic conclusions about the significance of index-number comparisons follow because we have made no assumptions whatsoever about the distribution of total budgets between consumers, nor about the nature of or the relationship between their tastes. Indeed, there is a close connexion between the interpretation of group index-numbers and the conditions for the existence of regular market demand curves discussed in sections **9.3** and **9.4**.

For example, if all consumers have equal budgets and identical tastes, then obviously if $p'.x' \geqq p'.x$ for the group the same inequality will hold for each and every consumer. Each consumer is better off in the current year than in the base year, and the current year is better by the Pareto criterion of section **16.1**.

As another example, suppose that consumers have identical tastes and indifference curves homothetic to the origin, then (see section **9.2**) the ratio of the quantities of x_1 and x_2 consumed will be the same for all consumers, and therefore equal to the ratio in which the totals $\bar{x}_1$ and $\bar{x}_2$ are available. Consider any proportional distribution among consumers of the total $p.x$ of base year budgets, and the same proportional distribution of the total of current year budgets. If $p'.x' \geqq p'.x$ the total quantities are related as, for example, in Figure 70. A consumer who had 1/1000 of the total of all budgets in each year would consume 1/1000 of the total of each commodity in each year, and his points x and x' would be related in exactly the same way (but of course on a smaller scale) as x and x' in Figure 70. Thus if the budgets were distributed in this way, each consumer would have $p'.x' \geqq p'.x$ and be better off in the current year.

What we have shown is that with identical and homothetic tastes, if the total quantities give $p'.x' \geqq p'.x$, then for *every* competitive distribution of the base year quantities x there *exists* a way of distributing the current year quantities x' which makes everyone better off. This is a much stronger statement than $x'Hx$ (and clearly implies that xHx' cannot be true).

It appears, therefore, that $p'.x' \geqq p'.x$ tends to mean more than simply $x'Hx$ the less the distribution of income changes and the more similar and the more nearly homothetic are the tastes of consumers. But even *strictly* identical and homothetic tastes do not permit us to conclude from $p'.x' \geqq p'.x$ that *social welfare* is higher in the current year. The *existence* of a distribution that makes everyone better off in the current year does not in itself justify such a conclusion, nor of course does it imply that such a distribution will be made.

In general if we are to conclude in *all* cases, from a comparison of index numbers of consumption within the restricted model of this section, that $W(u^{(A)}, u^{(B)},..., u^{(M)})$ has increased, it is necessary (i) that value judgements be made concerning the weights to be assigned to the individual utilities $u^{(A)}, u^{(B)},..., u^{(M)}$, (ii) that budgets be allocated in such a way as to achieve, for each set of total quantities, the maximum value of W in accordance with these value judgements. W may then be expressed as a function of $x_1, x_2,..., x_n$. Only then, strictly speaking, may we always conclude that social welfare has increased if $p'.x' \geqq p'.x$.

Exercises

1. Consumers A and B are at a competitive equilibrium in the conditions of section **16.2**. Each has a budget of £150, and pays £3 per unit for x_1 and £6 per unit for x_2. What would be the individual budgets and prices if exactly the same distribution of goods were to be achieved with the same total of £300, subject to the condition that A must pay twice as much per unit of each commodity as B?

2. Determine the relationship which must obtain between $\text{mrs}_{21}^{(A)}$ and $\text{mrs}_{21}^{(B)}$ if a Pareto optimum is to be achieved when A is consuming the total available amount, $\bar{x}_1$, of x_1, and B is consuming $\bar{x}_2$. Show that if the conditions for a Pareto optimum are satisfied when the goods are distributed in this way, there is a competitive equilibrium corresponding to the distribution.

3.

Commodity	*Base Year*		*Current Year*	
	Price	*Quantity*	*Price*	*Quantity*
x_1	£1	100	£1	200
x_2	£1	100	£2	20

(a) From these data, calculate the Laspeyres and Paasche price and quantity indices, expressing the current year prices and quantities as percentages of the base year prices and quantities.

(b) What conclusions would you draw if these data represented the purchases of (i) a single consumer, (ii) a group of consumers?

Notes on the literature

An excellent introduction to the subject-matter of this chapter is T. Scitovsky, *Welfare and Competition* (Irwin, 1952, ch. 4).

16.1 Welfare economics is a vast subject, and we shall not attempt to supply a bibliography. The reader may wish to consult E. J. Mishan 'A survey of welfare economics, 1939–59' (*Econ. J.*, vol. 70, no. 278, pp. 187–256, 1960), reprinted in *Surveys of Economic Theory*, vol. I (Macmillan, 1965) produced by the American Economic Association and the Royal Economic Society. The analysis of the problem of constructing, from individual preference orderings, a *social* preference ordering which satisfies certain conditions, is of considerable interest; see K. J. Arrow, *Social Choice and Individual Values*, Wiley, 1951 and 1963.

16.2 On this section the reader can profitably consult Newman's *Theory of Exchange*, chapter 3, and the ambitious reader may wish to persevere through chapters 4 and 5.

16.3 Our argument, that a competitive equilibrium is a Pareto optimum in a goods-characteristics model, takes the sting out of the *prima facie* rather disturbing remark by Lancaster ('A new approach to consumer theory', *J. polit. Econ.*, p. 152, 1966): 'The traditional marginal conditions for Paretian exchange optimum do not hold because the price ratio relevant to one consumer's decisions differs from the price ratio relevant to another's.' Problems of interdependence in welfare economics are extensively treated in J. de V. Graaff, *Theoretical Welfare Economics.* See also W. J. Baumol, *Welfare Economics and the Theory of the State* (London School of Economics, 2nd edn 1965).

16.4 The classic treatment of the subject of this section is Samuelson's 'Evaluation of real national income' (*Oxf. econ. Pap.*, new series, vol. 2, no. 1, pp. 1–29, 1950), reprinted in *The Collected Scientific Papers of Paul A. Samuelson*, vol. II, pp. 1044–72. Our argument is concerned only with the first twelve pages of this paper (the later parts take production into account), and at that only scratches the surface. The symbol H in the relation $x'Hx$ stands for Hicks. In the literature this relation is often lumped together with the quite distinct 'Kaldor criterion', according to which x' is better than x if one *can* redistribute the goods x' so as to make everyone better off than at the competitive equilibrium distribution of x. Our argument in the text implies that observation of total quantities and prices can never show that the Kaldor criterion is satisfied.

Another important paper, with a bearing on sections **9.3** and **9.4** of the text as well as **16.4**, is Samuelson's 'Social indifference curves' (*Q. J. Econ.*, vol. 70, no. 1, pp. 1–22, 1956), reprinted in *The Collected Scientific Papers of Paul A. Samuelson*, vol. II, pp. 1073–94.

Chapter 17
Conclusion

We shall resist the temptation to conclude this volume with a grand synthesis – a full model of the way in which the consumer makes his plans for all times and contingencies. The building blocks are available in the foregoing chapters for the reader who cares to undertake such an exercise. It is more likely, however, that if he finds this book useful in his thinking or research, it will be in its application to specific aspects of the consumer's behaviour, but it may be comforting to know that his work fits into a general model.

This model, as a conceptual structure, seems to me fairly impressive. The directions in which, I think, it should be and probably will be developed in the near future are: (i) exploration of the implications of the *goods-characteristics* relationship for the problems treated in all parts of the book; (ii) systematic treatment of the *information* at the consumer's disposal, and the ways in which he acquires it; (iii) fuller recognition of *external effects* in consumption – the impact of the choices of one consumer on the preferences of another; (iv) incorporation in the model of the *transactions costs* which we have frequently found to upset the tidiness of our formulations; (v) further derivation of specific *measurable demand relationships* from utility functions; (vi) empirical work designed to *measure central theoretical concepts* such as the characteristics of goods and assets, expectations of prices, earnings and interest rates, and subjective probabilities.

Technical Appendix

T.1 Own-price elasticity and expenditure

If the own-price elasticity of demand is unitary at all points on a demand curve, then

$$\frac{p_i}{x_i}\frac{dx_i}{dp_i} = -1,$$

so that $$\frac{dx_i}{x_i} = -\frac{dp_i}{p_i}.$$

Integrating both sides, and writing k for the constant of integration, we get

$$\log x_i = k - \log p_i,$$

so that $$x_i = \frac{C}{p_i}$$

or $$p_i x_i = C.$$

Thus unitary elasticity of demand means that total expenditure is constant at all points on a demand curve; if we start at any point (x_i, p_i) and reduce price ($dp_i < 0$), the increase in quantity dx_i is exactly enough to keep expenditure constant. But if demand is *elastic* $(p_i/x_i)(dx_i/dp_i) < -1$, so that if we start at the same point as before and reduce price by the same amount as before the increase in quantity dx_i must be *greater* than when demand is unit-elastic, and therefore total expenditure must *increase*. Hence if demand is elastic at all points on the demand curve, every reduction in price must increase total expenditure (as stated in the text, p. 56). Similarly, if demand is *inelastic*, $(p_i/x_i)(dx_i/dp_i) > -1$, a given reduction in price will increase quantity by *less* than when demand is unit-elastic, so that total expenditure will *fall.*

T.2 Average and marginal values

Let $f(x)$ be any function of x, with $x > 0$. We define

$$\text{Average value} = A = \frac{f(x)}{x};$$

$$\text{Marginal value} = M = f(x+1)-f(x).$$

We wish to show first that if A increases as we go from x to $x+1$, that is if

$$\frac{f(x+1)}{x+1} > \frac{f(x)}{x}, \tag{1}$$

then M is greater than either average value,

$$\text{i.e.} \quad f(x+1)-f(x) > \frac{f(x+1)}{x+1} > \frac{f(x)}{x}. \tag{2}$$

From **1** it follows at once that

$$x\,f(x+1) > (x+1)f(x). \tag{3}$$

If we subtract $x\,f(x)$ from both sides of **3**, and divide both sides by x, we get

$$f(x+1)-f(x) > \frac{f(x)}{x},$$

which is one part of **2**. If we add $f(x+1)$ to both sides of **3**, subtract $(x+1)\,f(x)$ from both sides, and then divide both sides by $x+1$, we get

$$f(x+1)-f(x) > \frac{f(x+1)}{x+1},$$

which is the other part of **2**.

We can also show that if A remains *constant*, M is *equal* to both average values by repeating the above argument exactly, but with '=' everywhere replacing '>'. And we can show that if A *decreases* as we go from x to $x+1$, M is *less* than either average value by repeating the argument with '<' everywhere replacing '>'. These results are stated on p. 57 of the text.

An alternative approach, relevant for average and marginal values at a *point*, is to note that $A = f(x)/x$ is (increasing/constant/decreasing) as

$$\frac{d}{dx}\left[\frac{f(x)}{x}\right] \gtreqless 0.$$

Now $f'(x) = d[f(x)]/dx$ is equal to M, interpreted as the marginal value of $f(x)$ at a point. Differentiation of A gives

$$\begin{aligned}\frac{dA}{dx} &= \frac{d}{dx}\left[\frac{f(x)}{x}\right]\\ &= \frac{x f'(x) - f(x)}{x^2}\\ &= \frac{1}{x}\left[f'(x) - \frac{f(x)}{x}\right]\\ &= \frac{1}{x}(M - A).\end{aligned}$$

With x positive, it follows that

$$\frac{dA}{dx}\begin{cases} > 0 & \text{as } M > A,\\ = 0 & \text{as } M = A,\\ < 0 & \text{as } M < A.\end{cases}$$

T.3 Utility maximization

In the immediate vicinity of a point where utility is maximized and the quantities of all commodities are positive, all changes in $x_1, \ldots, x_n$ permitted by the budget constraint leave utility unchanged. Hence the change in u (its total differential) is zero, so that

$$du = \sum_{i=1}^{n} u_i \, dx_i = 0, \tag{1}$$

where $u_i = \partial u / \partial x_i$.

This condition will define a maximum of u at the point x if, as we move away from x, u decreases for all changes in $x_1, \ldots, x_n$ permitted by the budget constraint. This will be so if *du*, which is zero at x decreases (and therefore becomes negative) as we move away from x. The differential *du* decreases if *its* total differential is negative, i.e. if

$$d(du) = d^2u = d\left(\sum_{i=1}^{n} u_i\, dx_i\right) = \sum_{i=1}^{n}\sum_{j=1}^{n} u_{ij}\, dx_i\, dx_j < 0. \qquad \mathbf{2}$$

The term u_{ij} means $\partial^2 u/\partial x_i \partial x_j$. We assume throughout that these second-order partial derivatives are continuous. On this assumption, there is a well-known mathematical proposition (Young's Theorem), which states that it makes no difference to the result whether we differentiate first with respect to x_i or first with respect to x_j;

$$u_{ij} = \frac{\partial^2 u}{\partial x_i\, \partial x_j} = \frac{\partial^2 u}{\partial x_j\, \partial x_i} = u_{ji}.$$

This, as we shall see in section **T.5**, has important economic implications. (It implies the symmetry of substitution effects,

$$\left(\frac{\partial x_i}{\partial p_j}\right)_S = \left(\frac{\partial x_j}{\partial p_i}\right)_S,$$

mentioned in section **5.4** of the text and elsewhere.)

The expression $\sum_i\sum_j u_{ij}\, dx_i\, dx_j$ in **2** is a *quadratic form*, and we seek the conditions in which it is *negative definite* subject to equation **1**. This means that we wish to know in what conditions the quadratic form will be negative for *all changes* in $x_1, \ldots, x_n$ which satisfy equation **1**.

The conditions (which we shall not attempt to prove) are expressed in terms of the following determinant, called the 'bordered Hessian'

$$U = \begin{vmatrix} 0 & u_1 & \ldots & u_n \\ u_1 & u_{11} & \ldots & u_{1n} \\ \ldots & \ldots & \ldots & \ldots \\ u_n & u_{1n} & \ldots & u_{nn} \end{vmatrix}.$$

It is formed by taking the Hessian determinant of the function $u(x_1, \ldots, x_n)$, – an $n \times n$ determinant composed of the second-order partial derivatives u_{ij} – and 'bordering' it with a new first row and first column consisting of $(0\, u_1 \ldots u_n)$.

The quadratic form in **2** is negative definite subject to **1** if and only if the *principal minors* of U (the determinants about the main diagonal $(0\ u_{11} \ldots u_{nn})$) of orders 3, 4, 5... are alternately positive and negative. If

$$\begin{vmatrix} 0 & u_1 & u_2 \\ u_1 & u_{11} & u_{12} \\ u_2 & u_{12} & u_{22} \end{vmatrix} > 0, \qquad \begin{vmatrix} 0 & u_1 & u_2 & u_3 \\ u_1 & u_{11} & u_{12} & u_{13} \\ u_2 & u_{12} & u_{22} & u_{23} \\ u_3 & u_{13} & u_{23} & u_{33} \end{vmatrix} < 0, \quad \text{etc.} \qquad \mathbf{3}$$

and the determinant U itself has the sign of $(-1)^n$, then although we have checked only *one* principal minor of each order, it will in fact be the case that *all* principal minors of order 3 are positive, *all* those of order 4 are negative, etc., so that the conditions for negative definiteness are satisfied.

These conditions are in fact equivalent to the assumption of smoothly and strictly convex-to-the-origin indifference surfaces made in chapter 3. This may be verified for the case of only two goods by deriving directly the conditions for convex-to-the-origin indifference curves stated on p. 90 of the text. Along an indifference curve (see section **6.4** of the text)

$$\frac{dx_2}{dx_1} = -\frac{u_1}{u_2}. \qquad \mathbf{4}$$

Convexity implies that as x_1 increases, mrs_{21} decreases (section **3.4**). But $\text{mrs}_{21} = u_1/u_2 = -dx_2/dx_1$. Hence as mrs_{21} decreases, dx_2/dx_1 must *increase*; $dx_2/dx_1 < 0$, and convexity requires it to come closer to zero as x_1 increases. The condition for convexity is therefore that $d^2x_2/dx_1^2 > 0$. Differentiating **4** with respect to x_1, we get

$$\frac{d^2x_2}{dx_1^2} = -\frac{u_2(u_{11}+u_{12}\ dx_2/dx_1)-u_1(u_{12}+u_{22}\ dx_2/dx_1)}{u_2^2}.$$

Substitution for dx_2/dx_1 from **4** gives

$$\frac{d^2x_2}{dx_1^2} = -\frac{u_2(u_{11}-u_{12}\ u_1/u_2)-u_1(u_{12}-u_{22}\ u_1/u_2)}{u_2^2}$$

$$= -\frac{u_2^2\ u_{11}-2u_1\ u_2\ u_{12}+u_1^2\ u_{22}}{u_2^3}.$$

This last expression is positive (since $u_2^3 > 0$) if and only if

$u_2^2 u_{11} - 2u_1 u_2 u_{12} + u_1^2 u_{22} < 0$, which is the condition given in the text (p. 90). And it is also the inequality we obtain if we multiply out the 3×3 determinant

$$\begin{vmatrix} 0 & u_1 & u_2 \\ u_1 & u_{11} & u_{12} \\ u_2 & u_{12} & u_{22} \end{vmatrix}$$

and find that it is positive.

Incidentally, although conditions **1** and **2** are *sufficient* for a maximum of u, the inequality $d(du) < 0$ is not strictly *necessary* for all problems and functions. $d^2u = 0$ (but not $d^2u > 0$) *may* be consistent with a constrained maximum. The situation is analogous to that of the function $y = -x^4$, which has a maximum at $x = 0$, even though $d^2y/dx^2 = 0$ at that point. However as we have just seen, the properties of the utility function in Chapter 6 ensure that the conditions for $d^2u < 0$ *are* in fact satisfied at a point where u is maximized subject to a linear budget constraint.

T.4 The composite commodity theorem

We wish to show (see p. 112 of the text) that if the convexity conditions of section **T.3** are satisfied by the utility function $u(x_1, \ldots, x_n)$, they are also satisfied by the utility function $v(x_1, x_c)$, in which the variables $x_2, \ldots, x_n$ have been replaced by

$$x_c = x_2 + \frac{p_3}{p_2} x_3 + \ldots + \frac{p_n}{p_2} x_n,$$

on the assumption that the price-ratios $p_3/p_2, \ldots, p_n/p_2$ are constant. It will be quite sufficient, and save a great deal of tedious algebra, to assume that $n = 3$, so that $u = u(x_1, x_2, x_3)$ and

$$x_c = x_2 + \frac{p_3}{p_2} x_3.$$

Now we know that when utility is maximized, $u_3/u_2 = p_3/p_2$. Therefore if condition **1** of section **T.3** is satisfied,

$$0 = u_1\,dx_1 + u_2\,dx_2 + u_3\,dx_3$$

$$= u_1\,dx_1 + u_2\,dx_2 + u_2\frac{p_3}{p_2}\,dx_3$$

$$= u_1\,dx_1 + u_2\left[dx_2 + \frac{p_3}{p_2}\,dx_3\right].$$

For those quantities x_1, x_2 and x_3 which are chosen when p_3/p_2 takes on its given constant value, the values of the functions $u(x_1, x_2, x_3)$ and $v(x_1, x_c)$ are equal.[51] The values of the partial derivatives of the two functions with respect to any of their arguments are also equal in these circumstances. Bearing in mind the definition of x_c, we deduce that:

$$u_1 = \partial v/\partial x_1 = v_1,$$
$$u_2 = (\partial v/\partial x_c)(\partial x_c/\partial x_2) = v_c,$$
$$u_3 = (\partial v/\partial x_c)(\partial x_c/\partial x_3) = (p_3/p_2)\,v_c.$$

Thus the first-order conditions for a maximum may be stated as:

$$u_1\,dx_1 + u_2[dx_2 + (p_3/p_2)\,dx_3] = v_1\,dx_1 + v_c\,dx_c = 0. \qquad \mathbf{1'}$$

The part of the composite commodity theorem we seek to prove is that if the quadratic form

$$\sum_{i=1}^{3}\sum_{j=1}^{3} u_{ij}\,dx_i\,dx_j$$

is negative definite, subject to $\sum_{i=1}^{3} u_i\,dx_i = 0$, (which is equivalent to **1′** when p_3/p_2 has its given value), then the quadratic form

$$v_{11}\,dx_1^2 + 2v_{1c}\,dx_1\,dx_c + v_{cc}\,dx_c^2 \qquad \mathbf{2'}$$

is negative definite, subject to **1′**.

When p_3/p_2 is given, the following equalities may be derived:

51. My colleague, John Craven, confirmed my suspicion that the "proof" given in the first printing was incorrect; the new proof is his. (The error in the earlier argument lay in the statement that $\partial(u_3/u_2)/\partial x_i = 0$; this should have read: $d(u_3/u_2)/dx_i = 0$, but this is not a fruitful line to pursue.)

$u_{11} = v_{11},$

$u_{12} = v_{1c}(\partial x_c/\partial x_2) = v_{1c},$

$u_{13} = v_{1c}(\partial x_c/\partial x_3) = (p_3/p_2)v_{1c},$

$u_{22} = v_{cc}(\partial x_c/\partial x_2) = v_{cc},$

$u_{23} = v_{cc}(\partial x_c/\partial x_3) = (p_3/p_2)v_{cc},$

$u_{33} = (p_3/p_2)v_{cc}(\partial x_c/\partial x_3) = (p_3/p_2)^2 v_{cc}.$

Thus **2′** may be written as:

$$\begin{aligned} v_{11}\, dx_1^2 &+ 2v_{1c}[dx_1\, dx_2 + (p_3/p_2)\, dx_1\, dx_3] + v_{cc}[dx_2^2 \\ &+ 2(p_3/p_2)\, dx_2\, dx_3 + (p_3/p_2)^2\, dx_3^2] \\ &= u_{11}\, dx_1^2 + 2u_{12}\, dx_1\, dx_2 + 2u_{13}\, dx_1\, dx_3 + \\ &+ u_{22}\, dx_2^2 + 2u_{23}\, dx_2\, dx_3 + u_{33}\, dx_3^2 \\ &= \sum_{i=1}^{3} \sum_{i=1}^{3} u_{ij}\, dx_i\, dx_j. \end{aligned}$$

The conditions for **2′** to be negative definite, subject to **1′**, when x_1, x_2 and x_3 are chosen with p_3/p_2 at its given value, are therefore simply that $\Sigma\, u_{ij}\, dx_i\, dx_j$ be negative definite, subject to $\Sigma\, u_i\, dx_i = 0$ (which is equivalent to **1′** in these circumstances); but this is precisely what is *assumed* to hold, *without* any restriction on prices. The satisfaction of the convexity conditions by the function $v(x_1, x_c)$ which contains the composite commodity is therefore implicit in their satisfaction by the function $u(x_1, x_2, x_3)$. It is straightforward but tedious to show that this holds for more complex cases.

T.5 The Slutzky equations

As we found in section **7.1**, it is necessary for a maximum of $u(x_1, \ldots, x_n)$, when all the x are positive and the budget constraint is

$$\sum_{i=1}^{n} p_i x_i = M,$$

that
$$\begin{aligned} u_1 - \mu p_1 &= 0, \\ \vdots \quad & \quad \vdots \\ u_n - \mu p_n &= 0. \end{aligned}$$

Taking the total differentials of all these equations, we obtain

$$p_1\,dx_1 + \ldots + p_n\,dx_n = dM - \sum_{i=1}^{n} x_i\,dp_i,$$

$$\begin{aligned} p_1(-d\mu) + u_{11}\,dx_1 + \ldots + u_{1n}\,dx_n &= \mu dp_1,\\ \vdots \qquad\qquad \vdots \qquad\qquad \vdots \qquad &\quad \vdots\\ p_n(-d\mu) + u_{1n}\,dx_1 + \ldots + u_{nn}\,dx_n &= \mu dp_n. \end{aligned}$$

It is convenient to write this result in matrix form, and to replace $p_1, \ldots, p_n$ by $u_1/\mu, \ldots, u_n/\mu$ (which of course we may do by virtue of the conditions for a maximum of u), as follows

$$\begin{bmatrix} 0 & u_1/\mu & \ldots & u_n/\mu \\ u_1/\mu & u_{11} & \ldots & u_{1n} \\ \vdots & \vdots & & \vdots \\ u_n/\mu & u_{1n} & \ldots & u_{nn} \end{bmatrix} \begin{bmatrix} -d\mu \\ dx_1 \\ \vdots \\ dx_n \end{bmatrix} = \begin{bmatrix} dM - \sum_{i=1}^{n} x_i\,dp_i \\ \mu\,dp_1 \\ \vdots \\ \mu\,dp_n \end{bmatrix}$$

The square matrix on the left-hand side is not singular, since its determinant is the non-zero determinant U of section **T.3** with the elements of the first row and first column divided by μ. We can therefore solve for any of the dx_i (say dx_1) by Cramer's rule

$$dx_1 = \frac{\begin{vmatrix} 0 & dM - \Sigma\,x_i\,dp_i & \ldots & u_n/\mu \\ u_1/\mu & \mu\,dp_1 & \ldots & u_{1n} \\ \vdots & \vdots & & \vdots \\ u_n/\mu & \mu\,dp_n & \ldots & u_{nn} \end{vmatrix}}{\begin{vmatrix} 0 & u_1/\mu & \ldots & u_n/\mu \\ u_1/\mu & u_{11} & \ldots & u_{1n} \\ \vdots & \vdots & & \vdots \\ u_n/\mu & u_{1n} & \ldots & u_{nn} \end{vmatrix}}.$$

In the expansion of the determinant in the numerator of the expression for dx_1, the coefficient of $dM - \Sigma\,x_i\,dp_i$ is the cofactor U_1 of the element u_1 in the bordered Hessian U of section **T.3** with the elements of the first column all divided by μ. The coefficient of $\mu\,dp_i$ is the cofactor U_{1i} of the element $u_{1i} (= u_{i1})$ of U, with each element of the first row *and* the first column divided by μ. (Of course, to divide all elements of a row or column of a determinant by μ is to divide the value of the determinant by μ). Finally, therefore, we have

$$dx_1 = \frac{(U_1/\mu)(dM - \sum_i x_i\, dp_i) + \sum_i (U_{1i}/\mu^2)\mu\, dp_i}{U/\mu^2}$$

$$= \mu\frac{U_1}{U}\left(dM - \sum_i x_i\, dp_i\right) + \mu\sum_i \frac{U_{1i}}{U}\, dp_i.$$

If only M changes, it follows that

$$\frac{\partial x_1}{\partial M} = \mu\frac{U_1}{U}. \qquad \mathbf{1}$$

And if only p_i changes we find (using **1**) that

$$\frac{\partial x_1}{\partial p_i} = \mu\frac{U_{1i}}{U} - x_i\mu\frac{U_1}{U}$$

$$= \mu\frac{U_{1i}}{U} - x_i\frac{\partial x_1}{\partial M}. \qquad \mathbf{2}$$

Of course the first term in **2** is the substitution effect and the second term is the income effect, as these were defined in section **5.2**.

The most important results are as follows. Firstly,

$$\left[\frac{\partial x_i}{\partial p_i}\right]_S = \mu\frac{U_{ii}}{U} < 0, \qquad \mathbf{3}$$

for any commodity x_i, since the argument given above applies to any commodity, not just to x_1. This negative own-price substitution effect, derived by another method in section **5.3**, follows in the present case because, by the convexity conditions of section **T.3**, the determinants U_{ii} and U, being principal minors of U of orders n and $n+1$ respectively, must have opposite signs, and $\mu = u_i/p_i > 0$. Secondly,

$$\left[\frac{\partial x_i}{\partial p_j}\right]_S = \mu\frac{U_{ij}}{U} = \mu\frac{U_{ji}}{U} = \left[\frac{\partial x_j}{\partial p_i}\right]_S. \qquad \mathbf{4}$$

This symmetry of cross-substitution effects, mentioned in section **5.4**, follows from the fact that, as mentioned in section **T.3**, it is assumed that for all i and j, $u_{ij} = u_{ji}$, so that the determinant U is symmetrical about its main diagonal, and therefore the cofactors U_{ij} and U_{ji} of the elements u_{ij} and u_{ji} are equal in value. Finally, using **4** and the relevant forms of **2**,

$$\frac{\partial x_i}{\partial p_j}+x_j\frac{\partial x_i}{\partial M}=\frac{\partial x_j}{\partial p_i}+x_i\frac{\partial x_j}{\partial M}, \qquad \mathbf{5}$$

a result which we shall use in our discussion of linear expenditure systems (sections **9.2** and **T.7**).

T.6 Concave and quasi-concave functions

The necessary conditions for a maximum of $u(x_1,\ldots, x_n)$ subject to one or more constraints, derived in sections **7.2** and **7.3** of the text for conditions more general than those of section **7.1** (or of sections **T.3** and **T.5**), are also sufficient if the following conditions are satisfied.

1. The function $u(x_1,\ldots, x_n)$ is *quasi-concave*;
2. The feasible region (the set of values of $x_1,\ldots, x_n$ permitted by the constraints) is *non-empty* (so that the constraints leave the consumer something to choose), *bounded* (otherwise u may have no finite maximum) and *convex*.

The convexity of sets was discussed in section **3.4**, and obviously the set of points permitted by the budget constraint (or by the budget constraint plus the rationing constraints of section **7.3**) is convex, bounded and (let us hope) non-empty. If *either* the feasible region is *strictly* convex (which in the present context it is not – see section **3.4**), *or* the utility function is *strictly* quasi-concave, there is a unique bundle of goods yielding a maximum of u. Let us therefore examine the concept of quasi-concavity.

Concavity is a special case of quasi-concavity. A function $f(x)$ of a single variable is concave if, given any two values x' and x'' and $0 \leqslant k \leqslant 1, f[kx'+(1-k)x''] \geqq kf(x')+(1-k)f(x'')$.

This implies that in Figure 71 the value of $f(x)$ at any point (say $\bar{x}$) on the line $x'x''$ is at least as great as the value of the ordinate at the point corresponding to $\bar{x}$ on the straight line joining C and D; $\bar{x} = kx'+(1-k)x''$; $f(\bar{x}) = \bar{x}A \geqq \bar{x}B = kf(x')+(1-k)f(x'')$.

$f(x)$ is *strictly* concave if, for $0 < k < 1$,

$$f[kx'+(1-k)x''] > kf(x')+(1-k)f(x'').$$

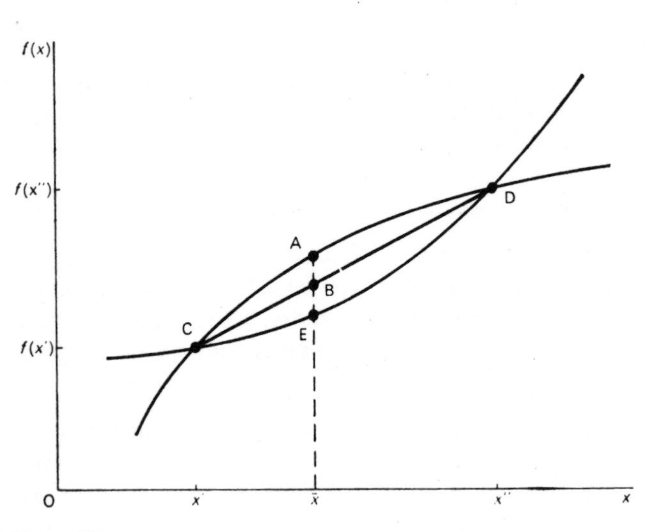

Figure 71

The curve CAD in Figure 71 is the graph of a strictly concave function, since at all points like $\bar{x}, \bar{x}A > \bar{x}B$.
The definition of a *convex* function is that

$$f[kx' + (1-k)x''] \leqq kf(x') + (1-k)f(x''),$$

with the strong inequality $<$ for strict convexity. The curve CED in Figure 71 is the graph of a strictly convex function.

In the case of a function $f(x_1, \ldots, x_n)$ of several variables, strict concavity means that, given $(x'_1, \ldots, x'_n)$ and $(x''_1, \ldots, x''_n)$, and $0 < k < 1$,

$$f[kx'_1 + (1-k)x''_1, \ldots, kx'_n + (1-k)x''_n] > kf(x'_1, \ldots, x'_n) + \\ +(1-k)f(x''_1, \ldots, x''_n).$$

When we are dealing with utility functions, all that we require for a unique maximum is that indifference surfaces be smoothly and strictly convex-to-the-origin everywhere. Strict concavity of the utility function implies this, as we shall see in a moment, but it also implies more. It implies that if we hold constant the quantities of all commodities but x_i, the behaviour of utility as x_i changes is as depicted by the curve CAD in Figure 71. This means that $u_{ii} = \partial^2 u/\partial x_i^2 < 0$, the diminishing marginal utility which, as we saw in section **6.4**, is not necessary for well-behaved demand functions.

All we require is that if a straight line is drawn between any two points x' and x'' on an indifference surface, every point between x' and x'' on that line lies on a higher indifference surface. It is sufficient, therefore, to make the weaker assumption (implied by strict concavity) that the utility function is *strictly quasi-concave*, which means that, for $0 < k < 1$,

if $\quad u(x_1', \ldots, x_n') = u(x_1'', \ldots, x_n'') = \bar{u}$,

then $\quad u[kx_1' + (1-k)x_1'', \ldots, kx_n' + (1-k)x_n''] > \bar{u}$.

T.7 Linear expenditure systems

We wish to prove several assertions made about linear expenditure systems in section **9.2**.

(a) If for each commodity $x_i \, (i = 1, 2, \ldots, n)$ the demand function is

$$x_i = a_{i1}\frac{p_1}{p_i} + \ldots + a_{ii} + \ldots + a_{in}\frac{p_n}{p_i} + b_i\frac{M}{p_i}, \qquad \mathbf{1}$$

then there exists a set of numbers $s_1, \ldots, s_n$ such that

$$x_i = s_i + \frac{b_i(M - \sum_{k=1}^{n} p_k s_k)}{p_i}. \qquad \mathbf{2}$$

Clearly this will be true if and only if in every such equation the constant term (the coefficient of p_i/p_i) and the coefficient of every price-ratio (p_j/p_i) is the same in **1** as in **2**. This means that in the demand functions for x_i and x_j

$$a_{ii} = s_i(1-b_i); \quad a_{ij} = -b_i s_j; \quad a_{jj} = s_j(1-b_j); \qquad \mathbf{3}$$
$$a_{ji} = -b_j s_i.$$

It is sufficient to show that for all i and j

$$\frac{a_{ii}}{a_{ji}} = -\frac{1-b_i}{b_j}, \qquad \mathbf{4}$$

for then we can *define*, for all i,

$$s_i = \frac{a_{ii}}{1-b_i}, \tag{5}$$

and **3** follows at once from **4** and **5**.

We make use of the symmetry proposition, cited in section **9.2** and proved as result **5** of section **T.5**, that

$$\frac{\partial x_i}{\partial p_j} + x_j \frac{\partial x_i}{\partial M} = \frac{\partial x_j}{\partial p_i} + x_i \frac{\partial x_j}{\partial M}. \tag{6}$$

First we perform the differentiations indicated by **6** on demand functions of the form **1** for x_i and x_j:

$$\frac{a_{ij}}{p_i} + \frac{b_i}{p_i}\left[a_{j1}\frac{p_1}{p_j} + \dots + a_{jj} + \dots + a_{jn}\frac{p_n}{p_j} + b_j\frac{M}{p_j}\right]$$
$$= \frac{a_{ji}}{p_j} + \frac{b_j}{p_j}\left[a_{i1}\frac{p_1}{p_i} + \dots + a_{ii} + \dots + a_{in}\frac{p_n}{p_i} + b_i\frac{M}{p_i}\right]$$

Multiply both sides by $p_i p_j$

$$a_{ij}p_j + b_i(a_{ji}p_1 + \dots + a_{jj}p_j + \dots + a_{jn}p_n + b_j M)$$
$$= a_{ji}p_i + b_j(a_{i1}p_1 + \dots + a_{ii}p_i + \dots + a_{in}p_n + b_i M)$$

and collect terms in $p_1, \dots, p_n, M$

$$(b_i a_{ji} - a_{ji} - b_j a_{ii})p_i + (a_{ij} + b_i a_{jj} - b_j a_{ij})p_j +$$
$$+ \sum_{k \neq i,j} (b_i a_{jk} - b_j a_{ik})p_k + (b_i b_j - b_j b_i)M = 0. \tag{7}$$

Since **7** holds for *all* values of $p_1, \dots, p_n$, and the expressions in parentheses multiplying the prices and M are all constants, it follows that they must all be zero. Therefore, to take the coefficient of p_i

$$(b_i - 1)a_{ji} = b_j a_{ii},$$

which is equivalent to **4** above, and the proof is complete.

(b) Secondly, we wish to show that if the consumer's budget permits him to buy more than the basic quantities $s_1, \dots, s_n$ (i.e. if $M > \sum_{k=1}^{n} p_k s_k$), then all goods are normal ($\partial x_i / \partial M > 0$) and all pairs of goods are net substitutes.

Recall from section **T.5** that for all i and j

$$\left[\frac{\partial x_i}{\partial p_j}\right]_S = \frac{\partial x_i}{\partial p_j} + x_j\left[\frac{\partial x_i}{\partial M}\right] \qquad \textbf{8}$$

and rewrite **2** above as

$$x_i = s_i(1-b_i) + \frac{b_i\left(M - \sum_{k \neq i} p_k s_k\right)}{p_i}. \qquad \textbf{9}$$

Perform on **9** the differentiations indicated by **8**, with $i = j$

$$\begin{aligned}\left[\frac{\partial x_i}{\partial p_i}\right]_S &= -\frac{b_i}{p_i^2}\left(M - \sum_{k \neq i} p_k s_k\right) + \frac{b_i}{p_i}\left[s_i(1-b_i) + \frac{b_i\left(M - \sum_{k \neq i} p_k s_k\right)}{p_i}\right] \\ &= \frac{b_i}{p_i^2}\left[(b_i - 1)\left(M - \sum_{k \neq i} p_k s_k\right) - (b_i - 1)p_i s_i\right] \\ &= \frac{b_i(b_i-1)}{p_i^2}\left(M - \sum_{k=1}^{n} p_k s_k\right).\end{aligned}$$

Since the own-price substitution term $(\partial x_i/\partial p_i)_S$ is negative, it follows from the last expression that if $M > \sum_{k=1}^{n} p_k s_k$, $b_i(1-b_i) > 0$. This implies that $0 < b_i < 1$, so that $b_i = p_i(\partial x_i/\partial M) > 0$, and therefore x_i and all other goods are normal.

Now differentiate **9** as indicated in **8** with $i \neq j$

$$\begin{aligned}\left[\frac{\partial x_i}{\partial p_j}\right]_S &= -\frac{b_i s_j}{p_i} + \frac{b_i}{p_i}\left[s_j(1-b_j) + \frac{b_j\left(M - \sum_{k \neq j} p_k s_k\right)}{p_j}\right] \\ &= \frac{b_i b_j}{p_i p_j}\left(M - \sum_{k \neq j} p_k s_k\right) + s_j\left[\frac{b_i(1-b_j) - b_i}{p_i}\right] \\ &= \frac{b_i b_j}{p_i p_j}\left(M - \sum_{k \neq j} p_k s_k - p_j s_j\right) = \frac{b_i b_j}{p_i p_j}\left(M - \sum_{k=1}^{n} p_k s_k\right).\end{aligned}$$

Since b_i and b_j, as shown above, are both positive, the last expression is positive if $M > \sum_{k=1}^{n} p_k s_k$. In these conditions $(\partial x_i/\partial p_j)_S > 0$ for all i and j, so that all pairs of goods are net substitutes.

(c) Thirdly, it can be shown that the demand for each commodity is inelastic with respect to its own price. Equation **2** above can be written as

$$x_i = s_i(1-b_i) + \frac{b_i\left(M - \sum_{k \neq i} p_k s_k\right)}{p_i}$$

or $$p_i[x_i - s_i(1-b_i)] = b_i\left(M - \sum_{k \neq i} p_k s_k\right). \quad \textbf{10}$$

Given M and all prices but p_i, the right-hand side of **10** is constant, so that $p_i[x_i - s_i(1-b_i)]$ is constant, and therefore the elasticity of $[x_i - s_i(1-b_i)]$ with respect to p_i equals -1. That is

$$\frac{p_i}{x_i - s_i(1-b_i)} \frac{\partial[x_i - s_i(1-b_i)]}{\partial p_i} = -1. \quad \textbf{11}$$

Since $s_i(1-b_i)$ is constant, $\Delta[x_i - s_i(1-b_i)] = \Delta x_i$, so that all the terms in **11** are the same as in the expression for the elasticity of x_i with respect to p_i, $(p_i/x_i)(\partial x_i/\partial p_i)$, except for the term $x_i - s_i(1-b_i)$ in the denominator. Since $x_i - s_i(1-b_i) < x_i$, $p_i/x_i < p_i/[x_i - s_i(1-b_i)]$, and therefore $(p_i/x_i)(\partial x_i/\partial p_i)$ is between zero and minus one.

(d) Finally, we wish to show that demand functions of the form **2** can be derived from a utility function of the form

$$u = (x_1 - s_1)^{b_1} \ldots (x_n - s_n)^{b_n}. \quad \textbf{12}$$

The necessary conditions for a maximum (sections **7.1** and **T.5**) are that

$$u_i - \mu p_i = \frac{b_i u}{(x_i - s_i)} - \mu p_i = 0. \quad \textbf{13}$$

If $b_i > 0$, which we have proved, and $x_i - s_i > 0$, which we assume to be the case, all marginal utilities are positive. We can also verify that the 'convexity' conditions of section **T.3** (or the strict 'quasi-concavity' of section **T.6**) are satisfied. For an alternative form of the utility function **12** is

$$u^* = \log u = \sum_{i=1}^{n} b_i \log(x_i - s_i).$$

In this additive function all marginal utilities are diminishing ($u^*_{ii} = -b_i/(x_i - s_i)^2$), so that indifference surfaces are convex-to-the-origin by the argument of section **6.5**.

It follows from **13** that

$$p_i(x_i - s_i) = \frac{b_i u}{\mu},$$

and therefore for all i and k

$$\frac{p_k(x_k - s_k)}{p_i(x_i - s_i)} = \frac{b_k}{b_i}$$

$$\text{or} \quad p_k x_k = p_k s_k + \frac{b_k}{b_i} p_i(x_i - s_i).$$

Summing the last expression over k, and remembering that

$\sum_{k=1}^{n} p_k x_k = M$ and $\sum_{k=1}^{n} b_k = 1$, we obtain

$$M = \sum_{k=1}^{n} p_k s_k + \frac{1}{b_i} p_i(x_i - s_i).$$

from which **2** can be very easily derived.

T.8 Additive utility functions with constant elasticity of substitution

We wish first to prove a result implied in section **12.4** (p. 201) (and the assertion in section **15.4**, p. 260) that in an inter-temporal utility function of the form

$$u = f[C(0)] + \frac{f[C(1)]}{1+p} + \frac{f[C(2)]}{(1+p)^2} + \dots, \qquad \mathbf{1}$$

if the elasticity of substitution η is everywhere constant, all indifference surfaces are homothetic with reference to the origin. If, and only if, this is the case, a given proportional change in the ratio of marginal utilities will lead to the same proportional change in the ratio of quantities whether the consumer remains on the same indifference curve or not.

If the function $y = f(x)$ has constant elasticity η (cf. section **T.1**) then

$$\frac{x}{y}\frac{dy}{dx} = \eta,$$

$$\frac{dy}{y} = \eta\frac{dx}{x},$$

$$\log y = k + \eta \log x,$$

so that finally $y = Kx^{\eta}$. **2**

The elasticity of substitution is the elasticity of (for example) $C(1)/C(0)$ with respect to $[\partial u/\partial C(0)] \div [\partial u/\partial C(1)]$. It follows from **2** that

$$\frac{C(1)}{C(0)} = K\left[\frac{\partial u/\partial C(0)}{\partial u/\partial C(1)}\right]^{\eta}, \qquad \mathbf{3}$$

so that $$\frac{\partial u/\partial C(0)}{\partial u/\partial C(1)} = \left[\frac{C(1)}{K\,C(0)}\right]^{1/\eta}.$$

Thus the mrs of $C(1)$ for $C(0)$ depends only on the *ratio* $C(1)/C(0)$, so that indifference surfaces are indeed homothetic with respect to the origin.

It is worthwhile to attempt to discover the *form* of the utility function $f(\;)$ in **1** which will yield a constant elasticity of substitution. From **1** and **3**

$$\frac{C(1)}{C(0)} = K\left\{\frac{f'[C(0)](1+p)}{f'[C(1)]}\right\}^{\eta},$$

so that $C(1)\{f'[C(1)]\}^{\eta} = C(0)K\{f'[C(0)](1+p)\}^{\eta}$.

This last equation must hold even if $C(1)$ changes while $C(0)$, and therefore the expression on the right-hand side, remains constant. Therefore $C(1)\{f'[C(1)]\}^{\eta}$ is a constant, so that

$f'[C(1)] = k_1[C(1)]^{-1/\eta}$. **4**

Integration of **4** gives (ignoring in this case the constant of integration, which has no economic significance)

$$f[C(1)] = \frac{k_1\eta}{\eta - 1}[C(1)]^{1-1/\eta} \quad \text{if } \eta \neq 1,$$

5

$$f[C(1)] = k_1 \log C(1) \qquad \text{if } \eta = 1.$$

The state-preference case of section **15** is mathematically identical. We may if we choose, however, replace $1/\eta$ by ρ, which we there propose as a measure of the degree of risk-aversion. Thus

$$E = \frac{\pi_a}{1-\rho} W_a^{1-\rho} + \frac{\pi_b}{1-\rho} W_b^{1-\rho} \quad \text{if } \rho \neq 1,$$

$$E = \pi_a \log W_a + \pi_b \log W_b \qquad \text{if } \rho = 1.$$

The elasticity of substitution η must be positive; otherwise indifference curves are not convex-to-the-origin. But if $\eta < 1$ ($\rho > 1$) total intertemporal utility (or expected utility) will be *negative*. This should cause no concern since marginal utilities, as can easily be verified, continue to be positive and diminishing. Indeed, it is *only* when $\eta < 1$ ($\rho > 1$) that a utility function of this form is bounded from above; its value cannot rise to or above zero. But it is only when $\pi > 1$ ($\rho < 1$) that it is bounded from below; if $\rho \geqslant 1$, utility approaches $-\infty$ as W approaches zero. As we saw on p. 215 above, it can be argued that the utility function is bounded both from above and from below. This led Arrow to propose the hypothesis of 'increasing relative risk-aversion'; our ρ must go from values below unity at very low levels of wealth to values above unity at very high levels of wealth. He is not, however, averse to the hypothesis that $\rho = 1$ over a significant intermediate range; this hypothesis underlies the simple portfolio formula at the end of section **15.4** of the text.

Incidentally, the utility function $u = x_1^{\beta 1} x_2^{\beta 2} \ldots x_n^{\beta n}$, labelled (U1) in section **9.2** of the text, displays unitary elasticity of substitution everywhere, since it gives rise to the same behaviour (in conditions of certainty) as $u^* = \log u = \sum_{i=1}^{n} \beta_i \log x_i$.

T.9 Existence of von Neumann-Morgenstern utility functions

Consider the prospect defined in the text (p. 218)

$y = (x, x'; \pi, 1-\pi)$.

It was established that there exist probabilities π_x and π_x' such that

$$x\,I(x^{(b)}, x^{(w)}; \pi_x, 1-\pi_x) \quad \text{and} \quad x'\,I(x^{(b)}, x^{(w)}; \pi_x', 1-\pi_x'),$$

and that

$$y\,I[x^{(b)}, x^{(w)}; \pi\pi_x+(1-\pi)\pi'_x, \pi(1-\pi_x)+(1-\pi)(1-\pi_x')].$$

Given another prospect,

$$y' = (x'', x'''; \pi', 1-\pi'),$$

by the same argument there exist probabilities π_x'' and π_x''' such that

$$x''\,I(x^{(b)}, x^{(w)}; \pi_x'', 1-\pi_x'') \quad \text{and} \quad x'''\,I(x^{(b)}, x^{(w)}; \pi_x''', 1-\pi_x''')$$

and that

$$y'\,I[x^{(b)}, x^{(w)}; \pi'\pi_x''+(1-\pi')\pi_x''', \pi'(1-\pi_x'')+(1-\pi')(1-\pi_x''')].$$

Now since $x^{(b)}Px^{(w)}$, it follows from the second postulate in section **13.2** that yRy' if and onlv if

$$\pi\pi_x+(1-\pi)\pi_x' \geqslant \pi'\pi_x''+(1-\pi')\pi_x'''.$$

Let us now arbitrarily assign the utility numbers

$$u(x^{(b)}) = 1, \quad u(x^{(w)}) = 0.$$

And let us assign to x, which is indifferent to $(x^{(b)}, x^{(w)}; \pi_x, 1-\pi_x)$, the utility number

$$u(x) = \pi_x u(x^{(b)})+(1-\pi_x)u(x^{(w)}) = \pi_x \times 1+(1-\pi_x)\times 0 = \pi_x.$$

Similarly $u(x') = \pi_x'$; $u(x'') = \pi_x''$; $u(x''') = \pi_x'''$.

If we now write the expected utility of $y = (x, x'; \pi, 1-\pi)$ as $E(y) = \pi u(x)+(1-\pi)u(x') = \pi\pi_x+(1-\pi)\pi_x'$,

and that of $y' = (x'', x'''; \pi', 1-\pi')$ as

$$E(y') = \pi' u(x'')+(1-\pi')u(x''') = \pi'\pi_x''+(1-\pi')\pi_x''',$$

will a comparison of $E(y)$ and $E(y')$ rank the prospects correctly?

The answer is clearly yes, since

$$E(y) \geqslant E(y')$$

if and only if

$$\pi\pi_x+(1-\pi)\pi_x' \geqslant \pi'\pi_x''+(1-\pi')\pi_x''',$$

which is precisely the necessary and sufficient condition given above for yRy'. Thus it is possible to assign to the objects $x, x', \ldots$ utility numbers such that the expected utilities $E(y)$, $E(y'), \ldots$ generate a ranking of prospects in accordance with the consumer's preference ordering.

T.10 Marginal utility, attitudes to risk and complex gambles

We wish to investigate the relationships among risk-aversion, risk-preference and the behaviour of marginal utility for gambles more complex than those considered in section **13.4**. We begin with the choice between the consumer's existing wealth $\overline{W}$ and the fair gamble $(W, W', W''; \pi, \pi', 1-\pi-\pi')$. Consider Figure 72, in which the utility function $u(W)$, with marginal utility everywhere decreasing, is clearly strictly concave according to the definition in section **T.6**.

Since the gamble is, by assumption, a fair one,

$$\overline{W} = \pi W + \pi W' + (1-\pi-\pi')W''$$

Its expected utility, $\pi\, u(W) + \pi'\, u(W') + (1-\pi-\pi')u(W'')$, can be written

$$E = (\pi+\pi')\left[\frac{\pi\, u(W) + \pi'\, u(W')}{\pi+\pi'}\right] + (1-\pi-\pi')u(W'').$$

The term in square brackets corresponds to the point F in Figure 72, found by dividing the straight line BC in the ratio $\pi:\pi'$. The expected utility of the gamble corresponds to the point E, found by dividing the straight line FD in the ratio $(\pi+\pi'):(1-\pi-\pi')$. Since the gamble is fair, the point E lies above $\overline{W}$, which represents the expected money value of the gamble. And as long as the utility function is strictly concave, the point E must lie below A, which represents $u(\overline{W})$, so that the gamble is rejected.

The point E is in fact the probability-weighted *centre of gravity* of the triangle B C D. It can therefore never lie above the graph of a concave function, and can lie on it only if the ' gamble ' is a certainty, with the probability of one of the prospects equal to unity.

If the fair gamble were $(W, W', \ldots, W^{(n)}; \pi, \pi', \ldots, \pi^{(n)})$, the point corresponding to E in Figure 72 would be the centre of gravity of an

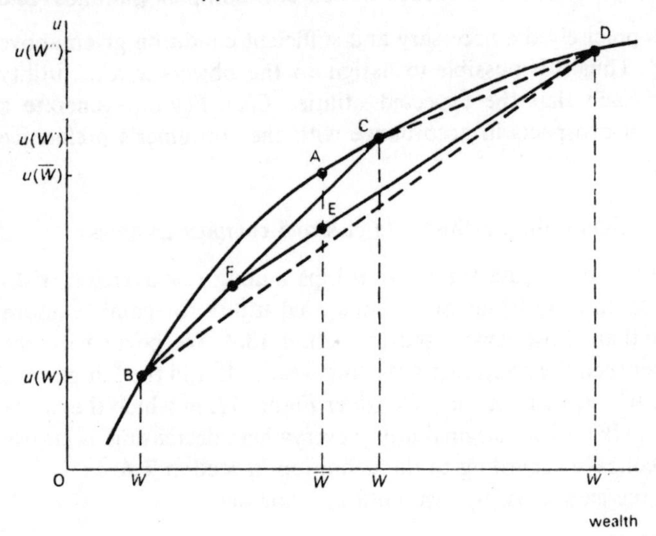

Figure 72

n-dimensional rectilinear figure, and again could not lie above the graph of a concave function. Clearly if $u(W)$ had increasing marginal utility everywhere and were therefore strictly convex (see section **T.6**), the point E for any fair gamble (certainties excepted) would lie *above* the graph of the function, and all fair bets of all degrees of complexity would be accepted.

We can *not*, however, show that if a complex fair bet is rejected, the utility function must be strictly concave everywhere in the range of the quantities of wealth included in the bet. It may be concave in some places and convex in others, and the decision to accept or reject a given fair bet depends on the precise form of the function and the quantities of wealth and probabilities involved.

T.11 Quadratic utility and inferior risky assets

In the portfolio problem of section **14.4**, let the size of the portfolio be P. Then expected utility is

$$E = \pi u[P(1+r)+Bg]+(1-\pi)u[P(1+r)-Bl].$$

If the utility function is quadratic, that is, $u = bx - cx^2$, then

$$\begin{aligned} E &= \pi\{b[P(1+r)+Bg]-c[P(1+r)+Bg]^2\}+ \\ &\quad +(1-\pi)\{b[P(1+r)-Bl]-c[P(1+r)-Bl]^2\} \\ &= bP(1+r)+bB[\pi g-(1-\pi)l]-c\{\pi[P^2(1+r)^2+2BPg(1+r)+ \\ &\quad +B^2g^2]+(1-\pi)[P^2(1+r)^2-2BPl(1+r)+B^2l^2]\}. \end{aligned} \qquad \mathbf{1}$$

To find the maximum of E we differentiate **1** with respect to B and set the result equal to zero,

$$\begin{aligned} \frac{\partial E}{\partial B} &= b[\pi g-(1-\pi)l]-c\{\pi[2Pg(1+r)+2Bg^2]+ \\ &\quad +(1-\pi)[-2Pl(1+r)+2Bl^2)]\} \\ &= b[\pi g-(1-\pi)l]-c\{2P(1+r)[\pi g-(1-\pi)l] \\ &\quad +2B[\pi g^2+(1-\pi)l^2]\} = 0. \end{aligned} \qquad \mathbf{2}$$

We then verify that **2** does indeed yield a maximum, since

$$\frac{\partial^2 E}{\partial B^2} = -2c[\pi g^2+(1-\pi)l^2] < 0$$

on the assumption, made in the text, that $c > 0$ (and $b > 0$).

Finally, we solve **2** to obtain the value of B

$$B = \frac{[b-2cP(1+r)][\pi g-(1-\pi)l]}{2[\pi g^2+(1-\pi)l^2]}. \qquad \mathbf{3}$$

As we saw in section **14.2**, if $\pi g-(1-\pi)l \leqq 0$, the investor holds no bonds. $b-2cP(1+r)$ is the marginal utility of wealth at the point where $W = P(1+r)$; unless this is positive, the marginal utility of wealth has ceased to be positive at (or below) the level at which the investor holds all his portfolio in money. Hence if the marginal utility of wealth is positive and some bonds are held, each term in the numerator of **3** is positive.

In these circumstances, partial differentiation of **3** with respect to P gives

$$\frac{\partial B}{\partial P} = -\frac{c(1+r)\{\pi g-(1-\pi)l\}}{\pi g^2+(1-\pi)l^2} < 0.$$

With given values of r, g, l and π, an increase in the portfolio reduces the quantity of bonds held, so that bonds are, as stated on p. 246 of the text, an inferior good.

T.12 Pareto-optimality and interdependent utility functions

The Pareto optima discussed in section **16.2** of the text may be described as situations in which $u^{(A)}(x_1^{(A)}, x_2^{(A)})$ is maximized subject to the conditions that $u^{(B)}(x_1^{(B)}, x_2^{(B)})$ is not less than a certain specified value $\bar{u}^{(B)}$, and that $x_1^{(A)}+x_1^{(B)} \leqq \bar{x}_1, x_2^{(A)}+x_2^{(B)} \leqq \bar{x}_2$. The function $u^{(A)}$ is strictly quasi-concave (see section **T.6**). The feasible regions permitted by the constraints $x_1^{(A)}+x_1^{(B)} \leqq \bar{x}_1$ and $x_2^{(A)}+x_2^{(B)} \leqq \bar{x}_2$ are convex (they are similar to the regions to which one is confined by a budget constraint). The feasible region permitted by the constraint $u^{(B)}(x_1^{(B)}, x_2^{(B)}) \geqq \bar{u}^{(B)}$ is strictly convex if $u^{(B)}$ is strictly quasi-concave; note that in Figure 66 the set of points on or above any indifference curve of B is strictly convex – it is one of the sets R(x) of section **3.4**. The set of points which make up the feasible region when all three constraints are satisfied is the *intersection* of (i.e. the set of points common to) three convex sets, and is therefore itself convex. (For if s and s' are in the intersection of the sets A and B, and A is convex so that $ks+(1-k)s'$ is in A, and B is convex so that $ks+(1-k)s'$ is in B $(0 \leqslant k \leqslant 1)$, then $ks+(1-k)s'$ is in the intersection of A and B, which is therefore also convex). By the argument of section **T.6**, therefore, since $u^{(A)}$ is strictly quasi-concave and the feasible region is convex, the conditions for a Pareto optimum derived in section **16.2** are sufficient.

When interdependence is present, as in the example in section **16.3**, p. 290, we are to maximize $u^{(A)}(x_1^{(A)}, x_2^{(A)}, x_1^{(B)})$ subject to $u^{(B)}(x_1^{(B)}, x_2^{(B)}, x_1^{(A)}) \geqslant \bar{u}^{(B)}$, with the quantities constrained as before. If, as in section **16.2**, we avoid corner solutions and bliss, all the constraints will be satisfied exactly ($u^{(B)} = \bar{u}^{(B)}$, $x_1^{(A)}+x_1^{(B)} = \bar{x}_1$, $x_2^{(A)}+x_2^{(B)} = \bar{x}_2$), and the necessary and sufficient conditions for a Pareto optimum will be similar in form to those derived in section **16.2**.

Since $x_1^{(A)}+x_1^{(B)} = \bar{x}_1, x_2^{(A)}+x_2^{(B)} = \bar{x}_2$, we can write the Lagrangean

$$L = u^{(A)}(x_1^{(A)}, x_2^{(A)}, x_1^{(B)}) + \mu[u^{(B)}(x_1^{(B)}, x_2^{(B)}, x_1^{(A)}) - \bar{u}^{(B)}]$$

as

$$L = u^{(A)}(x_1^{(A)}, x_2^{(A)}, \bar{x}_1 - x_1^{(A)}) + \mu[u^{(B)}(\bar{x}_1 - x_1^{(A)}, \bar{x}_2 - x_2^{(A)}, x_1^{(A)}) - \bar{u}^{(B)}]. \qquad \mathbf{1}$$

Setting the partial derivatives of **1** equal to zero,

$$\frac{\partial L}{\partial x_1^{(A)}} = \frac{\partial u^{(A)}}{\partial x_1^{(A)}} - \frac{\partial u^{(A)}}{\partial x_1^{(B)}} - \mu\frac{\partial u^{(B)}}{\partial x_1^{(B)}} + \mu\frac{\partial u^{(B)}}{\partial x_1^{(A)}} = 0;$$

$$\frac{\partial L}{\partial x_2^{(A)}} = \frac{\partial u^{(A)}}{\partial x_2^{(A)}} - \mu\frac{\partial u^{(B)}}{\partial x_2^{(B)}} = 0.$$

It follows that

$$\mu = \frac{\partial u^{(A)}/\partial x_2^{(A)}}{\partial u^{(B)}/\partial x_2^{(B)}} = \frac{\partial u^{(A)}/\partial x_1^{(A)} - \partial u^{(A)}/\partial x_1^{(B)}}{\partial u^{(B)}/\partial x_1^{(B)} - \partial u^{(B)}/\partial x_1^{(A)}}$$

$$= \frac{\partial u^{(A)}/\partial x_1^{(A)}}{\partial u^{(B)}/\partial x_1^{(B)}}\left[1 - \frac{\partial u^{(A)}/\partial x_1^{(B)}}{\partial u^{(A)}/\partial x_1^{(A)}}\right] \div \left[1 - \frac{\partial u^{(B)}/\partial x_1^{(A)}}{\partial u^{(B)}/\partial x_1^{(B)}}\right]. \qquad \mathbf{2}$$

On the assumptions, made on p. 290 of the text, that A and B pay the same price, p_2, for x_2, but different prices $p_1^{(A)}$ and $p_1^{(B)}$ for x_1, and that

$$\frac{p_1^{(A)}}{p_2} = \frac{\partial u^{(A)}/\partial x_1^{(A)}}{\partial u^{(A)}/\partial x_2^{(A)}} \quad \text{and} \quad \frac{p_1^{(B)}}{p_2} = \frac{\partial u^{(B)}/\partial x_1^{(B)}}{\partial u^{(B)}/\partial x_2^{(B)}},$$

we can derive from **2** the ratio of the prices $p_1^{(A)}$ and $p_1^{(B)}$ which will yield a Pareto optimum

$$\frac{p_1^{(A)}}{p_1^{(B)}} = \frac{p_1^{(A)}}{p_2} \div \frac{p_1^{(B)}}{p_2} = \frac{\partial u^{(A)}/\partial x_1^{(A)}}{\partial u^{(A)}/\partial x_2^{(A)}} \div \frac{\partial u^{(B)}/\partial x_1^{(B)}}{\partial u^{(B)}/\partial x_2^{(B)}}$$

$$= \left[1 - \frac{\partial u^{(B)}/\partial x_1^{(A)}}{\partial u^{(B)}/\partial x_1^{(B)}}\right] \div \left[1 - \frac{\partial u^{(A)}/\partial x_1^{(B)}}{\partial u^{(A)}/\partial x_1^{(A)}}\right],$$

as stated on p. 291 of the text.

Answers to the Exercises

2

1. (a) No.

(b) Yes.

(c) Clearly yes if we consider three different people. But if A is the brother of B and B is the brother of A, transitivity implies that A is his own brother. If we say that, by convention, every man is his own brother, then the relation is transitive.

(d) No. If A lies 120° east of B and B lies 120° east of C, then A lies 240° east, or 120° west, of C. By convention, we use the terms 'east of' and 'west of' to refer to angles of less than 180°. Thus A lies east of B and B lies east of C, but A does not lie east of C.

3

1. If $x \geqslant x'$ then xPx', and if $x' \geqslant x$ then $x'Px$, by Axiom **4**. Both xPx' and $x'Px$ are inconsistent with xIx', by Corollary (a) to Axiom **1**.
2. xRx'.
3. (a) Strictly convex.
(b) Convex, but not strictly convex.
(c) Not convex.
4. No. If $y = \sqrt{4}$, $y = +2$ or -2, so that a given value of x does not determine a *unique* value of y.

4

1. A horizontal straight line.
2. The function is homogeneous of degree one.
3. (a) See A. Marshall (*Principles of Economics*, Macmillan, 1920, p. 839).

(b) The ratios corresponding to AE/DA are always equal for the pair of demand curves in (i) at the same price, and in (ii) at the same quantity.

4. $\Delta Y =$ £50 as Y changes from £100 to £150. Other entries:

	(2)	(4)	(6)	(7)
Commodity 1	0·20	0·08	0·16	0·40
Commodity 2	0·60	0·72	0·64	1·20

5

1. Only (a) is true.

2. (a) x_i must be inferior, and therefore x_j must be normal.
(b) x_j must be normal.
(c) No conclusion can be drawn.

3. (a) Complement. (b) Complement. (c) Substitute.

6

1. (d) and (f) are inconsistent: u_1/u_2 must increase.

2. (a), (c), (e) and (f).

7

1. (a) It is halved.
(b) Yes.
(c) Homogeneous of degree *minus* one.

2. No. There is no reason why x_i and $u_i - \mu p_i$ should not both be zero; this would be true at x in Figure 32 if the slopes of the indifference curve and the budget line were equal.

8

1. $+0{\cdot}05$ for x_1, $-0{\cdot}04$ for x_2. Thus x_1 has an upward-sloping demand curve although a smaller fraction of the budget is spent on it.

2. (a) $u_1 = \partial u/\partial x_1 =$ limit as Δx_1 approaches zero of

$$\frac{\Delta x_1\, x_2}{\Delta x_1} = x_2;$$

similarly for u_2.

(b) $u_1 - \mu p_1 = x_2 - \mu p_1 = 0; u_2 - \mu p_2 = x_1 - \mu p_2 = 0$. Thus $\mu = x_2/p_1 = x_1/p_2$. Therefore $p_1 x_1 = p_2 x_2 = \frac{1}{2}M$.

(c) $\mu = x_2/p_1 = M/2p_1 p_2$.

(d) It decreases; cf. p. 119 of the text.

3. M must be reduced to £75.

9

1. (a) $x_1^{(r)} = 40$, $x_2^{(r)} = 30$.

(b) $x_1^{(r)} = 42$, $x_2^{(r)} = 29$.

2. < 1 for $x_1^{(r)}$, > 1 for $x_2^{(r)}$.

$$b_1^{(r)} = \frac{2}{5} < \frac{p_1 s_1^{(r)}}{p_1 s_1^{(r)} + p_2 s_2^{(r)}} = \frac{1}{2}, \quad \text{etc.}$$

3. $b_1 = 0{\cdot}45$, $b_2 = 0{\cdot}55$. ($b_1 = b_1^{(r)} h^{(r)} + b_1^{(s)} h^{(s)} = (2/5)\cdot\frac{1}{2} + \frac{1}{2}\cdot\frac{1}{2}$, etc.).

10

1. Quantity index $= x_1^{2/5} x_2^{3/5}$; price index $= \left(\frac{5p_1}{2}\right)^{2/5} \left(\frac{5p_2}{3}\right)^{3/5}$.

2. 18 p per pound.

3. (a) It will be scalloped, as in Figure 73. The lines joining A and C, C and E, etc., will be curves convex to the origin, not straight lines as in Figure 42.

(b) D, perhaps, if the curve joining C and E lies below or partly below (as in Figure 73) the curves CD and DE. B, only if the price of C falls more rapidly for larger quantities than the price of B.

(c) Not necessarily; it is possible for D to lie on the curve joining C and E. The point D could then be reached in two ways – by buying D alone or by buying a combination of C and E.

11

1. £945.

2. $x_1(0) + 3x_2(0) + x_1(1) + 5x_2(1) = 250$.

3. $x_1(0) = 75$; $x_2(0) = 25$; $x_1(1) = 50$; $x_2(1) = 10$. (The present values of expenditure on $x_1(0), x_2(0), x_1(1), x_2(1)$ are respectively 0·3, 0·3, 0·2, 0·2 of the present value of the consumer's wealth.)

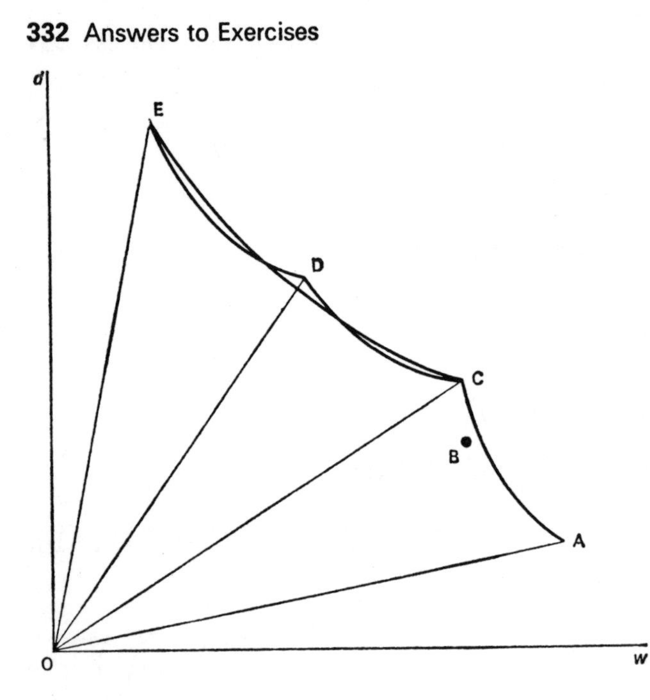

Figure 73

12

1. (a) $W_A(0) = £\left[200+\dfrac{250}{1+r_0}\right]$; $W_B(0) = £\left[150+\dfrac{150}{1+r_0}\right]$.

(b) $C_A(0)+\dfrac{C_A(1)}{1+r_0} = 200+\dfrac{250}{1+r_0}$;

$$C_B(0)+\frac{C_B(1)}{1+r_0} = 150+\frac{150}{1+r_0}.$$

(c) $C_A(0) = \frac{1}{2}W_A(0) = 100+\dfrac{125}{1+r_0}$;

$$C_B(0) = \tfrac{2}{3}W_B(0) = 100+\frac{100}{1+r_0}.$$

(d) No. It is sufficient to equate supply and demand in only *one* year. If we add together all the budget constraints (in this case only two) at a given set of prices, we have what is known as *Walras' Law*. In the present case the only price is $1/(1+r_0)$, and Walras' Law says that

$$E_A(0)+E_B(0)+\frac{E_A(1)+E_B(1)}{1+r_0} = C_A(0)+C_B(0)+\frac{C_A(1)+C_B(1)}{1+r_0}$$

For any given value of r_0, it follows that if total supply $E_A(0)+E_B(0)$ equals total demand $C_A(0)+C_B(0)$ in period 0, then total supply $E_A(1)+E_B(1)$ must equal total demand $C_A(1)+C_B(1)$ in period 1.
(e) 50%. $[200+150 = 200+225/(1+r_0)]$.
(f) A lends £16·67 to B. ($C_A(0) = 100+125/1{\cdot}5 = 183\frac{1}{3}$; $E_A(0) = 200$).

2. (a) Greater than unity. (x_2/x_1 must have fallen in a larger proportion than $p_1/p_2 = u_1/u_2$.)
(b) Unity. ($p_1 x_1 = \frac{2}{3}M$, $p_2 x_2 = \frac{1}{3}M$, so that $p_1 x_1/p_2 x_2$ is constant, and x_2/x_1 always changes in the same proportion as $p_1/p_2 = u_1/u_2$.)

13

1. ($\overline{W}+1$, $\overline{W}-1$; $\frac{3}{8}$, $\frac{5}{8}$).
2. Unfavourable.
3. Risk-preference.
4. -5.
5. Reject it. $[15(3/8)+10(5/8) < 12]$.

14

1. He will be indifferent; for each prospect $\mu = 5$ and $\sigma = 2$.
2. He will prefer y'; $1{\cdot}96+0{\cdot}2 = 2{\cdot}16 < 0{\cdot}6+1{\cdot}6 = 2{\cdot}2$.

15

1. (a) The present value of the portfolio must now be written as £$(100-0{\cdot}02\,B)$, where B is the *absolute value* of the present value of bonds held; whether B is, say, +£50 (£50 held in bonds) or −£50 (£50 in bonds sold short), brokerage charges are 0·02(£50) = +£1, Therefore:
$W_a=(100-0{\cdot}2\,B-B)(1{\cdot}05)+1{\cdot}15B=105+0{\cdot}1B-0{\cdot}21\,B$
$W_b=(100-0{\cdot}2\,B-B)(1{\cdot}05)+0{\cdot}95B=105-0{\cdot}1B-0{\cdot}21\,B$
Thus when $B > 0$, $W_a = 105+0{\cdot}079B$, $W_b = 105-0{\cdot}121B$, and when $B < 0$, $W_a = 105+0{\cdot}121B$, $W_b = 105-0{\cdot}079B$. The budget

line is as shown in Figure 74. The transactions costs of dealing in bonds cause it to bend backward from the straight line of slope -1 through the point (105,105).

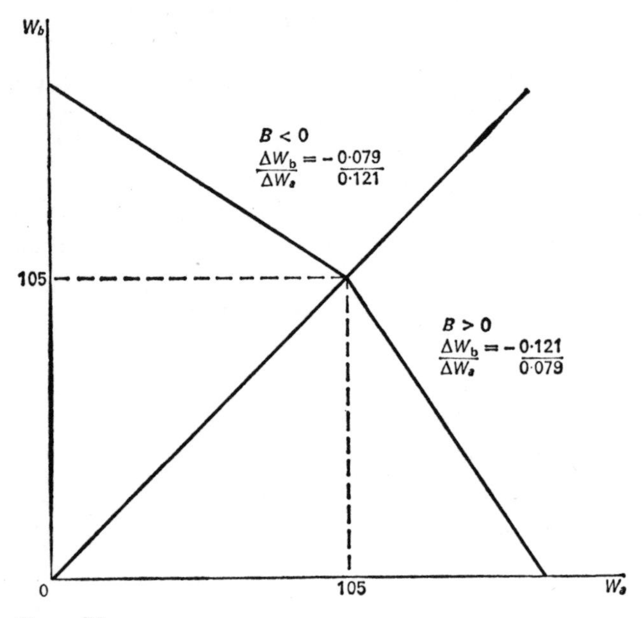

Figure 74

(b) $\pi_a > 0{\cdot}605$. $(\pi_a/\pi_b > 0{\cdot}121/0{\cdot}079)$.
(c) $\pi_a < 0{\cdot}395$. $(\pi_a/\pi_b < 0{\cdot}079/0{\cdot}121)$.

2 (a) $M = £216{\cdot}67$, $B = -£116{\cdot}67$;
(b) $M = £30$, $B = £70$.

16

1. $M^{(A)} = £200$, $p_1^{(A)} = £4$, $p_2^{(A)} = £8$; $M^{(B)} = £100$, $p_1^{(B)} = £2$, $p_2^{(B)} = £4$.

2. For a Pareto optimum at the bottom right-hand corner of the Edgeworth-Bowley box in Figure 67, where $x_1^{(A)} = \bar{x}_1 > 0$, $x_2^{(A)} = x_1^{(B)} = 0$, $x_2^{(B)} = \bar{x}_2 > 0$, it is necessary that A's indifference curve be tangent to or steeper than B's, i.e. $\text{mrs}_{21}^{(A)} \geq \text{mrs}_{21}^{(B)}$. If this is the case, it is clearly possible to draw one or more common budget lines

through that point, not steeper than A's indifference curve nor flatter than B's, such that $\text{mrs}_{21}^{(A)} \geqq p_1/p_2 \geqq \text{mrs}_{21}^{(B)}$.

3. (a) Laspeyres quantity index = 110(%);
Paasche quantity index = 80;
Laspeyres price index = 150;
Paasche price index = 109·1.

(b) No conclusion, since $p.x' > p.x$, $p'.x' < p'.x$.

Index